WITHDRAWN

D1071133

THE SLAVE SOUL OF RUSSIA

The Slave Soul of Russia

MORAL MASOCHISM
AND THE CULT OF SUFFERING

Daniel Rancour-Laferriere

NEW YORK UNIVERSITY PRESS

New York and London

NEW YORK UNIVERSITY PRESS
New York and London

© 1995 by New York University

All rights reserved

Library of Congress Cataloging-in-Publication Data
Rancour-Laferriere, Daniel.
The slave soul of Russia : moral masochism and the cult of
suffering / Daniel Rancour-Laferriere.
p.   cm.
Includes bibliographical references and index.
ISBN 0-8147-7458-X (alk. paper)
1. National characteristics, Russian.   2. Masochism—Russia
(Federation)   3. Self-destructive behavior—Russia (Federation)
4. Russia (Federation)—Civilization.   I. Title.
DK510.34.R36   1995
947—dc20   94-38519
                        CIP

New York University Press books are printed on acid-free paper,
and their binding materials are chosen for strength and durability.

Manufactured in the United States of America

10 9 8 7 6 5 4 3 2 1

DK
510.34
.R36
1995

052395-3080 H6

Господи помилуй, как мучительно трудно быть русским! Ибо ни один народ не чувствует столь глубоко тяги земной и нет на земле бо́льших *рабов божъих*, чем мы, Русь.

Lord have mercy, how agonizingly difficult it is to be Russian! For there is no other people which feels the earth's pull so profoundly, and there are no greater *slaves of God* on this earth than we, Rus'.

—Maksim Gor'kii

Contents

Acknowledgments

This book owes its title and chief inspiration to the Soviet Russian writer Vasilii Semenovich Grossman (1905–64). In his pessimistic novella *Forever Flowing* Grossman explains Russia's uniqueness by its "slave soul." Russia is a land of endless suffering, according to Grossman, because Russians typically cannot overcome their self-defeating slavishness.

If there was anything to what Grossman was saying, I thought when I first read him, then the psychoanalytic theory of moral masochism ought to apply to the Russians. Nearly one thousand footnotes later, I have become convinced that Grossman was correct, for I have been able to document the widespread occurrence of moral maoschism in various spheres of Russian culture.

Work on this book has been supported over the years by Faculty Research Grants (1988–93) from the University of California, Davis. The book also benefited from an International Research and Exchanges Board travel grant to the Soviet Union in 1990.

Portions of the book have been presented orally at meetings of the American Association for the Advancement of Slavic Studies (1992), the American Historical Association (1994), and the UC Davis Humanities Institute (1993).

Many individuals have offered constructive criticism of my work as it progressed. Barbara Milman listened incredulously but patiently as I tried to describe for her the things Russians do. Yuri Druzhnikov sat with me for hours explaining how to interpret certain mysterious Russian proverbs. My Moscow friends Vera Loseva, Aleksei Lunkov, Svetlana Kapelush, Lev Tokarev, Konstantin Pimkin, and Gayane Grigorian showered me with vivid anecdotes about masochism in Russia. Others who offered valuable comments include: Lois Becker, David Brodsky, Patricia Brodsky, Catherine Chvany, Toby Clyman, Robert O. Crummey, Joel Friedman, Jim Gallant, Musya Glants, Ben Hart, Kent Hart, Joanna Hubbs, Kathryn Jaeger, Gary Jahn, D. Barton Johnson, Lola Komarova, Ronald LeBlanc, Anna Leibovich, Yuri Mamleev, Karl Menges, Sidney Monas, Hugh Ragsdale, Steven Rosen, Gary Rosenshield, Charlotte Rosenthal, Anna Wierzbicka, and Elizabeth Wood. Helpful bibliographic assistance was provided by Opritsa Popa, as well as by Donald Beene, Frank Goodwin, Andre Janitzky, Shidan Lotfi, and Russel Schwartz. Special thanks go to Jackie DiClementine for her marvelous wordprocessing skills.

All translations into English are mine unless otherwise noted. A Russian translation of this book is in preparation.

THE SLAVE SOUL OF RUSSIA

O N E

Introduction

Russian history offers numerous examples of the exploitation and de-basement of human beings.

After the Mongols invaded in the mid-thirteenth century they ex-tracted obeisance, financial tribute, and military assistance from the princes of Rus' lands for at least the next century and a half. As the Mongols lost their grip, the Muscovite state expanded, its tsar enforcing unrestricted despotic rule over all citizens.

By degrees, starting roughly at the end of the fifteenth century, Russian peasants became more and more obliged to their landowning masters. From the late sixteenth century, they—that is, the vast majority of the rural Russian population—were bound from cradle to grave as serfs to their masters (or to the state directly), and they were not released from this form of involuntary servitude until 1861.

The Russian Orthodox Church, since the time of Peter the Great, was under the thumb of tsarist authority, and after the 1917 Revolution has endured periods of anti-religious persecution.

Russian women of all historical periods have been victimized by their men, whether they were being beaten for disobedience in accor-dance with the principles of the sixteenth-century *Domostroi,* or were holding down full-time jobs while at the same time being responsible for the bulk of household labor in the twentieth-century Soviet state.

For nearly three decades during the Soviet period of Russian history, forced labor was a way of life for the millions of inhabitants of the so-called gulag or system of concentration camps. Both Western and Soviet historians have acknowledged that this was outright slavery.[1] With the

onset of collectivization in the 1930s an aspect of serfdom was reinstated, for a large portion of the Soviet population was restricted by
means of an internal passport system to living in designated agricultural
areas.

To this day ordinary Russian citizens, who often have difficulty
obtaining the minimum goods and services necessary for subsistence,
contribute to the production of certain goods and services which only an
elite class, formerly known as the nomenklatura, has access to.

These facts are very diverse, and they are of course somewhat over-
simplified. But a general picture emerges which is accurate—and appalling. The sheer quantity and diversity of suffering that has gone on in
Russia, and still goes on there, boggles the Western mind.

The American psychoanalyst Edmund Bergler treated a class of
masochistic neurotics whom he termed "injustice collectors." I know of
no nation which has collected more injustices for itself than has Russia.

What are the causes of the great suffering that goes on in Russia?
Whence the Russian "need to suffer" ("potrebnost' stradaniia")[2]—as
Dostoevsky put it? Who is to blame?—to ask the perennial Russian
question.

Russia is customarily characterized as an "authoritarian" or "patriarchal" culture. This is no doubt true, but the very terms tend to attract
blame toward those exercising "authority," and draw analytic attention
away from those over whom "authority" is exercised, that is, away from
those who do the suffering and who might possibly be complicitous in
the "authoritarianism."

In the political and historical spheres, for example, this means (or
has meant in the past) undue attention to leaders and inadequate attention to the servile psychology of subordinates and ordinary Russians.
I am inclined to agree with Nicholas Vakar: "historians who have
written that the tyranny of the Tsars conditioned the nation to accept
the tyranny of the Communists have missed the fact that Russian habits of obedience have been the cause, not the result, of political autocracy."[3]

In the gender sphere exaggerated attention to authority has meant a
certain kind of male chauvinism, even among those feminist critics of
Russia who are so busy blaming the pampered Russian male ego for
female oppression that the female psyche goes unexamined.

Analogous statements could be made for other spheres of Russian life. Little effort has been made to understand just how the Russians manage to consistently get themselves into situations where they appear to have no choice but to submit and to suffer. How did Russians come to acquire their well-deserved epithet of "long-suffering people" ("terpelivyi narod")? Or, to utilize an alliterative epithet recently invented by poet Andrei Voznesenskii, why has Russia always been a "country of suffering" ("strana stradan'ia")?[4]

The Soviet prose writer Vasilii Grossman proffered his controversial notion that the "Russian soul" is by nature a "slave" ("raba").[5] This is a metaphorical characterization of the phenomenon in question, not an explanation of it. But, frankly, literary artists have exerted more effort in this area than anyone else, and their explorations have been very fruitful. Grossman is hardly alone. All of Dostoevsky's major novels, for example, offer insights into masochism. The poetry of Blok is filled with suffering welcomed by the sufferer. Much of Solzhenitsyn's writing glorifies suffering behind prison walls. And so on.

The literary imagery of Russian self-abnegation can be wide-ranging, even flamboyant. It is hardly falsifiable (in the Popperian sense), but at the same time it is highly interesting. Take, for example, the Russian Symbolist poet Viacheslav Ivanov, who in his essay on "the Russian Idea," declares: "our most attractive, most noble aspirations are imprinted with a thirst for self-destruction [zapechatleny zhazhdoiu samorazrusheniia]." "We" (Russians), Ivanov says, act as though other peoples are terribly stingy, and we try to prove ourselves a selfless people, a "self-immolating people," a "butterfly-Psyche" longing for a fiery death.[6] Ivanov uses the imagery of downward movement in an attempt to convey what he means. Russians have a "love for descent," they are inclined to voluntary subordination of the will to another (as in the religious practice of washing another's feet, or in the sectarian's utterance "You are greater than I"). The "law of descent" ("zakon niskhozhdeniia") is the essence of "Russian soul," and the lowly, humiliated, but enlightening Christ is the perfect model for this Russian tendency. It is as if the words "imitation of Christ" ("upodoblenie Khristu") were inscribed on the forehead of the Russian nation. It is as if Russians were *born* Christian: "Hic populus natus est christianus."[7]

These very heterogeneous images explain nothing, but they offer a treasure trove to the scholar seeking explanations. They make it easier to go about asking blunt questions: *How* do Russians endure their pain?

What *mental processes* permit them to go on living even as they perceive themselves as victims? Might there be a widespread *mentality* which encourages their victimization? Do they have some secret *need* or *wish* to suffer, or even to destroy themselves? If so, what is the *ontogenetic background* to the wish in individual Russians? Why is the wish so difficult to dislodge?

These are psychological questions, and they have not been answered in any substantive fashion in the past. They are of particular interest to the psychoanalytically oriented scholar. Of course other scholars, too, have taken an indirect interest. Considerable historical, philosophical, political, anthropological, and sociological research has been devoted to patterns of exploitation, subjugation, and even self-destruction in Russia. But psychological, and in particular, psychoanalytic study has been very scarce.

What I am proposing to do here is to construct a psychoanalytic model of the mentality behind both slavish behavior and its cultural signification in Russia.

The social practices and cultural phenomena in question exist at the level of the collective, not at the level of the individual. That is, they are sociocultural facts. But such facts depend on the actions of individuals, and individuals have feelings about what they are doing collectively. An individual who regularly participates in a social practice has a persisting attitude toward, a *mentality* concerning what he or she does (or signifies doing, or fantasizes doing) in his or her social environment. That mentality, or aspects of it, may be shared with other members of the collective. To the extent that sharing takes place, or to the extent that the shared mentality contributes to social developments and signifying practices, the mentality deserves the attention of historians, literary scholars, linguists, sociologists, anthropologists, and others who study human collectives.

But a mentality is first and foremost an object for psychological study. It persists in the face of historical and environmental change. For example, when Alexander II liberated the peasants from serfdom, the psychology of peasants did not just suddenly change—as Merezhkovskii understood when he said that "the liberty of slaves is a slavish liberty, little better than voluntary slavery."[8] Similarly, when Soviet power disintegrated, Russians did not suddenly become different people.[9]

What I am going to call a slave mentality[10] is something that psychologists, and in particular psychoanalysts, will be interested in. If I go so far as to speak of the *Russian* slave mentality, then I mean for historians, literary scholars, anthropologists, Slavists generally, and culture theorists to take an interest as well. But the primary focus of this study is nonetheless psychoanalytic.

One thing should be emphasized: in no way is the term "Russian slave mentality" (or the more poetic "slave soul of Russia," or the more clinical "Russian masochism") meant to imply that *only* Russians have such a mentality, or that *all* Russians have such a mentality, or even that the slave mentality is the most important psychological feature shared by significant numbers of Russians.

But there is a consensus among highly diverse observers—native Russians as well as foreign visitors, impressionistic literary artists as well as rigorous scholars, historians as well as commentators on the current scene—that there exists a widespread attitude of submissiveness toward authority and a tendency toward self-defeating and self-destructive behavior in individual Russians. Russians do not merely suffer. They have concocted for themselves a veritable cult of suffering.

It may be objected that masochistic attitudes and behaviors have simply been unavoidable in Russia, for reasons quite outside of the individual's control, and that it is therefore unfair to tag them with the derogatory-sounding epithets "slavish" or "masochistic." Why blame the victim? Why require heroism from an individual in an unbearable situation?

This objection is certainly valid when a victimized individual plays no role whatsoever in his or her victimization. An upstanding Soviet citizen who is suddenly and unexpectedly arrested by the KGB, for example, is not necessarily a masochist. But even a social system which is oriented toward victimizing individuals requires a certain amount of cooperation from those individuals, and to the extent that individuals do cooperate they are behaving more or less masochistically. Russian dissident V. Gorskii observed: "The rejection of freedom does not leave man unpunished. It turns him into a slave of necessity."[11] But (and I am sure Gorskii would agree) a slave of necessity is no less a slave. In other words, the easiest or most adaptive solution in a specific situation may well be the masochistic one, but that does not make it any less masochistic. Medical researcher V. D. Topolianskii emphasizes this important point in a recent interview with *Literaturnaia gazeta:*

In the context of a totalitarian government the nontraditional choice requires courage. Here an essential question arises: what do you call those people who attempted to fight the system? Were they people who behaved self-destructively (after all they knew they were in danger of being repressed), or were they persons who were trying to preserve their integrity amidst the general collapse? Official [Soviet] psychiatry insisted that the actions of Sakharov, Solzhenitsyn, and Grigorenko fell under the category of paranoia insofar as these individuals were characterized by an inability to make compromises. But I am strongly inclined, on the contrary, to label those who opted for compromise as the ones with self-destructive behavior. For, in a situation of unfreedom, compromise is always a betrayal of the self [predatel'stvo samogo sebia]. It has always seemed to me that a readiness to compromise and, consequently, to carry out assignments handed down from on high, is itself self-destruction [samorazrushenie].[12]

This is an essentially psychoanalytic insight. If in place of every occurrence of the word "self-destructive" we read instead "masochistic," then the passage would sound like a straightforward psychoanalytic interpretation of individuals acquiescing to the authoritarianism of the Soviet regime.

Masochism, like the heroic resistance Topolianskii speaks of, is an individual matter. Masochism is not a phenomenon of the faceless masses—although the self-destructive behavior of groups is itself an observable phenomenon in Russia, and a legitimate object of sociological study. Russians may sometimes seem to resemble a herd of lemmings headed into the sea, but that does not make the individual lemming any less interesting.

Psychoanalysis is, quite literally, analysis of the *individual* psyche. The collective is something else again. Many Russians feel that the collective is the most important thing in the world, but in psychoanalysis the individual reigns supreme. This is certainly one reason why there was a long history of hostility to psychoanalysis in Soviet Russia.

In any case, psychoanalysis understands that the individual who knuckles under to the collective is betraying himself or herself. The psychoanalyst cannot but observe that such submission, however understandable in context, is a form of masochism.

Masochism and the Slave Image

It is important to define the central concept of this book from the very start. Masochism, in the broadest sense (as opposed to the original, narrowly erotic sense),[13] is defined by psychoanalyst Anita Weinreb Katz as follows: "any behavioral act, verbalization, or fantasy that—by unconscious design—is physically or psychically injurious to oneself, self-defeating, humiliating, or unduly self-sacrificing."[14] This is roughly what Freud meant by his term "moral masochism."[15] Note that *enjoyment* is not part of this particular psychoanalytic concept, although the masochist, like anyone else, does *strive* for pleasure, and sometimes even achieves it. It should also be pointed out that, according to this definition, masochism can exist not only at a literal, behavioral level, but at other levels as well (one may wish to be beaten in reality, but one may also wish to be beaten only in fantasy—which means that masochism can occur in dreams, folklore, literary works, political commentary, religious teachings, etc.). The definition of masochism is not normally extended so far, however, as to include aggression directed outward, away from the self, for then we would be dealing with what psychoanalysts term sadism, or with the fuzzier and more problematical notion of the death instinct.[16] The definition of masochism utilized here also does not require a sadistic partner to participate in the masochistic act. Although sadomasochistic relationships are common, it is perfectly feasible to engage in masochistic behavior or fantasy without the participation of a sadist (e.g., one can beat oneself). Similarly, it is quite feasible to be a sadist without the participation of a masochist (e.g., one can beat others against their will).

Note also that no claim is being made here about whether masochism is "pathological," or "abnormal," or a "disorder." Western clinicians may use these terms, which are appropriate in their own cultural context. But I will try to avoid such evaluative epithets to characterize behavior in the Russian cultural context, even though the behavior in question may be fully comparable to what occurs in the Western clinic (and, by the way, in many areas of everyday life in the West as well).

I argue that the traditional submissiveness and self-destructiveness of the Russian slave mentality constitute a form of masochism. To say that the Russian soul is a slave is to say that Russians tend to injure themselves, defeat themselves, humiliate themselves, or sacrifice themselves unduly—all behaviors that characterize masochism in the Western clinical sense of the term.

And again, it is individual Russians who do these things. One may say that there is a culture of moral masochism in Russia, but it is individuals who enact that culture, who endow it with its masochism. Russia offers opportunities galore for suffering, as we will see, but it is individuals (even if fictitious individuals, such as Stavrogin or Ivan the fool) who take up the culture on its offer to suffer.

I am *not* going to argue that masochism is the essence of the so-called "Russian national character." If there is even such a thing as "national character" (or "modal personality," as some psychological anthropologists prefer to say), it has many aspects. The slave mentality is only one aspect. For personal reasons I became interested specifically in the masochistic feature of Russians. My task is not so much to "characterize" Russians as to examine a *particular characteristic*, masochism, as it occurs in individual Russians and in some established Russian sociocultural practices.

I want to emphasize that it is Russians who are being studied here, not any other Slavs such as Poles, Ukrainians, Slovaks, Czechs, Croats, Serbs, or Bulgarians. The terms "pan-Slavism" and "Slavophilism" (which all too often have meant pan-Russism and Russophilism) [17] have led to certain misunderstandings among non-Slavists. Some scholars— including psychoanalytic scholars—have tended to play fast and loose with the very term "Slavic," treating the highly diverse Slavic nationalities as if they were all homogeneous. But they are not. A Russian is not the same as, say, a Slovak—linguistically, politically, geographically— *and* psychologically. Some psychoanalytic scholars have even confused the *non*-Slavic ethnic groups of the Soviet Union with Russians (as when the acts of the Georgian Iosif Stalin are said to exemplify "Russian" behavior). The psychoanalytic scholar of Russian culture is just as obliged to learn the Russian language and survey the field of Russian studies as the Slavist is obliged to make an in-depth study of psychoanalysis before applying psychoanalysis to a Slavic topic.

Another sociocultural category that is *not* being studied here is the so-called *Homo sovieticus* who, as Mikhail Heller (Geller) and others have argued, possesses a relatively coherent set of (psychological and other) traits. [18] It is true that great changes occurred in Russia when the Soviets came to power, and that these changes could not but be reflected in the psyches of individual Russians residing there. Fear became a particularly important psychological factor, especially during the Stalin period. But my project is tightly focused on Russian masochism, which existed continuously before, during, and after the Soviet Union's seventy or so years of existence. *Homo sovieticus* may be a legitimate object of psychological study, just as "national character" may be. In particular, it would be interesting to find out which elements of *Homo sovieticus* are new and which merely derive from the old *Homo russicus* (or the old *Homo ucrainicus* or *Homo belarussicus*, etc., for that matter). But these questions would take us far afield.

I am not the first to apply the clinical term "masochism" to Russians. The most relevant work in this area was done by British psychiatrist Henry V. Dicks, a fluent speaker of Russian who interviewed Soviet soldiers who ended up in the West after World War II. Dicks refers to the "moral masochism," "intra-punitive tendencies," and "self-directed aggression" in his subjects.[19] He provides specific examples:

Frequently described reactions to threats by superiors, e.g., in the Army, are varying degrees of "self-immolation." A man berated by someone against whom he is powerless will suddenly, as it were, throw up his hands and say, "All right—shoot me then if you like—what do I care?"[20]

Russians have long experience of "absorbing" without rejoinder the insults and indignities of their masters and social superiors. The impassive exterior conceals a reaction which can be verbalized as follows: "You think me a fool and a knave. You think I am a feelingless clot and dumb beast. All right then, that's how I will act!" From this there result, according to my informants, countless acts of calculated clumsiness, spoiling of output or machinery, delays and muddles which are so contrived that while the perpetrators (often acting in silent collusion) are shown up as stupid and may be punished, they chiefly result in the vexation or heavy punishment of their superiors.[21]

The real focus of this author's research was not masochism, however, but "national character." As a result, his observations on Russian masochism were somewhat parenthetical and unsystematic. Similarly, others who have made assertions about the existence of masochism in Russia have not followed through with a detailed examination of this phenomenon.[22] Thus, although the hypothesis of Russian masochism does not originate with me, I do hope to contribute: (1) massive documentation of evidence for the hypothesis from a wide variety of spheres—historical, political, folkloric, literary, and so on, and (2) systematic, in-depth explorations in several narrowly defined areas, such as the folklore of Ivan the fool, the Russian bathhouse culture, the attitude of women toward men, and the attitude of Russians toward the collective. These explorations, in turn, will lead to a general claim about the maternal nature of the object toward which the Russian self takes a masochistic stance.

This book is about both images and realities. At one moment I may call up the emblem of the long-suffering Russian mother in a poem by Aleksandr Blok, the next I may cite statistics showing that the average Soviet woman put in nearly twice as many hours per week of labor as her husband did. The poetic image and the everyday reality are not always directly related, of course, but I think both need to be considered if there is to be an adequately broad psychological understanding of masochism in Russia.

The poetic versus the literal meanings of the very word "slave" offer an instructive example. Every person in traditional tsarist Russia was supposed to be a "slave of God" ("rab bozhii," as in the old proverb "Vse my raby Bozh'i [We are all slaves of God]").[23] This metaphor was very ancient and very ordinary. The Academy dictionary of Russian defines the expression not only as "a Christian," but also as "a human being generally (from the religious notion of the total dependence of a person on God)."[24] The corresponding feminine form, "female slave of God" ("raba bozhiia") referred not only to a woman Christian, but to a woman generally.[25]

The anarchist Mikhail Bakunin was thus only expressing a tautologous conclusion from ordinary Russian linguistic usage when he declared: "If God exists, the human being is a slave [Esli Bog est', chelovek—rab]."[26] Maksim Gor'kii, on the other hand, didn't mind God's existing as long as humans—Russian humans in particular—didn't have to be slaves into the bargain. Referring to the condescending generosity of God described in chapter 40 of the book of Job, Gor'kii exclaims: "Whenever I read this chapter, I shout out in my mind to my own fellow-Russians: just stop being slaves of God [da perestan'te zhe vy byt' rabami bozh'imi]!"[27]

The use of the word "slave" in these contexts is metaphorical and is intended to convey a certain psychological attitude of dependence and submissiveness before God. The metaphor is presumably based on intuitions concerning the attitudes and feelings that real slaves experience with respect to their real masters. As it turns out, these intuitions are quite accurate.

Real slaves existed in Russia well into our own century. There has been much variation over time and geographic location, of course, in the extent to which Russians have been enslaved. Technically, Russia has had both slavery (until 1723, then renewed in the Soviet period as forced labor) and serfdom (until 1861). Some scholars see little difference between true slavery and serfdom as it existed in Russia after the mid-eighteenth century. Under different sociopolitical conditions the Russian slave has been variously referred to as "rab," "kholop," "krepostnoi" (serf), and "zek" (convict, slave laborer). Curiously, the first two of these terms were also applied to Russian nobles in their relationship to the tsar during certain historical periods. The multifarious technical ways in which all these terms differ from one another will not be a concern of this book, nor will the socioeconomic, political, and demographic factors contributing to various enslavement practices in Russia.[28] Rather, my concern will be the masochism of Russians generally, many of whom happen to be literal slaves.

For the most part the Russian slave was indeed slavish. But the slave could also be defiant. This can be seen, for example, in various cultural practices, such as satirical folklore in which the peasant turns the tables on the landowner.[29] Defiance could also be manifested in criminal activity, such as stealing grain or timber from the landowner. Or there were more serious manifestations, such as the large uprisings (e.g., the famous one led by Emelian Pugachev in 1773–74), or smaller disturbances (so-called "volneniia"), or escapes. Sometimes rebellious peasants proffered the cunning excuse that the "tsar-father" was on their side.[30] But direct resistance to enslavement was, in any case, the exception, not the rule. As Peter Kolchin has pointed out, for example, *most* Russian serfs did not engage in "volneniia," otherwise serfdom could not have been maintained.[31]

Historians are understandably attracted to the various uprisings and rebellions which took place over the centuries in Russia. These are "events" which left extensive paper trails, while the ordinary, everyday slavishness of Russians constituted a distinct nonevent. From a psychoanalytic viewpoint, however, the rule is no less interesting than the exception.[32]

Much evidence is available on slavish attitudes in Russia, some of it going back centuries. In the mid-seventeenth century Adam Olearius, who had traveled in Russia, summed up his observations on Russian servility as follows:

They are all serfs and slaves. It is their custom and manner to be servile and to make a show of their slavish disposition. They bow to the ground to notables, and even throw themselves at their feet. They give thanks for beatings and punishments. All subjects, whether of high or low condition, call themselves and must count themselves the Tsar's *kholopi,* that is slaves and serfs. Just as the magnates and nobles have their own slaves, serfs, and peasants, the princes and the magnates are obliged to acknowledge their slavery and their insignificance in relation to the Tsar. They sign their letters and petitions with the diminutive form, such as Ivashka instead of Ivan, or *"Petrushka, tvoi kholop* [Petrushka, your slave]."[33]

About half a century earlier another traveler, Giles Fletcher, made rather similar observations:

Into what seruile condition their libertie is brought, not onely to the Prince, but to the Nobles, and Gentlemen of the Countrie (who themselues also are but seruile, specially of late yeares) it may farther appeare by their owne acknowledgments in their supplications, and other writings to any of the Nobles or chiefe officers of the Emperours. Wherein they name and subscribe themselues *Kolophey,* that is, their villaines, or bondslaues: as they of the Nobilitie doo vnder the Emperour. This may truely be saide of them, that there is no seruant nor bond slaue more awed by his Maister, nor kept downe in more seruile subjection, then the poore people are & that vniuersally, not only by the Emperour, but by his Nobilitie, chief officers, and souldiers. So that when a poore *Moujick* meeteth with any of them upon the high way, he must turne himselfe about, as not daring to looke him on the face, and fall downe with knocking of his head to the very ground, as he doth unto his Idoll.[34]

This behavior obviously signifies a masochistic psychological attitude in the slave who performs it. The kowtowing Fletcher describes was called "chelobitie" in Russian, literally "beating the forehead." Nowadays the word has acquired the metaphorical meaning of "petition" or "request." But it was originally—and in some contexts still is—a literal, physical bowing down, so low that the forehead would strike against the ground and possibly be injured. Other travelers' accounts from the sixteenth century, as Ronald Hingley points out, report that Russians "would happily exhibit the bumps on their foreheads raised through excess of zeal in executing the kowtow."[35] During the late Soviet period I actually observed athletic old women hammering a stone floor with their foreheads as they prayed before icons in one of the churches of Zagorsk. The Russian fool, according to a proverb, will go to extremes in this matter: "Make a fool pray to God, and he will break his forehead" ("Zastav' duraka Bogu molit'sia, on i lob razob'et").[36]

A particularly rich source of evidence about the masochistic attitudes of real slaves comes from Russian folklore gathered before 1861, for much of the peasantry before that date belonged to the serf category. The proverb just mentioned, for example, comes from the classic collection of Vladimir Dahl (1801–72), published originally in 1862. Here are some other lessons in slavishness from that copious work:

> Say you are guilty and bow down (or: lie down) (Govori vinovat, da poklonis' [ili: da lozhis']).
>
> He submitted and fell at his feet as well (Pokorilsia da v nozhki poklonilsia).
>
> Keep your head bowed and your heart submissive (Derzhi golovu uklonnu, a serdtse pokorno).
>
> Beat with your forehead lower: the sky is too high and the face of the earth is nearer (Bei chelom nizhe: do neba vysoko, do litsa zemli blizhe).
>
> Be quieter than water, and lower than grass (Tishe vody, nizhe travy).
>
> Crawl and grovel face down before him (Polzkom pered nim da nichkom).
>
> When they beat you, say thank you for the lesson (Pob'iut, tak skazhi spasibo za nauku).
>
> Do the work of seven, but obey one (Delai svoe delo za semerykh, a slushaisia odnogo).[37]

These utterances attempt to teach the peasant a sense of absolute submissiveness before authority. In pre-emancipation Russia this meant not only submissiveness before the peasant's landlord ("barin"), but servility before anyone powerful generally, such as a government bureaucrat, a military superior, and so on. Note that some of the items are in two parts, the second part being a reinforcement of the first. In effect: one act of submission may not be enough, two are needed to convince the dominant party of the slave's true servility, a servility of the heart as well as of gesture. Note also the "vertical" orientation of many of the sayings, the submissive party being well "below" the dominant party in the spatial configuration. Perhaps this is what Ivanov had in the back of his mind when he spoke of a Russian "law of descent."

Some of the proverbs describe masochism of a slightly different sort, that is, outright self-destructive behavior:

He offers up the rod to be used against himself (On sam na sebia palku podaet).

He is braiding a whip (or: a rope) to be used against himself (On sam na sebia plet' [ili: verevku] v'et).

The slave is beating herself if she does a poor job of reaping (Sama sebia raba b'et, koli ne chisto zhnet).

He covered his own beard with his spittle (Sam svoiu borodu opleval).

He stepped on the teeth of the rake and hit himself in the head (Nastupil na zub'ia—grabliami v lob).[38]

Such evidence for masochistic attitudes in the Russian peasant would of course have to be matched with evidence for *sadistic* inclinations ("It's fun to beat someone who is crying") or rebellious feelings ("A judge's pocket is like a priest's belly") in a balanced study of Russian proverbs.

Indeed, masochism is not the only feature of psychological interest in slaves. It is but one item in a spectrum of psychical phenomena which can be observed in the real slave, including that type of slave who lives in extremity in the forced labor camp, and who resorts to a variety of defenses—especially infantilization and identification with the aggressor—in order to overcome fear and survive physically.[39] The primary concern of this book, however, is masochism.

It should be granted that some aspects of masochism, such as extreme servility, may be appropriate in the situation of direct contact with a powerful master who holds the key to all resources. The shuffling, obsequious muzhik, like the American Uncle Tom in the antebellum south, had something to gain from his servility—which, by the way, is not to say that all muzhiki were docile all of the time, or that all southern black slaves were Uncle Toms in all contexts.

In the political realm servility can be especially useful for obtaining resources and even power (and hence, the possibility of acting on sadistic fantasies). The sycophant uses a form of masochism to manipulate a superior, and as a result can even appear to be in control of the superior. The relationship with the superior is not truly reversed, however. For example, all the tsar had to do was kill or arrest a few important people, or just withdraw resources, in order to remind his boyars *why* they were sycophants.[40] Or, all Stalin had to do was eliminate a few honest critics for most of the actors around him to turn servile.

In any case, masochism is no less masochism when it seems appropriate or adaptive in a given situation. It is important to recognize masochism for what it is, even as we never cease to be amazed by the multifarious uses to which it can be put.

What Is Russia?

Throughout this book *Russia* will be used not only as a metonymic designation of a geographic area occupied largely by ethnic Russians,[41] but as a collective personification of the Russian people as well. Here I simply follow tradition. Russians tend to think of their country as a collective representation of themselves, as a *person*. Numerous common epithets indicate that Russia belongs to this category: "Mother Russia" ("Rossiia mat'," "Matushka Rus' "), "Holy Russia" ("Sviataia Rus' "), "Motherland" ("Rodina"), "Fatherland" ("Otechestvo"), and many others which will appear in the following pages. Less common epithets are constantly being invented by Russian poets, but they have the same personifying effect, for example, Blok's "Beggarly Russia" ("Nishchaia Rossiia"), Belyi's "Deaf Russia" ("Glukhaia Rossiia"), Andreev's "Shabby Russia" ("Ubogaia Rus'"), and so forth.[42] Nowadays especially "sick Russia" is frequently encountered in the post-Soviet media.

The personification of Russia is a trope that is often extended, as when Russian soldiers are customarily referred to as "sons of the Fatherland," or "true sons of Russia." The poets especially are prone to take liberties in extending the personification. For example, Russia is a "female slave" ("raba") in the following stanzas from a somewhat sadistic poem titled "Russia" (1915) by Maksimilian Voloshin:

Люблю тебя в лике рабьем,
Когда в тишине полей
Причитаешь голосом бабьим
Над трупами сыновей.

Как сердце никнет и блещет,
Когда, связав по ногам,
На отмашь хозяин хлещет
Тебя по кротким глазам.

> I love you in the person of a slave,
> When in the quietness of fields
> You wail in a woman's voice
> Over the bodies of your sons.
>
> How the heart droops and shines
> When, having bound your feet,
> The master lashes wildly
> At your humble eyes.[43]

The poets are not alone here. Respected scholars too will extend the personification of Russia to considerable lengths. Literary historian Dmitrii Likhachev, for example, likes to dwell on the generosity and goodness ("dobrota") of a person called Russia:

> Russian culture did not copy, but creatively dealt with the riches of world culture. This huge country was always in possession of a huge cultural heritage, and managed it with the generosity of a free and rich person [s shchedrost'iu svobodnoi i bogatoi lichnosti]. Yes, namely a person, for Russian culture and all of Russia with it constitute a person, an individual [iavliaiutsia lichnost'iu, individual'nost'iu].[44]

Some authors, especially those with a nationalistic or Slavophile bent, extend the personification while at the same time refusing to recognize the poetics of the extension. Vadim Borisov, for example, speaks of the nation's person or personality ("lichnost' "), which is somehow distinct from the empirical and rationally analyzable manifestations of national life. In this view Russia is very much a literal human being:

> This sense of the nation as a *personality*, which has been expressed by individuals, corresponds with and confirms the people's awareness of its identity as embodied in folklore. Its image covertly governs our speech, for when we speak of the "dignity" of the people, its "duty," its "sins" or its "responsibility," we are making concrete, that is to say, unmetaphorical, use of terms that are applicable only to the moral life of a *person*.[45]

On the contrary, such usage is highly metaphorical, or, to be rhetorically precise, such usage constitutes the device of personification (Greek *prosopopoeia*, literally "face making"). A nation is not literally a person. A population of persons in a specific geographical area is not itself a person or a personality. It merely acquires some attributes of a person in the minds of its citizens (and the attributes it acquires reveal much about these minds). In the opinion of Russian philosopher Nikolai Berdiaev, anyone who actually falls for the idea that a given nation is a person ("lichnost'") is a nationalist, and is in some sense enslaved by that nation.[46]

The personification of a nation occurs in other countries besides Russia, of course, and is generally familiar to psychoanalysts:

We tend to regard our native land as a great mother who brings into being, nourishes, protects and cherishes her sons and daughters and inspires them with love and respect for herself and her traditions, customs, beliefs and institutions; in return for which her children are prepared to work and fight for her—and above all to protect her from her enemies; a good deal of the horror and disgust which is inspired by the idea of an invasion of one's native land by a hostile army being due to an unconscious tendency to regard such an invasion as a desecration and violation of the mother.[47]

There is a fairly extensive psychoanalytic literature on the personification of countries and other groups.[48] The (mostly non-psychoanalytic) literature specifically on "Mother Russia" is truly enormous, as will be seen below in chapter 7. Given the importance of parental imagery for characterizing Russia, it is not surprising that there is also a substantial (again, mostly non-psychoanalytic) literature characterizing the inhabitants of that country as collectively childlike, infantile, juvenile, adolescent, etc.[49]

Ultimately it is the real persons inhabiting personified Russia who are my quarry. Any personifying tropes these persons may create regarding their collective identity will here be read as projections or externalizations. The locus of the Russian culture of moral masochism is the mind of the individual Russian. For example, the unfortunate sufferings of "Mother Russia" and of her "true sons" cannot be understood without reference to the real sufferings of real mothers and real sons in a place called Russia.

TWO

Some Historical Highlights

I do not wish to relate the history of Russian masochism from the beginning, because the beginning is largely unknown. I also do not wish to tell this story in great detail, because it would be too distasteful for everyone involved, and besides there would not be nearly enough space in one volume. Nonetheless it is worthwhile at least to indicate some relevant high points, in roughly chronological sequence, before going into detail about specific, selected masochistic practices.

Religious Masochism

From the early days of Christian Rus' (an East Slavic area occupied not by Russians properly speaking, but by "Rusians," to use Horace Lunt's linguistic neologism),[1] there come reports of suffering welcomed by the sufferer. If, for example, the hagiographic accounts are to be believed, the princes Boris and Gleb permitted, even invited themselves to be murdered in 1015 by agents of their power-hungry elder brother, Sviatopolk. A variety of commentators have recognized the masochistic nature of this act (without using the psychoanalytic term). Soviet scholar S. S. Averintsev, for example, says that suffering was precisely what Boris and Gleb were up to ("Stradanie i est' ikh delo").[2] Soviet semiotician V. N. Toporov terms the act a "paired sacrifice" and a "voluntary sacrifice."[3] Philosopher Nikolai Berdiaev calls it a "feat of nonresistance" in which the "idea of sacrifice" predominates.[4]

Prince Iaropolk Isiaslavich, also assassinated by political enemies, is supposed to have uttered the following words: "O Lord my God! receive my prayer and *grant me a death from another's hand,* like that of my kinsmen Boris and Gleb, so that I may wash away all my sins with my blood and escape this vain and troubled world and the snares of the devil."[5] To Prince Andrei Bogoliubskii, another political murder victim, are attributed these last words: "I thank Thee, Lord, that Thou hast humbled my soul. . . . And now, O Lord, if they shed my blood, join me to the choirs of Thy holy martyrs."[6]

Examples could be multiplied. These "passion-sufferers" ("strastot-erptsy") are legion in the chronicles and other documents from ancient Rus'. Holiness ("sviatost'") was practically inseparable from sacrifice ("zhertva") of some kind.[7] Historian George Fedotov suspects that the accounts are distorted, however: "The voluntary character of the death is often contradicted by the circumstances related by the same author."[8] Many of the martyrdoms seem to have been concocted for political reasons.[9] Nevertheless, the *idea* of nonresistance to evil spread far and wide, and according to Fedotov began to be taken as a "national Russian feature."[10]

Ancient religious tracts are full of advice on the value of self-abnegation and suffering. For example, the *Izmaragd (Emerald,* which originated in the fourteenth century) characterizes humility as "the mother of virtues," advises children to serve their parents "with fear as a slave," and tells wives to obey their husbands "in silence." Misfortunes are sent by a loving God to give people an opportunity to save their souls or even gain glory: "Sorrows and pains make the sufferers glorious, as gold in fire becomes still brighter."[11]

The tradition of religious asceticism, which in Slavic lands began in about the tenth century and continues down to the present day, offers numerous examples of the active quest for suffering. The young Saint Theodosius (ca. 1108–74) mortified his flesh with iron chains hidden under his shirt, or exposed his body to stinging gnats. He was later known to sleep sitting, to eat a very meager diet, to beat his head against the floor while praying, etc.[12] Fedotov says that the "relatively moderate ascetic exercises" *(sic)* of this saint were supplemented by constant labor, such as grinding wheat, cutting wood, or hauling water.[13]

Saint Sergei of Radonezh (1314–92) wore uncouth garb, practiced heavy manual labor, would go for days without food, and adamantly refused to be elevated in the ecclesiastical hierarchy, according to his biographer Epiphanius the Wise. His holy ideal was poverty, and in this he "imitated his Master Jesus Christ our Lord." [14]

Saint Irinarkh of Rostov (d. 1616) always walked barefoot and wore chains and a hair shirt. Bolshakoff says: "After his death a collection of iron and copper chains, belts and helmets was found in his cell." [15]

Saint Seraphim of Sarov (1759–1833) was adept at fasting. One report has it that he ate nothing but grass for three years.[16] When consulted by the holy woman Anastasiia Logacheva (1809–75) he recommended that she wear chains to quell her carnal lust. Anastasiia evidently followed this advice, for upon her death penitential chains were found beneath her clothing.[17]

The masochistic practices of many of the holy monks were accompanied by paranoid fantasies or hallucinations ("demonology" is the theological euphemism for this). Theodosius said he was haunted by a "black dog" while praying. The recluse Isaac was pestered by demons who tricked him by taking the form of angels. The "much-suffering" John went about in nothing but chains and once tried to relieve his suffering by digging himself into the earth, where he experienced a terrible hallucination: "Over his head he saw the mouth of a horrible serpent belching flames. When the paschal night came, the serpent took the recluse's head and arms into its mouth and scorched his hair. Out of the serpent's mouth John cried to God, and the fiend disappeared." [18]

Perhaps the examples of religious suffering I have cited are extreme, and in some cases not credible. Yet it is generally acknowledged that the East Slavic holy men and holy women were indeed ascetic to a greater or lesser extent. Perhaps not all of them went to such great lengths at punishing themselves as the canonized saints were alleged to have gone. On the other hand, the less illustrious holy persons may have gone even further. Speaking of the relatively uneducated monks of the sixteenth century, Bolshakoff says:

Contemplation, the Prayer of Jesus and serious meditation on the Scriptures were replaced by extreme rigorism in the observance of a multitude of rites and by an astonishing severity in bodily mortifications. Long vigils, endless services, countless prostrations, extraordinary penances and fasting were de rigueur for every good monk, who, however, understood but little of the Scriptures and the Fathers.[19]

The population of these sufferers in old Russia must have been substantial during some periods. For example, in 1700, before Peter the Great imposed cutbacks, there were 1,200 monasteries in Russia. The figure for 1900 is 800 monasteries (300 of them nunneries), housing 17,000 professed monks and nuns, and nearly 30,000 novices of both sexes.[20] If religious suffering can be quantified (and even allowing for a decrease of asceticism over the centuries), these numbers are eloquent. They bespeak a religious masochism of massive proportions.[21]

Not without reason does James Billington speak of "an almost masochistic doctrine of ascetic discipline" and "the almost masochistic desire of the . . . monks to humble themselves."[22] Actually, the qualifier "almost" is quite unnecessary here. In similar fashion George Fedotov says: "The evaluation of suffering as a superior moral good, as almost an end in itself, is one of the most precious features of the Russian religious mind."[23] Again, the "almost" may be deleted. Suffering *is* masochistic in nature, it *is* an end in itself for the religious sufferers—which is not to deny that other ends also exist for such sufferers. In the case of monastic asceticism the most frequently mentioned end is of course spiritual perfection and union with God, and the eloquent writings of Nil Sorsky, Seraphim of Sarov, and some others testify to the mystical ecstasy which can sometimes be induced (in part) by self-denial and self-punishment.

There are signs of a revival of monasticism in Russia at the end of the twentieth century.[24] But it is not yet clear to what extent this revival will involve specifically ascetic/masochistic features.

Related (psychologically) to monastic asceticism is the Russian tradition of holy foolishness. The holy fool or fool in Christ ("iurodivyi Khrista radi") was a familiar figure in all Russian towns up until (and in some cases even after) the Bolshevik Revolution. Russians had a special fondness for the holy fools. As Slavophile philosopher Ivan Kireevsky said, "the Russian had a greater respect for the rags of the holy fool than the golden brocade of the courtier."[25]

Psychoanalytically viewed, the holy fool was a sufferer, part of whose masochism was specifically provocative or exhibitionistic in style. Giles Fletcher, English ambassador to Russia in 1588–89, describes the phenomenon:

They vse to go starke naked, saue a clout about their middle, with their haire hanging long and wildely about their shoulders, and many of them with an iron coller, or chaine about their neckes, or middes, even in the very extremity of winter. These they take as Prophets, and men of great holines, giving them a liberty to speak what they list without any controulment, thogh it be of the very highest himselfe.[26]

Often the "liberty" was paid for, however. Onlookers would verbally abuse or physically attack holy fools, or the authorities might arrest them. Holy fools would resort to all manner of scandalous behavior in order to provoke aggression: they sat on dung heaps, refused to wash, wore little or no clothing; they would dance about, shout obscenities or make incoherent utterances, smash objects, and so on. The sadistic impulse is unmistakable in all this, but the provocative-masochistic tendency overrides it. Kovalevskii demonstrates his awareness of this when he says of Pelagiia Ivanovna, the nineteenth-century holy fool from the Diveevo convent, that "she herself would provoke [vyzyvala] everyone in the community to insult and beat her."[27] Saint Procopii of Ustiug, who lived in the thirteenth century, thanked onlookers for their retaliatory jeers and blows. Vasilii Blazhennyi of Moscow (sixteenth century) was said to willingly accept the curses of those he provoked.

Maksim Gor'kii beautifully captures the exhibitionistic aspect of the holy fool's masochism: "Don't You see, Lord, how I torment and lower myself for the sake of Your glory? Don't you see? Don't you see, people, how I torture myself for the sake of your salvation? Don't you see?"[28]

Holy foolishness held an appeal not only for those who practiced it, but for many of those who witnessed it as well. Sometimes large crowds would gather around holy fools who were going through their masochistic routines. Impressionable children could not but be influenced by holy foolishness. The future narodnik writer Gleb Uspensky and his childhood friends, for example, admired and even imitated a holy fool named Paramon: "The children began to believe in the possibility of redemption and the happy life that would come in the next world. They followed Paramon around town, fasted, put nails in their shoes, and the child whose shoes first leaked blood became the envy of all the others."[29]

The *depiction* of holy foolishness in various art forms has its own attraction. Russian literature features numerous examples of holy fools, or characters who resemble holy fools, such as Pushkin's Nikolka, Nekrasov's Vlas, Dostoevsky's Prince Myshkin and Sonia Marmeladova, and Pasternak's Doctor Zhivago.[30]

Quite understandably, Billington associates holy foolishness with "masochistic impulses."[31] This is not to deny that holy fools were doing other things besides being masochistic (e.g., they sometimes offered a form of social protest, they prophesized, some suffered from an autistic disorder, etc.). Nor should we forget that folly for Christ's sake existed in other branches of Christianity, such as Greek Orthodoxy. It is curious, however, that thirty-six Russian fools have been canonized, while only six Greeks have. Saward is quite justified to speak of the "Russian enthusiasm" for holy foolishness.[32]

In the middle of the seventeenth century a new catalyst for masochistic practices developed on the Russian religious scene. It was at this time that a schism ("Raskol") arose between the official Russian Orthodox Church and a loosely affiliated group which eventually came to be called the Old Believers or Old Ritualists ("staroobriadtsy").[33] At issue were general questions of the growing secularization of Russian culture, the hierarchicalization of church authority, and the acceptability of foreign models for religious behavior. There were also some very specific issues of ritual, especially the question of how to make a proper Sign of the Cross. The Orthodox Patriarch Nikon, influenced by contemporary Greek Orthodoxy, issued instructions proscribing the old practice of using two fingers to cross oneself and requiring that this gesture be performed with three fingers instead. The theological doctrine behind this change is somewhat obscure (apparently three fingers signify the Holy Trinity, two signify the dual, divine-human essence of Christ). But the reaction to the new rule on the part of religious conservatives, such as the notorious Archpriest Avvakum (1620–82), was clear and categorical: "That wolf Nikon, in league with the devil, betrayed us through this crossing with three fingers." In particular the change in ritual was viewed by Old Believers as *an opportunity to become victims:*

In the instruction Nikon wrote: "Year and date. According to the tradition of the Holy Apostles and the Holy Fathers it is not your bounden duty to bow down to the knee, but you are to bow to the waist; in addition, you are to cross yourself with three fingers." Having come together we fell to thinking; we saw that winter was on the way—hearts froze and legs began to shake. Neronov turned the cathedral over to me and went himself into seclusion at the Chudovsky monastery; for a week he prayed in a cell. And there a voice from the icon spoke to him during a prayer: "The time of suffering hath begun; it is thy bounden duty to suffer without weakening!"[34]

And suffer the Old Believers did. *The Life of the Archpriest Avvakum Written by Himself* is filled with grisly scenes of flogging, burning, mutilation, starvation, forced labor, and other horrors—all welcomed in the name of Christ:

Down came the rain and snow, and only a poor little kaftan had been tossed across my shoulders. The water poured down my belly and back, terrible was my need. They dragged me out of the boat, then dragged me in chains across the rocks and around the rapids. Almighty miserable it was, but sweet for my soul! I wasn't grumbling at God. . . . The words spoken by the Prophet and Apostle came to mind: "My son, despise not thou the chastening of the Lord, nor faint when thou art rebuked of him. For whom God loveth he chasteneth, and scourgeth every son whom he receiveth. If ye endure chastening, God dealeth with you as with sons. But if ye partake of him without chastisement, then are ye bastards, and not sons." And with these words I comforted myself.[35]

Fortunately for Avvakum's reader, there is some occasional comic relief. Avvakum is capable of making fun of himself, he gently humiliates himself (this is part of his masochism) and his tormentors.[36] He is aware of his own narcissism, for he confesses to the pride which moved him to become self-appointed leader of his schismatic religious movement. As Priscilla Hunt observes, the revelation of this pride " . . . went beyond the conventional self-denigration of the humility topos."[37] There is a grandiose flair to Avvakum's masochism. His "voluntary suffering," his "self-abnegation and debasement"[38] entitled him to assume leadership of what he felt was the true spiritual way for Russia. And for this political prominence he paid precisely what he wanted to pay: he and three of his companions were placed in a pit filled with wood and burned to death.

Many lives came to a violent end during the apocalyptic days of the Russian schism. Avvakum and other leaders of the Old Believers sometimes even glorified suicide. Christ himself, after all, had welcomed the cup of death. There are numerous reports of both individual and mass suicides (usually by burning, sometimes by drowning) in the Old-Believer communities. A "deranged love affair with death," as Brostrom calls it, spread across the northern forests of Russia.[39] For example, in a village in the Ustiug region on October 8, 1753, 170 Old Believers—men, women, children—locked themselves in a large hut and would not let two Orthodox priests approach to dissuade them from their intention to "suffer in the name of Christ and for the two-fingered sign of the cross." Then, after shouting obscenities at the priests, they proceeded to set fire to the hut, and all inside died in torment.[40]

D. I. Sapozhnikov, who has written an entire book on this horrifying subject, provides a chart detailing fifty-three recorded incidents of individual or mass self-immolation in the seventeenth and eighteenth centuries. The chart indicates a grand total of 10,567 victims, although the actual figure is undoubtedly higher because it was impossible to record all incidents of group suicide in the far-flung Old-Believer communities.[41]

As historian Robert Crummey observes, "the Old Believers wanted martyrdom and were willing to go to great lengths to organize suitable circumstances." Their "urge for passive suffering" provides a striking illustration of a specific, religious type of masochism. The various instances of mass suicide among Old Believers had "psychological rather than social roots."[42] A psychoanalyst can only agree with this assessment by a professional historian.

Old Believer communities exist in remote parts of Russia to this day. The self-immolation practiced by some Old Believers eventually became an emblem of Russia's dark side. Mussorgsky's great opera *Khovanshchina,* for example, is based on events surrounding the Old Believer schism, and ends with a mass suicide by fire. Avvakum's autobiography exerted an enormous influence on the Russian radical intelligentsia, and on such literary artists as Merezhkovskii, Voloshin, and Nagibin.[43] There is probably an interesting article waiting to be written about the similarities between what Ziolkowski calls Avvakum's "auto-hagiography" and Aleksandr Solzhenitsyn's narcissistically charged *The Calf Butted the Oak.*

Christian Russia was (and in some respects still is) a land of myriad schismatic and sectarian groups, most of which arose in the seventeenth and eighteenth centuries. In addition to the Old Believers (including the numerous subgroups within this group, such as priested and priestless varieties, or those who "wander" and those who do not) there are, to name a few: the Dukhobors or "wrestlers for the spirit," who reject established churches and civil authority; the Molokans or "milk drinkers," whose asceticism is moderate and who eat dairy products on days of fasting; the Khlysty or "Flagellants"/"Christs," who attain religious ecstasy ("radenie") by various forms of self-mortification including possibly self-flagellation (depending on which expert you consult); the Postniks or "fasters;" and the Skoptsy or "castrators," who (the experts agree) mutilate themselves by removing their reproductive organs.[44]

Again, Billington refers explicitly to the "masochistic" qualities of Russian sectarianism.[45] The masochism is particularly obvious among the Skoptsy, although it does not appear to be erotogenic, even though the sexual organs are involved. That is, the mutilation does not involve sexual orgasm. Indeed, guilt over sexual feelings seems to be the cause of the mutilation, for such feelings were perceived as an obstacle to spiritual salvation. Among men one testicle might be removed ("polu-oskoplenie" [half castration]), or both ("malaia pechat'" [minor seal]), and sometimes the penis itself would be removed as well ("bol'shaia pechat'" [major seal] or "tsarskaia pechat'" [the tsar's seal]). Among women the nipple(s) or the entire breast(s) would be removed. The clitoris and/or labia would be cut out in some cases. Many, perhaps the majority of the Skoptsy, however, preferred "spiritual" castration, that is, sexual abstinence, to actual bodily mutilation.

As a result of their extreme practices members of some of the sects imagined that they became "Christs" (or, if women, "Bogoroditsy" or "Mothers of God"). This idea is actually a logical extension of a notion prevalent among all practicing Christians in Russia. The ideal sufferer in the "Russian religious mind" (to use Fedotov's expression) is, after all, Christ himself. Averintsev says that Russian saintliness is characterized by the most literal possible imitation of Christ, by a total willingness to "turn the other cheek," as Christ both practiced and preached.[46] For example, Saint Boris "imitated" Christ (the verb is "s"podobiti").[47] Epiphanius says of Sergei of Radonezh that "in all things and at all times he imitated his Master Jesus Christ our Lord. . . ."[48] Professor Brostrom has examined Avvakum's imitation of Christ in some detail.[49] The monastic director ("starets") Amvrosy (1812–91) repeatedly advised his listeners and correspondents to imitate Christ, for example: "You should . . . try in every way possible to pull out this root [of evil], through humility, obedience, and imitating the Lord Himself Who humbled Himself to the form of a servant and was obedient to death on the Cross and crucifixion."[50]

The poor and suffering peasantry of Russia were, by their very misery, often thought to be perfect imitators of Christ (cf. the tradition of confusing "krest'ianin" [peasant] with "khristianin" [Christian]).[51] To this day even not particularly religious Russians will, in a bad situation, utter the proverb: "Bog terpel, i nam velel" ("God [i.e., Christ] endured, and ordered us to [endure] too").[52] In suffering, a Russian is by definition imitating Christ.

Imitation of Christ is not some fuzzy, distant ideal for the religious Russian. It means concrete, physical and/or mental suffering. It can even entail a conscious search for humiliation. Dunlop says that starets Amvrosy "elected to spend his life hanging on a cross of self-abnegation."[53] The image of the cross is of course the Christian image *par excellence*. But here is a concrete example of just what that "cross" was for Amvrosy. The scene is the Optina Pustyn monastery in 1841, when Amvrosy was not yet a starets and was known as Alexander:

Once when . . . Alexander and Staretz Lev were together the Staretz suddenly intoned, "Blessed is our God, now and ever and unto ages of ages." Alexander, thinking that the staretz desired to commence the evening rule began to chant, "Amen. Glory to Thee, O God, Glory to Thee. O Heavenly King. . . . " Suddenly the staretz brought him up short, "Who gave you the blessing to read?" Alexander immediately fell down on his knees, prostrated himself and asked for forgiveness. The staretz, however, continued his tirade, "How dared you do that?" And Alexander continued his prostrations, murmuring, "Forgive me for the sake of God, Batiushka. Forgive me." By fighting down the instinct of self-justification Alexander was able to crucify the "old man" in him and put on the new.[54]

Such complete self-abnegation is the truest possible imitation of Christ.

Toward the end of his unhappy life the Russian writer Nikolai Vasil'evich Gogol (1809–52) became more and more attracted to religious self-abnegation. Christian humiliation became a goal for him. A great admirer of *The Imitation of Christ,* he gave advice such as the following to readers of his *Selected Passages from Correspondence with Friends:* "Pray to God . . . that someone should so disgrace you in the sight of others that you would not know where to hide yourself from shame. . . . That man would be your true brother and deliverer."[55] This advice Gogol applied to himself as well: "I myself also need a slap in public and, perhaps, more than anybody else."[56]

If a slap was what Gogol wanted, a slap is what he got, for even friends repudiated Gogol's book which, among other things, pretended to give religious advice to the tsar, requested that everyone in Russia pray for him (Gogol), advocated flogging for both the offender and the victim, and claimed that the common folk were better off illiterate. The publication of *Selected Passages* was followed by further masochistic acts. For example, Gogol burned the manuscript of a book on which he had been working for five years, the second part of *Dead Souls*. He grew increasingly religious, visiting Optyna Pustyn on several occasions, and developing a close relationship with an Orthodox priest by the name of Matvei Konstantinovsky. The latter recommended fasting and incessant prayer. Gogol followed this advice with a vengeance, and as a result he died of starvation and exhaustion on February 10, 1852.

There is a rich and ever-changing terminology for the various forms of religious masochism in Russia. For example, in the Russian theological literature Christ's voluntary relinquishment of divinity in order to experience human suffering is often termed "kenosis" (from the Greek, meaning "self-emptying"; cf. Philippians 2:6–8). The meaning of the term expands when scholars characterize the *imitation* of the self-humiliated Christ as "kenotic." [57] The meaning expands even further when, in her book *The Humiliated Christ in Modern Russian Thought*, Nadejda Gorodetzky says: "meekness, self-abasement, voluntary poverty, humility, obedience, 'non-resistance,' acceptance of suffering and death would be the expression of the 'kenotic mood'." [58] Fedotov, although resisting the breadth of Gorodetzky's conception, adds a spatial dimension: "It [kenoticism] is a downward movement of love, a descending, self-humiliating love, which finds its joy in being with the rejected." [59] Even Mikhail Bakhtin, whose dialogic theories would appear to have nothing to do with religion at all, gave kenoticism a central role. [60]

Kenoticism, asceticism, monasticism, holy foolishness, self-immolation, self-flagellation, and self-castration are different, if somewhat overlapping religious practices. Each is worthy of in-depth psychoanalytic study in its own right. Although all share the property of moral masochism, other psychoanalytic properties are involved in varying degrees and combinations as well (such as paranoia, narcissism, exhibitionism, depression, and intellectualization), and each practice will fit slightly differently into the psychobiography of any given religious masochist.

Early Observers of Russian Masochism

Serfdom was one of the first social phenomena to be attacked by the fledgling Russian intelligentsia at the end of the eighteenth century. Berdiaev goes so far as to say that the intelligentsia "was born" when Aleksandr Radishchev (1749–1802) expressed his outrage over the cruel treatment of Russian serfs in *A Journey from Petersburg to Moscow* (1790).[61] According to Radishchev, the peasant who works the field is the only one who has a real right to it, yet "with us, he who has the natural right to it is not only completely excluded from it, but, while working another's field, sees his sustenance dependent on another's power!"[62] The enslavement of the Russian peasant not only provokes moral indignation in Radishchev, but induces him to make interesting psychological observations, such as the following:

It appears that the spirit of freedom is so dried up in the slaves that they not only have no desire to end their sufferings, but cannot bear to see others free. They love their fetters, if it is possible for man to love his own ruination.[63]

Not only the literal slave, however, behaves slavishly. Members of the nobility can display extreme servility in their relations with others. Radishchev wonders whether those abused by a certain high dignitary know that

he is ashamed to admit to whom he owes his high station; that in his soul he is a most vile creature; that deception, perfidy, treason, lechery, poisoning, robbery, extortion and murder are no more to him than emptying a glass of water; that his cheeks have never blushed with shame, but often with anger or from a box on the ear; that he is a friend of every Court stoker and the slave [rab] of everybody, even the meanest creature, at Court? But he pretends to be a great lord and is contemptuous of those who are not aware of his base and crawling servility [nizkosti i polzushchestva].[64]

If the serf grows to love his chains, the nobleman wallows in servility. In both instances Radishchev identifies what appear, on their face at least, to be masochistic attitudes.

Poet Aleksandr Pushkin (1799–1837) reacted somewhat negatively to Radishchev's characterization of the peasant's plight in Russia. The French peasant, or the English factory worker is worse off, opines Pushkin in his 1834 essay on Radishchev's *Journey*. This is doubtful, however, and in any case is irrelevant. At one point Pushkin declares: "Take a look at the Russian peasant: is there even the shadow of slavish degradation [ten' rabskogo unichizheniia] in his behavior and speech?"[65] This rhetorical question is followed by praise of the Russian peasant's boldness, cleverness, imitativeness, generosity, etc.—none of which necessarily preclude slavishness at all.[66]

A particularly sharp critique of serfdom was made by the philosopher Petr Iakovlevich Chaadaev (1794–1856). In the first of his famous *Philosophical Letters,* written in French in 1829, he said:

Why . . . did the Russian people descend to slavery [l'esclavage] only after they became Christian, namely in the reigns of Godunov and Shuisky? Let the Orthodox Church explain this phenomenon. Let it say why it did not raise its maternal voice against this detestable usurpation of one part of the people by the other. And note, I pray you, how obscure we Russians are in spite of our power and all our greatness. Only today the Bosphorus and the Euphrates have simultaneously heard our canon thunder. Yet history, which at this very hour is demonstrating that the abolition of slavery is the work of Christianity, does not suspect that a Christian people of forty million is in chains.[67]

Chaadaev clearly disapproves of slavery, but he does not really direct his disapproval at the original enslavers, that is, at "our national rulers" who he believes inherited the spirit of "cruel and humiliating foreign domination" from the Mongols. Rather, he criticizes the Russian Orthodox Church for not intervening on behalf of the Russian people. For Chaadaev, official Russian Christianity is despicable for its failure to act. It is more backward, less truly Christian than Christianity in the West (he forgets the Christianity of the American South). He seems to suggest that the Russian Orthodox Church was itself behaving slavishly when it acceded to slavery in Russia.

Chaadaev utilizes an interesting familial image here: the Russian Orthodox Church did not raise its *maternal* voice ("sa voix maternelle") against serfdom. In effect, the Russian church *is not as good a mother* as the Roman Catholic Church which, since the time of Tertullian, had been known as *Domina mater ecclesia.*

Where there is a mother, a child cannot be far behind. For Chaadaev that child is Russia herself, or individual Russians:

We live only in the narrowest of presents, without past and without future, in the midst of a flat calm. And if we happen to bestir ourselves from time to time, it is not in the hope, nor in the desire, of some common good, but in the childish frivolousness of the infant, who raises himself and stretches his hands toward the rattle which his nurse presents to him.[68]

Chaadaev repeatedly resorts to the image of a child: "we Russians, like illegitimate children, come to this world without patrimony"; "We are like children who have never been made to think for themselves."[69]

Russian "children" lack not only a sufficiently maternal church, but a real legal system as well. As a result, according to Chaadaev, childish Russians come to expect, even welcome punishment from the paternal figure of the tsar, traditionally referred to as "little father tsar" ("tsar' batiushka") by Russians. The rule of law is utterly alien to Russians: "For us it is not the law which punishes a citizen who has done wrong, but a father who punishes a disobedient child. Our taste for family arrangements is such that we lavish the rights of fatherhood on anything that we find ourselves dependent on. The idea of lawfulness, of right, makes no sense to the Russian people." [70]

So, childish, inadequately mothered Russians live an abominable life. They willingly subject themselves to paternal authority. Incapable of asserting their rights, they only know how to ask permission: "Nous ne disons pas, p. e., j'ai le droit de faire cela, nous disons, telle chose est permise; telle autre ne l'est pas." [71]

Russians also enslave one another. Chaadaev, himself an owner of serfs, is racked with guilt. He has ideals of freedom, but he cannot live up to them, consequently his self-esteem is lowered: "Weighed down by this fatal guilt, what soul is so fine that it will not wither under this unbearable burden? What man is so strong that, always at odds with himself, always thinking one way and acting another, he does not in the end find himself repulsive?" [72] Given this attitude, it is not surprising that Chaadaev was subject to fits of depression.

The *First Philosophical Letter,* recalled Aleksandr Herzen, was "a shot that rang out in the dark night." [73] It provoked an uproar when it was published in Russia in 1836. The tsar got wind of the scandal and the journal in which Chaadaev's work had appeared was closed down. Chaadaev himself was placed under house arrest and— more than a century before psychiatric abuse was reinvented in the Soviet Union— Chaadaev was officially declared insane by the tsarist authorities. For over a year he endured daily examinations by a physician.

An essay ironically titled *The Apology of a Madman* (1837) was one result of this very frustrating situation. In it Chaadaev, among other things, takes back some of the criticism he had directed at Russian Christianity. The Russian Orthodox Church is now praised for its humility rather than castigated for its servility.[74] The Russians as a whole (not just serfs or the clergy) are characterized as submissive, but this feature now has a positive aura:

Fashioned, moulded, created by our rulers and our climate, we have become a great nation only by dint of submission [force de soumission]. Scan our chronicles from beginning to end: on each page you will find the profound effect of authority, the ceaseless action of the soil, and hardly ever that of the public will. However, it is also true that, in abdicating its power in favor of its masters, in yielding to its native physical climate, the Russian nation gave evidence of profound wisdom.[75]

Just what this "wisdom" was Chaadaev does not make clear in 1837. But in his later years he changes his mind again and criticizes the Russian slave mentality: "Everything in Russia bears the stamp of slavery [le cachet de la servitude]—customs, aspirations, enlightenment, even freedom itself, if such can even exist in this environment."[76] In 1854, during the Crimean War, he says:

Russia is a whole separate world, submissive to the will, caprice, fantasy of a single man, whether his name be Peter or Ivan, no matter—in all instances the common element is the embodiment of arbitrariness. Contrary to all the laws of the human community, Russia moves only in the direction of her own enslavement and the enslavement of all the neighbouring peoples. For this reason it would be in the interest not only of other peoples, but also in that of her own that she be compelled to take a new path.[77]

It is clear from his changes of opinion that Chaadaev must have harbored contradictory feelings about the submissiveness of Russians. A close reading of his works demonstrates that he experienced an intense ambivalence toward the idea of submissiveness generally. His psyche harbored both masochistic and antimasochistic impulses.[78]

Native Russians like Radishchev and Chaadaev were not the only ones to comment on the subject of Russian slavishness. Foreign visitors could not miss it either. A good example is the Polish poet Adam Mickiewicz (1798–1855), who was in Russia from 1824 to 1829. The "Digression" of his *Forefathers' Eve, Part III* (1832) offers, among other things, a satire of Russian servility. Mickiewicz tells an anecdote about a peasant servant found frozen to death on the field of Mars in Petersburg. It seems the peasant had been ordered by his master, a callous young army officer, to sit still and guard a fur coat. The officer had not come back for his coat, and the servant, rather than disobeying orders by donning the warm coat, literally froze on the spot. The narrator comments:

Oh, poor peasant! your heroism, a death like that,
Is commendable for a dog, but an offense for a human being.
How will they reward you? Your master will say with a smile
That you were loyal unto death—like a dog.
Oh, poor peasant! why do I shed a tear
And why does my heart quiver thinking of your deed:
Ah, I pity you, poor Slav!—
Poor nation! I pity your fate,
You know only one heroism—the heroism of slavery.[79]

As David Brodsky observes: "The anecdote shows the peasant's complicity in his own exploitation by a frivolous ruling elite."[80]

Another foreign visitor to Russia, Astolphe de Custine (1790–1857) had much to say on the subject of Russian slavishness. Custine was a French marquis who, having met Mickiewicz beforehand,[81] spent a summer traveling in Russia. His book, *La Russie en 1839,* was a great success in France and was very controversial in Russia, where it was read by many despite the ban on it there.[82]

Custine visited various Russian cities, including Petersburg (then the capital), Moscow, Iaroslavl, and the great trading center of Nizhnii Novgorod. He also stayed in the lice-infested roadside inns of many small villages. No matter where he traveled in "the empire of the tsar" the overwhelming impression he received was one of gloom and misery: "the life of the Russian people is more gloomy [triste] than that of any other of the European nations; and when I say the people [le peuple], I speak not only of the peasants attached to the soil, but of the whole empire."[83] Indeed, according to Custine, Russia is a society in which "no happiness is possible."[84]

The primary source of this unhappiness is the slavish attitude of Russians toward authority of any kind. This applies to all Russians, not just serfs (compare Olearius's previous declaration, "They are all serfs and slaves,"[85] or Chaadaev's assertion that there is no visible difference between a serf and a free person in Russia,[86] or Masaryk's later statement that "both slaves and lords have servile souls").[87]

Russian nobles, for example, are not like the cultivated, independent aristocrats of France and Germany, but are ambitious, fear-ridden individuals who are always trying to appease the tsar and other higher authorities. Thus the courtiers surrounding the Hereditary Grand Duke impress Custine with their hypocritical behavior: "What has chiefly struck me in my first view of Russian courtiers is the extraordinary submissiveness with which, as grandees, they perform their *devoirs*. They seem, in fact, to be only a higher order of slaves; but the moment the Prince has retired, a free, unrestrained, and decided manner is reassumed, which contrasts unpleasantly with that complete abnegation of self, affected only the moment before;" [88] "there are slaves everywhere," says Custine, "but to find a nation of courtly slaves it is necessary to visit Russia." [89]

Custine was an aristocrat whose father and grandfather were guillotined by French revolutionaries, so it is not surprising that he hoped to find evidence in Russia to support the idea of autocratic rule. But Russia changed his mind: "I went to Russia to seek for arguments against representative government, I return a partisan of constitutions." [90] Having now experienced a "nation of slaves" [91] Custine can declare that "a peasant in the environs of Paris is freer than a Russian lord." [92]

The idea of Russia as a "nation of slaves" seems to have been in the air by the late 1830s. Around the time the first edition of Custine's book appeared, the poet Mikhail Lermontov (1814–41) wrote a poem, now famous, about Russian authoritarianism:

Прощай, немытая Россия,
Страна рабов, страна господ,
И вы, мундиры голубые,
И ты, им преданный народ.

Быть может, за стеной Кавказа
Сокроюсь от твоих пашей,
От их всевидящего глаза,
От их всеслышащих ушей.[1]

Farewell, unwashed Russia,
Land of slaves, land of masters,
And you, blue uniforms,
And you, people, devoted to them.

Perhaps beyond the wall of the Caucasus,
I will hide from your pashas,
From their all-seeing eye,
From their all-hearing ears.[94]

Russia is here personified. She is "unwashed," as a person would be, she is spoken to ("Farewell"), as one would speak to a person. Her person is multiplied by the many who occupy her—the "slaves," the "masters," and the "pashas" (i.e., the tsarist gendarmes). She is despicable not only for her oppressors, but also for her oppressed who seem to welcome their oppression, who appear to be united in their willingness as one collective people ("narod") to obey the oppressors ("devoted people," or, in other variants, "obedient [poslushnyj] people" or "submissive [pokornyj] people").[95] Lermontov's contempt for the "land of slaves" is clearly very much in the spirit of Custine's critique of the "nation of slaves."

Given that so many accomplished writers—Radishchev, Chaadaev, Mickiewicz, Custine, and Lermontov[96]—had already dealt with the phenomenon of Russian slavishness by the middle of the nineteenth century, it is not difficult to understand why the definition of Russia as a "land of slaves" has stuck. It is now a topos taken for granted by many scholars of Russia. For example, writing in a 1992 issue of *The Times Literary Supplement* Leszek Kolakowski was able to speak of a "gloomy image of the eternal Russia, country of slaves,"[97] without bothering to use quotation marks or to mention his nineteenth-century predecessors in this matter.

Even the "iron tsar," Nicholas I, with whom Custine spoke personally, admitted to the sadomasochistic nature of his government's relationship with the Russian people: "Despotism still exists in Russia: it is the essence of my government, but *it accords with the genius of the nation.*"[98] For this despotic "essence" to accord with the nation's "genius" implies that Nicholas was indeed dealing with a "nation of slaves." The people ruled by Nicholas took, in his own view, a specifically masochistic stance with respect to his "despotism." Psychoanalysis offers a more straightforward terminology than the euphemistic phrase "genius of the nation [le génie de la nation]" uttered in French by the Russian tsar.

So, the Russian people have a genius for masochism. This talent, in Custine's estimation (although not in his terminology), applies to the lower as well as to the higher social orders, but in the former actual physical violence is very often involved as well:

Here, among a thousand, is another example. The postillion who brought me to the post-house from whence I write, had incurred at the stage where he set out, by I know not what fault, the wrath of his comrade, the head hostler. The latter trampled him, child as he is, under his feet, and struck him with blows which must have been severe, for I heard them at some distance resounding against the breast of the sufferer. When the executioner was weary of his task, the victim rose, breathless and trembling, and without proffering a word, readjusted his hair, saluted his superior, and, encouraged by the treatment he had received, mounted lightly the box to drive me at a hard gallop four and a half or five leagues in one hour.[99]

Custine seems to have witnessed such violence on a daily basis during his stay in Russia: "A man, as soon as he rises a grade above the common level, acquires the right, and, furthermore, contracts the obligation to maltreat his inferiors, to whom it is his duty to transmit the blows that he receives from those above him."[100]

The idea about transmitting blows down a dominance hierarchy is remarkable. In Fedor Dostoevsky's *Diary of a Writer* for the year 1876 the idea is expressed in a similar context. Dostoevsky as a young man had once observed how a government courier repeatedly struck his coachman on the back of the neck while the coachman, in turn, whipped his horse mercilessly:

This little scene appeared to me, so to speak, as an emblem, as something which very graphically demonstrated the link between cause and effect. Here every blow dealt at the animal leaped out of each blow dealt at the man.[101]

One could argue that Dostoevsky borrowed his image from Custine. But a merely literary approach would disregard the real contribution these authors make: Custine and Dostoevsky were depicting the same, objective social reality in Russia. People were beaten upon in old Russia, and those who were beaten upon tended to beat others.

Dostoevsky appends a further insight to his observation: "Oh, no doubt, today the situation is not as it used to be forty years ago: couriers no longer beat the people, but the people beat themselves [narod uzhe sam sebia b'et], having retained the rods in their own court."[102] What Dostoevsky has in mind here is the alcoholism prevalent among the common folk. He clearly understands that it is masochistic in nature, otherwise he would not metaphorize it as self-beating.

If Dostoevsky's reaction to the horrifying reality of Russians beating themselves and one other was to praise "the people" for its Christlike sufferings (see below, 240), Custine's response was to castigate the Russians for their essentially sadomasochistic social order:

Thus does the spirit of iniquity descend from stage to stage down to the foundations of this unhappy society, which subsists only by violence—*a violence so great, that it forces the slave to falsify himself by thanking his tyrant; and this is what they here call public order;* in other words, a gloomy tranquility, a fearful peace, for it resembles that of the tomb. The Russians, however, are *proud* of this calm. So long as a man has not made up his mind to go on all fours, he must necessarily pride himself in *something,* were it only to preserve his right to the title of a human creature.[103]

I have italicized two revealing aspects of this passage. First, there is an underlying masochistic attitude without which the sadistic practice could not continue. The one who is beaten upon "thanks" the one who beats (there are Russian proverbs on this topic, as we saw earlier), or at least accepts the beating without complaint. Second, the beating, which for what Custine would consider a normal person in a Western society would injure self-esteem, is instead consciously understood to *support* self-esteem. The victim pretends no damage has been done and experiences instead a special kind of pride. This compensatory or reactive pride is encountered time and again in accounts of Russian national character.

The Slavophiles

The notion of Russian slavishness was also taken up by the so-called Slavophiles ("slavianofily," who might more accurately have been characterized as Russophiles). For example, the philosopher Aleksei Khomiakov (1804–60) spoke of the "servility toward foreign peoples" ("rabolepstvo pered inozemnymi narodami") characteristic of Russians.[104] Generally the Slavophiles were uncomfortable with Russian slavishness. They looked forward to the liberation of the serfs, and they believed in something like free speech. At times they would even try to deny the existence of slavish attitudes in Russia. This led to some convolutions of thought which are quite fascinating for a psychoanalyst to consider.

It was asserted, for example, that Russians could be free even when enslaved (or even when subjected to what looked like slavery to a Western observer). Thus the ordinary Russian peasant was free even while being submissive to the government. Konstantin Aksakov (1817–60) expressed this paradox in 1855 as follows:

This attitude on the part of the Russian is the attitude of a *free* man. By recognizing the absolute authority of the state he retains his complete independence of spirit, conscience and thought. In his awareness of this moral freedom within himself the Russian is in truth not a slave, but a free man.[105]

According to Aksakov, Russians are essentially apolitical people who accede to authoritarian rule only because they have better things to do, namely, to develop their inner spiritual life: "And so the Russian people, having renounced political matters and having entrusted all authority in the political sphere to the government, reserved for themselves *life*—moral and communal freedom, the highest aim of which is to achieve a Christian society."[106]

The key idea for explaining this paradox, I think, is the adjective "communal" ("obshchestvennyi"), which appears again and again in Aksakov's discourse, as in the oxymoron "inner, communal freedom" ("vnutreniaia obshchestvennaia svoboda").[107]

The Slavophiles felt that intense communal interaction, especially of a religious sort, was the way to avoid enslavement by external, governmental power. The more Russians were enticed away from their native communal interaction (e.g., by the model of popular governments in the West, or by the westernizing reforms of Peter the Great), the more likely they were to be turned into "slaves." Only when Russians were being true to their essentially communal nature were they really "free."

Before further elucidating the peculiarly Slavophile understanding of "freedom," it is necessary to elaborate on the vital importance of communal action for the Slavophiles. I will begin by introducing a term which is frequently encountered in writings about Russian Slavophilism. *Sobornost'* (from "sobor," "council" or "synod") has been variously defined as "innate striving toward communality,"[108] "voluntary and organic fellowship,"[109] "sense of communality and unity freely acknowledged rather than externally imposed,"[110] and so on. Originally the term was religious or theological in nature, that is, it was an attempt to capture the idea of the "principle of conciliarism," or even the idea of the "catholicity" of Christ's church. But Aleksei Khomiakov and some of his Slavophile and neo-Slavophile followers broadened the notion, making it apply to secular collectives as well. For example, N. S. Arsen'ev utilized the term to characterize the congenial group spirit of the various literary salons and other social gatherings among the intelligentsia in Moscow during the nineteenth and early twentieth centuries.[111] Or, as recently as 1990, Aleksandr Solzhenitsyn proposed that a consultative body (a "Duma") be formed in Russia based not on mere "mechanical" voting, but on *sobornost'*.[112]

An example in Khomiakov's own work is an open letter he penned in 1860 to the people of Serbia which, among other things, glorified the communal decision-making process which allegedly characterized all Orthodox countries:

It is no accident that the commune, the sanctity of the communal verdict and the unquestioning submission of each individual to the unanimous decision of his brethren are preserved only in Orthodox countries. The teachings of the faith cultivate the soul even in social life. The Papist seeks extraneous and personal authority, just as he is used to submitting to such authority in matters of faith; the Protestant takes personal freedom to the extreme of blind arrogance, just as in his sham worship. Such is the spirit of their teaching. Only the Orthodox Christian, preserving his freedom, yet humbly acknowledging his weakness, subordinates his freedom to the unanimous resolution of the collective conscience. It is for this reason that the local commune has not been able to preserve its laws outside Orthodox countries. And it is for this reason that the Slav cannot be fully a Slav without Orthodoxy. Even our brethren who have been led astray by the Western falsehood, be they Papists or Protestants, acknowledge this with grief. This principle applies to all matters of justice and truth, and to all conceptions about society; for at the root of it lies brotherhood.[113]

The passage is replete with terms for the collective that Khomiakov and the other Slavophiles were fond of using: commune ("obshchina," roughly equivalent to "mir," another Slavophile favorite), local (land) commune ("zemskaia obshchina"), brethren ("brat'ia"), brotherhood ("bratstvo"), and society ("obshchestvo"). What holds the Orthodox collective together, according to Khomiakov, is an individual's submissive attitude toward it. Each member accedes humbly ("smirenno") and with love to some mysterious spirit of the collective, that is, to a unanimous resolution of "the collective conscience" ("sobornoi sovesti"). This is *sobornost'* in action.

Appropriately enough, the document from which this passage is quoted was itself signed by a collective of eleven individuals, including such well-known Slavophiles as Iurii Samarin and Konstantin and Ivan Aksakov.

Ivan Kireevsky (1806–56) was a Slavophile who described the alleged[114] communal life of ancient Rus' as follows:

You see an endless number of small communes [obshchin] spread out over the entire face of the Russian earth, each having its own manager of its laws, and each forming its own special accord [svoe osoboe soglasie] or its own small *mir*; these small *mir*s, or accords, fuse with other, large accords which, in turn, make up the regional accords which, finally, comprise the tribal accords, from which are formed one huge, general accord of the whole Russian land.[115]

There is much erasure of boundaries going on in this grandiose and hopelessly idealized picture. Not only is the communal *mir* equated with the agreement or accord ("soglasie") which brings it into existence and maintains it, but the smaller *mir* merges with ("slivaiutsia") the larger *mir* to which it belongs. This merging process proceeds on up the hierarchy of collectives, until all of ancient Russia is seen as one huge, harmonious collective.

Among the Slavophiles, Konstantin Aksakov was, as Walicki says, "the most ardent and uncritical admirer of the rural *mir*." [116] Aksakov was emphatic about the duty of the individual to submit to the will of this kind of collective:

> The commune [obshchina] is that supreme principle which will find nothing superior to itself, but can only evolve, develop, purify, and elevate itself.
>
> The commune is an association of people who have renounced their personal egoism, their individuality [ot lichnosti svoei], and express common accord [soglasie]: this is an act of love, a noble Christian act which expresses itself more or less clearly in its various other manifestations. Thus the commune is a moral choir [nravstvennyi khor] and just as each individual voice in the chorus is not lost but only subordinated to the overall harmony, and can be heard together with all the other voices—so too in the commune the individual [lichnost'] is not lost but merely renounces his exclusivity in the name of general accord and finds himself on a higher and purer level, in mutual harmony with other individuals motivated by similar self-abnegation [v soglasii ravnomerno samootverzhennykh lichnostei].[117]

The metaphor of the collective as a "moral choir" is quite appropriate in a context where the word "soglasie" (etymologically, "con-sonance") keeps coming up. The metaphor would later be picked up by the Symbolist supporter of *sobornost'* Viacheslav Ivanov (see Ivanov's notion of "khorovoe nachalo").[118] Here the image is elevated, sublime (as is Kireevsky's use of the term "soglasie"). But the corresponding "self-abnegation" of the individual does not recede from sight. There may be free speech in the Slavophilic commune, but when all is said and done there is no such thing as a minority opinion, or a loyal opposition. *Everyone* has to agree, the decisions of the commune have to be *unanimous*. One mustn't spoil the music. There is an ever-present threat that the personality ("lichnost'") will assert itself, "like a false note in a choir." [119]

We may return now to the Slavophile notion of "freedom." It is a remarkable fact that, despite all their emphasis on submission to the collective, the Slavophiles still believed the individual member of the collective to be "free." For example, according to Khomiakov only the individual Christian has authority. Even God does not have authority. Participation in Christian life must come freely, from within. It can never be coerced in any way. The true Christian is *not* a slave, says Khomiakov repeatedly. The true Christian is free.

Of course if an individual Christian decided not to exercise the option to submit freely to the will of the collective, then a problem could conceivably arise. That is, an individual, without necessarily becoming the "slave" of some external authority, might still reject unanimity and *sobornost'* as well. Khomiakov does not consider this possibility. Indeed, there is no room for dissidence in Khomiakov's Christianity. The true Christian is free *only* to go along with the collective.

This can be best characterized as a masochist's idea of freedom. It fits in with the general Russian tendency to characterize freedom in a paradoxical way. Dostoevsky's famous character Kirilov, for example, asserts that the highest form of free will is suicide. Or, there is philosopher Nikolai Fedorov's idea that the Russian tradition of obligatory state service actually fosters freedom. George Young comments: "While Westerners may look upon the Russians as a weak, slavish people who allow themselves to be herded like cattle by dictators who for some reason are best loved when most oppressive, Fedorov interprets the Russian lack of self-assertion as a subtler and more advanced understanding of freedom."[120] Another example is the bold oxymoron "free theocracy" ("svobodnaia teokratiia"), which is how philosopher Vladimir Solov'ev characterizes his ideal of social organization. As Billington says, Solov'ev's task was "to reconcile total freedom with a recognition of the authority of God."[121] In the twentieth century we have conservative thinker Aleksandr Solzhenitsyn asserting that "Freedom is *self-restriction!* Restriction of the self for the sake of others!"[122]

Examples could be multiplied. Here it is sufficient to indicate that neo-Slavophile thought regarding freedom is consistent with the inconsistent attitudes expressed by the Slavophiles on the same theme.

Without an understanding of the masochistic element in the Slavophile notion of freedom one might well argue that the Slavophiles *either* advocated submissiveness *or* advocated freedom, but not both. There have been endless debates on which of the alternatives is correct.[123] In fact, because of the underlying masochism of their ideology, Slavophiles were in a position to advocate *both* with good conscience.

There was some question as to whether the freedom advocated by Khomiakov was individual or was a property of the larger, supra-individual collective.[124] But the problem of the distinction between individual and collective itself perfectly reflects the poor demarcation which typically results when an individual takes a masochistic stance with respect to an object (see the clinical discussion below).[125]

The questionable distinction between individual and collective is also apparent in Ivan Kireevsky's formulaic characterization of life in an idealized ancient Rus': "The person belonged to the *mir*, the *mir* belonged to the person." [126]

In general, the constant references to "inner" freedom in Slavophile writings about the (by definition external) collective testify to a confusion between self and collective object in the Slavophile imagination. There can of course be no "inner" freedom when the *only* choice is to go along with the wishes of the collective. Or rather, there can be "inner" freedom, but only if it is consistently masochistic in its aims. In the West this would not normally be considered to be "freedom," although in Russia it is often what is meant by "volia" or "svoboda"— two words often unavoidably but misleadingly translated as "freedom."

Masochistic Tendencies among the Russian Intelligentsia

Although many in the Russian intelligentsia ever since the late eighteenth century have commented directly or indirectly on the masochistic tendencies of Russians, there is also a masochistic tradition within the intelligentsia itself. This is particularly true of those members of the intelligentsia who were politically engaged, the so-called radical intelligentsia.

In 1851, for example, the liberal emigré journalist Alexander Herzen characterized the powerlessness of the "thinking Russian" in the face of tsarist oppression as follows: "This is the source of our irony, of that anguish which eats away at us, drives us to fury, and urges us on until we reach Siberia, torture, exile, or untimely death. We sacrifice ourselves without hope, from bitterness and boredom [ot zhelchi; ot skuki]." [127] This sounds like self-sacrifice for the sake of self-sacrifice. It is really no different from the general Russian masochism Herzen was hinting at when he spoke of Russian slavery: "A long period of slavery is no accident, for it corresponds to some feature of national character."[128] Yet Herzen did not want to recognize the masochistic element specifically in traditional communal life, preferring instead to view it as a native Russian "communism" capable of protecting the peasant from exploitation by landowners and others.[129] Subsequent populist thinkers followed Herzen in ascribing great potential to the peasant commune for the future of Russian socialism and communism.[130]

Nikolai Chernyshevsky (1828–89) was a radical journalist who spent nineteen years in Siberia—and could have spent fewer years there if he had been willing to petition for a pardon after ten years. He was apparently not being ironic when he referred to his Siberian period as the happiest in his life (the "Bless you, prison" theme reverberates to this day in Russian literature, e.g., in the works of Solzhenitsyn).[131] When Chernyshevsky married he made it clear to his wife that she was free to commit adultery (she obliged him). The ideal revolutionary in his novel *What is to Be Done?* (1863) sleeps on a bed of nails. Harvard scholar Adam Ulam says that there was something in Chernyshevsky's obstinate endurance of suffering that "borders on masochism."[132] Not so. This *was* masochism.

Petr Kropotkin (1842–1921), although born into the privileged Russian aristocracy, was a champion of the exploited peasantry and a revolutionary best known for his theoretical writings on anarchism. As a young man he volunteered for military service in Siberia—when he could have remained instead in the capital. Once, when languishing in a French jail for his revolutionary activities, he refused to accept an offer of bail from friends. William H. Blanchard, in a very interesting study on revolutionary morality, is explicit about Kropotkin's moral masochism: "Kropotkin is difficult to understand without the assumption of some motive of moral masochism, a feeling of guilt that requires some compensatory behavior."[133] According to Blanchard, Kropotkin illustrates a thesis that may be made about revolutionaries generally: "Revolutionaries must be prepared to suffer if they are to advance their causes. They must show the government they cannot be broken, even by imprisonment. Perhaps the only people suited for such long ordeals of suffering are those who derive some satisfaction from the experience of suffering itself."[134]

The intelligentsia's will to self-sacrifice found its first full-scale outlet

in the so-called "going to the people" ("khozhdenie v narod") movement which took place starting in the mid-1870s. This was a joint effort
primarily by upper-class young people to serve their social inferiors, the
Russian peasant folk ("narod"). Some of these populists (sometimes
called "narodniki"—although this term is somewhat vague and has a
convoluted history) [135] wanted simply to help the peasants by educating
them and their children, giving them medical treatment, and so on, while
others (especially followers of the sadistic Bakunin) wanted to foment
anti-tsarist revolution. As it turned out, most of the peasants themselves
were not interested in achieving the social progress intended for them. In
some cases they even turned over the agitators to the police. There were
mass trials. The populist movement, initially at least, was a gross failure.

Perhaps this failure was not itself an unconsciously intended self-
punishment, but the original goal of political action by the Russian
intelligentsia did involve a form of self-sacrifice, even self-punishment.
Billington says these activists—especially during the so-called "mad
summer" of 1874—were "swept away by a spirit of self-renunciation." [136] Fedotov sees "something irrational" in the movement, adding
that "sometimes the motive of sacrifice was everything and the positive
work had but a secondary importance." [137] Tibor Szamuely says:
"Atonement for serfdom became the collective mission of the intelligentsia." Szamuely speaks of "the overpowering guilt-complex of the Russian intelligentsia, its obsession with the ideas of collective sin and social
redemption." [138]

Nadejda Gorodetzky translates from the memoirs of a "man of the
seventies," M. Frolenko:

> Youth brought up on the ideas of the 'sixties was imbued by the idea of
> serving the people and sacrificing personal career or goods. Many had, in their
> childhood, sincere [religious] belief. The teaching of Christ: to lay down one's
> soul, to give away one's possessions, to suffer for one's faith and ideal, to leave
> father and mother for their sake, to give oneself wholly for the service of others,
> was a testament of God. It was not difficult with such a background to take in
> the teaching of the 'sixties about one's debt to the people and the necessity to
> pay back for all the privileges received in their childhood. [139]

The reasoning here is not at all unlike that of guilt-ridden individuals
who entered monasteries. To the extent that some narodniki, in addition
to dressing as peasants, actually managed to share the unaccustomed
miserable life of the peasant—to work long hours, eat poorly, live

among vermin, and so forth—they paradoxically achieved for themselves the very humiliation which they longed to liberate the peasant from. According to Gorodetzky, the "desire for self-abasement" extended to the realm of education, for many of the narodniki felt that they did not deserve to become educated off the backs of the starving peasants: "If we wait and finish our studies, we may become bourgeois-minded and no longer wish to go down among the people."[140]

Although some of the narodniki admired Christ, Gorodetzky does have difficulty fitting them to the procrustean bed of Christianity. The psychoanalytic category of masochism is more appropriate as an explanatory, or at least just a descriptive category. Similarly, Fedotov has a hard time determining "what kind of Christianity . . . dominated the subconscious mind of the Narodniks."[141] Christianity is not an inherent property of the "subconscious mind," however. Again, masochism is.

One does not have to be a Christian to be a moral masochist. One can be an atheistic Russian *intelligent*, for example. It is simply false to attribute covert Christianity to a declared atheist. Scholars would not be so astonished that the narodniki resemble Christian monks if they were willing to admit masochism as a legitimate *tertium comparationis*.

It goes without saying that the narodniki were doing many other things besides being masochistic: they were reacting to odious tsarist authoritarianism; they were providing some education at least to peasants; they were identifying with the peasants; they were escaping from their parents; they were preparing the way for large-scale revolutions in Russia, and so on. The identification with the peasantry is of particular psychoanalytic interest, and is closely associated with masochism. This identification has often been expressed in Russian as "soedinenie" (union) or "sliianie" (merging). Richard Wortman (without mentioning psychoanalysis) speaks of an "identification with the peasant" among the intelligentsia of the fifties and sixties.[142] Paraphrasing the "anthropological principle" of Chernyshevsky, Wortman explains: "To understand the peasant, one had only to understand oneself."[143] Wortman also points to Aleksandr Engel'gardt's advice to fellow narodniki to acquire peasant humility (for then one is more likely to succeed in living and working with the peasants).[144]

Not all the Russian intelligentsia went as far as the narodniki in the masochistic direction (and even fewer went as far as the terrorists among them in the sadistic direction, e.g., those who assassinated Tsar Alexander II in 1881).[145] But the self-destructive or humiliating idea surfaces again and again in the literature about the intelligentsia. Berdiaev, in his contribution to the controversial *Vekhi (Signposts)* symposium of 1909, states paradoxically: "The best of the intelligentsia was fanatically ready for self-sacrifice [samopozhertvovanie]—and no less fanatically preached a materialism which negated all self-sacrifice." G. P. Fedotov says of the intelligentsia that "heroic death [was] more important than a life full of labor." Joanna Hubbs believes that "the intelligentsia assumed the role of the 'Humiliated Christ,' sacrificing their personal ambitions for the salvation of their motherland." [146]

Particularly eloquent on the subject of the intelligentsia's masochism is Tibor Szamuely in his book *The Russian Tradition*. Following in the footsteps of Dostoevsky, Sergei Bulgakov, and others, Szamuely sees the Russian intelligentsia as a kind of loosely organized religion:

The intelligentsia ... represented something in the nature of a revolutionary priesthood, a subversive monastic order. Its way of life was founded on a genuine asceticism, an aversion to worldly riches, a scorn for the ordinary "bourgeois" creature comforts. Self-abnegation became second nature; the Russian *intelligent* was easily recognizable by his utter and un-selfconscious disregard for material considerations, his fecklessness and impracticality, his indifference to appearances and cheerfully disorganized existence.

The intelligentsia regarded this hand-to-mouth existence as an admirable and highly moral condition. In part it reflected their voluntary renunciation of conventional values—it also went a long way towards satisfying the search for martyrdom which, whether consciously or not, underlay so much of their activity. In autocratic Russia martyrdom, in prison or exile, was not difficult to come by; it was accepted not merely courageously, but often, it seemed, eagerly. The cult of suffering, the idea of the necessity of sacrifice—sacrifice of oneself no less than of others—formed a vital element in their ethos. Suffering cleansed one, brought one nearer to the tormented people; the sacrifice of personal happiness, of the best years of one's life, and, if need be, of life itself, was the price that had to be paid for the achievement of a new Golden Age; only through suffering and sacrifice could the guilt of privilege ever be expiated.[147]

There is considerable psychoanalytic insight here. Without mentioning Freud, Szamuely not only perceives the moral masochism of the Russian intelligentsia (he calls it "search for martyrdom" or "cult of suffering"), but grants that it might be unconscious ("whether consciously or not"). Szamuely also detects the role of guilt ("suffering cleansed one," "guilt of privilege") and the issue of separation from/merging with another suffering object ("brought one nearer to the tormented people"). These are all topics that are familiar to the clinician, as we will see in chapter 5.

Speaking specifically of the masochism of the literary intelligentsia, Vera Dunham says: "Fiction of social concern was inclined to paint a dark picture of contemporary society, much darker than might have been realistically warranted. The black tone was added by the intelligentsia's need to be tormented."[148]

Some scholars have been reluctant to accept the idea of a self-lacerating, masochistic Russian intelligentsia. In his essay on "The Birth of the Russian Intelligentsia," Isaiah Berlin rejects "the generally held view of the Russians as a gloomy, mystical, self-lacerating, somewhat religious nation," preferring to regard Russian intellectuals, at least, as possessing "extremely developed powers of reasoning, extreme logic and lucidity." The problem here is that these two things are in no way mutually exclusive, as Berlin seems to think they are. The gloomy, self-punishing Stavrogin—to take a well-known literary example—certainly possesses "extremely developed powers of reasoning." Yet Stavrogin is a cold calculator *and* a guilt-ridden masochist all wrapped in one. He eventually commits suicide, which is the most masochistic act possible.

Berlin says: "If you study the Russian 'ideologies' of the nineteenth and indeed the twentieth century, I think you will find, on the whole, that the more difficult, the more paradoxical, the more unpalatable a conclusion is, the greater is the degree of passion and enthusiasm with which some Russians, at any rate, tend to embrace it."[149] In other words, the Russian *intelligent* is capable of acting in accordance with perceived logical truthfulness, even if the logical conclusion harms someone—including the logical Russian who is reasoning so well! Berlin's own Herzen offers Siberian exile as an example, as we saw above.

Berlin, too, offers an example, namely, the odd behavior of the social critic Vissarion Belinsky during his period (1839–40) of Hegelian resignation to the forces of tsarist autocracy. Nothing was more contrary to Belinsky's own natural inclination to resist autocratic power and help the downtrodden, which is to say nothing could have been more masochistic for him personally: "Belinsky gloried in the very weight of the chains with which he had chosen to bind his limbs, in the very narrowness and darkness which he had willed to suffer; the shock and disgust of his friends was itself evidence of the vastness, and therefore of the grandeur and the moral necessity, of the sacrifice." [150]

Perhaps the most eloquent *Russian* spokesman for the idea of a masochistic Russian intelligentsia was the writer and critic Dmitrii Merezhkovskii (1865–1941). In that volume of his collected works titled "Sick Russia," Merezhkovskii repeatedly asserts that Russians—especially members of the intelligentsia—are slavish by nature. Russians cannot be "holy," he says, without being slavish, because when they are free they are sinful: "In freedom they are sinful, in slavery they are holy"; "Holy Russia is a land of holy slaves." [151] Merezhkovskii advances the idea that the numerous rebellions in Russian history never amounted to much because the rebels (Pugachev and his crew, the Decembrists, etc.) always *wanted* to be defeated. The long line of Russian uprisings constitutes "an eternal rebellion of eternal slaves." [152] Characterizing the memoirs of the famous serf-turned-censor Aleksandr Nikitenko (1804–77), Merezhkovskii says: "A slavish book about a slavish life. The writer is doubly a slave, both by birth and by calling— a serf and a censor." [153]

Merezhkovskii, writing under the influence of Viacheslav Ivanov (1866–1949), describes Russians in a way that strongly suggests the modern psychoanalytic conception of moral masochism: "Self-denunciation and self-humiliation [Samooblichenie—samooplevanie, literally "spitting on the self"] are generally characteristic of Russian people." [154] Among Russians there is a "terrible will to descent, to disrobing, to self-destruction, to chaos." [155] Merezhkovskii (unlike Ivanov) actually uses the word "masochism" ("mazokhizm"). It occurs in reference to the suddenly repentant attitude of some of the intelligentsia after the events of January 9, 1905 (so-called "Bloody Sunday," when tsarist police fired on a crowd of peaceful demonstrators in Petersburg, killing over a hundred people). Here is how Merezhkovskii describes a "former Marxist" who was castigating the "ignoble Russian revolution":

His eyes shone with that delight of self-flagellation, self-destruction [samoistrebleniia], that voluptuousness of shame which in the moral realm correspond to the physical voluptuousness of blows, to masochism [sootvetstvuiut fizicheskomu sladostrastiiu poboev, mazokhizmu].[156]

These words, written in 1909, predate Freud's writings on moral masochism by some fifteen years.[157] The similarity is remarkable. Both

Merezhkovskii and Freud take the self-destructive element in (the original, erotogenic sense of) the term "masochism" as a model for self-defeating attitudes and behaviors *generally*.

Even more remarkable, however, is the primordial maternal imagery Merezhkovskii utilizes to depict the attitudes of failed revolutionaries. He refers to a passage in the story "The Holy Wanderer" by Zinaida Gippius.[158] A little child named Vasiuta is dying. For several days Vasiuta has been in agony, and is so worn out he cannot even cry. His mother takes him into her arms. He looks into her eyes, she asks what she can give him. His little head hanging limp, he replies softly: "You could give me a bit of milk, Mamka, but I don't feel like it [da ne khotstsa]."[159] The child is so totally defeated by his illness that he does not even want his favorite milk.

The defeatist former revolutionaries, says Merezhkovskii, are like this little Vasiuta. They hang their heads. There is nothing left for them, their former desires are meaningless. The attitude of a defeated adult is like the attitude of a defeated child, a child that no longer even wants milk from its dear mother. The image is primal, it refers the reader back to a very early stage in the child's relationship with the nurturing mother. Psychoanalytically speaking, the image is pre-Oedipal. Merezhkovskii anticipates what *post*-Freudian analysts will have to say about the ontogenetic origin of masochistic attitudes (see below, 94ff.).

Curiously, the maternal imagery returns in Merezhkovskii's depiction of something that would seem to be the very opposite of defeatism, namely, rebelliousness: "We [Russians] no longer believe the testimony of Saint Hippolytus that 'The Antichrist will ascend into the heavens.' *Yet we sucked this in with mother's milk*; it's in our blood, even amongst nonbelievers: treachery, sinfulness, the demonism of any kind of escape upward into flight [kainstvo, okaianstvo, liutsiferianstvo vsiakoi voobshche voli k voskhozhdeniiu, k poletu]."[160] Tolstoy's philosophy of reductive simplification, Pisarev's nihilism, and Bakunin's anarchistic tendencies are all examples of this upward-directed defiance, says Merezhkovskii.

Rebellious Russians did indeed "suck in" their rebelliousness "with mother's milk"—if the psychoanalytic view is to be believed (below, 106, 119). The primal rebellion was against the controlling mother in Russian matrifocal society. But the primal submission was also submission to that mother. Defiance and masochism are the two necessary poles of life's earliest ambivalence. Merezhkovskii senses this, even though he is not altogether explicit. The maternal imagery puts him just next door to psychoanalysis.

According to Merezhkovskii, wild, barbaric faces peep out from behind the ascetic mask of the Russian Christ. When Christ rises from the dead on Easter Sunday Russians customarily proclaim their holy joy to one another, saying: "Christ has arisen!" (Easter is a very special holiday—more important than Christmas—in Russian Christianity).[161] But Merezhkovskii tells us that he has heard drunken Russians mix *mother oaths* with their ritualized utterances celebrating Christ's resurrection.[162] Again, maternal imagery accompanies the vertical motif.

"What if the Russian idea is Russian insanity?" asks Merezhkovskii. This is not a very precise diagnosis, clinically speaking. But Merezhkovskii clearly wants us to understand that there is something wrong, something pathological in the slavish attitude of Russian intellectuals toward authority. Russia is like a man being buried alive. He screams in protest, but the dirt just piles up on the coffin, a cross is placed there, and the great Russian thinkers do nothing but find ways to justify what is happening:

Dostoevsky writes on the cross: "Resign yourself, proud man [Smiris', gordyi chelovek]!" L. Tolstoy writes: "non-resistance to evil [Neprotivlenie zlu]." Vl[adimir] Solovyev writes: "This is not the point [Delo ne v etom]." Viach[eslav] Ivanov writes: "Through the Holy Spirit we rise from the dead [Dukhom Sv. voskresaem]."[163]

A caricature, to be sure. But Merezhkovskii has understood something essential, something masochistic about the very "Russian" worldviews of Dostoevsky, Tolstoy, Solovyev, and Ivanov.

Masochism and Antimasochism

Vasilii Rozanov (1856–1919) was a contemporary of Merezhkovskii's who also cultivated hostile sentiments toward Russian masochism. His antimasochism is most clearly expressed in his writings about religion and sexuality. According to Rozanov, religious belief and erotic feelings should overlap with one another. There is too much asceticism and glorification of suffering in Christianity. Christ essentially castrated and made slaves out of his followers.[164] Russians should have more reverence for their pagan roots. The Russian Orthodox church should recognize that human beings are sexual creatures. Withered, impotent old monks should not be held up as shining examples for young people. The sexual activity of a newly married couple should be encouraged. Indeed, it should begin right in the church where the wedding takes place, and the young couple should live on the church premises until the wife is pregnant.[165]

Rozanov is fond of using maternal imagery to convey his ideas: "Christianity is the sweat, pain, and joy of a mother who is giving birth, it is the cry of a newborn child." But here Rozanov wants to emphasize the joy ("radost'"), not the pain ("muki"): "One cannot insist enough on the fact that Christianity is joy, only joy, and always joy."[166]

In contrast to his antimasochistic religious stance, however, are Rozanov's equally strong masochistic inclinations. For example, even though the Church refused him permission to marry the woman he loved (and with whom he had five children), Rozanov continued to praise the Church in his writings, for example: "The Church is the soul of society and of the people."[167] Rozanov's servile attitude toward tsarist power is also well known, and was essential to his extreme conservatism.[168] As for Russia herself, Rozanov never failed to see her in a bad light, yet he never stopped loving her either. Russia was condemned to sin and to suffer immense pain for her sins (here Rozanov is, as Lisa Crone says, a "prophet of doom").[169] *Because* Mother-Russia is a sinner one is obliged to love her:

It's no great accomplishment to love a fortunate and grand motherland. It is when she is weak, small, humbled, even stupid, even depraved—that we should love her. Precisely, exactly when our "mother" is drunk, when she tells lies, when she gets all tangled up in sinfulness—that is when we are obliged not to leave her. But this is not all: when finally she dies and is picked at by the Jews until nothing but her bones are left, then that person who weeps by her useless, spat-upon skeleton will be a real Russian.[170]

With this thoroughly disgusting imagery Rozanov not only idealizes Russian masochism, but reveals his own necrophilic and anti-Semitic tendencies.

Another Russian thinker who strayed into antimasochistic territory—and whose maternal imagery is equally interesting—is the religious philosopher Nikolai Fedorovich Fedorov (1828–1903). Fedorov lived ascetically, but advocated a view profoundly opposed to the fatalistic attitudes normally met with in Russia. Fedorov believed that it would one day actually be possible to restore life to people who have died, that is, to all those previous generations that have succumbed to what Fedorov termed "the blind force of nature." *The Philosophy of the Common Task*, a posthumously published treatise that Fedorov was writing for most of his life, has been called brilliant by some, half crazy by others.[171] There can be no doubt, however, that the theory of human resurrection advocated in this complex work is fascinating.

Death is the source of all unhappiness. "Why does what is living die?" Fedorov repeatedly asks. Or, to personify the issue: "Why is nature not a mother to us, but a stepmother, or a nurse who refuses to feed us?"[172] Nature is even an "executioner" of those who are willing to sacrifice themselves for the sake of their fellow human beings. But Fedorov resists death, he is disgusted by "altruists" who have a "passionate desire to be martyrs," that is, who in psychoanalytic terms engage in masochistic behavior. Fedorov's "project" for the resurrection of all humankind is a rejection of both the masochistic welcoming of death as well as the not particularly masochistic acceptance of death that all aging human beings develop. For Fedorov, death is simply not acceptable—not for one's self, not for one's fellow humans with whom one wants to connect ("rodstvennost'"), not for previous generations of humans to whom one is connected by the all-important bonds of kinship ("rod"). "Blind nature," who deals in death, must be conquered, must be "regulated" by means of scientific understanding. She must be given eyes to see us with, and only we humans, the highest and most intelligent form of life, can give her those eyes. Thus, to extend Fedorov's imagery to its logical conclusion, nature will no longer be the mere stepmother who tends to fail in looking after us orphans (cf. Russian "besprizornye"), but will be the ideal mother we all knew before we knew death, the first organism we deigned to personify, to give a face.

In fact, however, Fedorov tends to "patrify" rather than "matrify" the natural universe (he invents the Russian term "patrofikatsiia").[173] The earth tends to be seen as a graveyard of our fathers ("kladbishche ottsov") rather than our mothers (or rather than both). The face we will confront when we reach the ultimate spiritual summit will be the face of God the Father. These are just a few of the many side-effects of Fedorov's ordinary Russian sexism (his insistence that a wife's place is in the home, and his frequent references to "feminine caprice" require no comment).

Particularly interesting is Fedorov's denigration of mothers—this despite his extensive and life-affirming vocabulary of words based on the Russian root meaning "birth" ("*rod*," "*rod*stvo," "*rod*stvennost'," "*rod*noe ia," etc.). Once everyone is resuscitated no further childbirths will be necessary. Mothers are among the masochistic "altruists" whom Fedorov disapproves of. Christ did not admonish us to be like mothers, but rather to be "like children." Contradicting Saint Anthony's idea that the model of Christian love is the mother's total devotion to her child, Fedorov says that the son's love for the father is a better model. Even among animals mothers are totally devoted to offspring, and "the human race ... would be no higher than animals if its morality were limited to maternal love." [174]

Thus, even if nature *were* a mother rather than a stepmother, she would not meet Fedorov's high standards. It seems that even real mothers cannot protect their children from eventual death. Therefore it is up to children to take matters into their own hands, to work together on the "common task" of eliminating death through education and science.

Fedorov's great enmity toward death may seem exaggerated, but it is also very Russian. Other Russian thinkers have tried to find ways to resurrect the dead in one form or another, and many aspects of Russian culture manifest a preoccupation with resistance to death. In a very interesting 1965 article Peter Wiles viewed such varied phenomena as the Soviet slogans about Lenin's immortality ("Lenin is more alive than all the living"), the Orthodox tradition of preserving a saint's remains whole and intact, the Russian religious emphasis on Christ's resurrection from the dead, the folkloric figure of Koshchei the Deathless, the hyperdevelopment of gerontology in Russian medicine, Lev Tolstoy's obsession with death—and of course Fedorov's philosophy—all as manifestations of the Russian preoccupation with death.

The Russian fascination with resurrection is, in essence, a preoccupation with a special form of masochism: does one or does one not *submit* to death? The ultimate enslavement for every Russian is enslavement to death.

Of course for everyone—Russians and non-Russians alike—death is a serious issue, to put it mildly. But for someone living in a culture of moral masochism death is, in addition, viewed through the filter of masochistic motivation. One does not only feel anxiety, or dread, or eventual philosophical acceptance. One goes further, one *welcomes* death with open arms, or, on the contrary, one *denounces* it in disgust. Fedorov's "project" may be understood as an extended denunciation of death.

The polarity of attitudes toward death may be illustrated by an aspect of the difficult personal relationship between Fedorov and Lev Tolstoy. The great novelist and moralist was always saying things that irritated Fedorov. Tolstoy's "love of death" was particularly intolerable to Fedorov. On one occasion Tolstoy expressed his affection for the human skull lying on a desk at Fedorov's house. On another occasion Tolstoy said to a colleague of Fedorov's: "here I am standing with one foot in the grave, and all the same I'll say that death is not a bad thing." [175] As Young points out, these remarks apparently led Fedorov to break off personal relations with Tolstoy.

On his deathbed Fedorov did not admit that he was dying.[176] He carried his antimasochism to the ultimate extreme.

Viacheslav Ivanov, apparently reacting to Fedorovian ideas about death, had a more accepting, Tolstoyan attitude. In his philosophical discussion of the inseparability of humanity from nature ("Priroda," in this case not "blind") Ivanov quite spontaneously lapses into maternal imagery:

From the time that he is conscious of himself, Man remains true to himself in his secret wish: to conquer Nature. "I am alien to you," he says to her, but he himself knows that he does not speak the truth, and that she, welcoming the future with an inescapable embrace, answers: "You are mine, for I am you [ty moi, ibo ty—ia]." And thus speaks the oracle: you will not be victorious over the Mother [ne pobedish' Materi] until you yourself turn to her and take her into your arms, saying: "You are mine, for you are I myself [ty moia, ibo ty— ia sam]." [177]

There is an antagonism between Mother Nature and Man, and Man cannot win until he admits that he and Mother Nature are one and the same. But the victory will be Pyrrhic, once fusion with this particular mother is achieved, for Ivanov is clearly referring to death at her hands. The danger of being dominated by her, of welcoming her masochistically, is not escaped after all. Unlike Fedorov, Ivanov is willing to give up the wish to conquer Nature, to defy death. Ivanov's masochism in this context contrasts with Fedorov's antimasochism.

Nikolai Berdiaev (1874–1948) was a Russian philosopher so preoccupied with masochistic and antimasochistic ideas that he came to view practically the entire world as a would-be slave driver of the individual. In his 1939 book *Slavery and Freedom* he argues that a great variety of things—God, nature, the collective, civilization, individualism, the state, the nation, war, money, revolution, sex, beauty, and even "Being" itself—all are capable of "enslaving" the individual. This view may be characterized as slightly paranoid.

According to Berdiaev, the individual human being is inclined to cooperate in his or her own enslavement: "man likes being a slave and puts forward a claim to slavery as a right." [178] But one must resist enslavement. The existence of one's very personality ("lichnost'") depends on a persistent *refusal* to be enslaved. This resistance, however, leads to suffering, for in most cases, according to Berdiaev, it is easier to go along with whatever pressures are exerted on the personality than to be assertive or to seek freedom ("svoboda"). The truly free personality therefore cannot avoid suffering. Indeed, Berdiaev says, "in a certain sense personality is suffering." [179]

Berdiaev's advocacy of "free personality" would thus, on its face, appear to be an advocacy of masochism. This is not true *a priori,* however, for not *all* suffering has to be self-destructive or humiliating (e.g., temporary suffering in order to obtain something advantageous to the self would not be considered masochistic by the clinicians, as we will see below). Besides, there are very few people who go in for such suffering: "Free personality is a flower that blooms but rarely in the life of the world." [180] It is obvious from reading his books that Berdiaev himself was one of those rare flowers.

All Russians have a talent for suffering, asserts Berdiaev. Our philosopher is perhaps not such a rare flower after all. This is evident from his discussion of Dostoevsky in *The Russian Idea,* a book originally published in 1946: "The problem of suffering stands at the center of Dostoevsky's creation. And in this he is very Russian. The Russian is capable of enduring suffering [vynosit' stradanie] better than the Westerner is, and at the same time he is exceptionally sensitive to suffering, he is more compassionate [bolee sostradatelen] than the Western person." [181]

Suffering is much too important to the Russian to be separated from what Berdiaev sees as the traditional slavishness of the Russian: "The understanding of Christianity was slavish," he says of the Russian Orthodox Church's centuries-long subordination to tsarist will. [182] Russians are characterized by a "love of freedom," but they also demonstrate an "inclination to slavery" ("sklonnost' k rabstvu"); "Russians ... either riot against the government or they submissively bear its yoke."[183] Russians are thus a contradictory, ambivalent people, in Berdiev's view (and in the view of many others of course, from Merezhkovskii to Freud, from Belinsky to Brodsky). But the positive side of this particular contradiction, the striving for freedom, does not eliminate the negative side, the "inclination to slavery," nor does it eliminate the ability "to endure suffering" entailed by *both* sides.

There is a curious family background to Berdiaev's obsession with freedom and slavery. In his autobiography Berdiaev repeatedly speaks of his alienation from his family, especially his French-speaking mother: "The expression 'bosom of the mother [materinskoe lono]' said nothing to me—neither that of my own mother nor that of mother earth."[184] Here Berdiaev, by his own terms, is being very un-Russian for elsewhere he had said: "The Russian people have always liked living in the warmth of the collective, in a sort of dissolution in the earthly element, in the bosom of the mother."[185]

Berdiaev's sense of alienation ("chuzhdost'") extends to the whole world, yet the imagery he uses is persistently maternal, often involving *birth:* "I cannot remember my first scream, elicited by my encountering a world alien to me. But I know for certain that from the very beginning I felt that I had fallen into an alien world."[186] The positive result of this perpetual alienation was a quest for freedom ("svoboda"), a quest which is imaged as resistance to the familiar and familial. The verbal root -*rod*-, meaning "birth," occurs again and again:

Everything familial [rodovoe] is opposed to freedom. My repulsion against familial life [rodovoi zhizni], against anything connected with the birthing element [rozhdaiushchei stikhiei], is most likely explained by my insane love of freedom and of the source of personality. Metaphysically this is mine most of all. Kin [Rod] always struck me as an enslaver of the personality. Kin [Rod] is the order of necessity, not freedom. Therefore the fight for freedom is the fight against the power of the familial [rodovogo] over the human being. The opposition of birth [rozhdeniia] to creativity was always very essential to my philosophical thinking.[187]

The linguistic play here is striking, it is a kind of bad poetry. Berdiaev is *too* concerned with notions expressed by means of the root -*rod*-, that is, by the overall idea of birthing. He can barely bring himself to mention his mother, yet a mother is precisely the one who gives birth. The last sentence is particularly revealing, for it suggests that Berdiaev set his own personal independence, expressed as creativity, over and against his mother's ability to give birth. Yet the strength of the opposition only indicates the extent of the identification with the person opposed, that is, with the "birther" who would "enslave" him. Berdiaev's beloved freedom is itself a mother: "I issued from freedom, she is my female parent [Ia izoshel ot svobody, ona moia roditel'nitsa]." [188]

In his early writings (during the First World War) Berdiaev was as interested in Russian ambivalence about being enslaved as in his late works. But the earlier writings reveal a greater preoccupation with the Russian willingness to be enslaved, and they contain a remarkable personification *cum* gendrification of Russia. Not only is Russia a slave, she is a female slave. The "slavish" ("rab'e") in Russian character may be equated with the "womanish" ("bab'e"). Writing under the direct influence of Rozanov, Berdiaev says that there is not so much an "eternal feminine" in Russia as an "eternally womanish" ("vechno-bab'e"):

The Russian people does not want to be a masculine builder, its nature may be defined as feminine, passive, and submissive [zhenstvennaia, passivnaia, i pokornaia] in governmental matters, it always awaits its bridegroom, its husband, its master. Russia is a submissive, feminine land. A passive, receptive femininity with respect to governmental power is so characteristic of the Russian people and of Russian history. There is no limit to the humble endurance of the long-suffering Russian people [Net predelov smirennomu terpeniiu mnogostradal'nogo russkogo naroda]. [189]

This gendered imagery of Russia's slavishness eventually became a commonplace in Russian cultural commentary. For example, writing at about the same time as Berdiaev, the poet Maximilian Voloshin characterized Russia as a "bride" and a "female slave." Unlike Berdiaev, however, Voloshin metaphorized Russia's self-destructiveness specifically as sexual promiscuity:

Поддалась лихому подговору,
Отдалась разбойнику и вору,
Подожгла посады и хлеба,
Разорила древнее жилище
И пошла поруганной и нищей
И рабой последнего раба.

So you listened to the evil counsel,
Gave yourself to burglars, thieves and scoundrels,
Burned your towns and crops and would not save
This, your ancient home. And from this wasteland
You went out—embarrassed and a beggar
As the least slave of the lowest slave.[190]

Approximately half a century later Vasilii Grossman, in his bitter novel *Forever Flowing,* would pick up on this sexist metaphor and would even specify Russia's bridegroom, namely, Vladimir Ilych Lenin: "The Great Slave [Velikaia raba] rested her seeking, questioning, evaluating gaze on Lenin. He became her chosen one."[191]

Lenin himself showed some appreciation of the Russian slave mentality. In his 1914 article "On the National Pride of the Great Russians" he says that the Russian people are oppressed by "tsarist butchers, nobility, and capitalists."[192] This is possible, in part, because of the Russian nation's "great servility [velikoe rabolepstvo] before priests, tsars, landowners, and capitalists." Lenin quotes, with approval, words he attributes to Nikolai Chernyshevsky: "a pitiful nation, a nation of slaves, all slaves from top to bottom."[193]

True, admits Lenin, Russia also produced great liberals and revolutionaries, such as Radishchev, the Decembrists, Chaadaev, and others (there was antimasochism as well as masochism). Russia gave rise as well to a "powerful revolutionary party of the masses" in 1905. But, according to Lenin, the existence of "overt and covert Great Russian slaves," that is, "slaves in relationship to the tsarist monarchy" cannot be denied. Lenin is particularly incensed by the use of slavish Russian peasants to stifle freedom in neighboring countries:

No one who is born a slave can be held responsible for that fact. But the slave who not only avoids striving for freedom, but justifies and embellishes on his slavery (for example, he calls the suffocation of Poland, Ukraine, etc. a "defense of the fatherland" of the Great Russians), such a slave is a lackey and a boor who elicits a legitimate feeling of indignation, contempt, and loathing.[194]

For Lenin, it is the duty of Russian social democrats to despise Russia's "slavish past" and her "slavish present"—the latter most prominently exemplified, in Lenin's opinion, by Russia's role in the ongoing First World War. The best thing is for tsarist Russia to be defeated, because tsarism enslaves Russians and other nationalities. The best way to "defend the fatherland" is to revolt against one's *own* monarchy, landowners, and capitalists. They are, after all, the *"worst* enemies of our moth-erland [*khudshikh* vragov nashei rodiny]."[195]

One can of course reach one's own conclusions as to whether the subsequent defeat of Russian monarchism resulted in a lesser or greater quantity of "overt and covert Great Russian slaves." I think, however, that anyone acquainted with the history of the Stalin period would estimate that the sheer quantity grew.

Custine would have agreed. He would have asserted that, *in principle,* the Bolshevik seizure of power in 1917 could not eradicate the Russian slave mentality:

> Tomorrow, in an insurrection, in the midst of massacre, by the light of a conflagration, the cry of freedom may spread to the frontiers of Siberia; a blind and cruel people may murder their masters, may revolt against obscure tyrants, and dye the waters of the Volga with blood; *but they will not be any the more free: barbarism is in itself a yoke.*
>
> The best means of emancipating men is not pompously to proclaim their enfranchisement, but to render servitude impossible by developing the sentiment of humanity in the heart of nations: that sentiment is deficient in Russia.[196]

Custine understood that political revolution is not enough. There also has to be a change in the way people think, in their very psychology. Otherwise political repression just comes back. The "iron tsar," Nicho-las I clamped down (and got away with it) after the Decembrist uprising. In our century it was Stalin and his henchmen who managed to re-enslave the Russian nation after the bloodshed of the late teens and early twenties. In George Kennan's opinion, even if we grant that Custine's book is not a very good characterization of Russia in 1839, it is nonethe-less "an excellent book, probably in fact the best of books, about the Russia of Joseph Stalin."[197] This statement, we should keep in mind, comes from a former ambassador to the Soviet Union who had exten-sive dealings with Stalin. Kennan adds: "Whatever else may be said about Custine, and whichever of his many weaknesses may be held against him, his readers of the present age must concede that he detected, in the glimpse he had of Russia in the summer of 1839, traits in the *mentality* of Russian government and society, some active, some latent."[198]

An external, political yoke will always be possible as long as the Russians are weighed down with their internal, psychological yoke, that is, their masochism together with any reactive antimasochistic strivings.

Custine understood this implicitly. He stepped right up to the brink of psychoanalysis.

Recent Developments

During most of the Soviet period it was impossible to discuss Russian masochism openly in Russia. Abroad, however, discussion was possible (e.g., Berdiaev, Fedotov, and some others, as we have seen). Particularly interesting are the publications of Russian dissidents in the West from the 1970s. Julia Brun-Zejmis has recently analyzed the works of such thinkers as Andrei Amal'rik, Igor' Shafarevich, Iurii Glazov, Aleksandr Solzhenitsyn, Dmitrii Dudko, Vasilii Grossman, and others in light of their highly diverse views of "Russian subservience" and "Russia's martyrdom under the Soviet regime."[199] Brun-Zejmis finds fascinating parallels between the writings of these thinkers and the works of Chaadaev long before them. I will have more to say about some of these writers below. Here it is sufficient to quote one of the dissidents Brun-Zejmis discusses, namely, O. Altaev, who makes a very interesting argument about the "dual consciousness" of the servile Soviet intelligentsia:

The intelligentsia does not accept the Soviet regime, it tends to shun it and at times even despises it. Yet, on the other hand, there is a symbiosis between them. The intelligentsia feeds the regime, it cherishes it and fosters it. It awaits the collapse of the Soviet regime and hopes this collapse will come sooner or later, but it also co-operates with it. The intelligentsia suffers because it is forced to live under Soviet rule, yet it strives toward prosperity. We have here a combination of the incombinable. It is not enough to call it conformism, for conformism is a completely legal compromise of interests by means of mutual concessions accepted in human society everywhere. It is also not enough to call it opportunism. That would be a narrow interpretation, for opportunism is a result of deeper processes. It is servility, but not of an ordinary kind, but an *ostentatious servility with suffering*, with "a Dostoevskian touch" to it. Here we have at the same time a horror of the fall and enjoyment in it; no conformism, no opportunism knows of such refined torments.[200]

Such suffering is clearly an example of moral masochism, although Altaev of course does not use the psychoanalytic term and tends to emphasize its collective aspect.

Within Russia it became possible to consider the question of Russian masochism openly only after the mid-1980s. The reforms initiated by Mikhail Gorbachev were the key to this process. Whether Gorbachev intended to or not, his institution of glasnost stimulated intellectuals to grapple with the issue of Russianness itself.

One of the first to publicly recognize the traditionally slavish attitude toward authority in Russia during this period was the noted poet Evgenii Evtushenko. Writing in a 1988 issue of *Literaturnaia gazeta,* Evtushenko argued that "slavish blood" has accumulated to such an extent in his culture that " . . . today it must not be squeezed out drop by drop but pumped out by the bucketful." [201]

In his article Evtushenko attempts to explain the recent Russian coinage *priterpelost'*. According to Evtushenko, *priterpelost'*—rendered as "servile patience" by the resourceful Antonina W. Bouis [202]—is an attitude which has for many decades allowed Russians to tolerate chronic shortages of ordinary consumer goods and services:

Priterpelost is capitulation before "infinite humiliations" [Pasternak's phrase]. First we humiliate ourselves [unizhaemsia] to get an apartment. We humiliate ourselves hunting in the jungles of commerce for wallpaper, faucets, toilet bowls, latches. The sight of a Yugoslav lamp fixture or a Rumanian sofa bed brings fireworks to our eyes. When a child is born, we humiliate ourselves to obtain day care and kindergartens, finding nipples, crawlers, disposable diapers, carriages, sleds, playpens. We humiliate ourselves in stores, beauty parlors, tailor shops, dry cleaners, car-repair garages, restaurants, hotels, box offices and Aeroflot counters, repair shops for TVs, refrigerators and sewing machines—stepping on our pride, moving from wheedling to arguing and back to wheedling. We spend all our time trying to get something. It's humiliating that we still can't feed ourselves, having to buy bread and butter and meat and fruit and vegetables abroad. [203]

Evtushenko was not describing a merely current or temporary situation. Seventy-one years after the Bolshevik Revolution, and forty-three years after defeating a by now affluent Germany, Evtushenko's Russia was *still* a country of widespread consumer deficits. Since the fall of the Soviet Union the economic situation has only become worse, of course.

How has it been possible for Russians to endure their economic deprivation for so long? The answer, Evtushenko seems to suggest, is a chronically low self-esteem: "Every queue, every shortage shows our society's disrespect for itself [neuvazhenie obshchestva k samomu sebe]." Custine, too, had noticed the low self-esteem of the Russians when he observed that living in Russia "renders characters melancholy, and self-love distrustful [les amours-propres défiants]." [204] A society that thinks so little of itself, says Evtushenko, will tolerate being victimized, or will only grumble mildly at the authorities and avoid real insight into its situation. Above all, it will not act. The authorities alone are not responsible, says Evtushenko, and blaming them is no excuse for inaction. The people ("narod") themselves are, in part, responsible. They do not respect themselves enough to protest, to support perestroika, to take concrete action against "humiliating queues."

Anyone who has ever stood in a line for long knows the feeling of frustration that comes with this experience. But for Russians there is more than frustration. There is surrender, surrender which becomes chronically intertwined with self-identity and self-respect.

Evtushenko says that Russians passively accept their bad situation because they feel they deserve a bad situation: "If we put up with it, then we deserve it." Anyone who accepts humiliation deserves humiliation. Russians ask for it, they get it, and it is appropriate that they get it. Evtushenko approves of the punishment. But he says "*we* deserve it," which is to say he invites it for himself as well. He is a Russian, he knows himself, he knows that there is a part of himself that wants to be humiliated. He wants to overcome that part of himself, he wants Russians to overcome that part of themselves. But that masochistic part is nonetheless still there, and as long as it is there self-esteem will be low: "most of all, I want our country to like itself"—which is to say that, at present, it still does not like itself.

Russians love their country, Evtushenko says: "We are proud of its traditions. But not all traditions are good. And *priterpelost'* is a bad tradition that must be rejected."[205] National self-esteem is reduced by masochistic *priterpelost'*. It is only a rather perverse, that is, reactive, concept of national pride that would include a traditional wish to be humiliated.

During the late Soviet and, now, the immediate post-Soviet period there have been abundant discussions of the self-destructive variant of masochism in the Russian press. It is not difficult to see why. Many political, economic, and cultural structures have come tumbling down, as if on purpose, as if their destruction were somehow intended.

An anonymous 1992 editorial in *Nezavisimaia gazeta* states that society ("obshchestvo") is in such extreme disarray that "it is capable of only a more or less rapid self-disintegration [samoraspadu]."[206] In a poem on the front page of a 1992 issue of *Literaturnaia gazeta* poet Andrei Voznesenskii declares that "Russia is a suicide" ("Rossiia—

samoubiitsa").[207] In a January 1991 issue of the same newspaper Lidiia Grafova speaks of "the bacchanalia of our self-destruction."[208]

Perhaps the most eloquent portrayal of self-destructiveness was offered by the former dissident Aleksandr Solzhenitsyn. In a now famous essay predicting the breakup of the Soviet Union Solzhenitsyn says:

We have forfeited our earlier abundance, destroyed the peasant class together with its settlements, deprived the raising of crops of its whole purpose and the soil of its ability to yield a harvest, while flooding the land with man-made seas and swamps. The environs of our cities are befouled by the effluents of our primitive industry, we have poisoned our rivers, lakes, and fish, and today we are obliterating our last resources of clean water, air, and soil, speeding the process by the addition of nuclear death, further supplemented by the storage of Western radioactive wastes for money. Depleting our natural wealth for the sake of grandiose future conquests under a crazed leadership, we have cut down our luxuriant forests and plundered our earth of its incomparable riches—the irreplaceable inheritance of our great-grandchildren—in order to sell them off abroad with uncaring hand. We have saddled our women with backbreaking, impossibly burdensome labor, torn them from their children, and have abandoned the children themselves to disease, brutishness, and a semblance of education. Our health care is utterly neglected, there are no medicines, and we have even forgotten the meaning of a proper diet. Millions lack housing, and a helplessness bred of the absence of personal rights permeates the entire country. And throughout all this we cling to only one thing: that we not be deprived of our unlimited drunkenness.[209]

So: we have done this, we have done that, the destruction is *our* fault, it is really *self*-destruction. This sounds very much like masochism. But there is a catch. A society is not a person. The "we" is not an "I"— however much the Russian imagination strives to equate the two (see below, chap. 9). Real masochism is about individual persons, not societies. Russian society may be falling apart in many respects, but the locus of masochism is in its self-destructive citizens—the alcoholics, drug addicts, suicides, overburdened wives, envious peasants, unproductive workers, and so on. And of course there are other reasons for the disintegration of Soviet Russia besides the masochism of individuals. Indeed it could be argued that individual masochism was greater in the more stable periods of Russian history than during Russia's troubled times, for it was then that individuals knuckled under to authority.

The topic of masochism has even become fashionable, and sometimes even the formerly rare Russian word "mazohkizm" is used in these discussions. In a recent interview in *Moskovskie novosti* writer Vl.

Sorokin uses the word to refer to the fondness for the camp theme in the writings of Solzhenitsyn and Shalamov.[210] More often than not the Russian word is used in a metaphorical sense of the self-destructiveness of a group rather than of the individual, as in an article which appeared in *Moskovskie novosti* in 1991: "We must oppose the masochistic slogan [mazokhistskomu lozungu] about the immediate disintegration of government with a slogan about the freedom of downtrodden nations."[211] Sometimes, although the word "mazokhizm" is not used, that is nonetheless what is meant. For example, a series of articles on "self-destructiveness" ("samorazrushenie") appeared in *Literaturnaia gazeta* in 1992. In one article Vasilii Golovanov interviews medical researcher V. D. Topolianskii, who argues that Russia's totalitarian past fostered self-destructive behavior:

A totalitarian society needs the self-destructive person [samorazrushaiushchii-sia], meaning a person who can be controlled. Therefore totalitarianism creates an unusually subtle system for achieving the seduction, corruption, and, ultimately, the self-destruction of the personality. The final product is a person who has so lost track of himself, and has squandered his abilities and attachments to such an extent that he gains pleasure from the fact that he is scum [podonok].[212]

Every normal person, according to Topolianskii, has a need to do some useful, even creative activity. If this need is repressed externally the individual may start to behave in a self-destructive way. A worker's negative attitude toward work is an example. The shoddy workmanship of Soviet industrial products harmed not only consumers, but did psychological harm to the workers themselves, or induced them to harm themselves. Tatiana Zaslavskaia, in her secret "Novosibirsk Report" of 1983, spoke of the "low value attached to labour as a means of self-realization" among Soviet workers.[213] Anyone who lived in Russia during the late Soviet period knows the proverb, "They pretend to pay us, and we pretend to work." But in behaving according to this proverb one was really betraying oneself, one was acting in a self-destructive fashion. The worker's "I don't care" attitude—which translates Topolianskii's very oral Russian expression "naplevatel'stvo," literally, "spitting on [something]"—could only lower one's own opinion of oneself and make one feel like "scum." One might just as well have been one of the most extreme forms of masochist, that is, an alcoholic, as in the proverb: "If vodka interferes with your work, give up work!"[214]

Another recent commentary on masochism in Russia comes from

the president of the recently founded Russian Psychoanalytic Society, psychiatrist Aron Isaakovich Belkin. In an article that appeared in the newspaper *Sovetskaia kul'tura* in July of 1991, Belkin discusses the negativism of the contemporary Soviet media ("Everything is bad, everything is horrible, and everything will become even more horrible!"), comparing it to the attitude of a normal adolescent who is trying to break free from the parents by constantly finding fault with them. He points to alcoholism, endemic boorishness ("khamstvo"), and the widespread I-don't-care attitude as examples of "self-destruction of the personality" ("samodestruktsiia lichnosti").[215]

Curiously, Belkin does not use the psychoanalytic term "masochism," and demonstrates no awareness of the recent psychoanalytic research on masochism that has been going on in the West (see chap. 5, below). In the newly emerging psychoanalytic literature, on the other hand, masochism is explicitly discussed in light of recent Western research. These discussions are for the most part confined to erotogenic masochism, however.[216]

THREE

Two Key Words
in the Vocabulary
of Russian Masochism

It would be difficult to move any further in this psychoanalytic treatise without an explication of two items which are very difficult to translate into English. Indeed, I will not translate them, but will refer to them in transliterated form for the duration.

Smirenie

The ethical notion of *smirenie* falls into the same semantic ballpark occupied by such English terms as "humility," "meekness," and "submission," but the Russian term is more affectively loaded for Russians than the English terms are for most English speakers. *Smirenie* is primarily a religious (specifically, Russian Orthodox) feeling. Typically one submits oneself to a high dominance male called "God" ("Bog"), but other powerful figures, such as the peasant commune ("mir"), may also elicit this emotion.

Smirenie (together with etymologically related items) is generally evaluated in a positive way by traditional Russians. For example, most of the proverbs gathered on this topic by Dahl express approval:

> *Smirenie* is pleasing to God, is enlightening to the mind, is salvation for the soul, is a blessing to the home, and is a comfort to people (Smiren'e—Bogu ugozhden'e, umu prosveshchen'e, dushe spasen'e, domu blagosloven'e i liudiam uteshen'e).

> *Smirenie* is a girl's necklace to a young man [is becoming to her] (Smiren'e devich'e [molodtsu] ozherel'e).

The Lord saves the humble of spirit (Smirennykh Gospod' dukhom spasaet).

Quietly is not bad, the more humbly the more profitably (Tikho ne likho, a smirnee pribyl'nee).

God opposes the proud, but gives abundance to the humble (Gordym Bog protivitsia, a smirennym daet blagodat').[1]

In her semantic analysis of *smirenie* linguist Anna Wierzbicka speaks of "serene acceptance of one's fate, achieved through moral effort, through suffering, and through realization of one's total dependence on God, an acceptance resulting not only in an attitude of non-resistance to evil but also in profound peace and a loving attitude towards one's fellow human beings."[2] Thus, although *smirenie* implies a certain degree of psychological calm, it is not the same thing as passivity or inaction. It is attained only after great internal effort, even struggle. From a psychoanalytic viewpoint, the resolution of the struggle may well be self-abasing or self-destructive, that is, may be masochistic in certain situations.

Some Russian thinkers, sensing the masochistic potential in *smirenie*, take exception to the majority's positive evaluation of this phenomenon. Many among the intelligentsia at the beginning of our century rejected *smirenie*, as Sergei Bulgakov indignantly observes in his contribution to the *Vekhi* symposium,[3] although as we saw earlier, the intelligentsia were quite capable of finding other routes to masochism. Nikolai Berdiaev, a strong advocate of individual freedom as we have seen, is disgusted with the "slavish doctrine of *smirenie* [rab'e uchenie o smirenii]."[4] He feels that Russians use *smirenie* as an excuse for disgraceful behavior: "The Russian is accustomed to thinking that dishonor is not a great evil, as long as one is humble in one's soul [smirenen v dushe], is not proud, and does not put on airs." "Better to sin humbly [smirenno greshit']," says Berdiaev with tongue in cheek, "than proudly to seek self-perfection." Even for the most horrible crime one may "humbly repent [smirenno kaiat'sia]."[5]

Berdiaev does not mention any specific criminal here, but Freud in his essay on Dostoevsky does, and at the same time expresses a view quite similar to Berdiaev's:

A moral man is one who reacts to temptation as soon as he feels it in his heart, without yielding to it. A man who alternately sins and then in his remorse erects high moral standards lays himself open to the reproach that he has made things too easy for himself. He has not achieved the essence of morality, renunciation, for the moral conduct of life is a practical human interest. He reminds one of the barbarians of the great migrations, who murdered and did penance for it, till penance became an actual technique for enabling murder to be done. Ivan the Terrible behaved in exactly this way; indeed this compromise with morality is a characteristic Russian trait. Nor was the final outcome of Dostoevsky's moral strivings anything very glorious. After the most violent struggles to reconcile the instinctual demands of the individual with the claims of the community, he landed in the retrograde position of submission both to temporal and spiritual authority, of veneration both for the Tsar and for the God of the Christians, and of a narrow Russian nationalism—a position which lesser minds have reached with smaller effort.[6]

The "submission" Freud speaks of here would very well render the Russian *smirenie*. And the "lesser minds" Freud refers to might well be ordinary Russian peasants who have at their fingertips so many proverbs about the virtues of *smirenie*.

One does not have to actually mention God or the tsar to get into the spirit of *smirenie*. For example, Slavophile philosopher Aleksei Khomiakov says:

The reverence felt by the Russian who passes through Europe is quite understandable. Humbly [smirenno] and with bowed head he visits the Western sanctuaries of everything beautiful, in full awareness of his personal—and our general—impotence. I would even say that there is a kind of joyful feeling in this voluntary humility [v etom dobrovol'nom smirenii].[7]

The one before whom one feels *smirenie* does not even have to be male. Khomiakov's great reverence for his powerful mother is apparent in these words he wrote shortly after her death:

As far as I am concerned, I know that, however useful I may be, I owe to her both my direction and my steadfastness in this direction, although she did not intend this. Happy is he who had such a mother and such a mentor in childhood, and at the same time what a lesson in *smirenie* is given by this conviction! How little of what is good in a person belongs to that person![8]

As we saw earlier, Khomiakov advocated *smirenie* of the individual primarily in relation to the collective, be that collective religious or secular (the extended notion of *sobornost'*). However, the collective, I will argue below, is itself an icon of the mother.

A curious thing about *smirenie* is that the one who achieves it is often proud of it, or is at least not deprived of self-esteem because of it. One submits, yet one is not lowered in one's own eyes. On the contrary, one may be elevated, one may be narcissistically gratified. Khomiakov even speaks of an undesirable "proud *smirenie*" ("gordoe smirenie").[9] In his book on Dostoevsky Berdiaev says that "often Russians take pride in their special *smirenie* [gordiatsia svoim iskliuchitel'nym smireniem]."[10] Dostoevsky's personifying statement about Russia's greatness (in *The Brothers Karamazov*) is a perfect example: "Russia is great in her *smirenie*" ("velika Rossiia smireniem svoim").[11] But a peasant proverb admonishes: "Self-abasement (excessive *smirenie*) is worse than pride" ("Unichizhenie [izlishnee smirenie] pache gordosti").[12]

The apparent logical anomaly indicates that a reactive psychological process of some kind is taking place. Custine, too, noticed this: "Conforming to this social devotion, he [the typical Russian peasant] lives without joy, but not without pride; for pride is the moral element essential to the life of the intelligent being. It takes every kind of form, *even the form of humility,*—that religious modesty discovered by Christians."[13] The French word which Custine uses here is "humilité,"[14] which in context seems to be a reasonable translation of *smirenie*.

The process is familiar to psychoanalysis. Otto Fenichel speaks of the "pride in suffering" and "ascetic pride" which accompany certain masochistic practices.[15] The extreme form is what Charles Sarnoff calls "masochistic braggadocio."[16]

Not all Russians take pride in their *smirenie*. But it is clear that *smirenie* itself is a psychological state widespread in Russia, and that this state offers abundant opportunities for masochistic enactment.

Sud'ba

The most total form of resignation to events in the universe is fatalism. Such an attitude was endemic among the peasant masses of Russia. This is recognized by very different kinds of scholars. Historian Richard Pipes says, for example: "The true religion of the Russian peasantry was fatalism. The peasant rarely credited any event, especially a misfortune, to his own volition. It was 'God's will,' even where responsibility could clearly be laid at his own doorstep, e.g. when carelessness caused a fire or the death of an animal."[17] Compare K. D. Kavelin who, in his 1882 polemic titled *The Peasant Question*, declared: "The peasant may be happy, or sad, he may complain about his fate [sud'bu], or he may thank God for it, but he accepts good and evil without so much as a thought that one might be able to attract the former or fight against and defeat the latter. Everything in his life is given, predetermined, preestablished." [18]

It is easy to see the relevance of such attitudes to masochism. A peasant who failed to act on his or her own behalf because of fatalistic ideas was more likely to be victimized than the peasant who did not. The fatalistic peasant was more likely to be behaving self-destructively than the realistic peasant.

The relevant lexical item here is *sud'ba*. Most dictionaries render this word as "fate" or "destiny," but Wierzbicka shows that the Russian concept is holistic, referring to a person's entire life which seems utterly predetermined, while the English words refer to more limited situations and occupy a fairly minor place in English-speaking cultures. Wierzbicka found that, in comparable corpora of Russian and English, *sud'ba* occurs much more frequently than *fate* and *destiny* combined. [19]

Sud'ba is taken for granted. The philosopher Vladimir Solov'ev described it as a "fact" that is "beyond question." [20] It is also unavoidable. One's *sud'ba* is something one must accept with total resignation and passivity. "You can't walk away from *sud'ba*" ("Ot sud'by ne uidesh'"), says the proverb. [21] It is a proverb all Russians know, not just peasants.

A person is, in a sense, sentenced forever to a specific *sud'ba*. There is no choice. There can never be two of them, there can be only one: "Dvum sud'bam ne byvat', a odnoi ne minovat'" ("There is no such thing as two *sud'ba*s, and one there is no escaping"). [22] The same can be said of death, as in Count Rostopchin's words to Muscovites about to be invaded by Napoleon: "Dvum smertiam ne byvat'. Chemu byt' togo ne minovat'" ("One cannot die twice. What is to be cannot be escaped"). [23]

Wierzbicka makes a good argument for her thesis that the phraseology of *sud'ba* stresses "an attitude of acceptance and resignation." [24] Here are some of the phrases and expressions she culls from Aleksandr Zholkovskii's extensive entry in the Mel'chuk-Zholkovskii combinatorial dictionary [25] and from Dahl's dictionary [26] of peasant Russian:

Chto sud'ba skazhet, khot' pravosud, khot' krivosud, a tak i byt' ("Whatever *sud'ba* decrees, be it just or unjust, will come to pass").

Sud'ba ruki sviazhet ("*Sud'ba* will tie your hands/arms").

neumolimaia sud'ba ("inexorable *sud'ba*").

v rukakh sud'by ("in the hands of *sud'ba*").

ruka/perst sud'by ("the hand/finger of *sud'ba*").

voleiu sudeb/sud'by ("by the will of *sud'ba*").

slepaia sud'ba ("blind *sud'ba*").

These lexical collocations (and many others like them) have the effect of personifying or anthropomorphizing *sud'ba*. Typically one is resigned not to some impersonal force, but to a quasi-human being.

By personifying *sud'ba* it is easier to lay credit or blame at its— her—door. Personification is here a setup for psychological displacement and potential masochism. To blame some event harmful to the self on "blind *sud'ba*" is a way of not having to take responsibility for it. In effect, "I am not the cause, blind *sud'ba* is the cause." In some cases "I" may in fact not be the cause; in others, however, "I" may be responsible, but also unconsciously unwilling—for whatever reasons—to admit responsibility. It is in the latter situation that the individual is behaving masochistically.

Wierzbicka presents an impressive array of evidence to support her thesis that "Russian grammar is quite unusually rich in constructions referring to things that happen to people against their will or irrespective of their will." Some of the grammatical constructions in question reflect, in her opinion, "a folk philosophy at the heart of which appear to lie a kind of 'fatalism' and a kind of resignation." [27] I will not repeat Wierzbicka's lengthy linguistic analyses here, but it is worth noting that the infinitive form of a verb is often involved in such constructions, as in the sequence type *negation + infinitive + dative (person):*

Ne vidat' tebe etikh podarkov ("Alas, you'll never see these presents").

Ne raskryt' tebe svoi ochen'ki iasnye ("Alas, you'll never open those bright little eyes"—folkloric).

Ne vidat' Egoriu ottsa-materi ("Egor wasn't fated ever to see his father or mother again").

Ne byt' tebe burzhuem/ Ne byt' tebe Frantsuzom ("You are not fated to be a bourgeois/ You are not fated to be a Frenchman"— Marina Tsvetaeva).

The infinitive of the verb "byt'" ("to be," as in the last example) can participate in a variety of "fatalistic" constructions. Sometimes the words *suzhdeno* or *sud'ba* (or both) are brought in, as when Tat'iana surrenders herself to Evgenii Onegin in Pushkin's famous poem: "No tak i byt'! Sud'bu moiu/ Otnyne ia tebe vruchaiu." ("But so be it! My *sud'ba*/ Henceforth I place in your hands.").[28]

There is something childlike about Russian fatalism. Or, to put it another way, there is something motherly about fate itself. Joanna Hubbs says: "Among the Russian peasantry, there was a firm belief that a mother controlled a child's development and growth by conferring a particular fate upon it." [29] The fatalistic expression "na rodu napisano," literally "it was inscribed at birth" is ancient and widespread in Russia.[30] The lullabies a mother sang to her child were believed capable of casting a spell upon the child ("baiukat'," "to sing lullabies to," is related to "baiat'," "to charm," "to cast a spell").[31]

Usually what the mother wished for the child was positive—that it grow up to be big and strong, for example. But Russian peasant mothers sometimes wished a much worse *sud'ba* upon their child, namely, death. Folklorist Antonina Martynova found that, out of a corpus of 1,800 lullabies collected, 80 expressed the mother's wish that the child should die.[32] An example may be taken from a recently published collection of folklore about children:

Баю, баю да люли!
Хоть теперь умри,
Завтра у матери
Кисель да блины —
То поминки твои.
Сделаем гробок
Из семидесяти досок,
Выкопаем могилку
На плешивой горе,
На плешивой горе,
На господской стороне.
В лес по ягоды пойдем,
К тебе, дитятко, зайдем.[33]

Baiu, Baiu da liuli!
May you die now,
Tomorrow at mother's
There will be kissel and pancakes,
This—your funeral repast.

We'll make a little casket
Of seventy boards,
We'll dig a little grave
On bald hill,
On bald hill,
Where the Lord lives.
When we go gathering berries,
We'll drop by to see you, little child.

It is probably safe to say that the majority of peasant mothers did *not* feel this way, at least consciously, and that they regarded their little children instead as a precious blessing.[34] But one should keep in mind that mothers, like anyone else, are capable of feeling conscious or unconscious ambivalence toward those whom they love: "Children are a joy, children are also a sorrow," says a proverb.[35] In any case, there *is* substantial evidence that many Russian peasant mothers, under certain very trying conditions, actually wished their children would die. But what were these conditions?

One of the prominent demographic features of tsarist Russia was the extraordinarily high childhood mortality rates among the peasantry. In the eighteenth century Mikhail Lomonosov estimated that half of the 500,000 infants born annually died before the age of three.[36] David L. Ransel has gathered statistics demonstrating that nearly half of the children born in late nineteenth-century Russia died before the age of five. To explain this appalling figure, Ransel points to the unsanitary conditions and cruel practices surrounding childbirth (see below, 190–93). He also observes that infants were often put on solid foods from the first days of life, that is, at a time when their bodies could not possibly handle the pathogens thereby introduced. Infants were often fed by means of a "soska," an unsanitary rag containing food that had been partially chewed by another member of the family. With time the "soska" would putrefy, and even larger quantities of pathogenic bacteria would enter the child's gastrointestinal tract.

One reason why this was happening was that mothers were absent all day during the summer work season. Having an infant to care for—even a very sick infant—was no excuse to stop working in the fields (here a mother submitted to pressure from the family and commune), so someone else in the family had to look after the child. The child was breast-fed only early in the morning and late at night—if it was breast-fed at all. In the daytime the deadly "soska" was in the child's mouth almost continuously. Even when the mother was more often available for breast feeding, the "soska" was still used as a source of food and as a pacifier.

The *sud'ba* of very many of these children was early death. In some areas during the summer months up to 80 percent of children born failed to survive. They died largely from the extreme dehydration produced by "summer diarrhea." [37]

Ransel notes the understandable guilt which some mothers felt about their neglect. He also discusses the resigned, fatalistic attitude which parents developed as a result of the "carnage" that was going on around them. Some proverbs expressed the psychical distance that parents tried to gain from their horrible experiences, for instance, "It's a good day when a child dies," or "The death of a child is a mere chip off your knife blade, but that of a mom or dad leaves a gaping hole." [38] The death-wish lullabies would have to be included with this kind of lore.

What about the children who survived the high childhood mortality rates? They, as they became old enough to understand, must have been deeply disturbed by the deaths of siblings and other children around them. They must have realized that they too were potential victims, and that their parents were somehow responsible. They also must have sensed that their parents were trying not to become too attached to them, or wishing for their death outright. As we will see in the clinical discussion below (chap. 5), a child who perceives a parent (especially the mother) as hostile, withdrawn, or otherwise inadequate may develop in a masochistic direction. Certainly a child whose mother openly expresses a death wish against the child will be adversely affected. One can easily imagine a masochistic fantasy arising out of this situation, and perhaps persisting into adulthood, in effect: "very well, then, my mother wants me to die, so I *will* die—or commit some self-destructive act." Such a person might needlessly get into dangerous, suicidal situations. But when something bad actually happened, *sud'ba* would be blamed. It would be too painful to think badly of one's own mother.

The peasant child who died left its natal mother and went back to "mother earth." Everyone who lives must die. Everyone's fate is death. But it is not immediately obvious why death should be imaged by the survivors as a return to the mother. Why not the father—or a second cousin for that matter? Why any person at all? One's lifeless body goes into the earth, but why personify the earth in this context?

That Russians did (and still do) personify the earth as a mother is well known. The peasant topos "mother moist earth" ("mat' syra zemlia") refers to the mother specifically as a place one goes to after dying, or in order to die (as opposed to a fertile place which gives birth to a harvest—for which there are other topoi). Ransel speaks of peasant beliefs about the earth pulling the child back to itself, inviting death. A child born face down was expected to die soon.[39] There are several proverbs of the type "We are born not for life, but for death [Ne na zhivot rozhdaemsia, a na smert']."[40]

To resist death too much is to resist "mother moist earth." Jesus Christ was the only one to succeed at this, for he underwent a resurrection ("voskresenie") which is celebrated on Easter Sunday, the most important holiday in the Russian Orthodox Church. In view of this, is it surprising that Merezhkovskii heard *mother*-cursing mixed in with the happier utterances of an Easter celebration? (see above, 50). An eloquent religious proverb captures the contrast: "For some it's 'Christ has arisen!,' but for us it's 'Do not weep for me, mother!'" ("Komu: 'Khristos voskrese!', a nam: 'Ne rydai mene, mati!'").[41] The words in the first half of the proverb are traditionally spoken by Orthodox Russians to one another on Easter Sunday. They signify great joy. The words in the second half, which derive from portions of the Russian Orthodox liturgy and from the folkloric spiritual songs, were spoken by Christ to his Blessed Mother as he was dying on the cross.[42] They mean utter misery. The alternatives expressed by the proverb are thus: arise and live versus die in the presence of the mother. Resurrection is not only opposed to death, but is in some sense contrasted with the mother. In rising from the dead one emerges from the mother, in dying one re-enters the mother. In the spiritual songs, for example, the Mother of God experiences a *quickening of her womb* ("Utroboiu svoei razgoraiuchi")[43] as she sees her son dying on the cross.

Psychoanalyst Theodor Reik offers, I think, the clearest explanation for the fateful association of death with the mother, although he is not speaking specifically about Russians:

For all of us the mother is the woman of destiny. She is the *femme fatale* in its most literal sense, because she brought us into the world, she taught us to love, and it is she upon whom we call in our last hour. The mother as a death-dealing figure became alien to our conscious thinking. But she may become comprehensible in this function when death appears as the only release from suffering, as the one aim desired, the final peace. It is in this sense that dying soldiers call for their mothers. I can never forget a little boy who, in the agonies of a painful illness, cried: "Mother, you have brought me into the world, why can't you make me dead now?"[44]

Mothers bring children into the world. Therefore the possibility of leaving the world, of death, ought also to be associated with the mother. One's inescapable fate is personified as a mother everywhere, not just in Russia. A mother who is neglectful, or outright infanticidal,[45] only intensifies a personification which already exists in the minds of those who observe her. Some Russian peasants no doubt understood that children were dying all around them in part because of maternal neglect. But, as children themselves, they had already understood that their mothers had given them life, and that they therefore "owed Mother Nature a death" (to use Freud's expression).

When people die in droves, or for no apparent reason, life does not seem to be worth much. That is, when *sud'ba* is behaving in "stupid" fashion, an individual's life holds little value, as in the proverb: "*Sud'ba* is a turkey, and life is a kopek" ("Sud'ba—indeika, zhizn'—kopeika").[46] When one feels mistreated generally, fate may be represented as a *bad* mother, that is, a stepmother, as in songs about "*sud'ba*-stepmother, bitter lot" ("sud'ba-machekha, gor'kaia doliushka").[47]

Nikolai Nekrasov's poem "Mother" features a "martyr-mother" who says to her children:

«Несчастные! зачем родились вы?
Пойдете вы дорогою прямою
И вам судьбы своей не избежать!»

Unfortunate ones! What were you born for?
You will set off along the straight road,
And you will not be able to escape your *sud'ba!*[48]

It is as if this poor mother were predetermining the *sud'ba* of her poor children by her very utterance. The lines have a distinctly performative ring.

Nadezhda Durova (1783–1866), the famous noblewoman who dressed as a man and fought in the Russian army against the Napoleonic invaders, also heard about the unhappy *sud'ba* in store for her specifically from her mother: "She spoke to me in the most horrible terms about the *sud'ba* of this [i.e., female] sex [o sud'be etogo pola]: a woman, in her opinion, is obliged to be born, to live, and to die in slavery [v rabstve]; eternal bondage [nevolia], burdensome dependence, and all sorts of oppression are her lot [dolia] from the cradle to the grave."[49] Only Durova, unlike most Russian women of her day, rebelled. She was one of the notable Russian antimasochists. Slavery was no *sud'ba* for her.

Soviet social psychologist V. V. Boiko says that the immense burden on modern mothers consists, in part, of "a large moral responsibility for the *sud'ba* of her children."[50]

I hope these diverse examples sufficiently indicate that the idea of *sud'ba* is very often associated with the *mother*. In the clinical discussion of masochism below (chap. 5) I hope to show that this association is not an accident.

FOUR

Masochism in Russian Literature

Dmitrii Merezhkovskii once observed that the best Russian writers, however rebellious they may have been in their youth, repented. They ended up preaching *smirenie* to their readers. Pushkin turned away from his Decembrist friends to write an ode to Nicholas I, Gogol blessed Russian serfdom, Dostoevsky declared, "Humble thyself, proud man! [Smiris', gordyi chelovek!]" in his famous Pushkin speech, Tolstoy advocated "nonresistance to evil," and so on. The only exception, according to Merezhkovskii, was Lermontov.[1] Perhaps that was because Lermontov died so young.

Selected Masochistic Characters

Whether or not Russian writers themselves were advocates of moral masochism, it may truly be said that Russian literature is filled with *characters* who welcome their unhappy fate—suffering, punishment, humiliation, even death. But literary scholars have not paid much attention to masochistic literary characters as a category. One has to go to the chapter on Russian fiction in Nadejda Gorodetzky's opinionated theological treatise *The Humiliated Christ in Modern Russian Thought* (1973 [1938]) to find something like a survey.[2] Gorodetzky's book is not psychoanalytic at all. But her theme—the humiliated Christ—draws her precisely to characters who are interesting for the psychoanalytic scholar of masochism. Not all masochists in Russian literature are Christian, of course, but all truly Christian characters are moral masochists.

Also very helpful is Margaret Ziolkowski's *Hagiography and Mod-*

ern Russian Literature, a literarily more sophisticated study which pays particular attention to "kenotic characters" in nineteenth-century Russian fiction.[3] In her insightful discussions of characters in the fiction of Dostoevsky, Leskov, Uspenskii, and others Ziolkowski often uses the term "kenoticism" in a way that psychoanalysts would immediately recognize as meaning moral masochism.

Here I wish merely to point to some of the more obviously masochistic characters in nineteenth- and twentieth-century Russian fiction, without repeating too much of what the theologically oriented scholars have said already.

Turgenev's peasants, for example, are often very humble and accepting of their sad fate, and they usually explain their situation in Christian terms. "The beginning of faith is self-abasement, humiliation," says the heroine of "A Strange Story."[4] Beautiful Lukeria in "The Living Relic," paralyzed by a fall from a porch, accepts her lot wholeheartedly and asks no favors from God: "Why should I worry the Lord God? What can I ask of Him? He knows better than I do what I need. He has sent me a cross which signifies that He loves me."[5] Gorodetzky cites numerous other instances of this kind of thinking from Turgenev. Each of Turgenev's masochistic characters is unique, however, and many of them constitute complex and fascinating subjects for potential psychoanalytic case histories.

Tolstoy too depicted many Christian sufferers. One thinks of the rich merchant in "God Sees the Truth but Waits" who is falsely accused of murder and is sent to Siberia, where he learns to accept his sad fate with Christian humility and gratitude, even after the true murderer has been found. Or there is the monk Sergii who, when sexually aroused by the presence of a seductive woman in his cell, chops off one of his own fingers with an axe (later he becomes a wandering beggar with no name other than "slave of God"). Platon Karataev, the famous peasant in *War and Peace,* sits beneath a birch tree with a look of joyful solemnity on his face as he waits for a French soldier to shoot him (cf. Vasilii Shukshin's character Egor in *Snowball Berry Red,* who obligingly permits a gang leader to shoot him in a grove of his beloved birches).

There are some not particularly Christian masochists in Tolstoy as well, such as Prince Andrei, who seems determined to die before his time, or Anna Karenina, whose behavior becomes increasingly self-destructive as the novel named after her progresses. Of course all these characters, even the ones in the stories written for peasants, are more interesting and complex than the simplifying label "masochist" would suggest. Each of them deserves in-depth psychological study. Indeed one of them, Pierre Bezukhov of *War and Peace*, who occasionally behaves in self-destructive fashion, struck me as deserving an entire book.[6]

Dostoevsky is of course *the* master when it comes to depicting masochism in literature—Russian or otherwise. His novels are filled with characters who wallow in guilt, crave punishment, or seek injury or humiliation of one kind or another. For example, in *Crime and Punishment* Raskolnikov, after protracted agonizing over his murder of the pawnbroker woman, confesses to his crime, is exiled to a Siberian prison, and eventually welcomes his prison sufferings as the road to spiritual regeneration. Aleksei Ivanovich, hero of *The Gambler,* likes to humiliate himself for the sake of women, and repeatedly punishes himself by losing at roulette. The underground man in *Notes from Underground* manages to be insulted and humiliated by practically anything anyone around him does. Nastasia Filippovna of *The Idiot* runs off with Rogozhin, a man she knows will abuse her (and who in fact eventually murders her). The Christlike Prince Myshkin of the same novel invites all sorts of aggression and cruelty from those around him. In *The Possessed* Stavrogin withstands a physical blow from Shatov without responding. And so on.

Welcomed injury or humiliation in Dostoevsky's works is augmented by body language which seems to prime the characters for outright masochistic acts. For example, Dostoevsky's characters have a strong tendency to *bow down* before others. Psychoanalytic critic Steven Rosen counts seventy-five bows, kneelings, earth-kissings, and other gestural abasements in *The Brothers Karamazov.*[7]

To be sure, there is more to Dostoevsky's characters than their masochism. Stavrogin, for example, is a highly intelligent and complex sado-masochist. There are also major psychological differences in what these characters do, even within the masochistic sphere. Both Stavrogin and Myshkin are capable of accepting a physical blow, for example, but the motivation is quite different in each case. Yet the self-destructiveness is also there as a common feature. There is an underlying psychological similarity to many of Dostoevsky's characters, which may be characterized as a need to be injured in some way. As critic Edward Wasiolek says: "The Dostoevskian hero not only pays back for the hurt he suffers, but he looks for hurt to suffer. He likes being hurt. When he cannot find it, he imagines it, so that it will sting in his blood with the pungency of real hurt. He has a stake in being hurt: he seeks it, pursues it, and needs it." [8] The hurt very often takes the form of narcissistic wounding ("obida" is a key Dostoevskian word, as in the case of the underground man). But it can manifest itself in various other ways as well, such as gross physical punishment, guilt feelings, humiliation, and of course the most self-destructive act possible, that is, suicide (Dostoevsky's novels are littered with suicides).

Dostoevsky is thus remarkably inventive at finding ways for his characters to attract punishment or to get into humiliating situations. Both conventional and psychoanalytic critics have observed this.[9] Moreover, Dostoevsky himself was perfectly aware of what he was doing. Of Stavrogin's decision to publicize in writing the fact that he had sexually abused a little girl, the narrator says: "The fundamental idea of the document is a grim, naked need for punishment, for a cross, for public execution." Father Tikhon, to whom Stavrogin confesses, also detects Stavrogin's masochistic motive: "Yes, it is a penance and your natural need for it has overcome you. The suffering of the creature you wronged has so shattered you that it has brought home to you the problem of life and death, so there is still a hope that you are now on the great, still-untrodden path of calling disgrace and universal scorn down upon yourself." [10]

Tikhon, who is a perceptive (but intrusive) psychoanalyst, sees that Stavrogin's is not a straightforward Christian masochism, but a masochism that is heavily laced with narcissistic and exhibitionistic elements: "your intention to do this great penance is ridiculous in itself." Stavrogin must not only make a spectacle of himself, he must also be sincerely humble in consequence. "You will triumph," says Tikhon, "as long as you sincerely accept their spitting at you and trampling upon you—if you can endure it!" [11] As it turns out, he cannot endure such humiliation, and opts for suicide, a different sort of masochistic act.

Less religious in orientation than the writers I have mentioned thus far is the bitter satirist Mikhail Saltykov-Shchedrin, whose novels are strewn with masochists. The inhabitants of Glupov ("stupidville"), for example, are moved by an "ardent love of authority [siloiu nachal'stvoliubiia]." [12] They invent all kinds of ways to harm themselves. For example, they refrain from fighting a fire which is burning down their town, and instead rant and rave at their governor for what is happening. A later governor of the town is confronted with a crowd of protesters, all of whom are on their knees however. The ancestors of the Glupovites are characterized as follows:

There was in olden times a people called the Headbeaters [golovotiapami], and they lived in the far north, in that region where the Greek and Roman historians thought the Hyperborean Sea to be. These people were called Headbeaters, because it was their habit to beat their heads against anything that came in their way. If they came to a wall, they beat their heads against it; if they wished to pray, they beat their heads against the floor.[13]

The History of a Town (1869–70), from which these passages are quoted, is also full of sadistic fantasies to match the masochistic ones (e.g., under a certain governor Borodavkin "there was not a single Glupovite who could point to any part of his body which had not been flogged"; the governor Ugrium-Burcheev "beat himself not feigning," although he is otherwise the arch-sadist of the novel).[14] The laughter which Saltykov-Shchedrin elicits from his reader is itself sadistic in nature, being a form of aggression against the Glupovites. But to the extent that Russians recognize *themselves* in the Glupovites (just as they recognize themselves in the figure of Ivan the Fool—see below, chap. 6) they are laughing at themselves, that is, they are engaging in a mildly masochistic fantasy of their own.

In the twentieth century Russian writers continued to invent masochistic characters. The hero of Vladimir Mayakovsky's long poem "Cloud in Trousers" mocks himself, nails himself to a cross, and compares himself to a dog which licks the hand that beats it. D-503, the hero-number of Evgenii Zamiatin's futuristic novel *We,* explicitly welcomes the pain and punishment doled out by the dominatrix-number I-330. Boris Pasternak's Doktor Zhivago never fails to infuriate my American students with his willing abandonment of his beloved Lara, and his subsequent self-willed going to seed at the end of the novel. Andrei Platonov's works are full of mildly depressed, slightly childish characters who seem to welcome their abasement, for example, Nikita Firs of "Potudan River," who descends to begging and cleaning latrines. Los Angeles Slavist Thomas Seifrid has written a fascinating analysis of Platonov's later works, which he terms "literature for the masochist."[15]

Igor Smirnov explicitly deals with the "masochistic culture," "masochistic ideals," and "kenosis" promoted by Soviet socialist realist fiction. Many heroes in this genre efface themselves totally in order to carry out instructions from on high or to fulfill "the plan" dictated by revolutionary authority. For example, the fanatic Pavel Korchagin (in Nikolai Ostrovsky's *How the Steel Was Tempered,* 1935) repeatedly puts himself in great danger, or subjects himself to great deprivation for the sake of the Party. He emerges from the Civil War disabled and incapable of normal physical activity, but doggedly searches for new ways to serve the Bolshevik cause.[16]

Slavist Katerina Clark has also written on masochism in the Stalinist novel, although she prefers to use anthropological imagery rather than psychoanalytic terminology. Many socialist realist heroes go through what Clark calls a "traditional rite of passage" involving some sort of mutilation, ordeal, or sacrifice. Literal or metaphorical death may occur in the rite, and the result is fusion with some higher collective: "when the hero sheds his individualistic self at the moment of passage, he dies as an individual and is reborn as a function of the collective." [17]

Aleksandr Solzhenitsyn has created some masochistic characters in his fiction. Many of Solzhenitsyn's women are slavishly devoted to their husbands, for instance, Alina Vorotyntseva, Irina Tomchak, and Nadezhda Krupskaya in *August 1914.* Gleb Nerzhin of *The First Circle* is no slave, but he does something which, although perhaps noble, is very dangerous and potentially self-destructive: he spurns a cushy job in a special camp for mathematicians and scientists, and decides to plunge instead into the horrible depths of the gulag. Another of Solzhenitsyn's characters, the quintessentially Russian General Samsonov of *August 1914,* marches submissively toward death when he realizes his army has been defeated:

> The commander's voice was kindly, and equally friendly were the looks that followed him as he rode on after thanking the men and wishing them well. There was not a hostile glare to be seen. The bared head and the solemn grief, the unmistakable Russianness, the unalloyed Russianness of his face [opoznavaemo-russkoe, nesmeshanno-russkoe volosatoe litso], with its bushy black beard and its homely features—big ears, big nose—the heroic shoulders bowed by an invisible burden, the slow, majestic progress, like that of some old Muscovite Tsar, disarmed those who might have cursed him.
>
> Only now did Vorotyntsev notice . . . the doomed look imprinted on Samsonov's face from birth [otrodnuiu obrechennost']: this was a seven-pud sacrificial lamb led to the slaughter. He kept raising his eyes to something slightly, just slightly above his head as though he were expecting a great club to descend on

his meekly upturned bulging brow. All his life, perhaps, he had been expecting this, without knowing it. Now he was resigned to it.[18]

This characterization of Samsonov as an "unmistakably Russian" masochist is quite appropriate, historically. The real Samsonov led a Russian army to sure defeat at the hands of the Germans in East Prussia during the opening weeks of the First World War. Nearly a quarter of a million Russian soldiers were lost. Supposedly the idea was to help the French by forcing the Germans to withdraw troops from the Western front. Historian Richard Pipes quotes a statement made by the Grand Duke Nikolai Nikolaevich to a French military representative at Russian Headquarters: "We are happy to make such sacrifices for our allies."[19]

A list of masochistic characters in Russian literature would be long indeed. I have only begun to scratch the surface. Rather than continue with a list, however, I would like to look closely at some specific (but diverse) literary passages which offer interesting hints about the deep structure of Russian masochism.

Dmitrii Karamazov

Readers of Dostoevsky's *Brothers Karamazov* assume that old man Karamazov was killed by his illegitimate son Smerdiakov. But Dmitrii (Mitya) Karamazov is unjustly accused of the crime instead. There is a long investigation, and the authorities decide to try Dmitrii. At first he is rebellious, but then, as he is about to be led away to prison, he makes an abject speech in which he welcomes his sad *sud'ba:*

I understand now that such men as I need a blow, a blow of destiny [udar sud'by] to catch them as with a noose, and bind them by a force from without. Never, never should I have risen of myself! But the thunderbolt has fallen. *I accept the torture of accusation, and my public shame, I want to suffer and by suffering I shall be purified.*[20]

In order to understand this clearly masochistic declaration, a psychoanalyst would want to know something about the events leading up to it. As it turns out, Dmitrii had taken a nap before his speech because he was so exhausted by the long interrogation of the investigators into his alleged crime. While asleep he had a vivid dream, and this dream tells us much about Dmitrii's motivation.

In the dream Dmitrii sees depressing sights—a cold, November steppe, a village in which half of the huts are gutted by fire, poor peasant women standing about, cold, thin and wan. Particularly striking is the image of a mother with her extremely unhappy child:

In her arms was a little baby crying. And her breasts seemed so dried up that there was not a drop of milk in them. And the child cried and cried, and held out its little bare arms, with its little fists blue from cold.

"Why are they crying? Why are they crying?" Mitya asked, as they [Mitya and his driver] dashed gaily by.

"It's the babe [ditë]," answered the driver, "the babe weeping."

And Mitya was struck by his saying, in his peasant way, "the babe," and he liked the peasant's calling it a "babe." There seemed more pity in it [zhalosti budto bol'she].

"But why is it weeping," Mitya persisted stupidly, "why are its little arms bare? Why don't they wrap it up?"

"The babe's cold, its little clothes are frozen and don't warm it"

"But why is it? Why?" foolish Mitya still persisted.

"Why don't they feed the babe?" Dmitrii asks desperately. Feeling "a passion of pity [umilenie], such as he had never known before" Dmitrii wants to cry, he wants to do something "so that the babe should weep no more, so that the dark-faced, dried-up mother should not weep, so that no one should shed tears again from that moment."[21] Then he hears the reassuring voice of his beloved Grushenka, who promises to remain with him for the rest of his life (implicitly, even in Siberia). He wakes up, a radiant smile on his face.

Given that Dmitrii has just had such a dream, it is not surprising that he immediately begins his speech with the following words: "Gentlemen, we're all cruel [vse my zhestoki], we're all monsters, we all make people weep, *including mothers, and babes at the breast.*"[22] But what has this persisting image of an unhappy babe at the breast got to do with Dmitrii's own current unhappiness? He continues: "but of all, let it be settled here, now, of all I am the lowest reptile! Every day of my life, *beating my breast,* I've sworn to amend, and every day I've done the same filthy things. I understand now that such men as I need a blow of destiny."[23] — that is, a blow of *sud'ba,* and so on, as we saw above.

The breast imagery thus carries over into Dmitrii's castigation of himself. He beats his own breast ("biia sebia v grud' ") right after saying that he is guilty of making women and babes at the breast ("grudnykh detei") cry, which in turn is right after his dream about an extremely unhappy baby crying at its mother's inadequate breast ("grudi-to . . . takie issokhshie").

All of this business about breasts constitutes extraordinarily primal psychical material. Dmitrii's dream seems to have carried him very far back in time. Dmitrii is miserable in his present situation, just as a child at the breast is miserable when the breast/mother does not feed it. Previous psychoanalytic readers of the dream agree that the mother and child in the dream represent Dmitrii's dead, abandoning mother and Dmitrii himself as a child.[24] Whether or not one agrees with such an interpretation, it has to be admitted that some kind of connection exists between Dmitrii's masochistic welcoming of a blow of *sud'ba* and the mother/breast imagery of the immediately preceding dream. This connection will be explored below, after the relevant clinical considerations have been raised.

Tat'iana Larina

If Dmitrii Karamazov's *sud'ba* is to suffer in prison for a parricide he desired to commit but in fact did not commit, the *sud'ba* of Tat'iana Larina, heroine of Aleksandr Pushkin's verse novel *Eugene Onegin,* is simpler. It is to suffer rejection by the man she loves. But she welcomes his rejection of her and her subsequent suffering quite as much as Dmitrii welcomes the opportunity to purify himself in prison. Vasilii Rozanov classifies her as a "passion sufferer" ("Strastoterpitsa").[25]

True, Tat'iana does not initially wish to be rejected, to be punished. That was not the enterprise she originally had in mind. Rather, she had wished to be sexually united with the man who has swept her off her feet. But so profound is the attraction to Onegin, so totally does she commit herself to him, that she is prepared to accept anything he deems appropriate as a response, including rejection. She hands over control of her *sud'ba* to Onegin, as we saw earlier in a passage quoted from her love letter to him. Other passages as well in the letter depict the extent of her surrender:

> Другой!.. Нет, никому на свете
> Не отдала бы сердца я!
> То в вышнем суждено совете...
> То воля неба: я твоя;
> Вся жизнь моя была залогом
> Свиданья верного с тобой;
> Я знаю, ты мне послан богом,
> До гроба ты хранитель мой...[3]

Another! . . . No, to nobody on earth
would I have given my heart away!
That has been destined in a higher council,
that is the will of heaven: I am thine;
my entire life has been the gage
of a sure tryst with you;
I know, you're sent to me by God,
You are my guardian to the tomb.[27]

The sympathetic narrator tells us that poor Tat'iana's *sud'ba* is in the hands of a "fashionable *tyrant.*" But after a while we begin to get the impression that Tat'iana, whom Dostoevsky called "the apotheosis of the Russian woman,"[28] *likes* to be tyrannized. She feels that she will "perish" because of Onegin, but also that "perishing from him is lovely."[29] Her soul, "avid of sadness" ("pechali zhadnoi") after being rejected by Onegin, continues to ache for him.[30] She suffers much, and her suffering is very Russian.[31] Hers is the same soul, the same "dusha," that the narrator had previously characterized as Russian: "Tat'iana (being Russian, in her soul [russkaia dushoiu]."[32] The critics agree that Tat'iana's folksy Russianness is one of her essential features.[33]

In Tat'iana's dream, one of the most famous in Russian literature, Onegin takes the form of a bear, chases her across a snowy landscape, then appears as the "master" ("khoziain") of a gang of grotesque wild animals which terrify her. Onegin is at this moment both dear and frightful to Tat'iana ("mil i strashen ei")—an indication of her ambivalence. She desires him, but fears terrible consequences. She is laboring under what psychoanalysts would recognize as the infantile conception of sex as a terrible act of violence.[34] Yet she then permits the "master" to take her to a bench, deposit her there, and start to make love to her, and would without objection have allowed him to take away her virginity were it not for the fact that two other characters suddenly enter upon the scene.[35]

From the dream it is clear that Tat'iana wants Onegin to master her sexually. But in reality he is the master of her fate. By means of the love letter she throws herself at him, and it is then up to him to decide what will become of her. Because he rejects her, her *sud'ba* is to marry another man, an honorable man, yet a man she does not love, a man by whom (as Rozanov observes) she apparently has no children. It is as if Onegin were her father who, in the venerable Russian tradition, marries off his daughter to some stranger.

Indeed, Onegin is more of a parental figure than his Byronic, worldly-wise image would suggest. Tat'iana *makes* him a parent by her insistently childlike stance.[36] Her love is not that of a sophisticated coquette, it is no game. Rather, it is innocent, trusting. In love Tat'iana is as dependent as a child: "Tatiana . . . unconditionally yields/ to love like a dear child [kak miloe ditia]." [37] When she tries, naively, to explain her feelings for Onegin to her old nurse, she fails. The nurse thinks that she is ill. Repeatedly referring to Tat'iana as "my child" ("ditia moe"), the nurse tries to take care of her, as a solicitous mother would (the office of nurse or "niania" was the typical means of parent-surrogation among the nineteenth-century Russian nobility).

In frustration Tat'iana sharply orders the nurse out of the room, and commences to write the love letter already quoted above. If the nurse does not understand, perhaps Onegin will. One parental figure is replaced by another.

But, although Tat'iana is willing to play the child, Onegin plays at best a very distant and inadequate parent. After receiving the letter he comes to her in the family garden and commences to deliver a cold, standoffish sermon. Tat'iana, a "humble little girl" ("smirennoi devochki") "humbly" ("smirenno") hears out the lesson of Pushkin's pseudomature, narcissistic hero.[38] She is in tears as he escorts her back to her mother. She will be unhappy for the rest of the novel, indeed she will cherish her secret unhappiness for the rest of her life. That is her *sud'ba,* and it is Onegin—she believes—who has determined that *sud'ba.*

Even when Onegin comes crawling back to Tat'iana in the end there is no change in her attitude. She admits that she still loves him, but she is now properly married (to a man she does not love) and will not be unfaithful. More important, her *sud'ba* had been decided by his response to her initial, abject declaration of love to him. She now is even *grateful* to him for the way he behaved:

> в тот страшный час
> Вы поступили благородно,
> Вы были правы предо мной.
> Я благодарна всей душой...[4]

> at that terrible hour
> you acted nobly,
> you in regard to me were right,
> to you with all my soul I'm grateful.[40]

Again, it is her soul, her Russian "dusha" which accepts the abjection. What is more, she would still prefer that he be the strict disciplinarian with her:

> колкость вашей брани,
> Холодный, строгий разговор,
> Когда б в моей лишь было власти,
> Я предпочла б обидной страсти
> И этим письмам и слезам.[5]

>   the sharpness of your scolding,
> cold, stern discourse,
> if it were only in my power
> I'd have preferred to an offensive passion,
> and to these letters and tears.[42]

How can he be the slave ("Byt' chuvstva melkogo rabom") when *sud'ba* has already determined that *she* be the slave? No, she will remain severed from him, as *he* had originally decided ("You must, / I pray you, leave me"). She would rather be enslaved by the memory of a lost, inadequate object than gain a present object. She would prefer that Onegin be dead for her, as is her poor nurse ("niania"), the mother-surrogate whom he had replaced, and who now sleeps in the "humble churchyard" near her childhood home.

Vasilii Grossman's Thousand-Year-Old Slave

Vasilii Grossman (1905–64) was a writer very much preoccupied with the notion of fate (*sud'ba, rok*). His novel *Life and Fate* (*Zhizn' i sud'ba,* 1980) offers a panoramic view of the sometimes intersecting, sometimes parallel fates of its countless characters—Russians and Germans, Jews and Gentiles, soldiers and civilians, the living and the dead. Grossman has been called the Soviet Tolstoy, and *Life and Fate* is regarded by some as the *War and Peace* of the twentieth century.

But it is Grossman's incomparably pessimistic novella *Forever Flowing* (*Vse techet,* first published abroad in 1970) that is relevant here. In this work Grossman explicitly connects the idea of fate to Russian masochism.

In several chapters toward the end of the work the reader encounters Grossman's somewhat loose but fascinating theses concerning "the myth of Russian national character" and "the fate [rok] and character of

Russian history." [43] According to Grossman's narrator, "inexorable repression of the individual personality" and "slavish subjugation [kholopskoe podchinenie] of the individual personality to the sovereign and to the state" accompanied the "thousand-year history of the Russians." This external force produced a Christian strength and purity of national character that was unlike anything in the West. Russian observers, such as Chaadaev, Gogol, and Dostoevsky, had understood this, and had honestly believed that Russia would eventually have something very special to offer to the West. But they had not understood something else, namely, that "the characteristics of the Russian soul were born not of freedom, that the Russian soul is a thousand-year-old slave. And what could a thousand-year-old slave give to the world . . . ?" [44]

Grossman's ideas of "Russian soul" and "thousand-year-old slave" are personifications of the Russian people. They are not persons, properly speaking, but they resemble persons. They are metaphors for the many submissive persons in Russia, or for the submissive characters in Grossman's novel. For example, the "thousand-year-old slave" is like the character Nikolai Andreevich, a Soviet scientist whose "entire life consisted of one long act of obedience, with no trace of disobedience." [45]

Grossman has clearly been influenced by Chaadaev, Custine, Lermontov, Berdiaev, and other writers on the slave soul of Russia. His contribution is to wield the notion of Russian masochism as a weapon against Bolshevism, and against Lenin in particular.

Grossman repeats and extends his personification of the "thousand-year-old slave." At one point she is a "great slave" ("Velikaia raba") who, having recently cast off the chains of tsarism, marries Lenin. She follows after him with obedient step. Seeing that she is so pliable, Lenin begins to lord it over her. Gradually he becomes alarmed and frustrated by her "soft Russian submissiveness and suggestibility." [46]

Lenin could not change Russia's age-old slavish essence. For this reason, according to Grossman, he was not a *true* revolutionary: "Only those who encroach on the very foundation of old Russia—her slave soul [ee rabskuiu dushu]—are revolutionaries." [47]

Lenin was victorious, yes, but the Russian soul remained a slave. The narrator says that there is nothing mysterious about the "Russian soul," for slavishness is no mystery. The real riddle is why Russia seems fated to be slavish:

What is this, really, an exclusively Russian law of development? Can it be that the Russian soul, and only the Russian soul, is fated to develop not in direct proportion to the growth of freedom, but in proportion to the growth of slavery? Do we have here, after all, the destiny [rok] of the Russian soul?[48]

"Of course not," retorts the narrator to himself. There are other countries which have slavish traditions, too. But still, for Russia there is indeed no hope. Russia's slavishness is predestined. Such is the fate of history ("rok istorii"). Even Lenin, who valiantly attempted to absorb Western ideas of freedom, failed to liberate Russians. Lenin—with his fanatic Marxist faith, his iron will, his intolerance of dissent, his cruelty toward his enemies—was himself a product of the slavish Russian mentality. Lenin only managed to re-enslave the peasants, the proletariat, the intelligentsia. He could not overcome Russian slavishness because he was a part of it. He, like Dostoevsky and the other "prophets of Russia," "was born of our unfreedom." In Grossman's view, there simply is no possibility for Russians to escape their enslavement.

It is difficult to imagine a more pessimistic, fatalistic, and, for some, even offensive attitude. Many of Grossman's readers were disturbed. He was doing something much more radical than criticizing the great Lenin. When it was published in the West, his novella offended Russian chauvinists of both the pro-Soviet and anti-Soviet bent.[49] When more recently it was published in Russia, some writers accused Grossman of "Russophobia."[50] Anatolii Anan'ev, who was responsible for publishing it in the journal *Oktiabr'*, defended Grossman: "the phrase about Russian soul being a thousand-year-old slave provoked fury. But if we are not slaves, then why have we been submissively standing in lines for seventy years, why have we been applauding any dogma that happens to be spoken from the rostrum?"[51]

What the psychoanalyst is likely to notice in Grossman's text is the association of masochism ("soft Russian submissiveness and suggestibility," "slave soul") with the notion of fate (here *rok*). In Grossman's formulation, there is a predestined quality to Russian masochism.

The analyst also cannot miss the repeated images of *birth* in Grossman's text: "the characteristics of the Russian soul were born [rozhdeny] not of freedom"; "the birth [rozhdenie] of the Russian state system"; Lenin was "born [rozhden] of our unfreedom;" "anywhere slavery exists, such souls are born [rozhdaiutsia]," etc.[52] This kind of imagery suggests that the fatedness of Russia's slave soul originates specifically *from birth*.

The one who gives birth is, of course, the mother. What Grossman seems to be saying in these philosophical passages is that *the very earliest relationship with a mother of some kind is what predetermines Russian slavishness*.

Three things, then, are connected for Grossman: masochism, fate, and the mother. This triple connection, as we saw earlier, also applies to Dostoevsky's character Dmitrii Karamazov (and to some extent it applies to Tat'iana Larina, with Onegin a mother-surrogate rather than a literal mother).

Why should masochistic inclinations be connected to both fate and the image of the mother? This is a question that cannot be answered without a detailed consideration of the unconscious psychodynamics of masochism.

For that matter, many other aspects of the slave soul of Russia will remain a mystery until—at last—we delve into the psychoanalytic literature on masochism.

FIVE

Ontogeny and the Cultural Context

From a psychoanalytic perspective, the slave soul of Russia is best understood as an example of something Freud called moral masochism. Unlike erotogenic masochistic practices (sometimes called perversion masochism) in which an individual may need to be bound, beaten, or otherwise mistreated in order to achieve sexual orgasm, and unlike severe self-destructive and self-mutilative behavior based on a pervasive disintegration of psychic structures, moral masochism is a relatively mild disturbance in which the otherwise healthy individual searches for opportunities to suffer, to be humiliated, or to be defeated.

It does not matter, according to Freud, who it is that satisfies the "need for punishment": "The suffering itself is what matters; whether it is decreed by someone who is loved or by someone who is indifferent is of no importance. It may even be caused by impersonal powers or by circumstances; the true masochist always turns his cheek whenever he has a chance of receiving a blow."[1]

Karen Horney says that the masochist may be overwhelmed by a "feeling that good and evil come from outside, that one is entirely helpless toward *fate*, appearing negatively in a sense of impending doom, positively in an expectation of some miracle happening without one's moving a finger."[2]

The ideas of "impersonal powers," "circumstances," or "fate" in these formulations sound remarkably like the Russian ideas of *sud'ba* and *rok*. Freud discusses human acceptance of "the dark power of Destiny" elsewhere in his essay on masochism, and in his *New Introduc-*

tory Lectures on Psychoanalysis he dwells further on the predestined quality of some forms of moral masochism:

There are people in whose lives the same reactions are perpetually being repeated uncorrected, to their own detriment, or others who seem to be pursued by a relentless fate [Schicksal], though closer investigation teaches us that they are unwittingly bringing this fate on themselves. In such cases we attribute a 'daemonic' character to the compulsion to repeat.[3]

Ultimately, says Freud, the sense of unavoidable fate in such cases is determined by previous experience of the parents, which is to say that fate is not so impersonal after all: "The last figure in the series that began with the parents is the dark power of Destiny which only the fewest of us are able to look upon as impersonal"; "all who transfer the guidance of the world to Providence, to God, or to God and Nature, arouse a suspicion that they still look upon these ultimate and remotest powers as a parental couple."[4]

If the power which threatens the masochist ultimately emanates from the "parental couple," then the ontogenetic origin of masochism must lie in childhood. As Loewenstein says, "masochism seems to be the weapon of the weak—i.e., of every child—faced with the danger of human aggression."[5]

Clinical Developments since Freud

Although Freud speaks of the "parental couple" as the ultimate source of any internal need for suffering and punishment, he more often than not specifies the *father* as the model for the psyche's internal disciplinarian (superego, conscience), and in his article on Dostoevsky he declares outright that "Fate is, in the last resort, only a later projection of the Father."[6] Freud also tends to focus on the *Oedipal* dimension of internal needs for suffering (e.g., "through moral masochism morality becomes sexualized once more, the Oedipus complex is revived and the way is open for a regression from morality to the Oedipus complex").[7]

These two tendencies of Freud's are, in my opinion and in the opinion of many other modern psychoanalysts and psychologists, mistaken. The *mother* has a crucial role to play in the origination of the child's masochistic tendencies, and she plays her role specifically in the *pre-Oedipal* period. These considerations do not exclude, but complement the later role of the father and of Oedipal dynamics.

The importance of the mother in early development has been emphasized in many post-Freudian theories of human ontogeny. The child begins its existence in a sort of symbiosis with the mother. There follows what some psychoanalysts term a separation-individuation process, which takes place very roughly from about the fourth to the thirty-sixth month of age. The child acquires the fundamentals of its "mother tongue" specifically in the context of its early relationship with the mother. It is in this context that the child also learns the elementary moves of give and take required for all subsequent reciprocal interaction with persons. The child has its first erotic experiences in the pre-Oedipal situation. And so on. In many respects the mother-child dyad is the prototype of all significant social interaction the child will ever have. There is an enormous literature (not only psychoanalytic) on the fundamental importance of the mother in early child development.[8]

How does this literature contribute to our understanding of masochistic practices? What role does the pre-Oedipal mother play in the child's acquisition of masochistic tendencies? The existing theories on pre-Oedipal mother-child relations are very heterogeneous, and they do not always deal with the problem of masochism. But from those which do, it is possible to tease out a thread of common concerns as regards the ontogenetic origin and adult manifestations of masochism.

Many psychoanalysts hold that the adult masochist has suffered some form of deprivation or trauma at the hands of the pre-Oedipal mother. The mother may not have been sensitive enough to the child's need for milk, she may have been emotionally unresponsive (or responded inappropriately) in dyadic interaction with the child, or she may have physically abused the child. Such a mother has, in a sense, defeated her child, and the child, having had no adequate experience of what it means to be victorious, grows up to be someone who tends to engage in self-defeating behavior. The masochist *repeats* prior defeats. In effect: "I shall repeat the masochistic wish of being deprived by my mother, by creating or misusing situations in which some substitute of my pre-Oedipal mother-image shall refuse my wishes."[9]

Masochism should not be blamed entirely on mothers, however. Life is not easy even for the infant whose mother is doing everything humanly possible to care for it. Anxiety is unavoidable in infancy. Also, some infants may simply be constitutionally incapable of withstanding the treatment they receive from perfectly normal mothers.[10] There are defective infants as well as defective mothers. I want to avoid the kind of stigmatization of mothers that resulted from the once-popular term "schizophrenogenic mother." Psychoanalysts do not always seem to be aware of how much they blame their patients' mothers.

In any case, it is the psychoanalytic consensus that *something* went wrong in the masochist's early interaction with his or her mother— regardless of who was "at fault." As Kerry Kelly Novick and Jack Novick assert, "the first layer of masochism must be sought in early infancy, in the child's adaptation to a situation where safety resides only in a painful relationship with the mother." [11]

Something may later go wrong in the relationship with the father as well, of course, or with other individuals. But usually masochistic problems originate in interaction with the mother, if only because the mother is usually the child's primary caretaker—in Russia, as elsewhere—in the crucial early phases of development.

Indeed, by virtue of her uniquely powerful position in the young child's life, the mother enormously influences all of the child's subsequent thinking and fantasizing about dominance and submission. The pre-Oedipal mother is the prototypical "master," the child is the prototypical "slave." Psychologist Dorothy Dinnerstein has written on this topic:

In our first real contests of will, we find ourselves, more often than not, defeated: The defeat is always intimately carnal; and the victor is always female. Through woman's jurisdiction over child's passionate body, through her control over what goes into it and what comes out of it, through her right to restrict its movements and invade its orifices, to withhold pleasure or inflict pain until it obeys her wishes, each human being first discovers the peculiarly angry, bittersweet experience of conscious surrender to conscious, determined outside rule.[12]

When the child—for whatever reason—has this "bittersweet experience" more often than it can bear, then it is in some sense permanently injured. Its sense of itself (as distinct from others), its evaluation of itself (narcissism) is affected. The masochist is, among other things, forever trying to repair old injury to the self.

Only the repair fails. What is more, this failure seems to be planned. The masochist seeks out failure, sometimes even seems to enjoy it. How can this be?

Paradox lies at the heart of masochism. The masochist achieves what Thoedore Reik calls "victory through defeat." [13] Arnold Cooper speaks of "the paradox of pleasure-in-unpleasure." [14] Anita Katz finds it paradoxical that "the masochistic person contradicts himself or herself, speaking and acting against self-strivings and self-fulfillment in a seemingly absurd manner." A striking clinical example is offered by Katz:

> After several years of our work, she [a self-deprecating, self-defeating patient] said: "I want you to be my mother." When I asked her what that would be like, she startled both of us by beginning to hit herself on her face and head. She screamed, "Do you see what I did? I beat myself when I think of being mothered."

On another occasion, when the patient was again beating herself, the analyst told her to sit up and stop it. The patient then asked, in complete innocence: "That's not good for me, is it—beating myself?" [15] Masochists can be surprisingly ignorant of the harm they do to themselves.

Various attempts have been made to explain the paradox of masochism. Daniel Stern, in his discussion of the "paradoxical stimulation" offered to infants by relatively unresponsive and neglecting mothers, offers a behaviorist rather than a psychoanalytic model. According to Stern, there is a class of mothers who seem able to reinforce only the self-hurtful behavior of their infants:

> All infants have a "repertoire" of common self-hurtful or discomforting mishaps, such as losing their balance in the chair and falling "slow motion" to one side; or missing their mouth with a spoonful and landing the stuff in the eye, ear, or chin; or misjudging a reach for something and falling forward on their face; or miscalculating the trajectory of an object they are bringing toward their face and bumping it against their forehead. Many of these misoccurrences are in fact funny in the way that slapstick is funny, and most caregivers may laugh (if there is no real injury) and also give some soothing "there-there" behaviors.
>
> What is unusual about this group of mothers is that only when one of these mishaps befalls the infant do they come alive. Only when inspired by the "funny" circumstances of the infant's discomfort does the mother perform lively infant-elicited social behaviors. At those moments she shifts from her deadpan uninvolvement and becomes an effective social partner. At that point, the infant usually rapidly recovers from his mishap in response to his "transformed" mother, and they then share one of their rare moments of mutually pleasurable and exciting stimulation. The problem of course is that the infant's main moments of interactive delight and liveliness with his mother are dependent upon and perhaps become associated with an immediately preceding unpleasurable feeling. A more ideal learning paradigm could hardly be devised for acquiring the basis of masochism: pain as the condition and prerequisite for pleasure. (The maternal behavior of these mothers is not without obvious sadism.) [16]

Stern does not suggest that this is the only route to masochism, but clearly this particular route is in some sense the "fault" of the mother.

Another—more psychoanalytic—idea is that masochistic practices derive from the child's defiant, sadistic feelings initially directed toward an external object such as a parent, but which have then been redirected inward as a result of identification with the object.[17] In this view, masochism is sadism turned inwards. An example would be the little boy who becomes enraged and bites himself instead of the parent when the parent imposes some restriction.[18]

Another approach focuses on the individual's need to *control* the people who administer pain. Irving Bieber describes a three-and-a-half-year-old girl who attempted to control her mother's punishing behavior by punishing herself:

During the preceding year, whenever one parent, especially the mother, punished the girl physically, the child would inflict or threaten to inflict self-injury. She would strike her hands or head on solid objects with sufficient force to produce hematomata; or she would burn her hand on a radiator, or over an open gas flame if she could get to it. By these maneuvers she was largely successful in preventing physical punishment.[19]

To be more precise: she was successful in preventing punishment *by the parent,* for she did nonetheless punish herself. She gained a measure of control over the situation by taking that control away from the parent. Her masochistic actions constituted a narcissistic assertion, in effect: "*I* did it." Control requires a self who controls.

Related to control is the notion of *mastery.* Otto Fenichel, for example, discusses "repetitions of traumatic events for the purpose of achieving a belated mastery."[20] In *Beyond the Pleasure Principle* Freud describes a little boy who was trying to overcome the anxiety of being separated from his mother. The boy developed a game in which he threw objects away and then, with great pleasure, "found" them again. The game was repeated again and again. The apparently compulsive nature of the play led Freud to his concept of the repetition compulsion ("Wiederholungszwang").[21] Not all such repetition is necessarily masochistic, although most analysts agree that masochistic practices do tend to be repetitive in nature.

According to Edmund Bergler, the future masochist initially masters the painful aspects of the pre-Oedipal situation by "sugarcoating" them, that is, by reversing their real significance: "No one frustrated me against my wishes; I frustrated myself because I like it."[22] Again, the shift of control is away from an outside agent to the asserting self. This shift is based on an illusion, of course, for it would never have had to take place if the self were *really* in control. But it does give the developing child a means to reduce anxiety, as well as a potential source of pleasure. The child actively tries to obtain pleasure, even if the conditions are inappropriate and success is unlikely.[23] As Cooper puts it: "the infant claims as its own, and endows with as much pleasure as possible, whatever is familiar, whether painful experiences or unempathic mothers."[24]

Masochistic behavior in adults is not always obvious to the outside observer. It may even appear as a normal striving for goals. But a little free association on the couch reveals what is going on, at least to the attentive analyst. Here is one of the numerous clinical examples offered by Bergler:

> A young man had developed an amorous attachment for a girl outside his financial and social sphere, and was very conscious of the obstacles. *He constantly reiterated the hopelessness of the situation and stated that the inevitable day must come when the family would convince the girl to give him up.* One evening the girl told him that an old friend of hers was going to be in town shortly and asked him whether he would object to her seeing him. This trial balloon, testing his "notorious" jealousy, was immediately used by the young man for a violent scene, with which he unconsciously hastened the inevitable end.[25]

The young man, in effect, planned the unhappy ending of an affair that might actually have turned out well (or might have turned out well if a different girl had been chosen). Other psychoanalysts have observed other kinds of pathological infatuation and masochistic patterns of falling in love. Otto Kernberg, for example, describes patients who receive "narcissistic gratification and fulfillment in the enslavement to an unavailable object."[26] The gratification is narcissistic in the sense that the patient is rewarded with an implicit feeling of grandiosity or moral superiority over the rejecting object. In effect: "I am the greatest sufferer of the world."[27]

This is also a somewhat exhibitionistic (Reik would say "demonstrative") idea. The masochist is always posturing. Psychoanalysts have noted the theatricality of masochism, the masochist's need for a "public" of some sort. It is unusual for a masochistic act to take place without a witness, at least an imaginary witness. In the deepest layers of the masochist's psyche this witness is always the pre-Oedipal mother.

In the immediate clinical situation, however, the witness is the therapist. Masochists love to perform self-destructive acts in the presence of the person who is trying to prevent them from performing such acts. One of Bergler's patients, a depressed, unemployed woman of means who regarded working women as "silly slaves," consistently showed up late for her psychoanalytic sessions. Yet she was always disappointed that the analyst could not devote more time to her. Sometimes she was so late that only five minutes of the session remained, yet she insisted on having a full session of treatment. She could not understand that the doctor had to send her away, even though she knew another patient was waiting. She perceived the doctor as an unjust tyrant, when in fact she was punishing herself. She was also incapable of making any connection between her feelings about the analyst and her hatred of her mother, whom she regarded as some kind of monster.[28]

Masochistic behavior is often accompanied by feelings of self-righteousness or self-pity. "Poor me," the patient seems to say, "I am always getting mistreated." Yet the patient somehow always manages to end up in a situation that results in suffering. The patient wallows in suffering, even while complaining constantly about it.

Such patients become what Bergler calls "injustice collectors." They go about the world searching for ever-new ways to be "kicked in the jaw." On the surface they appear to be aggressive, they seem to have a "chip on the shoulder," but they are only trying to provoke aggression from others by their behavior—and they often succeed.

Many masochists are desperately in need of love. They *use* suffering to obtain sympathy and love from others. This is evident, for example, in one subtype of what Otto Kernberg calls "depressive-masochistic personality disorder" in which there are "traits reflecting overdependency on support, love, and acceptance from others." These traits reveal "a tendency to excessive guilt feelings toward others because of unconscious ambivalence toward loved and needed objects, and an excessive reaction of frustration when their expectations are not met." For these patients the "sense of being rejected and mistreated as a reaction to relatively minor slights may lead them to unconscious behaviors geared to making the objects of their love feel guilty."[29]

As Bernhard Berliner puts it, such patients try to "extort love" from others.[30] Otto Fenichel speaks of the "accusing, blackmailing tone" of the masochist.[31] Or, to use an American slang expression, masochists like to "lay guilt trips" on the people around them, and often suffer (or rather, try to enjoy) rejection as a result.

The love which the masochist ultimately seeks is a mother's love—often metonymically represented as the pre-Oedipal mother's breast. One self-pitying, self-deprecating masochist wrote the following in a note to her analyst:

I was about to say that I think I over-love my mother, and am afraid of this, also afraid of her love because there is something disgusting about it. I don't know why it should be disgusting, but it is . . . I would say large, flopping breasts come into the picture, over-earthiness.[32]

To "over-love" the floppy-breasted mother is to need her love too much, and the feeling of disgust in this case is clearly a compensatory reaction (the technical term is reaction formation). Bernhard Berliner says that "the masochist hangs on, so to speak, to a breast which is not there and which he has to repudiate when it could be there, symbolically."[33] Esther Menaker also emphasizes the background of felt oral deprivation by the mother in masochistic behavior:

The normal development of the ego is as directly dependent on getting love from the mother at the earliest infantile level, as is the physical development on getting milk. If mother love on the oral level is absent or insufficient, the individual suffers a psychic trauma which must eventuate in a malformation and malfunction of the ego. The masochistic reaction is one form of an attempt on the part of the ego to deal with this trauma. It sacrifices itself, that is, its own independent development and the sense of its own worth, to sustain the illusion of mother love—an idealized mother image—without which life itself is impossible.[34]

This idea is illustrated by the case of a masochistic woman patient who was literally deprived of her mother and cared for by a busy uncle for the first four or five months of her life. This masochist certainly had inadequate mothering during the crucial pre-Oedipal period.

An even more graphic example is the dream Dmitrii Karamazov has shortly before his masochistic declaration of guilt (see above, 84). Recall that the mother in the dream is unable to feed her child. Her breasts are dried out, and the child is crying pitifully. Dmitrii is very moved by this. He wants to cry himself. He identifies with the child, he understands how the child must feel, since he himself had been abandoned by his mother when he was three years old. He must feel the child's own rage against the mother for not providing nourishment. But hostility against the beloved mother is bound to produce guilt, which is to say that the hostility is redirected back against the self. Guilt feeling is, by psychoanalytic definition, an imagined experience of aggression directed against the self: " . . . the self-reproaches are reproaches against a loved object which have been shifted away from it on to the patient's own ego." [35]

Not for nothing, then, does Dmitrii guiltily beat his *own* breast after the dream, for his unhappy dream child (i.e., he himself as a child) had raged against the *mother's* dried-out breasts. The masochistic declaration of guilt ("of all I am the lowest reptile," "I need a blow, a blow of *sud'ba,*" etc.) *is* this rage, redirected away from the inadequate mother and toward the self.

When later Dmitrii repeatedly says "It's for that babe I am going to Siberia now," [36] he is rationalizing his guilt feelings, explaining to himself and to those around him why he welcomes the punishment of Siberia. If there weren't any children deprived of the mother's breast, there wouldn't have to be any sought-for Siberia. If mothers were (perceived as) adequate, there wouldn't be any masochism. Here Dostoevsky achieves an essentially psychoanalytic insight by means of literary images.

Is Masochism Gendered?

As is evident from the variety of clinical examples I have given, both males and females may engage in masochistic practices. It is not clear *a priori*, then, whether the slave soul of Russia might or might not be a gendered object. There is reason to believe, however, that certain of these practices under certain conditions are more prevalent in one sex than in the other.

Fighting wars, for example, is an arguably masochistic activity practiced almost exclusively by males in all cultures. One may debate what constitutes a reasonable cause for taking the extreme risk of charging an enemy position—the motherland and Stalin, freedom and justice, oil in the Persian Gulf, or whatever—but one cannot doubt that men do these things more often than women do, and that they often die as a result. Perhaps this masochistic aspect of warfare has been neglected because the sadistic aspect is so obvious. The feuding princes of ancient Rus' understood it quite well, however, for they interpreted death in battle as a deserved *punishment*. In effect: "I believe I am right; if I am wrong God will punish me."[37]

Sexual masochism is also more common among males than females. Morton Hunt found, for example, that nearly twice as many males as females in his sample obtained sexual pleasure from receiving pain.[38] Males, incidentally, are also more likely than females to be sexual sadists.[39]

Curiously, it is almost always male sexual masochists who don the clothes of the opposite sex. This makes sense in light of the fact that women generally have a lower social status than men do.[40] If one (whether male or female) needs to be spanked, or bound, or otherwise humiliated in order to achieve orgasm, one may as well choose gender signs that "go" with the occasion (e.g., an apron rather than a jock strap).[41]

In some nonsexual contexts women appear to be more masochistic than men. Psychotherapists are familiar with a pattern of victimization that many women seem to gravitate toward. As Lynn Chancer observes, if such a pattern did not really exist, it would be difficult to explain the popularity of such self-help titles as *Women Who Love Too Much* or *Men Who Hate Women and the Women Who Love Them*.[42]

The notion that women are inherently masochistic, however, has been controversial, to say the least, and Freud did not help matters with his unclear ideas about "female masochism."[43] Within the psychoanalytic community there have been conflicting views on the extent to which women are masochistic.[44] Some feminist psychologists have vigorously attacked "the myth of women's masochism."[45]

There are some empirical data to go on. For example, Frederic Kass, in a study of what is nowadays called "self-defeating personality disorder" by many in the American psychiatric community, found that the following "masochistic personality criteria" were significantly more frequent in female patients than in male patients:

Remains in relationships in which others exploit, abuse, or take advantage of him or her, despite opportunities to alter the situation.

Believes that he or she almost always sacrifices own interests for those of others.

Rejects help, gifts, or favors so as not to be a burden on others.

Responds to success or positive events by feeling undeserving or worrying excessively about not being able to measure up to new responsibilities.

Thinks only about his or her worst features and ignores positive features.[46]

It is possible, however, that many of the women in Kass's sample were living in abusive home situations. After all, when spouse abuse occurs, it is women, not men, who are usually the victims. The higher figures for self-defeating attitudes in women could reflect, in part, a natural reaction to being traumatized or to having been traumatized: "There is no justification for labeling as a core part of someone's personality pattern the reactive behavior which victims develop," says feminist therapist Lynne Rosewater.[47]

When Rosewater assessed a group of battered women using the Minnesota Multiphasic Personality Inventory (MMPI), she found remarkably high scores for anger *directed inward*. This anger, moreover, was "often experienced as guilt—a feeling of being personally responsible for the bad things that happen." [48] Such findings are in keeping with the general tendency for women to direct feelings inward and to blame themselves (whereas men tend to direct feelings outward and blame others).[49]

Battered women who direct anger inwards clearly exhibit masochism (in Freud's sense of sadism directed inwards). But feminist psychologists prefer to avoid both the term "masochism" and the expression "self-defeating personality disorder" in making a diagnosis: "To label victims as self-defeating personality disorders is simply to revictimize them." [50] "To perpetuate victimization in the name of nosology is unconscionable." [51]

I doubt that most masochists read diagnostic manuals or are given access to their diagnosis by their therapists, and therefore they are not likely to be harmed by the diagnosis itself. It is possible, however, that some therapists are so insensitive as to allow the diagnosis of "masochism" or "self-defeating personality disorder" to adversely influence the way they treat their women patients. That is, some therapists may be tempted to blame the patient rather than help the patient get out of a traumatic situation. For such therapists—and there are many of them, if the feminists are to be believed—it is probably better to speak of battered woman syndrome,[52] learned helplessness,[53] or some other term that does not in any way lead the therapist to make a negative evaluation of the victim. Such an approach should also be taken to judges and juries, for they are in a position to do legal harm to women.[54]

For purposes of this book, however, it is possible to call a spade a spade. Battered women do tend to stay in their abusive relationships, that is, they behave in accordance with the definition of masochism given at the beginning of this book (p. 7). But no therapy is being proposed here, nor is any expert opinion being offered to a court. I am doing applied psychoanalysis, not therapeutic or forensic psychoanalysis.

In any case, I am quite aware that victims are not *necessarily* responsible for their victimization. Iosif Stalin, for example, is at least partially responsible for the terrible things that befell the Soviet people (including his second wife), as I have argued elsewhere.[55] One may legitimately study how some victims (abused women, slavish Russians, etc.) allow themselves to be victimized without denying that (1) sadists and other victimizers do exist, and (2) some victims play no welcoming role whatsoever in their victimization, that is, some victims are not masochists at all. Also, having an inferior social status (e.g., female or serf) does not necessarily mean that one is a masochist. Masochism may help one endure low status, but tolerating low social status does not necessarily mean one is masochistic, or masochistic all of the time.

Even when victims are behaving masochistically they are not necessarily suffering from a "personality disorder" (this is why I prefer the simple term "masochism" to the gratuitously evaluative "self-defeating personality *disorder*"). Masochistic behaviors can be adaptive, both in the clinical and Darwinian senses of the word. For example, initiation of dangerous physical combat may lead to self-destruction, yet it may be the only reasonable thing to do in certain situations. It may both enhance the probability of survival and eliminate the unbearable emotional tension of waiting for the enemy to attack. Similarly, a battered woman may in effect welcome further injury by staying with her abusive mate, but she may also be gaining the advantage of some fathering for her children, and the abusive situation may satisfy emotional needs of her own that other situations cannot.

The Masochist's Questionable Self and Unquestionable Other

Masochists can be extremely resistant to psychotherapy. In this connection Freud spoke of a "negative therapeutic reaction." Stuart Asch describes what he (after Bergler) calls the "malignant" masochist: "These masochistic characters are extremely resistant to analyzing behavior and attitudes that they maintain in order to perpetuate a primitive attachment to an internal object, a preoedipal conflict. The attachment is a residual of incomplete separation-individuation from the early mothering object." [56] According to Asch, these patients are still so influenced by the internal representation of a "devouring, sadistic mother" that they try to *appease* that image by sabotaging the therapy:

The gratification in failure, with its associated aim to make the therapist or parent or surrogate helpless to stop the patient, is often tied to a specific fantasy. The primary love object, usually the preoedipal mother, is somehow aware of this jousting and is watching and approving of the defeat of the analyst. The patient experiences it as *reuniting him with his preoedipal object*. The negative therapeutic reaction in these instances is intended to defeat the analyst's aim of disengaging the masochist from his death embrace with the internalized preoedipal, engulfing mother figure. [57]

Sometimes these patients do succeed in bringing the therapy to a complete halt. The analyst simply has to give up, and the patient may walk out, never to return.

Helen Meyers takes a somewhat more optimistic attitude toward malignant masochists. She, like many other analysts, recognizes the importance of the pre-Oedipal mother: "Unconsciously, the masochist continues to 'seduce' his internalized, critical, maternal object and repetitively reenacts, in current relationships and in the transference, the old scenario learned at his mother's knee." [58] But Meyers also pays particular attention to the important role that masochism can play in the child's attainment of self-definition and separateness from the mother, and this leads her to be tolerant of the masochist's need to be negativistic:

The "no" of the two-year-old toddler helps him define himself, even when it involves getting into trouble. Unpleasure is experienced as a necessary accompaniment or condition for the pleasure in and drive for separateness and individuation. The adult masochist's "I will, too, be self-destructive and you can't stop me" asserts his control, but also defines him as an independent agent, separate, autonomous, and individuated. "I am the sufferer" defines his identity, though a negative one.[59]

"As difficult as this may be for the therapist," says Meyers, "it may be necessary for the patient to fail on his own, before he can give up this masochistic stance without fear of merger."[60]

This "fear of merger," which derives from an insufficient sense of separateness and individuality, is important in certain forms of masochism. It is as if the masochist does not have a separate identity unless he or she is suffering: *Doleo ergo sum*, I suffer, therefore I am—to quote a Cartesian neologism that has appeared more than once in the psychological literature on masochism.[61]

An insufficient sense of individual identity is as much the masochist's narcissistic problem as is low self-esteem. When the masochistic act is designed to show that "*I* am in control, not someone *else*" (see above, 98), then there is an implicit danger that the "I" might be confused with the "someone else." Similarly, when the masochistic act is aimed at mastery of a previous trauma (above, 98), the implication is that the trauma has threatened the very being of the masochist. The boundaries of the self who masters are clearer than those of the self who is traumatized.

Daniel Kriegman and Malcolm Slavin (1989) suggest that repetitively self-defeating behavior in the clinical situation is aimed at the completion of a previously interrupted construction of the self. In this Darwinian view the self is an "organ" which has been produced by natural selection, and which reflects the inclusive genetic interests of the individual.

Robert Stolorow believes that "masochistic activities, as *one* of their multiple functions, may serve as abortive efforts to restore, repair, buttress and sustain a self-representation that had been damaged and rendered precarious by injurious experiences during the early pre-oedipal era, when the self-representation is developmentally most vulnerable."[62] To illustrate this thesis, Stolorow points out that some masochists are relieved of anxiety when they experience skin contact with a beloved person, or when their skin is stimulated in some unusual way: "the structurally deficient masochist . . . seeks erotic stimulation and warming of the skin surface, because it highlights the outlines of his precarious body image and restores his sense of self-cohesion."[63] Stolorow argues that the well-known exhibitionistic tendencies of masochists (e.g., concern with martyrdom) also serve to shore up a failing self-image. Some masochists feel they do not even exist unless they are observed.

Roy Baumeister has offered a theory of (erotogenic) masochism that seems to be the opposite of Stolorow's. According to Baumeister, masochistic practices do not facilitate cohesion of the self, but provide an avenue of *escape* from it:

Masochism may appeal to psychologically normal people as a way of escaping from the self. That is, masochism divests the person of awareness of self in high-level, symbolic, meaningful terms, extending into the past and future. In its place, masochism focuses awareness on the self at extremely low levels; as a physical entity existing in the immediate present, passively experiencing sensations and simple movements. Masochism deconstructs the self, providing escape from identity into body.[64]

If one needs to escape from the self, however, there must be a problem with that self. It does not naturally cohere, it would fall apart without periodic relief of some kind (Baumeister focuses on powerful politicians and responsible corporate executives who periodically come to a domi-nator or a dominatrix for a beating). I suspect, moreover, that the "elaborate self-concept" which needs to be "deconstructed" in the scene of humiliation is originally formed in early interaction with the mother, although Baumeister himself says almost nothing about ontog-eny. At least *something* went wrong in the formation of the masochist's self.[65]

Before Baumeister, some psychoanalysts had also viewed masochism as an attempt to escape from the self. Karen Horney is an example. She made it clear that the self to be escaped from is highly problematical: "The obtaining of satisfaction by submersion in misery is an expression of the general principle of finding satisfaction by losing the self in something greater, by dissolving the individuality, by getting rid of the self with its doubts, conflicts, pains, limitations and isolation."[66]

Another example is Erich Fromm. In his important treatise *Escape from Freedom* (1965 [1941]), written in response to the rise of mass fas-cism in Germany, Fromm expresses the idea that individual responsibility and freedom are frightening. The self is insignificant and alone in the world. Consequently there is an inclination to "escape" from or "forget" the self, to fall into submissive dependence on some larger, controlling so-cial entity such as a mass religious or ideological movement (e.g., Calvinism, Nazism). One component of this process is masochistic in nature. "Escape" from the self is very likely to be self-destructive.[67]

It should be clear by now that, within the psychoanalytic field, there are diverse and sometimes contradictory views on the relationship of masochism to the self. The major contradiction has to do with the direction the masochist seems to be moving with respect to the pre-Oedipal mother. Some analysts (e.g., Meyers, Stolorow) see masochistic behavior as an attempt to achieve a separate identity or self-definition with respect to an external, maternally significant reality. Others (e.g., Asch) view masochism as a way *not* to be separated from the engulfing, pre-Oedipal mother, as even a means of achieving merger with her. The "escape" theories seem to fit the latter category, as they involve submersion in a larger other that is implicitly maternal (e.g., the highly idealized and ideologized group).

Perhaps these two apparently conflicting views can be resolved by positing two different grades of masochism, or two different extremes of the masochistic spectrum (much as manic-depressive illness is now regarded as a unitary phenomenon in the psychiatric community). At one extreme the self revives the old delusion of independence from the pre-Oedipal mother, at the other extreme it entertains the even older delusion of fusion with her.

The closest thing to a synthesis of these extremes that I have been able to find in the psychoanalytic literature is made by Lane, Hull, and Foehrenbach. Speaking of behavioral negativity generally (which includes masochism), these authors say: "One of the most important functions of negativity in later life is to *simultaneously express and defend against* unconscious symbiotic longings, wishes to return to the earliest relationship with the mother, a relationship that bore the stamp of negativity." [68] Adducing specific examples such as self-mutilation and headbanging, Lane et al. state: "These actions . . . may represent unconscious enactments of a primitive fantasy of merging with the destructive mother. The ensuing physical sensations restabilize the patient's uncertain body image *and provide assurance against the underlying fantasy.*" [69] In other words, the masochist simultaneously expresses longing for symbiotic merger with the mother *and* defends himself or herself against such longing. The fantasy of fusion is there, but so also is the self-defining defense against the fantasy—both wrapped up in the one masochistic act. In some acts the fantasy may appear more obvious, while in others the defense against the fantasy seems to take center stage.

In any case, it is clear that the self—whether aiming for further individuation and coherence, or headed back toward the old symbiotic union with the mother—is what is at issue in masochism. The masochist has a questionable sense of self, no matter what form the attempt to resolve that question takes.

Also, whatever the ultimate theoretical solution turns out to be, *Russian* masochism can turn up at either end of the spectrum. The exhibitionistic holy fool, for example, seems to utilize suffering primarily to achieve self-definition, while the submissive member of the tsarist peasant commune apparently loses his or her self in that commune, which has many maternal features as we will see below.

With the masochist's very identity or sense of self a major issue, it should not be surprising that masochistic habits are not easily extirpated. To stop being masochistic is to be a different person, a different self. If Russians were to emerge from their past shorn of their masochism, they would not be Russians anymore. They would be someone else. As Virginia Warren says, "masochists *could* change their identity, so that in the future they could cast off their self-inflicted pain and still have a (different) sense of self." [70]

But traditionalist Russians, at least, have not wanted to become someone else. Slavophile Konstantin Aksakov wrote: "Russians should be Russians, should take the Russian path, the path of faith, meekness, and the inner life." [71] For Aksakov, to take the path of "meekness" is to *be* Russian. Or, since the self is confused with Mother Russia anyway, to take this path is to *be* Russia: "Yes, Russia's only danger is that *she will cease to be Russia,* and this is where the present Petrine system is leading us." [72]

Similarly, the right-wing, anti-Semitic nationalist Igor' Shafarevich (1923–) fears that Russia's essential identity will change if Russians accept what he calls "russophobic" attitudes, such as the idea (among others) that Russia is "a nation of slaves [narod rabov] always bowing down before cruelty and grovelling before strong power." Shafarevich declares: "a people [narod] that evaluates its history *this way* can no longer exist." [73] This is perfectly correct, although Shafarevich would no doubt be perturbed to realize that he has achieved a psychoanalytic insight: for Russians to evaluate themselves as masochistic is, indeed, to stop being Russians. The self-aware masochist is already a different self from the unconscious masochist (including the masochist who denies masochism).

If the self of the masochist is problematical and fragile, the masochist's *other* is often unquestionable, solid, and grand—for example, the incomparable, eternal Mother Russia. According to psychoanalysis, this other is the parent (usually the mother) returned, but impossibly idealized, transformed into what Heinz Kohut would call an "idealized parent imago." [74] She may in fact have been abusive, but in the mind of the masochist she is now an angel. Stolorow, summarizing the work of several other psychoanalytic scholars, says, "The masochistic character stunts his own independent ego development, sacrifices his competence, and creates a debased and depreciated perception of his own self in order to sustain the image of an idealized, all-good, all-powerful maternal object on whom he can depend for nurture and protection." [75] Many masochistic patients periodically treat their analysts this way, for example. Highly religious individuals behave in a similar manner. The famous *Ad maiorem Dei gloriam* of the Jesuits is an essentially masochistic proposition. [76] The great Russian masochist Avvakum was constantly seeking to displace glory from himself onto divine figures: "Speak, seeking glory not for yourself but for Christ and the Mother of God." [77]

Here it is important to remember that the aggrandizement of the other toward whom one takes a masochistic stance is entirely projective in nature, that is, not based on the real status of that other. Nydes describes one patient who

sought to assuage his guilt for having divorced a devoted but dominating wife by constantly berating himself for his ingratitude. His tearful self-flagellation reached its height just a few weeks before his marriage to what seemed to him to be a much more desirable woman. One day in the midst of the painful experience of his self-inflicted suffering, it suddenly occurred to him that his sadness was really quite useless since his former wife could not possibly know anything about it. That simple reality fact served to remind him that it was his infantile superego and not his former wife whom he was really attempting to appease. [78]

Today's Russia, like this self-flagellating patient, is a country going through a sort of divorce and remarriage. Much of the masochistic posturing seen in the recent Soviet and post-Soviet media reflects not the reality of the situation, but personally archaic attitudes toward a previously idealized, domineering mother.

Normalcy and Cultural Variation

Ordinary, "normal" individuals may sometimes behave in masochistic ways. Almost all the recent psychoanalytic scholars of masochism assert, at one point or another, that masochism is ubiquitous in human fantasy and behavior. Patients who come in for treatment of their masochistic practices or who end up in hospital emergency wards are just the extreme end of a continuous spectrum. As Charles Brenner says, "the difference between the normal and the masochistic character is one of degree rather than of kind."[79] Everyone is a potential masochist because everyone has had some masochistic experience in early development.

Indeed, anyone who is capable of feeling guilt, of inducing guilt in others, of delaying gratification, of being devoted to a child, of working hard to achieve a goal, of subsuming personal interests to a larger cause, is by definition fulfilling some need for—or gaining some degree of satisfaction from—the experience of pain.

Consider, for example, the completely normal phenomenon of guilt. Having committed—in imagination or in reality—a transgression, one may punish oneself inwardly, that is, feel guilty. The feeling is not necessarily conscious, and is induced by a relatively autonomous internal agency traditionally termed the superego.[80] The feeling of guilt can lead to corrective external action (e.g., an apology or restitution), maladaptive external action (e.g., committing a crime in order to experience the relief of punishment), or to internal maneuvering of some kind (e.g., rationalization or repentance). When guilt feelings persist they may develop into a kind of masochism in statu nascendi. For example, a person with a lingering sense of guilt may develop a tendency to welcome misfortune. In certain religious attitudes this is even explicit. Interpreting the scriptural admonition to turn the other cheek, that is, to actually welcome misfortune, the nineteenth-century Russian elder ("starets") Ambrose wrote:

If anyone begins to tell lies about you or molests you without provocation, this is a blow to the right cheek. Do not murmur but endure this blow with patience, turning the left cheek, that is, *remember your own unjust deeds* [= feel guilty].

And even if at the moment you are faultless, you have sinned much in the past. You will quickly realize that *you merit this punishment* [i.e., feel guilty some more].[81]

This rationalization of misfortune by means of guilt, if habitualized, can obviously have self-destructive effects. In isolated instances, however, it may be a perfectly adaptive and normal response. The Archpriest Avvakum, who often utilized such rationalization in his autobiography, was also often the victim of beatings and eventually was burned to death, while Aleksandr Solzhenitsyn, who only rarely resorts to it (namely, in his *Gulag Archipelago*)[82] was actually quite adept at escaping victimization.

Avvakum and Solzhenitsyn were two different individuals with differing degrees of masochism in (roughly) the same culture. In addition to individual variation in masochistic behavior, however, there is also cultural variation. Different cultures offer quantitatively and qualitatively different opportunities to feel guilty and to be victimized. There is precious little discussion of this cultural dimension in the psychoanalytic literature proper.[83]

No two cultures have identical expectations regarding guilt. In late twentieth-century America, for example, the typical individual earns a relatively honest living, obtains goods and services for the prices advertised, loses or gains wealth in reasonably understandable and orderly fashion, etc. True, this may sound like an idealized caricature to an American law-enforcement officer who is busy chasing criminals. But anyone who has ever lived in, say, Soviet Russia—and who consequently has experienced the pressing need to be illegally employed in order to make an adequate living, to give bribes in order to obtain goods and services, to engage in various forms of falsification and corruption in order to accomplish the simplest of life's tasks—will understand how much more common the experience of guilt must have been under the Soviet regime. As Nancy Condee and Vladimir Padunov put it: "From the lowest menial worker to the highest party official, everyone survives because everyone breaks the rules. Being alive is proof of guilt."[84] This insight, which is of considerable psychoanalytic value, was apparently a commonplace among the Muscovite intelligentsia during the late Soviet period.

The Soviets, however, did not invent Russian guilt. Guilt has always been a hallmark of Russian culture. Consider, for example, the way

Russians say goodbye. One expression, "Do svidaniia," is fairly superficial and rather like English "See you," or French "Au revoir." The more traditional "Proshchai," however, expresses deep emotion. There is no English equivalent. Etymologically, the word is a request to be forgiven, an exhortation that the addressee relieve the addresser of an accumulated burden of guilt. The one who says "Proshchai" may or may not have committed certain sins, but nonetheless acts as though the sins are there, and hopes that the other person will nonetheless not think badly of him or her. This guilty attitude inherent in uttering "Proshchai" has been analyzed in a very interesting article by the philologist V. N. Toporov.[85]

"Proshchai" fitted into a general pattern of asking forgiveness ("prosit' proshcheniia") on certain threshold occasions among the peasantry. Ethnographer M. M. Gromyko devotes an entire chapter to this practice in her recent book. She observes, for example, that when a peasant set out on a long journey, he customarily gathered together all who were close to him and, bowing down before them, asked each one for forgiveness. At the end of the Maslenitsa holidays (which often included considerable sexual licentiousness), individuals were supposed to beg each other's forgiveness. This usually occurred on the last Sunday before Lent, a day which was termed "proshchenyi den'" (forgiving day) in many areas.[86]

"Only God is without sin," according to traditional peasant belief, and everyone else is guilty of some sin or other. "There is no getting away from guilt," asserted the peasant. Numerous such proverbs may be found in Dahl's collection, and in other collections:

> Even the righteous one falls/sins seven times per day (I pravednik semidzdy v den' padaet [*ili:* sogreshaet]).
>
> The day (spent) in sinning, the night in tears (Den' vo grekhakh, noch' vo slezakh).
>
> Unintended sin lives in everyone (Nevol'nyi grekh zhivet na vsekh).
>
> Everything in the world happens because of our sins (Vse na svete po grekham nashim deetsia).[87]

If indeed everything happens because of one's sinful nature, then one is motivated to welcome, or even provoke misfortune, that is, one is more likely to behave masochistically than if this guilt-ridden attitude were absent.[88]

These internal psychological attitudes are important, but external social structure can also foster masochistic events. Chronic guilt seeks an object. In most Western countries, for example, the average middle-class masochist has to exercise some ingenuity, short of hiring a dominatrix, stepping out onto a busy freeway, or committing a crime outright, in order to find punishment. In Russia, on the other hand, you don't have to be very provocative at all. There's always a line to stand in, a restaurant to refuse you admission, a bureaucrat to abuse you, an icon to bow before, a sin to repent for, a bathhouse to beat yourself in, an informer to report on you, an official who demands a bribe, and so on. Indeed, unless you are a privileged member of Russian society (e.g., you are included in the Soviet *nomenklatura* or its post-Soviet derivatives), it is very difficult to go about daily life *without* experiencing considerable pain. One might almost say that, in such a cultural environment, it helps to be a masochist.

This is precisely my point. In a country where the opportunities for experiencing guilt and suffering are legion there is strong psychological pressure on individuals to choose masochistic solutions to everyday problems. The Russian soul is a slave not only because certain psychological dynamics in early ontogeny universally favor the development of masochistic attitudes (they do), but also because cultural expectations and social organization in the adult world push the individual toward masochism.

Americans who go to Russia (either Soviet or post-Soviet) for an extended period of time like to say they are there "for the long haul." Whatever their motives for being there, they do recognize that they are going to experience hardship and deprivation. Russians who come to the West, on the other hand, express no such sentiment about the West. They may miss their homeland, they may even disapprove of many aspects of life in the West, but I have never heard a Russian visitor or emigré say that life in the West is a hardship, or that they are in "for the long haul."

Ergo, Russian society and culture must offer an overall greater opportunity for suffering than does the West. This is true regardless of whether any given individual who happens to be living in Russia actually

takes advantage of the opportunity. Moral masochism may be a phenomenon intrinsic to the individual psyche, but it can also be encouraged
or discouraged by the sociocultural milieu. Moral masochism is an
individual matter, but a culture of moral masochism is constituted by
individuals in their interaction with an environment that encourages
specific tokens of that masochism.

The Swaddling Hypothesis Revisited

There is a feature of *early* ontogeny in Russia that, although not
unique to Russia, is not often encountered (anymore) in the developed
countries of the West. I have in mind another potential source of masochism, the traditional Russian practice of swaddling infants.

Among the peasantry since time immemorial, and even today among
most urban dwellers, mothers customarily wrap up their infants in narrow strips of cloth ("pelenki") from birth. These swaddling bands serve
both to contain the child's excretions and to severely restrict bodily
motion. The arms and legs of a swaddled child are rendered immobile.
When fully swaddled the entire child (except for its face) is tightly
embraced in a kind of womb-substitute.

Lev Tolstoy, in an autobiographical fragment of 1878, tells us how
this can feel:

I am bound [ia sviazan], I want to stick my hands out and I cannot. I cry and
weep, and my cry is disagreeable even to me, but I cannot stop. Some people are
standing bent over me, above me . . . I remember that there are two of them, and
[crossed out: they feel sorry for me, but because of some strange misunder-
standing they] my cries have an effect on them: they are alarmed by my cries but
do not untie me [ne razviazyvaiut menia], which I wish they would, and I cry
still louder. To them this seems necessary (that is, that I be bound), while I know
it is not and I want to prove this to them [crossed out: and it is this misunder-
standing that tortures me most of all and forces me] so I let forth a cry repellent
to myself but irrepressible. I feel the unfairness and cruelty not of people,
because they feel sorry for me, but of *sud'ba* and I feel sorry for myself.[89]

Tolstoy may not actually be remembering the experience of being swaddled, that is, he may be having what psychoanalysts would term a screen
memory.[90] Nonetheless, this description is written by one of Russia's
greatest authors, an acknowledged master in the depiction of human
emotions. It is not unreasonable to assume that a swaddled child feels
much the way Tolstoy says it feels.

There is an enormous anthropological, psychoanalytic, and medical literature on swaddling practices worldwide.[91] In Russia medical specialists and journalists have denounced swaddling ever since the middle of the eighteenth century—but largely in vain.[92] Psychoanalyst Geoffrey Gorer made the Russian version famous when he advanced his "swaddling hypothesis" in 1949:

> When human infants are not constrained they move their limbs and bodies a great deal, especially during the second six months of life; it seems probable that much of this movement is physiologically determined, as an aspect of biological maturation. Infants tend to express emotion with their whole body and not merely their face, for example arching their back or thrashing about or hugging. They also explore their own body and the universe around them with their hands and their mouth, gradually discovering what is edible and what inedible, what me and what not-me. While they are swaddled in the Russian manner, Russian infants can do none of these things; and it is assumed that this inhibition of movement is felt to be extremely painful and frustrating and is responded to with intense and destructive rage, which cannot be adequately expressed physically.

Tolstoy's remembered experience certainly confirms this idea that swaddling generates rage in the child. Gorer goes on to say:

> These feelings of rage and fear are probably made endurable, but also given emphasis, by the fact that the baby is periodically loosed from the constraints, and suckled and petted while unswaddled. This alternation of complete restraint without gratifications, and of complete gratifications without restraint, continues for at least the first nine months of life. It is the argument of this study that the situation outlined in the preceding paragraphs is *one* of the major determinants in the development of the character of the adult Great Russians.[93]

According to Gorer, swaddling contributes to such supposedly Russian adult characteristics as: the need for authoritarian constraint alternating with total gratification of impulses (e.g., orgiastic feasts, prolonged drinking bouts); the ability to endure pain and deprivation for long periods; a generally inward orientation and great concern with matters of the soul; persisting guilt feelings which require periodic absolution or purging; and others.

Unfortunately it is not always clear just what the connection is between swaddling and whatever psychological phenomenon Gorer happens to be discussing. Nor does Gorer always get his facts about Russia right. But it does not seem unreasonable, on the face of it, to expect that swaddling would have some effect on the child's (particularly emotional) development, or that it be *one* of the determinants of the character of adult Russians.

Subsequent empirical studies have shown that swaddling does not usually retard motor or cognitive development, and that it does not *necessarily* provoke a rage reaction in the child. Indeed, once the swaddling bands are in place (after some initial fussing by the child), and as long as the infant is not too old or has had no experience of this treatment, then swaddling seems to have at least a temporary calming effect.[94] This is clearly a boon to an overworked mother.

I once ran into a couple with their swaddled child in a Moscow elevator. I asked the mother if the child was swaddled tightly. She replied: "Yes, he is such a little bandit!"

Ninety-six of Kluckhohn's sample of 172 Russians stated that they had been swaddled. Twenty-two said they did not know, and twenty-six reported that they definitely had not been swaddled. The remaining subjects evaded the question or equivocated. Kluckhohn noted that most subjects tended to feel very uncomfortable about discussing this topic.[95] I have noticed the same discomfort in conversations with Russian colleagues and friends.

From my own casual observations of swaddled children in Russia over the last fifteen years or so, and from conversations with urban Russians who have children, it would appear that swaddling is still a widespread practice. The Russian mother is still more likely than not to swaddle her infant. The severity of swaddling seems to have decreased, however. Often the arms are left free, and the bands are not tight ("tugo"). Swaddling also seems to be terminated early in urban areas, that is, after two or three months.

Highly educated Russians still give the same old, peasant-style answers when asked why the child is swaddled in the first place: "so that his legs will not grow crooked"; "so that he will not scratch his eyes"; "so that he will not tear off his ears" (a child whose arms are not swaddled may have to wear special little mittens). These statements are absurd, but psychologically revealing. Since they are manifestly untrue, they probably apply to the adults who make them rather than to the infants. In declaring that infants will *harm themselves* unless swaddled, that is, in declaring that their infants are natural masochists, adults are revealing that they themselves are preoccupied with masochistic ideas. The same goes, incidentally, for grown-ups who are generally oversolicitous and overprotective of children (Urie Bronfenbrenner has noted the extreme solicitousness of adults toward children during the high Soviet period).[96] Indeed, the same applies to intrusive altruists in Russia generally, for example, the complete stranger who approaches you on the street and tells you to button up your coat.

Fathers, it should be noted, do not swaddle. Mothers do. The swaddling scene is pre-Oedipal, or at least a-Oedipal.

Swaddling is an aspect of the pre-Oedipal mother's control over the child. Although swaddling may calm the child for a time, initially the child fusses, and later, when the child becomes hungry or otherwise agitated, there is obvious discomfort with the swaddling bands. Only a prompt unswaddling by the mother can prevent a full-fledged rage reaction. But what if the mother does not react, or is not able to react soon enough, or is not available to react? It seems unlikely that rage and defiant feelings can be averted, even with good-enough mothering. Or more precisely: it seems unlikely that rage and defiance of the mother herself can be averted.

If, in addition, the infant is regularly "steamed" by its mother in a bathhouse (including whipping with birch switches—see below, chap. 8), then it is difficult to imagine how the child could avoid rage at its mother. Also, if the child is later (as a toddler) tied for several hours with a rope to a table or a shelf for misbehavior—as was known to happen among the peasantry[97]—then again it seems very likely that the child must become enraged at its mother. Finally, in times and places where there were high childhood mortality rates, surviving children may have developed ambivalent and problematical attitudes toward their mothers (see above discussion of *sud'ba*, 74).

While mothers in all cultures exercise considerable control over the movement and actions of their infants, mothers who in addition swaddle their infants exercise considerably more control. Initially this control may seem rather impersonal, both because the infant has little idea of what a person is, and because the control is exercised "at a distance" from the mother. The mother does not directly hinder the child's movements, the swaddling bands do. The bands are inexorable. Perhaps at first the child is incapable of making a mental connection between the bands and the mother. But the repeated experience of being unbound and bound up by the mother, especially if this extends well beyond the commencement of the separation-individuation process (i.e., around four months), must eventually make it evident to the child that the mother is the one who does the hateful restraining.

With swaddling, then, there is an enhanced potential for the mother-child relationship to become problematical, and a problematical relationship with the pre-Oedipal mother itself offers an opportunity for the development of masochistic feelings and behaviors, as we saw above. From the child's viewpoint, there is pain and anger (as if there weren't already enough pain and anger when swaddling is absent!). The mother's control and authority must seem utterly absolute. At the same time the child must feel abandoned by the mother, all alone with powerful emotions that, initially directed against the mother, may then be directed against mother-substitutes (e.g., defiant rebellion against Mother Russia), or turned around against the self (giving rise to guilt, as Gorer argued). Here it is rage turned against the self which is of primary interest.

Swaddling may be said to encourage masochism in the sense that it stimulates the child to "give up" any resistance to constraint by the swaddling bands (this is in fact the physiological response in very young infants—they tend to go limp). But swaddling also fosters masochistic feelings. Tolstoy says that he felt extremely sorry for himself, that he let out a scream that was repellent even to himself (yet he kept screaming). He did *not* blame those who swaddled him (possibly his mother and nurse together)—which was already a first step toward blaming himself. But even if he did not blame himself, he blamed *sud'ba*—that is, a mental construct which, as we saw earlier, is ripe with masochistic possibilities.

It appears, then, that swaddling—especially when severe ("tugo") and prolonged—contributes to masochism in Russia. Whether it contributes to other adult psychological characteristics is another question which I will not deal with here.

According to psychoanalytic theory, masochism has its roots in the pre-Oedipal period of early childhood. This is probably true cross-culturally, although there is great sociocultural variation in the quantity and quality of opportunities for adults to behave or to fantasize in masochistic fashion. In Russia there are opportunities galore. In addition, there is a climate of guilt which pushes adult individuals toward masochistic solutions to life's problems. Add to this the traditional Russian abuse of infants by swaddling and associated practices, and it becomes difficult to imagine how masochism can be avoided in Russia.

SIX

The Russian Fool and His Mother

The fool (masculine "durak," feminine "dura") is a species of masochist. He or she deliberately does things which do not seem to make good sense, at least from the viewpoint of an outside observer. In particular, the "stupid" things a fool does are harmful *to the fool*. Observers laugh—sometimes even the fool laughs—because the fool's acts are self-destructive, self-defeating, and humiliating. What the fool does thus fits the clinical definition of masochism given at the beginning of this book.

A Surplus of Fools

Foolishness is a universal phenomenon. Many Russians claim, however, that Russia has more than her share of fools. Russia has so many fools, according to an old proverb, that the supply should last for the next one hundred years ("Na Rusi, slava Bogu, durakov let na sto pripaseno").[1] Although this proverb is itself more than a hundred years old, there is no indication that the attitude reflected in it has changed. In the late Soviet press, for example, the phrase "country of fools" ("strana durakov") was very often encountered, and no one but extreme right-wingers (e.g., Igor' Shafarevich)[2] seemed to mind it. Consider the following item from a 1991 issue of *Moscow News:*

An organizing committee for the formation of the Russian Foolish Party [Org-komitet po formirovaniiu Duratskoi partii Rossii] has been created in Tiumen. Its chair, Iu. Alekseev, declared that only his party can count on success in this "country of fools." In the upcoming mayoral election he is challenging the current head of the city soviet.[3]

There was some hope that things would change after the coup of August 1991 was foiled by democratically minded forces. On the front page of an issue of *Literaturnaia gazeta* published on 21 August of that year, poet Evgenii Evtushenko declared:

Мы сегодня — народ,
                  а не кем-то обманутые дурачки.[4]

Today we are a people,
                  and not fools deceived by someone.

Finally, it seemed, Russians were not being submissive, self-destructive fools, but were resisting harmful orders handed down from above.

One year later, however, in an issue of *Moskovskie novosti*, we find Russian journalist-playwright Aleksandr Gel'man asserting that foolishness is alive and well in Russia. Engaging in a playful masochism of his own, Gel'man calls himself a "fool" and declares: "Stupidity [glupost'] is a large social force which has been neglected for a long time. We stupid ones, after all, are in the majority." Gel'man goes on to say:

Oh, that stupidity of ours! It is not huge or measureless, but it is inescapable. Once in a while it seems like we might just be saved from it, we might just shake it out of our heads after all—but then we wake up the next day (next year, next century) and there it is, the little mother is right there in her place [matushka na svoem meste].[5]

There is no escape, for "we are in love with our stupidity, and love is blind," says Gel'man. Stupidity is thus personified, she is a beloved "matushka," and no other "dama" can possibly substitute for her. This "matushka," to judge from our earlier discussion of the important role of the mother in the ontogeny of masochism, is an utterly appropriate personification.

Foolishness has historical roots deep in medieval Russia.[6] Synchronically speaking, the Russian idea of the fool is a peasant idea. In every village there was supposed to be a "derevenskii durachok"[7] (cf. English "village idiot"). Russian peasant lore is rich with the imagery of stupidity. To select just a few items from the folktale motif-index compiled by Barag et al. in 1979:

They attempt to milk chickens.

He cuts the branch out from underneath himself and falls.

They pull on a log in order to make it longer.

A simpleton kills his own horse.

A fool is afraid of his own shadow, throws things at it.

A fool traps and accidentally kills his mother.

Foma and Erema do everything wrong—they ruin a house they are building, fail to plow a field, catch no fish, and eventually both drown.[8]

These ideas, however gruesome some of them may seem, elicit laughter in the appreciative Russian listener. The Russian peasant laughs *at* the fool, that is, permits a momentary and merely symbolic outburst of violence directed against him. The fool may do something actually violent against himself (or sometimes against someone else as well), but the listener remains in effective control while the fool does his thing. The listener's laughter is violence contained. In psychoanalytic terms, the laughing listener expresses sadistic feelings when confronted with the fool's masochistic behavior. The interaction of fool and listener is thus sadomasochistic in essence.

Sadistic attitudes toward the fool are very common in Russia. In general, it is assumed that a fool is someone who is beaten often, or who ought to be beaten or otherwise abused: "Beat a fool, do not spare the fist!"; "You can't save up enough fists for all the fools"; "They'll beat a fool even in church."[9] Although the fool cannot be taught anything by beatings ("Teaching a fool is like curing the dead"),[10] there is nonetheless a powerful contradictory assumption as well, that is, that the fool (or anyone else, for that matter) needs to be "taught" by violent means:

In order to teach fools, do not spare fists (Uchit' durakov—ne zhalet' kulakov).

He's grown to the size of the devil, but he hasn't been beaten with a knout (i.e., he is stupid) (S cherta vyros, a knutom ne bit *[t. e., glup]*).

I'll smarten you up. Let's be humbly thankful for brains *(said after punishment)* (Ia tebe dam uma. Blagodarim pokorno za um *[govoriat posle nakazaniia]*).[11]

The knout is not torture, but knowledge in advance (Knut ne muka, a vpred' nauka).

The rod is dumb, but it will give intelligence (Palka nema, a dast uma).[12]

Violence is thus an essential "pedagogical" technique in the peasant imagination (and in social reality as well, to judge from the abundant evidence for corporal punishment in traditional Russia).[13]

There is a strong temptation to beat the fool (sadism), while at the same time there is an urge to get the foolishness beaten out of oneself (masochism). In both processes there seems to be a fear of actually *being* a fool, that is, of crossing some dangerous boundary separating the self from the fool. The fact that there are so many proverbs advising one not to get involved with fools suggests that there was a real possibility that one might regard oneself as a fool (I quote just a few here from the many in the Dahl collection):

God forbid that you get mixed up with a fool (Ne dai Bog s dura-kom sviazat'sia).

Get mixed up with a fool, and may your soul rest in peace (S durakom sviazat'sia—vechnaia pamiat').

You can ward off the devil with a cross and a bear with a pestle, but there is no way to get rid of a fool (Ot cherta krestom, ot medvedia pestom, a ot duraka—nichem).[14]

The fool is such a threat that one is in danger of *becoming* one just by having some relationship with one. To observe two fools fighting, for example, means that you are a fool. To accuse someone of being a fool is to risk being called a fool in return ("Ty durak" can provoke "Ot duraka slyshu").[15] The danger is general: "He who gets mixed up with a fool is a fool" ("Durak, kto s durakom sviazhetsia").[16]

Among Soviet intellectuals the issue of whether one was a "smart" person or a fool was still important. Bulat Okudzhava wrote a famous song on this subject, titled "Song about Fools." It seems that one day the fools (read: stupid bureaucrats, plodding hacks, neanderthal police agents, etc.) began to get embarrassed about being fools, so they had special tags attached to them which read "smart." The song ends with the following quatrain:

Давно в обиходе у нас ярлыки,
по фунту на грошик на медный.
И умным кричат: "Дураки, дураки!"
А вот дураки незаметны.

Long, long ago we got used to these tags,
They aren't worth a penny a pound.
Now they shout at the smart men, "You fools, oh you fools!"
And so the fools go unnoticed.[17]

One hesitates here, because for a moment it is not clear what Okudzhava now means by "smart" and by "fool." But that is precisely the message. It is easy to confuse a "smart" person with a "fool." The boundary is not clear. As with the nineteenth-century peasant, the twentieth-century intellectual is very concerned about how to distinguish the two. There is always a danger that the "smart" person will be mistaken for a fool, or vice versa.

For the "smart" person a fool is someone who endangers the boundary between self and other. A fool is a self who threatens fusion with other selves. The ridiculed object just *might* be a subject, especially if the subject is (as most Russians are) in the habit of fighting off masochistic impulses. There, but for resistance to masochism, go I.

It is easier to live with the idea that fools exist if one thinks they do not really mind their situation in life. The fool is a masochist, after all. One should not feel guilty about mistreating the fool because he *likes* or *enjoys* abuse:

Spit/piss in the eyes of a fool, and he'll think it's heavenly dew (Duraku khot' pliui/stsy v glaza, a on: bozh'ia rosa).

A fool is pleased at the hole in his side (Liubo duraku, chto chirii [dyra] na boku).[18]

Were it not for the fool's apparent "stupidity," these latter proverbs would be a straightforward characterization of the fool's masochism. As for those who are inclined to beat on fools, they have no need for a "stupidity" to conceal their sadism. Apparently concealment is not necessary in the case of sadism. This suggests that masochism is psychologically more disturbing to Russians than is sadism.

Ivan the Fool

All Russians know about the folktale ("skazka") character Ivan the fool ("Ivan durak" or "Ivanushka durachok," sometimes just "Ivan" or just "durak" or "duren' ").[19] As Andrei Siniavskii has recently pointed out, Ivan the fool is the favorite of all Russian folktale heroes.[20] He is a "low" hero who is always getting into scrapes for doing something that appears foolish or stupid. Folklorist Eleazar Meletinskii asserted that Ivan the fool is remarkably deep, psychologically, and that the humor of this fool's actions is much more developed than in corresponding Western tales (e.g., German, Norwegian) or Eastern tales (e.g., Turkic).[21] Already at the beginning of our century A. M. Smirnov argued that the great appeal of Ivan the fool throughout Russia over many generations indicates that a profound psychological truth is tapped by this figure.[22]

The psychology of Ivan the fool is revealed by the variety of ways in which he manages to get punished. In one tale, for example, he is supposed to deliver dumplings to his brothers. But on the way he notices his shadow following him and, thinking the shadow is hungry, throws the dumplings at it. As a result, his brothers beat the living daylights out of him. In another tale he takes the creaking sounds made by a birch tree for spoken words, and is later ridiculed by his "smart" brothers. Sometimes his foolish act brings punishment without even the intervention of another person, as when he cuts the tree limb he is perched on. In some of the tales the fool gains no reward for his troubles, and merely moves from one punishing situation to another. In other stories he does attain a worthy goal, such as gold or a beautiful wife. Ivan the fool sometimes turns out to be Ivan the prince.[23] In the meantime, whatever the outcome, the fool is always punished in some direct or indirect fashion for his manifestly stupid actions. The descriptions of the punishments are remarkably detailed, they tend to be repetitious, and they are clearly intended to elicit sadistic outbursts of laughter from the listener.

Russians laugh at their folkloric fool. He seems to deliberately provoke punishment (even though, logically speaking, he is not responsible, for he is retarded, i.e., too "stupid" to understand what he is doing). His apparent masochism cannot but gratify the addressee's sadistic impulses. But the laughter also reveals a kind of recognition. Some previously repressed information about the *self* is released by the fool.[24] In laughing at their folkloric fool, Russians are laughing at themselves. He is, after all, often named Ivan—a favorite name among Russians,[25] a name that may even be considered metonymic for Russians.[26] When Ol'ga Semenova-Tian-Shanskaia titled her ethnographic monograph "The Life of 'Ivan,' " she was counting on this metonymy.[27] As Maksim Gor'kii argued, Ivan the fool represents the Russian peasant's own willingness to take a beating, to be passively resigned in the face of whatever *sud'ba* has to offer.[28]

The listener's laughter is thus a doubly masochistic phenomenon. Ivan the fool does things which provoke ridicule upon himself, and laughing Russians are in effect ridiculing themselves. Ivan's provocative style of masochism finds resonance in the Russians' habit of laughing at themselves.

The folkloric fool either does not know his acts will get him into trouble because he is too retarded to understand what is going on, or he *does* know but is slyly biding his time ("sebe na ume," as the Russians say). Scholars have tended to focus on the latter. The masochism is easier to ignore that way, and emphasis can be put on the tales in which Ivan is covertly clever, and in which there is a happy ending (although sometimes the happy ending is just a matter of luck, with the fool remaining truly naive). It is in any case important to keep in mind that tales about the fool do not always have a happy ending (in such instances the fool is likely to be nameless). In these tales the listener is treated to nothing but a series of masochistic incidents. Even when the ending is happy (e.g., the fool gets the princess and the gold), what comes before the ending is in any case overtly self-destructive for the fool.

The apparent masochism of the Russian folkloric fool sometimes shades over into altruism. As Smirnov observes, Ivan is "ready for any self-sacrifice."[29] Dmitrii Likhachev considers the fool specifically in the context of his discussion of Russian kindness ("dobrota").[30] The fool can be very kind—to animals, to the poor, to his family. For example, he permits a swarm of mosquitoes to suck his blood. Or he gives alms to beggars. In such behavior, as Meletinskii observes, the fool is "the embodiment of the great potentialities inherent in the simple man of the people."[31]

In his altruistic function Ivan the fool seems almost holy. Likhachev uses the terms "durak" and "iurodivyi" almost interchangeably.[32] The fool is capable of loving his enemies in a curiously Christ-like fashion. He can be, as the Russians say, stupid to the point of saintliness ("glup do sviatosti").[33]

The Fool and His Mother

Joanna Hubbs prefers to view the fool's altruistic behavior as "motherly."[34] A quite explicit example is the foolish general who sits naked on some eggs in order to hatch out the chicks—a hen is a mother, after all.[35] In an early Soviet literary variant titled "Van'ka Dobroi" ("Van'ka the Good) the fool lives happily ever after with his mother and two of the animals he has saved.[36]

The Russian folkloric fool tends to be strongly attached to his family, especially his mother. Altruism in Russia, as everywhere else,[37] is learned on mother's knee. But the foolishness as well as the altruism should be characterized as "motherly," or at least as having to do with the mother. In many variants the problem is that the fool cannot seem to make a *break* with his mother. He is often the youngest child, which means he is the last one to have emerged from his mother's body, and no one else has since occupied his position as mother's little boy.[38] He is very passive and dependent on his mother. His closeness to her is part of what makes him laughable. He is an adult, but is developmentally retarded. Sometimes he is speechless, like an infant. He is a lazybones, a stay-at-home, usually remaining in his mother's hut and lying on (or behind) the stove. Sometimes even his name suggests the stove to which he is so attached: "Ivan Zapechnik" ("Ivan Behind-the-Stove") or "Kniaz' Pechurinskii" ("Prince Stovish").[39] The image of the stove ("pech'," a feminine noun) is decidedly maternal, and reinforces the idea of the fool's continuing dependence on his mother ("The stove is our dear mother," says a peasant proverb).[40] Like a little child, the fool is often without britches, he is dirty,[41] does not clean himself, has a runny nose, and so forth. His mother is more or less forced to take care of him.[42] When he does get up the energy to go out and do some daring, stupid deed, he often follows this with a return home to his mother and a reversion to his former passivity and nearly symbiotic union with his mother. The behavior of the Russian folkloric fool thus exemplifies that grade of masochism in which the individual, when behaving masochistically, is attempting to move *away* from the mother (see clinical discussion, above, 109). In any case, the boundary of the foolish self with the mother is at issue.

Russian proverbs often implicate the mother (but not the father) in the fool's foolishness. There are many ways, for example, to excuse a fool by saying he was *born* that way (e.g., "Ne durak, a *rodom* tak," or "Kak *rozheny*, tak i zamorozheny").[43] These are hints that the mother somehow gave birth badly, or made some kind of mistake in giving birth to the fool. She compensates for this by taking pity, by devoting special attention to her defective child (in the tales he is often the favored third child). But sometimes she will neglect or abuse the child.[44] Sometimes she will admit that her child is a fool.[45] One proverb has her formerly speechless son call *her* a fool ("Tri goda ne bail parnishko, da: 'dura mat'").[46]

Here we should note the traditional sexist attitude which portrays women as not too bright: "Long on hair, but short on brains" ("Volos dolog, da um korotok").[47] There are quite a few such proverbs, and Russia is indeed a male chauvinist nation in the extreme (as will become clear in the discussion below on the slave soul of Russia as a gendered object). But the quintessential Russian fool is nonetheless a man, not a woman, a "durak," not a "dura." There is many an "Ivan durak," but no "Tatiana dura." If in the folkloric imagination there is some foolishness in women (including mothers), nonetheless it is men who go to extremes in this matter.[48]

Laughter is essential to the fool's appeal, but this laughter can become rather gruesome by Western standards. The grown-up fool's closeness to his mother is mildly funny, but non-Russians are likely to be shocked when the fool insists on keeping his mother's corpse nearby because he cannot part with it.[49] Russians laugh when the fool mistakenly takes his mother for a thief and kills her with a club.[50] They laugh when the fool (in several variants) uses his mother's corpse to force various people to pay him for allegedly murdering her.[51] They are delighted when the fool throws the mother-figure of Iaga-Baba into an oven and cooks her.[52]

It is difficult to avoid the impression that the fool feels hostile toward his mother in many of the tales (despite, or perhaps because of his dependence on her), and that sympathetic (laughing) Russians are finding an outlet for archaic, childish hostility they once felt toward their own mothers. Their laughter at the fool implies approval of what the fool is doing to his mother.[53]

Consider an example of the very abundant motif-type known as the "arrant fool," [54] who tests his mother's patience rather severely:

In a certain family there was an arrant fool. Not a day passed on which people did not complain about him; every day he would either insult someone or injure someone. The fool's mother pitied him and looked after him as if he were a little child; whenever the fool made ready to go somewhere, she would explain to him for half an hour what he should do and how he should do it. One day the fool went by the threshing barn and saw the peasants threshing peas, and cried to them: "May you thresh peas for three days and get three peas threshed!" Because he said this the peasants belabored him with their flails. The fool came back to his mother and cried out: "Mother, mother, they have beaten up a fellow!" "Was it you, my child?" "Yes." "What for?" "Because I went by Dormidoshkin's barn and his people were threshing peas there." "And then, my child?" "And I said to them: 'May you thresh peas for three days and get three peas threshed.' That's why they beat me up." "Oh, my child, you should have said: 'May you have such an abundance that you have to be hauling it for ever and ever.' "

The fool was overjoyed. The next day he went to walk in the village and met some people carrying a coffin with a dead man in it. Remembering yesterday's advice, he roared in a loud voice: "May you have to haul this for ever and ever!" Again he was soundly thrashed. The fool returned to his mother and told her why he had been beaten up. "Ah, my child," she said, "you should have said: 'May he rest in peace eternal!' " These words sank deep into the fool's mind.

Next day he went wandering again in the village and he met a gay wedding procession. The fool cleared his throat, and as soon as he came up to the procession, he cried: "May you rest in peace eternal!" The drunken peasants jumped down from the cart and beat him up cruelly. The fool went home and cried: "Oh my dear mother." [55]

This goes on for two more identically silly episodes. Finally the mother gets fed up and forbids her fool to go to the village any more, and the tale ends. In other variants there is either no resolution (the tale ends *in medias res*), or the fool eventually dies from his many wounds.

What is the point of such a narrative? What is funny about it, and why does it strike home for Russians?

The two chief players are mother and child. Their back-and-forth interaction is what is important (the ending varies, and is largely irrelevant). The mother seems normal, while the grown-up son is a fool that she looks after "as if he were a little child" ("kak za malym rebenkom").

Indeed the fool's behavior is childlike—comparable to that of a two-year-old, to be precise. Mothers in all cultures know about the "terrible twos," an age when the child is first asserting its independence from her by constantly getting into scrapes, always saying "no," often ending an adventure in tears. This is an important stage in the formation of the *self*. Often the child knows perfectly well when something is wrong or harmful, but pretends not to and gets into trouble anyway. Of a child that is behaving in this obstreperous fashion Russians will use the same expression as they use for characterizing a fool: "He is on his mind to himself" ("On sebe na ume").[56] Mothers do not necessarily love their children any less as a result of such behavior, however. The narrating mother in Natal'ia Baranskaia's *A Week Like Any Other* declares of her children: "I love our little fools so much." [57] This is generally in keeping with the affectionate attitude Russians have toward the fool figure ("Akh ty moi glupen'kii," or "Akh ty moi durachok").[58]

What is going on in the Afanas'ev tale is very much like a misbehaving toddler's interaction with the mother. Just as the rebelling child repeatedly runs off and hurts itself, the fool here keeps going into town and doing something that elicits abuse from others. And just as the little child always runs back to its mommy for comfort, the fool here runs back repeatedly to his "matushka."

From the viewpoint of the tale's addressee, as I observed above, the fool appears to be inviting abuse, that is, he appears to be behaving masochistically. This impression is difficult to shake in this particular tale because the fool is thrashed so many times—not just the magical number three, but five times. In another variant, the mistreatment occurs nine times in a row.[59] In a literary variant by Lev Tolstoi the beatings occur seven times, with the fool being beaten to death the last time.[60] Note also the fool's epithet, "*nabityi* durak," translated as "*arrant* fool" by Guterman, but etymologically better rendered as "*very beaten* fool," or more colloquially as "stuffed full," as in "nabityi meshok" ("a bag stuffed full").[61] Another way to convey this fool's foolishness is to say that, no matter how much he gets beaten, the foolishness does not get beaten out of him.

The repetitiveness of the beatings is suggestive. The fool is being *particularly* rebellious. He is not only punishing himself, he seems to be punishing his mother as well (she becomes quite frustrated). If he cannot do anything to please her, he will punish her. His willfulness is directed at her as well as at himself—or *would* be if he were not so "stupid." His foolishness is a cover that permits the Russian addressee to indulge in both self-destructive and mother-destructive fantasies. Punishing the self and punishing the mother are not very different when there is a lingering boundary problem between mother and child.

And the attempt may fail. At the deepest level, the Russian folkloric fool invites the addressee to indulge in a disturbing fantasy of remaining merged or fused with the mother. When the fool does try to make the break, his mother usually encourages him. But his efforts are in vain, at least initially, and in many variants the fool never does succeed. He must remain with his mother till the end of his days. Nothing could be more humiliating. The unseparated self is the lowest form of self. It deserves all the punishment it gets from funny storytellers and laughing listeners.

SEVEN

Is the Slave Soul of Russia a Gendered Object?

I am a slave.
　　—*Soviet housewife*[1]

The "slave soul of Russia" is a metaphorical characterization of a mentality that pervades Russia on all cultural levels. But in the depths of the individual Russian psyche, this "slave soul" is a specific, personified, and gendered entity: it is a woman, most commonly the first and foremost woman in every Russian's life, namely, the mother. At the national level, as we saw earlier, the "great [female] slave" (Grossman) is "Mother Russia" herself.

Any responsible mother is in some sense enslaved by her children, especially by very small children who require constant attention. Vasilii Rozanov characterized a mother as a slave ("sluzhit rabyneiu") in a touching vignette about a sick child and its attentive mother.[2] But there is nothing particularly Russian about sacrificing oneself to the needs and whims of what Freud liked to call *sa majesté l'enfant*.

In Russia, however, there has always been a gross inequality of the sexes which served to intensify a woman's enslavement. A traditional Russian woman was, in effect, the slave of her man. Among the peasantry, for example, a daughter was expected to be obedient to her father until he married her off, whereupon she was required to submit to the will of her husband. The husband became her "father" within the patriarchal peasant culture, as in the proverb "A husband is the wife's father, a wife is the husband's crowning glory" ("Muzh zhene otets, zhena muzhu venets").[3] Among the gentry the situation was not very different, as can be seen from Professor Stites's discussion of "the subservience of married women to their husbands in nineteenth-century Russia." Stites goes so far as to make an analogy with the institution of serfdom: "In many ways, the wife-daughter's status under the husband-father was analogous to that of the landlord's serf."[4]

Among the peasantry the husband himself was likely to be a slave (literally until 1861, metaphorically both before and after). There is a famous passage about the complexities of the serf wife's enslavement in Nikolai Nekrasov's folkloristic poem *Red-Nose Frost:*

> Три тяжкие доли имела судьба,
> И первая доля: с рабом повенчаться,
> Вторая — быть матерью сына раба,
> А третья — до гроба рабу покоряться,
> И все эти грозные доли легли
>   На женщину русской земли.

> Fate held three heavy parts:
> The first was to be married to a slave,
> The second was to be the mother of a slave's son,
> The third was to submit to a slave to the grave.
> All of these terrible lots fell upon
> The woman of the Russian land.

Here Nekrasov sympathizes with the downtrodden Russian woman, and understandably so. But the picture was really more complicated. The inequality of the sexes was affected in important ways by the fact that both spouse abuse and child abuse were common in the peasant family.

When a peasant wife did not submit to the will of her husband, that is, did not behave in accordance with the ethical principle of *smirenie,* she could expect to be beaten by him. When her children did not submit to his will, they too could be beaten by him. They could also be beaten by their mother, although mothers tended to beat their children for different reasons than fathers did.[5] Nevertheless, both parents were abusive. The abuse was accomplished in a variety of ways: the child was whipped with a rope, hit with a fist, a stick, or a nettle switch, dragged by the ear or the hair, or kicked.[6]

Although from a small child's viewpoint the mother is a dominating, enslaving figure in any culture (above, 96), as the Russian child grows it becomes increasingly clear that the father is the family slave driver. Among the Russian peasantry the father's abuse of the mother would often take place right in front of the children. For example, ethnographer Ol'ga Semenova-Tian-Shanskaia reports on one muzhik who, when drunk, used to threaten his wife with an axe, or beat her on the head with a threshing-flail as the children cried and screamed nearby.[7]

It must be quite an epiphany for the growing Russian child to discover that its master has a master (especially if this occurs in the context of the primal scene—see below). The original enslaver is, after all, a slave. Any hostile wishes that the child may have had against the mother—and even children who have not been swaddled Russian-style have hated their mothers at one point or another—must be reactivated by a male adult who himself lords it over the child's mother. At the same time, having been lorded over in the past, the child must also be able to identify with a mother who now appears to be a victim. In other words, the child must be torn. At some moment in development the child has the affective makings of both master and slave, both sadist and masochist.

Within the traditional peasant family the father was a harsh disciplinarian who had a right to beat his children, to decide who they married, to determine where they would live, etc. Christine Worobec provides a very typical example in her excellent recent book on post-emancipation peasants:

On 12 September 1871, in Ivanovo canton, Shuia district, Vladimir province, a father charged his son with leaving home and not being respectful of parental authority. When the son defended his action by accusing his father of severely beating him, the father replied that it was a parent's right to punish a disobedient son. The father reasoned that such beatings were merely instructive; they could not lead to maiming. The cantonal court sided with the father, sentenced the son to twenty lashes, and ordered that he return to his parents' home.[8]

Such familial authority has always had its political analogue in Russia. Political authoritarianism is expressed with specifically paternal metaphors. The Russian tsars, for example, had since the seventeenth century been affectionately referred to by the naively monarchistic peasantry as "little father" ("Batiushka"). Peter the Great was "Father of the Fatherland" ("Otets Otechestva").[9] Iosif Stalin, who far outstripped the tsars in the degree to which he enslaved Russia (and the rest of the Soviet Union), was called "Father," "Father of the Peoples," "Wise Father," "Beloved Father," and so forth.[10]

In the religious realm, as in the political, the paternal metaphor reigned, and continues to reign. For example, a nineteenth-century Russian monk writes: "We must not try to find out why this happened in this way, and not in that, *but with childlike obedience* we must surrender ourselves to the holy will of *our heavenly Father* and say from the depth of our soul: '*Our Father,* Thy will be done.' " [11] The Russian Orthodox "God" is most definitely a father, not a mother.

The childlike quality of Russian obedience is manifested in the very pronouns Russians used in addressing the authorities. Russian has two second person pronouns, the familiar *ty* and the polite *vy* (cf. French *tu* and *vous,* German *Du* and *Sie*). Initially the Russian child uses only *ty,* whether the interaction is with adults or with peers. The familiar pronoun is the pronoun of childhood. Among peasants this pronoun remained predominant in adulthood as well, however. *Vy* was used on certain formal occasions (e.g., matchmaking), or in situations where deliberate distance was desired, or in addressing some members of the gentry (e.g., the landlord's wife). But *ty* was used toward those in authority, as Paul Friedrich has pointed out:

The household chief, the landlord, Tsar, and God were all addressed with *ty* and the quasi-kinship term, *batjushka* ("little father"). Thus a striking feature of authority in Russia as against the West was that *vy* generally did symbolize greater power, but that when the greatness passed a certain point the speaker switched back to what might be called the *ty* of total subordination or of an intimacy that could not be jeopardized. From another point of view, *ty* to God, Tsar, and squire emphasized the fatherly aspect of their jural authority.[12]

In the Soviet period childish familiarity with authority figures decreased, of course. But the paternal metaphor continued to reign. A Soviet woman physician and hospital section head writing a letter to sociologist Larisa Kuznetsova, describes a confrontation she had with another physician who was supposed to be working *under* her: "Once I permitted myself to make a joke: 'Which of us in this section is the Mama—me or you?' Pedantically he raised his index finger and replied harshly: 'Remember that I am everywhere the Papa.' " [13] Eventually this woman quit her job as section head and went back to being an ordinary physician. As another Moscow woman said: "Inequities don't always give rise to anger. Sometimes they make you subservient." [14]

Patriarchy Conceals Matrifocality

Despite the overt patriarchal orientation of adult Russian culture, the child's *early* viewpoint should not be neglected. Small children are preoccupied with their mothers, not their fathers. They cannot eat, drink, clothe themselves, clean themselves, or move about without the mother's assistance and/or permission. The "barin" may not allow you to leave the borders of his estate, and the paternalistic Russian bureaucrat may not permit you to leave the borders of the Soviet Union, but your mother did not even let you out of her arms, or the swaddling bands, or the cradle, or the hut.

To a traditional Russian child the world must seem very "matriarchal" (and even more so if the father is absent or indifferent). Patriarchs do not mother. They can take neither credit for caring for the infant nor blame for subjugating it. Indeed, mothers in all cultures are in charge of their children until they are weaned.[15]

Actually, a much better term than "matriarchal" here would be *matrifocal,* meaning that the emphasis in Russia is on the mother-child relationship at the expense of the father-child or father-mother relationships.[16] There is in fact no such thing as a "matriarchal" society anywhere on our planet, and there probably never has been one.[17] But it is possible for a society, such as Russia, to be intensely matrifocal while at the same time being patriarchal to varying degrees at various time periods.

Even after the Russian child has grown up, the mother remains extremely important. Ivan Petrovich Sakharov, writing in the middle of the nineteenth century, quotes a long peasant incantation designed to neutralize the effects of a mother's anger against her grown-up son.[18] Referring to interviews with Soviet Russian soldiers, Henry Dicks says: "On the whole the impression was gained that a Russian man's mother remained his most important love-object even though he was married."[19]

In Russia, according to philosopher Nikolai Berdiaev, "the fundamental category is motherhood."[20] This statement is not just about individual Russians and their mothers. The matrifocality of the Russian family has spilled out into the culture as a whole. Maternal imagery permeates all levels of Russian society and culture. To the Westerner, there seems to be an excess of signification about mothers in Russia, and this excess indicates that the average Russian needs to continue dealing, even in adulthood, with the experience of having been mothered.

For example, mother earth is the place where, in the native lore, all crops grow ("mat' zemlia-kormilitsa") and all Russians are eventually buried ("mat' syra zemlia"). Russians speak of the "bosom of the earth" ("lono zemli"). More than one Dostoevsky character has been known to flop down upon the earth, kiss it as if it were a person, and moisten it with tears of joy or grief. On various ceremonial occasions among the peasantry the earth was kissed. Russian peasants sometimes swore oaths by swallowing a handful of earth. Land disputes were decided by peasants who paced boundaries with a clump of earth on their head. In the absence of a priest, peasants would sometimes confess their sins to mother earth.

The Volga, the Oka, and various other Russian rivers, Moscow and some other cities, plants such as rye ("rozh' ")—all have "mother" or the pleonastic "natal mother" ("mat' rodnaia") as their epithet. "Mother Russia" ("matushka Rus'," "Rossiia mat' ") is a very normal way for the Russian to personify his or her country, while "Fatherland," that is, "otechestvo" is less common and less significant (except in contexts of extreme nationalism or war). Some lines from Nikolai Nekrasov provide a famous example:

Ты и убогая,
Ты и обильная,
Ты и забитая,
Ты и всесильная,
Матушка Русь!..

Thou pitiable,
Thou prosperous,
Thou downtrodden,
Thou almighty
Mother Russia.[21]

"Motherland" ("Rodina," literally "Birthland") is another widespread designation, as in the famous recruitment poster from World War II, "The Motherland Mother Calls" ("Rodina mat' zovet"); this term can also refer to the village or general locale one was born in.

The "Mother of God" ("Bogoroditsa" or "Bogomater'," unlike the "Blessed Virgin Mary" of Western Christianity) is quite as important as the male divinities in Russian Orthodoxy and popular Russian Christianity. She pities those who suffer and who sin, she is a protector, she works miracles, she aids women in labor, churches are consecrated in her name, she was the guarantor of military pacts, her icon was worshipped by soldiers before battle, and so on. Mary is not only Christ's mother, she is the metaphorical mother of all religious Russians, even of all humankind. Historically, she seems to have inherited some features of the old Slavic fertility goddess Makosh', the "mother of the harvest."

In the religious lore, there are repeated allusions to the "three mothers" in every person's life: the Mother of God, Mother Moist Earth, and the natal mother. It is as if one mother were not enough, or not adequate enough. Mother cults, both Christian and pagan, can be traced back to earliest Russia. A central figure of Russian folktales is the maternal hag Baba Yaga, who threatens to eat little children.

The Soviet government traditionally rewarded prolific mothers with the title of "Heroine Mother" (423,000 Soviet mothers had received this award by 1990). The Communist Party itself ("partiia") was often characterized as the "mother" of Soviet citizens in both official and unofficial lore.[22]

Ambivalence toward Mothers

There are widespread hostile, even sadistic attitudes toward the maternal image in Russian culture. These attitudes are all too often neglected by scholars of Mother Russia.

The most common way to swear in Russian, for example, is to make a nasty sexual reference about someone's mother. This language is colloquially referred to as "mat" (which is related by folk-etymology to the Russian word for "mother," i.e., "mat' "). The most widespread and ancient expletive in the vocabulary of mat is "eb tvoiu mat'," which has many nuances of meaning and considerable linguistic peculiarity, and which may be very loosely translated as "go to hell!" or "goddamn it!"[23] But the phrase literally means "[I] fucked your mother," and it is obviously this underlying meaning which stirs emotion in both the addresser and addressee—so much emotion that, until only recently, the phrase was taboo in the Russian press, even for purposes of quotation or linguistic analysis. The attitude of Soviet authorities toward mat was essentially the same as that held by the Russian Orthodox Church and the tsarist censorship.

The Oedipal dimension of mat is not far below the surface, because it is usually spoken by a male to another male, and the third party is somebody's mother. In effect, the most common mother oath may be translated as: "I fucked your mother, and therefore I might even be your father." Such an expression automatically creates an Oedipal triangle, with antagonism between the father and child figures, as well as hostility toward the mother. A variant form, "Fuck your mother!" ("Ebi tvoiu mat'!") admonishes the addressee to commit incest—also a clearly Oedipal idea.

The Oedipal suggestiveness of mat is expressed by an explicitly Oedipal legend from the Smolensk area about its origin:

Every person has three mothers: his natal mother and two great mothers, moist mother earth and the Mother of God. The devil "disturbed" one person. This person killed his father and married his mother. From that time on humankind has been swearing, mentioning the name of the mother in curses, and from that time this evil has spread about the earth.[24]

Boris Uspenskii cites numerous religious folkloric texts in which one's own mother, mother earth, or the Mother of God is horrified and suffers greatly upon hearing mat spoken.[25] An inescapable consequence of mat—at least in the fantasy life of the religious Russian—is maternal suffering. All of these texts are of course designed to induce guilt in the addressee. One should, like one's mother, suffer.

This brings us to the pre-Oedipal aspect of Russian obscenities. When mat is used aggressively, the direct target (given in the accusative case) is the mother. But mat is always *understood* as being directed at the mother's child as well. That is, to insult a person's mother using mat is the same as to insult the person. The person's honor depends on the mother's honor. Why this should be so makes sense, psychoanalytically. After all, the person's self-esteem or core narcissism itself derives from pre-Oedipal interaction with the mother. Indeed, it was during a period when the self was not yet clearly distinguished from the mother, when the boundary with her was not yet clearly established, that the child's narcissistic core was formed. The insult "I fucked your mother" injures self-definition as much as it injures self-esteem.

A common variation on "I fucked your mother" is "I fucked your soul-mother" ("Eb tvoiu dushu mat' "). This adds a sacral or religious tone, as Uspenskii observes.[26] But the extension is psychoanalytically revealing as well. The word "soul" stands in grammatical apposition to "mother" (they are both in the accusative case). Thus the soul as well as the mother are "fucked." But the "soul" in question is that of the addressee, so the expletive's target is equally the mother and the mother's child. From the viewpoint of the addressee the self and the self's mother are equally insulted. Again, mother and self are difficult to distinguish—which is a specifically pre-Oedipal problem.

Writer Andrei Siniavskii, when asked recently for a definition of freedom by a correspondent of *Literaturnaia gazeta*, replied: "Freedom is when someone tells you to go to hell [lit., go to your fucked mother— k edrennoi materi], but you go where you please."[27] This definition is perhaps not so whimsical as it seems. The insult calls on the addressee to return (psychoanalytically, regress) to the mother he or she was once bound to, but the addressee instead rejects that mother.

Apart from mat, there is much other evidence for hostility toward mothers in Russian culture. Russian autobiographers (e.g., Andrei Belyi in *Kotik Letaev*, Gork'ii in his *Childhood*) have a tendency to portray their mothers as psychologically treacherous, as has been established by the late Richard Coe.[28] Matricidal fantasies abound in Russian literature, especially in Dostoevsky's novels.[29] Various Russian writers have expressed their extreme disillusionment with "Mother Russia," including Dmitrii Merezhkovskii, who wrote an article characterizing Russia as "The Pig Mother" ("Svin'ia Matushka"),[30] and Andrei Siniavskii, who castigated Soviet Russia for driving out its Jews: "Mother Russia, Bitch Russia [Rossiia-Suka], you will answer for this child too, raised and then shamefully dumped by you."[31] Maksimilian Voloshin characterized Russia as a "cruel infanticide" ("gor'kaia detoubiitsa") for the way she treated Pushkin and Dostoevsky.[32] Aleksandr Solzhenitsyn quotes anti-Russian lines that were supposedly popular in the early Soviet period:

Мы расстреляли толстозадую бабу Россию,
Чтобы по телу ее пришел Коммунизм-мессия.

We shot fat-assed, old-lady Russia
So that messianic Communism could climb onto her.[33]

Similarly, Aleksandr Blok's marching revolutionaries in his famous poem "The Twelve" shoot "Holy Russia" in her fat rear end.[34]

More examples could be adduced. Of those given, mother-cursing is probably the most important, because (mostly) men of all social categories everywhere in Russia do it. What is more, they do it from an early age, when interaction with the mother is still intense. According to

Ol'ga Semenova-Tian-Shanskaia, for example, the Russian peasant child learned how to swear before it was even capable of speaking complete sentences. Such behavior was not only not discouraged in the peasant family, it was actively fostered. When the mother refused the child something, the child might call her a "bitch" ("suka") right to her face—and the mother herself might then brag to her friends about her energetic little "ataman." If a child beat on its mother's apron with a switch, grown-ups would express their approval.[35] A child might be beaten for many reasons, but swearing was not one of them ("Za skvernye slova ne bili").[36]

Expressions of hostility toward the mother should not be separated from the adoration of Mother Russia—and of Russian mothers generally—that is more commonly and more openly discussed in the literature on Russian national attitudes. It can at least be said that *ambivalence* characterizes the Russian fascination with maternal imagery. The image of the mother can arouse feelings of both love and hate, submission and rebellion. What this ambivalence springs from in individual ontogeny is most probably the overwhelming control exercised by the person on whom one is totally dependent in early development.

The matrifocality of Russian experience is what makes women such a threat to men in Russia. There is a whole series of proverbs which indicate that the peasant male felt inescapably tied down or restricted by his wife, yet at the same time he fatalistically accepted such restriction:

A wife is not a boot (not a bast shoe), for she cannot be kicked off (Zhena ne sapog [ne lapot'], s nogi ne skinesh').

A wife is not a mitten, for she cannot be thrown off (Zhena ne rukavitsa, s ruki ne sbrosish').

A wife is not a gusli: having played, you cannot hang her up on the wall (Zhena ne gusli: poigrav, na stenku ne povesish').

A wife is not a saddle, for she cannot be taken off your back (Zhena ne sedlo: so spiny ne symesh').[37]

A wife is not this, a wife is not that, but most important a wife is not your *mother:*

A wife is not a mother, whose body should not be beaten (Zhena ne mat', ne bit' ei stat').[38]

The wife and mother thus form a kind of equivalence class, with the wife functioning as a stand-in for the more forbidding and dangerous mother. Semiotically speaking, a man's wife is a maternal icon.[39] One may wish (have wished) to beat the mother, but in fact one is only allowed to beat the iconic signifier of the mother.

Here we are dealing with phenomena which are familiar to the psychoanalytic anthropologist. Mother-cursing, wife-beating, heavy drinking, and generally hypermasculine behavior are characteristic of men in matrifocal cultures everywhere.[40] Referring specifically to the Russian culture, psychiatrist Henry Dicks says that Russian men repress the "mother's boy" inside themselves in favor of "rugged, swaggering, 'masculine' behavior."[41]

The traditional Russian patriarch may from time to time exercise abusive force over his wife (especially when under the influence of alcohol), but he tends to slip back into a submissiveness and passivity that characterized his early experience with his mother.[42] His wife is then in a position to run his life for him, as if she owned him along with their children. In these periods she will seem a "matriarch" to the outside observer. But in reality she is enslaved by her husband, for taking care of both his physical and psychological needs is a considerable burden. She pays for her imagined control with labor, and besides, the illusion of control is itself shattered every time he flies into a rage and beats her up, or steps in to make an important family decision, or any time she tries to exercise power outside of the family.

Suffering Women

Whether the Russian mother is loved or hated, worshipped or beaten (or both), controls or is controlled by her spouse, she *suffers*. It is important that she suffer. The Russian mother is almost by definition a sufferer, whereas there is no notion of a suffering *father*.[43] Mothers sacrifice themselves with their enduring patience, they redeem themselves and others with their misery. Sometimes—not always—their suffering is masochistic in nature. Sometimes also the *representation* of their suffering seems exaggerated, as though the suffering of their children were being projected upon them.

Mother Russia herself suffers, as in these lines from Nikolai Nekrasov:

> В минуты унынья, о родина-мать!
> Я мыслью вперед улетаю.
> Еще суждено тебе много страдать,
> Но ты не погибнешь, я знаю.

> In moments of dejection, O motherland-mother,
> I fly forward in my thoughts.
> You are still fated to suffer much,
> But I know you will not perish.[44]

Similarly, writer Aleksandr Solzhenitsyn utilizes in his novels what Ewa Thompson terms the "topos of Russia-as-victim."[45] In Boris Pasternak's *Doktor Zhivago* Mother Russia is characterized as a martyr ("muchenitsa").[46] Ordinary Russians, too, perceive Russia as suffering. In his psychoanalytic study Dicks says: "It was remarkable how often my interviewees expressed the postwar state of Russia in terms of their 'starving, neglected mother.'"[47]

Mother Russia's suffering is so great that she needs to be "saved"—especially if one is a Russian nationalist. Hence the anti-Semitic commonplace: "Beat the Jews and save Russia!" ("Bei zhidov, spasai Rossiiu!"). The conservative tsarist censor Aleksandr Nikitenko lamented: "Poor Russia, they insult you so cruelly! God save us from revolution!"[48] Even the liberal newspapers in today's poverty-ridden post-Soviet Russia constantly speak of "saving" Russia. Because her customary epithet actually is "Mother," Russia offers a particularly direct example of Richard Koenigsberg's thesis that "the wish to 'save the nation' is the projective equivalent of the wish to *restore the omnipotence of the mother*."[49]

Billington says of ancient Russia: "Women quietly encouraged the trend in Russian spirituality which glorified non-resistance to evil and voluntary suffering."[50] In his *Diary of a Writer* Dostoevsky heaped praise upon the Russian woman, "that self-renouncing martyr for the Russian man."[51] Nikolai Nekrasov praises suffering mothers throughout his poetry, for example, the "martyr mother" ("muchenitsa-mat' ") in a poem titled "Mother."[52] Contemporary fashion designer Viacheslav Zaitsev attributes part of his success to his "sainted mother," to her "heroic patience, and a saintly capacity for self-sacrifice."[53]

The Russian mother does not necessarily suffer *for* her child. The important thing is to suffer. An overworked Soviet mother interviewed by Hansson and Lidén said: "She [a mother] has to suffer the sorrows of her people. Then her child will turn out well. I'm quite convinced of that."[54]

In the religious folklore the maternal image is a suffering image. The Russian Madonna tends to be very somber. She is, as Siniavskii says, "suffering incarnate."[55] Icons of her are said to shed tears or blood. Mary's chief sorrow is of course the suffering and death of her son, Jesus. This is not a particularly Russian idea, but there are some associated ideas which might seem odd to Western Christians.

For example, Christ's own suffering tends to be viewed primarily through the prism of his mother's suffering.[56] Indeed, as Strotmann points out, it is icons of the Mother of God that are the most venerated in Russia.[57] Icons of Christ do not get as much attention as those of his mother. Yet icons of the Holy Mother tend to include Christ anyway, in the form of a child. The divine child is, in effect, inseparable from his mother, is practically *implied* by the mother: "il ne faut pas oublier que l'icone de la Vierge est toujours celle de la Mère et du Fils, unis par un lien indestructible."[58]

In Russian Orthodox theology Jesus and his mother are extremely close. They are close in the sense that they are very often together, with Mary showing special sympathy for everything that her son undergoes. They are also close in the sense that they are similar. Father Isaiia of the Troitse-Sergieva Lavra says, for example:

Just as Her Divine Son did, She [the Mother of God] carried Her cross Her entire life. This cross consisted of the scandalous discrepancy between the greatness befitting Her as the Mother of God, and the condition of humiliation in which She lived right up until Her death.[59]

At the foot of the cross on Mount Golgotha this woman suffered intensely with her son. After three days he rose from the dead. Similarly, according to tradition, she herself rose up into heaven three days after she died. This event, the Assumption ("Uspenie") is the greatest church holiday associated with Mary,[60] just as Easter (celebrating Christ's "voskresenie") is the greatest festival for Christ in Russia.

The similarity between the Mother of God and God the Son can give rise to situations where one might be confused with the other. In his 1898 essay on the idea of humanity in Auguste Comte, philosopher Vladimir Solov'ev describes the remarkable icon of Sophia, or the divine Wisdom, in Novgorod. She sits on a throne at the center of the icon, with a Mother of God in the Byzantine style on her right, John the Baptist on her left, and Christ rising above her with uplifted arms. According to Solov'ev, this central, feminine figure cannot be the Mother of God, nor can she be Christ: "If this were Christ, then it could not be the Mother of God, but if it were the Mother of God, then it could not be Christ."[61] This very jumping back and forth between alternatives, however, suggests some higher semantic equivalence between the two, as if the Sophia represented some principle of unity between the divine Mother and her Child.

Christ is so similar to his mother that he sometimes "mothers" her. Andrei Siniavskii refers to an icon of the Assumption in which Christ, standing before his mother's body, takes her soul into his hands in the form of a swaddled child.[62] There may be a revenge fantasy lurking here.

Another aspect of Russian religiosity that will not be familiar to Western Christians is a tendency toward blending the pagan mother earth with the Christian Mother of God. Both of these maternal images suffer because of the sinfulness of Russian people. Boris Uspenskii quotes a spiritual song from the mid-nineteenth century:

Как расплачется и растужится
Мать сыра-земля перед Господом:
Тяжело-то мне, Господи, под людьми стоять,
Тяжелей того — людей держать,
Людей грешныих, беззаконныих,
Кои творят грехи тяжкие....

Thus mother moist-earth cries out
And laments before the Lord:
It is hard for me, Lord, to stand under the people,
It is harder still to hold up the people,
Sinful people, lawless people,
Who commit grave sins.[63]

According to the religious lore, both mother earth and the Mother of God suffer terribly whenever people swear using mother-oaths (so-called "mat").[64]

The suffering Mother of God is supposed to come to the aid of those in need, that is, those who, like her, are suffering. She has great power as an "intercessor and protector," according to Joanna Hubbs. But just how "powerful" is she in fact? She is powerless to protect her son from being crucified, and the perpetual sorrow of her expression encourages the worshiper to *accept* the trials and tribulations of life. Hubbs says: "Mary is the Tree of Life upon which her son hangs."[65] This is a protector?

Closely related to the Christian cult of the Mother of God in Russia is the old Slavic cult of Paraskeva-Piatnitsa. This cult appealed even more directly to masochistic impulses. Worshipers (women), among their other activities, would beat themselves violently.[66]

Russian proverbs attest to the abundant suffering of mothers (and women generally). In Vladimir Dahl's classic collection one can find such items as the following:

> A young wife cries till the morning dew comes, a sister cries till she gets a golden ring, but a mother cries till the end of her life (Moloda zhena plachet do rosy utrennei, sestritsa do zolota kol'tsa, mat' do veku).

> A mother's crying is like a flowing river, a wife's crying is like a running brook, a bride's crying is like falling dew—as soon as the sun comes up, it dries the dew away (Mat' plachet, chto reka l'etsia; zhena plachet, chto ruchei techet; nevesta plachet—kak rosa padet; vzoidet solntse—rosu vysushit).

> A mother cries about her own handful (child), not someone else's (Mat' plachet [po detishchu] ne nad gorstochkoi, a nad prigorshnei).[67]

> It is a woman's habit to help out matters by means of tears (Zhenskii obychai—slezami bede pomogat').[68]

Some of the proverbs—evidently spoken by men—suggest that women cry more than is really necessary (e.g., "In women and drunkards tears are cheap"). Still, on the face of it, more tears do suggest more suffering.

Russian literature is rich with the imagery of suffering and self-sacrificing women, some of whom are masochistic, some of whom are not. Pushkin's Tat'iana Larina has already been mentioned. Nikolai Nekrasov's long poem *Russian Women* (1872) features a noblewoman who follows her husband to a Siberian mine and, at the poem's climax, falls on her knees to kiss her husband's chains.[69] Many of Dostoevsky's female characters suffer on behalf of their men. Barbara Heldt characterizes one of Dostoevsky's best-known heroines as follows: "Nastasia Filippovna allows Rogozhin to murder her"; "she is given a multitude of opportunities to cast aside her role as femme fatale or fallen woman; she is shown to be capable of living quietly; but she is ultimately unwilling to live."[70]

In Lermontov's *Hero of Our Time* Vera declares to Pechorin: "I am your slave [ia tvoia raba]"[71]—and after suffering great emotional torments over Pechorin, has the good sense to leave him. Tolstoy's Natasha in *War and Peace* gives up her aggressive charm entirely when she marries Pierre Bezukhov, degenerating into an unkempt "fertile female" and "slave to her husband."[72] Pasternak's lecherous old Komarovsky seduces the young girl Lara, making her his slave ("nevol'nitsa") and causing her great suffering. She then imagines herself to be among the "poor in spirit" who are blessed by Christ.[73]

Anna Akhmatova, author of the long poem *Requiem*, which depicts the terrible sufferings of the wives of those arrested during the 1930s, takes pride in having been "with the people," "unprotected by foreign wings."[74] Solzhenitsyn's Matriona loses her life while helping rapacious relatives haul away a portion of her house.

These are all very different examples, of course, but women's suffering is seen as somehow exemplary in all of them. Men sacrifice themselves in literary art too, but their suffering lacks a certain emblematic quality. The righteous Matriona can stand for all of Russia, but Nerzhin, or Kostoglotov, or even Ivan Denisovich cannot.

Women's folklore is a particularly rich source of information on women's suffering. For example, any self-respecting peasant woman in tsarist Russia knew how to keen. Men, on the other hand, did not. All of the various forms of laments ("plach," "prichitanie," "prichet," "voi") were sung exclusively by women. In many areas of Russia a woman who did not possess the "art of the lament" was held in reproach.[75]

Does this mean that women had more to lament about than men did? Or were men just more restrained emotionally?

The answer is yes to both questions. Men were not supposed to wail on those occasions when wailing by women was called for: the death of a loved one, the drafting of a loved one into the tsarist army, the loss of livestock or property, etc. These events, theoretically, should have been just as upsetting to men as to women. On the other hand, mothers were closer to their children than men were, daughters were closer to their parents than sons were, and so on. A correspondingly greater degree of suffering at the loss of loved ones could therefore be expected from women.

In addition, there was one event in life which was much more tragic for women than for men, namely, marriage. With good reason Pushkin declared that "our wedding songs are melancholy, like a funereal howl."[76] Here a woman, unlike a man, was being torn from her family and was entering into a form of virtual enslavement by the spouse and in-laws. She had every reason to lament this fate—although normally she also accepted it. Indeed, the wedding laments assisted her in accepting it. They served as an instrument for gaining mastery over the idea that she no longer had freedom ("volia"), that she must now obey everyone in the new, patrilocal household (for detailed consideration of the prenuptial bathhouse laments, see below, 195–99).

For the traditional peasant woman to marry was truly to embark upon a life of suffering. The remarkable nineteenth-century anthropologist Aleksandra Efimenko writes that the Slavic (including the Russian) peasant woman is "worn down by slavery and heavy labor," and that she "by her own admission sanctions this abnormal relationship [with the husband]."[77] Efimenko quotes a folk song in which a Russian woman sings "I, of my own will, am an eternal servant [vekovechnoiu slugoiu] to my dearly beloved."[78]

Soviet sociologist Larisa Kuznetsova says that a Russian woman's willingness to "bend her back" is a habit that has "become overgrown with its own psychology over the centuries [privychka gnut' spinu obrosla v vekakh svoei psikhologiei]."[79] She says that women in some parts of Russia before the revolution were, for all intents and purposes, "house slaves and concubines" who had to be dragged out of the abyss of ignorance and servility "often against their own will."[80] Kuznetsova characterizes the old patriarchal idea of femininity as "concern for a man, submissiveness to him, obligingness."[81]

Soviet sociologist A. Kharchev refers to the alienation which occurred between the proverbial "enslaver-man and enslaved woman" in the Russian family of tsarist times.[82] Marriage for love was rare in those days, says another Soviet sociologist V. A. Sysenko, who also speaks of the "humbled" ("prinizhennoe") position of the woman in the old, patriarchal Russian family.[83]

Among contemporary Western scholars, Christine Worobec has

gone far in the direction of recognizing that Russian peasant women were complicitous in their own oppression. She characterizes the position of the post-emancipation peasant woman as follows in her recent book *Peasant Russia:*

Despite their position as second-class citizens, Russian peasant women supported or, at least, accommodated themselves to the patriarchy. The isolated individual might resist her subjugation, but peasant women did not stand up as a group to protest their oppression. This accommodation may be explained by the nature of the patriarchy itself, which was careful to give women some rewards, power, and safeguards. Russian peasants honored women as mothers and diligent workers. Because men were dependent on their wives' labors in the household and its environs, they gave women a good deal of latitude in managing their affairs. The patriarchy also placed great store in women's honor, so intricately tied to family and male honor. It protected women's reputations, rigorously punishing those who falsely slandered a woman.[84]

Recognizing that "accommodation" did take place, Worobec does not, however, consider the possibility that a psychological factor such as masochism might have facilitated it. It is true that peasant women gained "some rewards, power, and safeguards" for "accommodating" to their abject position, but these do not have to be the only features that contributed to an acceptance of that position.[85] Worobec herself provides numerous examples of female abjection which must surely have had a psychological basis. Thus, during a typical peasant wedding ceremony the bride was at one point obliged to throw herself at the feet of the groom as a sign of submission and obedience. Later in the ceremony she was obliged to remove his boots for him. She was not supposed to get into the nuptial bed with him until she obtained his permission to do so[86] (these secular rituals corresponded perfectly with the bride's *legal* obligation "to obey her husband as the head of the family" and render "unlimited obedience" to him).[87] Certainly a masochistic attitude would make such behaviors easier for the bride to perform. Even if the groom threw in some symbolic economic incentive, such as placing money in the boot removed by the bride,[88] the bride's masochism should not be ruled out. Indeed, if such a gift were perceived as humiliating, then accepting it would also be masochistic.

Worobec also points to the deferential attitude of the peasant wife toward her husband. While a wife might address her husband using the respectful first name and patronymic, or sometimes call him "father," the husband would typically use just the first name or such derogatory terms as "baba" (woman) or "starukha" (old lady).[89]

Worobec observes that a husband had the right to beat his wife (even publicly), and quotes proverbs such as: "A husband is the law for his wife"; "Beat your wife like a fur coat, then there will be less noise"; "The more you beat the old woman, the tastier the soup will be"; "There is no court for women and cattle."[90] Such proverbs have, as Worobec says, "a decidedly male voice," and there are many of them. A few from the Dahl collection may be added here:

> The one I love is the one I beat (Kogo liubliu, togo i b'iu).
>
> Beat your wife before dinner, and again before supper (don't sit at the table without beating) (Bei zhenu k obedu, a k uzhinu opiat' [bez boia za stol ne siad']).
>
> If you let a woman off, you'll become a woman yourself (Babe spustish'—sam baba budesh').
>
> Freedom spoils even a good woman (Volia i dobruiu zhenu portit).
>
> A chicken is not supposed to crow like a rooster, a woman is not supposed to be in charge of a husband (Ne pet' kure petukhom, ne vladet' babe muzhikom).
>
> A wife is always guilty before her husband (U muzha [pered muzhem] zhena vsegda vinovata).
>
> Cry, young wife, but tell your sorrow to no one (Plach', moloda zhena, da pro svoe gore nikomu ne skazyvai).[91]

These proverbs are perhaps more indicative of male sadism than female masochism. A wife did not necessarily *want* to be beaten, even if there was pressure to accept such behavior. Indeed, there is evidence of some resistance to being beaten. As Worobec points out, women chanted incantations to safeguard against beatings. Sometimes they would run away from husbands who were prone to "excessive violence."[92]

Yet there was generally an attitude of *smirenie*. Violence that was not considered "excessive" was nonetheless tolerated. Efimenko tells us that "wives lodge complaints [in court] only for severe beatings," meaning that "the lighter ones thus pass without any action being taken."[93]

These words ought to be seriously considered by those scholars who think that litigation records, however detailed, are an indication of what was *typical* in old Russia. Here one proverb is worth many court cases.

Worobec points to the general social approval of wife beating:

Russian peasant society did not countenance a woman's flight to her parents as a justifiable response to wife beating. In directly challenging her husband's authority, she threatened the entire power structure of the village. The display of a man's strength vis-à-vis his wife was important both inside and outside the household. It maintained his propriety as an upright community member and brought honor upon his household.[94]

Worobec cites cantonal court cases lost by women who attempted to run away from their violent husbands. Only women whose husbands were completely irresponsible about managing the household economy or paying taxes were granted any legal relief—and even then these women were expected to continue living with their dangerous husbands.

Nancy Shields Kollmann, writing of an earlier period in Russian history (fourteenth- through seventeenth-century Muscovy), observes that "women could seek defense against abusive husbands and other male kin." However, husbands were abusive nonetheless, and wives tolerated the abuse, as we must conclude from the immediately following sentences in Kollmann's article:

Although men were *allowed* to discipline their wives, Orthodox teaching urged them to inflict *only just and moderate beatings*. Litigants declared that *excessive* beating invalidated a husband's conjugal authority over his wife.[95]

Here I have taken the liberty of italicizing some items in order to point up the obvious.

All scholars of peasant Russia in tsarist times agree that wife beating was common. Ol'ga Semenova-Tian-Shanskaia asks, for example, "how often" a husband would beat his wife, not *whether* he beat her (the answer: often if he was drunk, rarely if he was sober). Semenova-Tian-Shanskaia goes on to observe that, after taking a beating, a peasant wife was more likely to be concerned about whether the object the husband had used to beat her was broken than about the condition of her own body.[96]

The absence of wife beating was considered abnormal. The fact that most women remained married nonetheless (and only uncommonly sought recourse with the village assembly or cantonal court) strongly suggests that women accepted a bad situation. Some of Dahl's proverbs bear this out:

This has nothing to do with me, whatever my husband says is correct (Moe delo—storona, a muzh moi prav).

My Ustim is bad, but it's better being with him (Khud moi Ustim, da luchshe s nim).

With him there is sorrow, but without him it's twice as bad (S nim gore, a bez nego vdvoe).

He (my husband) won't beat me, but he won't leave either (On [Muzh] bit' ne b'et i proch' neidet).[97]

The last item suggests an unclear domestic situation. A man who is not beating his wife would normally be expected to leave, for he must not love her anymore. There were some women, in other words, who felt unloved if they were not beaten. Apparently this was not *just* a male fantasy. Efimenko, a woman with enlightened views who had plenty of experience living with peasants, states that "Russian [peasant] women regard the blows of the husband as proof of his love."[98] This does not mean that they were enjoying the blows, but that they were semiotizing them in a certain way.

Sexologist Krafft-Ebing, citing a seventeenth-century German source, tells of a certain German visitor to Russia who took a Russian wife and settled with her there. The German noticed that his new wife was unhappy, and asked her what was wrong: " 'I want nothing,' was the answer, 'but what is customary in our country—the whip, the real sign of love.' When [he] adopted the custom his wife began to love him dearly."[99]

Maxime Kovalevsky, in his lectures delivered at Oxford in 1889–90, writes: "In more than one popular song the wife is represented as bitterly complaining of the indifference of a husband who never on any occasion gives her a good beating."[100] Earlier, in his 1872 book *Songs of the Russian People* W.R.S. Ralston translates a series of lyrics sung by a young man and a girl (or more frequently, by two girls) on the subject of "A Wife's Love." First one of the singers (representing the husband) declares that he is going to the bazaar to get some fine cloth for his wife. The other (representing the wife) rejects this present, however. Then the husband sings that he is going to get a golden ring, but the wife rejects this too. Finally the husband comes back from the bazaar with a "silken whip" and proceeds to deliver a blow to the wife with it. The wife's attitude changes completely. She now looks upon her husband with affection as the chorus sings:

> Good people, only see!
> How well she loves her Lord!
> Always agrees with him, always bows down to him,
> Gives him kisses.[101]

He has won her love by abusing her.

To repeat: Russian peasant women did not necessarily get pleasure from being mistreated. On the other hand, as was made clear at the beginning of this book, pleasure is not a necessary ingredient of masochism in the first place. I think, therefore, it is best to interpret the evidence as supporting the existence of masochism among peasant women. This is not to say that the Russian peasant woman was continually masochistic in all contexts, but that she was at least capable of on-again, off-again masochism to deal with her mate's intensely ambivalent feelings toward her, as well as to deal with her own emotional needs.

To read beatings as a sign of love indicates a need for love. The ethnographer or anthropologist might object that Russian peasant women did not marry "for love" in the first place. Even granting that this might be true (and keeping in mind that these women often did not have much say in the matter), it has nonetheless never been demonstrated by any ethnographer that peasant women had no need for love. Certainly any chrestomathy of Russian folk songs will contain love lyrics sung by women. To assume that peasant women had no emotional needs would be condescending indeed. On the other hand, to assume that they had a need to love or to be loved (as is the case with normal women and men in the twentieth-century West) is to raise the possibility that they might have accepted abuse as a next-best substitute for the love they needed.

The idea that beating signifies love may seem strange to the Western mind, but if we consider the connections which Russian culture makes between violence and sexual intercourse (which in turn can be related to love), the idea will not seem so strange.

It was Freud's Russian patient Sergei Pankeev, better known as the

Wolf Man, who inspired the famous linkage of sex and violence now known in the psychoanalytic literature as the *primal scene*. By this term is meant the "scene of sexual intercourse between the parents which the child observes, or infers on the basis of certain indications, and phantasies. It is generally interpreted by the child as an act of violence on the part of the father." [102] According to Freud, Pankeev by chance witnessed parental intercourse at the age of one and a half (or two and a half) years, and mistakenly interpreted what was going on as something terrible for his mother. Yet the mother did not react as if she were being mistreated at all: "He assumed to begin with, he said, that the event of which he was a witness was an act of violence, but the expression of enjoyment which he saw on his mother's face did not fit in with this; he was obliged to recognize that the experience was one of gratification." [103] Pankeev's mother thus *seemed* to be behaving masochistically—not because she was apparently enjoying sex, but because she was welcoming what appeared to the Wolf Man to be violence directed against her.

When one considers the extremely crowded living conditions of the typical Russian peasant hut, it is difficult to avoid the conclusion that the primal scene must have been a banal occurrence for every peasant child, not just Freud's Russian aristocratic patient. Parents and children did not have the luxury of sleeping in separate rooms of the peasant's log hut. Rather, sleeping was a communal matter. The whole extended family typically slept together on the "polati," which was a large raised platform. Normally this sleeping bench extended over the stove, which provided warmth for the sleepers in winter.

The crowded communal apartments of the Soviet period must also have been conducive to primal scene experiences. Even apart from the "kommunalka," living arrangements in the Soviet period fostered the primal scene experience. According to psychotherapist Valerii Maksimenko it was recommended that the child not be taken out of the parents' bedroom until the age of three years, while a Western childrearing manual suggested six months. [104]

Living conditions in Russia have generally fostered a sexualization of the child's discovery that, as I put it earlier, the master has a master. That is, sleeping arrangements have encouraged a sadomasochistic idea of parental sexuality.

At one point in his discussion Freud says of Pankeev: "He understood now that active was the same as masculine, while passive was the same as feminine." [105] This is not a particularly psychoanalytic idea, but is traceable at least as far back as Aristotle and other ancient thinkers, [106] and may be found in Russian theoretical writing about sexuality as well. Thus the early Soviet gynecologist A. V. Nemilov, in his very popular book *The Biological Tragedy of Woman,* states: "In the specialization of the reproductive process man has been given the active part (just as the male gamete or sperm cell is active and mobile), while to woman has been allotted a more passive role." [107]

Certainly this dichotomy is biologically valid in the narrow sense that a male has to have an erection and an ejaculation in order for intercourse to take place (while the female does not even need to have an orgasm). But, in a Russian context at least, the male's sexual "activeness" may be thought of more broadly, in part because of the widespread primal scene experience, and in part because of the overall high level of violence against women. That is, the "activeness" of the male encompasses both notions of sexuality and violence.

Linguistic examples of this association may be adduced. There is a Russian verb, "trakhat' " (perfective "trakhnut' ") which means "to bang," "to strike." This original meaning of the verb clearly refers to violence. But the verb also has a slang meaning, "to fuck." [108] Only a man can perform this action, however (cf. English "Bill banged Jane," but "Jane banged Bill" is impossible in the sexual sense). Striking a woman is here the lexical equivalent of having sexual intercourse with her.

The common Russian verb "ebat' " (to fuck) also has very aggressive overtones, and cannot normally have a feminine subject. [109] A man does it to a woman, but a woman does not do it to a man. A woman who utters the ordinary Russian insult "Eb tvoiu mat' " is using the masculine form, even though she is a woman, for she literally says "I, a man, fucked your mother."

These linguistic examples are in consonance with the overall cultural expectation that wife beating is normal. The connection of male sexuality with violence is embedded in the Russian culture on more than one level. From the viewpoint of a Russian woman trapped in this culture it is very easy to interpret the connection masochistically, that is, to accept it as an invitation to masochism. A Russian woman is prepared by her cultural experience (including possibly witnessing the primal scene) to expect a certain amount of violence to go along with sexual intercourse, or more generally, to go along with living with a man. If she wants sexual intercourse with a man (and, apart from potential autoerotic and lesbian inclinations, we have to assume she does at least on occasion), she may feel that she has to endure some pain into the bargain. If she wants love from a man as well (and again we have to assume she is perfectly capable of falling in love), she may feel that the only way she can get love is to be on the receiving end of the man's hatred too, that is, she may reconcile herself with his explosive ambivalence. Finally, if she lives with the chronic, low-level guilt experienced by most Russians (as we saw earlier), she may accept spousal violence as a form of expiation.

In this masochistic reasoning sex and love *mean* violence, but the direction of the semiosis can also be reversed, so that violence *means* love and sex. Thus a Russian woman may even come to assume that a man who does not beat her does not love her, and that a man who does not have an underlying contempt for her (and all other women) is sexually impotent (see below, 174).

Impotence was indeed a problem among the Russian peasantry. It is a well-known medical fact that excessive intake of alcohol renders a man temporarily incapable of sexual intercourse. A peasant returning home after a spree in the local tavern might have *wanted* to have sex with his wife, but he could not if he was too drunk.[110] So instead he might beat her (recall Tian-Shanskaia's observation that the peasant was most likely to beat his wife when drunk). From the wife's viewpoint there would have been an understandable inclination to interpret her husband's disgraceful behavior in some positive light, especially if she loved him. When drunk he was incapable of expressing love for her in the normal way, that is, by having sexual intercourse with her. So he only did what he could instead, he beat her. Sex and violence were already in a kind of equivalence class for her, so why not interpret his violent behavior in a positive way? Such an interpretation was of course masochistic in nature, but in some respects it made life easier for her.

There is a revealing expression in Russian: "slave of love." This can only apply to a woman, however (it is "raba liubvi"—as in the title of Nikita Mikhalkov's 1976 film—not "rab liubvi"). Similarly, the phrase "slave of the husband" ("raba muzha") is a commonplace, while "slave of the wife" ("rab zheny"?) does not occur.[111] In Russia it is women, not men who are thought of as being enslaved when loving someone of the opposite sex.

Suffering from Equality

In her paper on "The Problem of Feminine Masochism" (1935) psychoanalyst Karen Horney makes a curious statement about women in Russia. Reacting to other psychoanalysts (Helene Deutsch, Sandor Rado) who had made exaggerated claims about the universal presence of masochism in women, Horney emphasizes the role of cultural factors in determining the prevalence of masochism. Under the tsars, she says, women tended to be masochistic, but then a major social upheaval completely altered this attitude:

Masochistic phenomena in women can be detected as a result of directed and sharpened observation, where they might otherwise have passed unnoticed, as in social rencontres with women (entirely outside the field of psychoanalytic practice), in feminine character portrayals in literature, or in examination of women of somewhat foreign mores, such as the Russian peasant woman who does not feel she is loved by her husband unless he beats her. In the face of this evidence, the psychoanalyst concludes that he is here confronted with an ubiquitous phenomenon, functioning on a psychobiological basis with the regularity of a law of nature.

The onesidedness or positive errors in the results obtained by a partial examination of the picture are due to a neglect of cultural or social factors—an exclusion from the picture of women living under civilizations with different customs. The Russian peasant woman of the Tsaristic and patriarchal regime was invariably cited in discussions aimed at proving how deeply masochism is ingrained in female nature. Yet this peasant woman has emerged into the self-assertive Soviet woman of today who would doubtless be astonished if beatings were administered as a token of affection. The change has occurred in the patterns of culture rather than in the particular women.[112]

There can be no doubt that an immense sociocultural change took place in Russia in the early decades of the twentieth century. But this does not necessarily mean that masochism disappeared (or even lessened) in Russian women. Perhaps wife beating per se did become less accepted, especially as women moved to urban areas and became more educated than their mothers and grandmothers were. But the Sovietization of Russia also brought vast new opportunities for women to suffer. Women achieved some degree of equality with men but, as one Soviet woman interviewed in Moscow said, "it seems to me that our women *suffer* from equality." [113] How is this possible?

Lynne Attwood explains: "the emancipation [Soviet women] have supposedly enjoyed for the past 70 years has saddled them with a hefty double burden of work inside and outside the home, unassisted by husbands or by many of the labour-saving devices of the West." [114] This "double burden" ("dvoinaia nosha," "dvoinaia nagruzka") which most Soviet Russian women bore is well known. Even the conservative Soviet leader Leonid Brezhnev recognized it in a 1977 speech in which he asked the members of his audience to express their gratitude for the "self-sacrificing labor" of their female comrades. [115] The typical Soviet Russian woman handled the bulk of domestic-related tasks (cooking, cleaning, laundry, shopping) *and* held down a *full*-time job. In the words of the same Muscovite woman quoted above, "it's obvious that the woman suffers the most." [116]

What drove Soviet women to increase their labor by entering the workforce? The answer to this question is complex, and depends in part on historical context. In the troubled early decades of Soviet power many women simply had to work because there was a severe deficit of males (many women lost their men during the First World War, the civil war, the purges, and the Second World War). [117] Women were also encouraged to work by an ideology of emancipation that glorified those women who worked side-by-side with men in building Communism (the ideology itself was fueled, in part, by labor shortages). More recently two primary factors, according to Gail Lapidus (on the basis of Soviet data), motivated women to be employed: economic pressure to make adequate provision for the family, and the attraction of enhanced status and independence for those who could claim to be gainfully employed. [118] The salary of one spouse was simply not enough to meet expected living standards for a family of dependents, and besides, a job was itself of intrinsic value. This last factor was particularly important, as some studies showed that most women would continue working even if it became economically feasible for them not to, or at least they would continue in part-time employment. [119] A very typical statement was made by a Moscow woman named Natasha: "I think it's essential for a woman to work. If I don't work for a period of time, I lose my feeling of self-esteem." [120]

Although a Soviet woman's employment brought her positive feelings about herself, she was not necessarily treated equally with men in the workplace. Women were generally paid less than men who had the same amount of education, they held jobs of lesser status, and were underrepresented in managerial positions. This is documented by a variety of Soviet statistical sources.[121]

Russians like to refer to women as "the weak sex" ("slabyi pol"). But in some areas, such as agriculture, Soviet women were not permitted to operate heavy machinery and had to do the bulk of the manual labor instead (98 percent of the field workers in agriculture were women).[122] More than one quarter of construction workers and about a third of road workers were women.[123] Overall, more than half of all the manual laborers in the Soviet Union were women.[124] L. T. Shineleva wrote: "Our pain and our shame is women pouring asphalt and laying railway cross ties." [125]

If women were as active as men in the workforce, they were even more active than men in the household. Lapidus summarizes some of the Soviet sociological studies: "Although men and women devote roughly equal time to paid employment and physiological needs, working women devote on average 28 hours per week to housework compared to about 12 hours per week for men; men enjoy 50% more leisure time than women." [126] The differences may even have been greater than this, especially in rural areas.[127] To some extent the differences extended into grandparenthood: the Soviet Russian grandmother ("babushka") was much more likely to be involved in the care of her children's offspring than was the grandfather.

The imbalance between hours spent by men and hours spent by women on household tasks was very roughly similar across developed countries, such as the United States, the Soviet Union, France, Germany, and Great Britain.[128] What was different about Soviet women is that they endured the imbalance *and* typically worked full-time. In a time-use study comparing the residents of Jackson, Michigan, with those of Pskov, USSR, it was found that 80 percent of the Pskov women were employed, while only 55 percent of the Jackson women were. In addition, while employed women in Pskov worked forty-eight hours per week on average, employed Jackson women worked only forty-one hours.[129]

As Vladimir Shlapentokh and others have pointed out, the main concern in a Soviet woman's life was lack of time to do all the tasks she expected of herself. It is no wonder that she fell ill much more often than her male counterpart.[130]

There were of course other things in life that weighed heavily on Soviet women besides their double burden. Women menstruate, get pregnant, have abortions, give birth, and go through menopause. Not for nothing did Dr. Nemilov speak of "the biological tragedy of woman." Russian men, Soviet or otherwise, do not have to do any of these things. True, neither do men from other cultures, but Russian men seem to bend over backward to avoid getting involved, or are prevented in one way or another from getting involved. For example, a man would never have been seen in a Soviet abortion clinic where, because of inadequate educational and contraceptive practices, the average sexually active Soviet woman went two to four times by the end of her reproductive cycle.[131] As for childbirth, it was a lonely, frightening, and painful experience for the Soviet woman. She was obliged to give birth in a special, unhygienic place called a birthing house ("roddom"). There she was typically not given anesthesia, was often treated rudely by the personnel, and was forbidden visits by her husband. Postpartum sepsis was not uncommon, and maternal mortality and infant mortality occured at rates up to seven times greater than in the developed countries of the West.[132]

As far as their "female" physiological functions were concerned, then, Soviet women bore a heavy, risky burden alone, without the help of their men. It is not surprising that, in the context of a questionnaire about childbirth practices, a sample of ex-Soviet women were much more likely than American women to agree with the statement that "women must be strong and accept the fact that they carry most of life's burdens."[133]

Of the various "female" physiological functions, childbirth was the one most directly related to the double burden. A woman without children did not really have a double burden yet. A sudden increase in a woman's tasks came with the birth of her first child. As Iankova pointed out, although a wife's household burdens multiplied enormously at this stage, the husband's schedule changed relatively little.[134]

The Double Burden and Masochism

Who imposed the double burden on Soviet women? To speak merely of "dual roles" is to avoid the question of who assigned or accepted those roles.

Generally there was a reluctance to blame anyone personally, including the women who took on the double burden. Rather, it was the fault of the "system," as in this statement by Leningrad feminist Ekaterina Aleksandrova: "by attracting women to the work place and simultaneously preserving the traditional family, the system deliberately condemned women to dual exploitation, at home and at work." [135] Just how a "system" might "deliberately condemn" women to their double burden is a personification that Aleksandrova does not explain. Later in her paper she blames the "superpatriarchy" created by the Soviet government.

In similar fashion Bonnie Marshall says: "Unfortunately, the women interviewed [in a book about Soviet women] have been programmed by the society to which they belong, so that they take part in their own denigration." Here "society" is the victimizer, although Marshall is granting that women participated in their victimization as well. Indeed, women even thrived under the patriarchy that oppressed them: "As second class citizens within a patriarchy, women have become accustomed to bad treatment. They have learned to deal with oppression and to thrive under it. Their spirits fail to wither." [136] The women Marshall refers to seem almost proud of what they endure. This comes very close to what psychoanalyst Charles Sarnoff calls "masochistic braggadocio." [137]

One of the effects of women's willingness to work so hard at household-related chores was that men profited in the workplace. Lapidus says: "By freeing males from the performance of routine household and child-care chores, which would otherwise divert time and energy from educational, professional, and political pursuits, women workers in effect advance the occupational mobility of males at the cost of their own." [138] The phrasing here suggests that women were the agents of the behavior which ended up defeating them ("women workers . . . advance"), that is, they were not forced by men to do what they did. In other words, women engaged in self-defeating behavior, behavior which is masochistic by definition.

Commenting on some of the available statistics, feminist demographer Jo Peers said: "Women's huge contribution to Soviet power, both in the workforce and in servicing the population at home, brings her unequal rewards in terms of money, time, status and political power." The Soviet man, meantime, gained greater rewards while remaining "a relative parasite within the home." [139] Again, to look at the language: one who "services" a "parasite" would seem to be someone who is very close to a willing slave.

How did Soviet women feel about their double burden? They certainly noticed it, and many admitted to feeling oppressed by it. To the question of whether it was easy to combine professional and family roles addressed to a group of Moscow working women, 10 percent said "It is very hard," 10 percent said "It is hard," and 52 percent said "It is bearable" [140]—which is to say that a total of 72 percent of the women questioned recognized the difficulty of their double task. In another sample, roughly half to two-thirds of working mothers reported feeling "extremely tired" toward the end of a work day, depending on how many children they had. [141]

Today these figures would no doubt be larger, given the economic deterioration that has been going on in what used to be the Soviet Union. One estimate has it that, whereas a few years ago women had to stand in line for basic goods an average of ninety minutes per day, more recently they have to stand in line for three hours per day. [142] And of course it *is* primarily women who stand in line. As Kuznetsova points out, the only line in which men predominate is the line for vodka. [143]

Yet, until rather recently, women have been reluctant to complain about their unfair lot. Old-fashioned *smirenie* prevailed. True, some resentment was expressed in the Soviet press, even in those media aimed at rural women, that is, at women who had traditionally been most accepting of traditional values. [144] But, by Western standards, Soviet Russian women were very accepting of their lot, their *sud'ba* or *dolia*. For example, a woman's marital satisfaction was only very weakly correlated with the extent of her husband's participation in everyday household activities, according to S. I. Golod's survey of 500 Leningrad couples. [145] In a sample of 1,343 married Moscow women with two children, 85.3 percent actually approved of the extent of their husbands' participation in shopping, 74.8 percent approved of their husbands' participation in cooking and washing dishes, and 85.9 percent approved of their husbands' participation in taking care of the children (from these and similar data Viktor Sysenko drew the entirely fallacious conclusion that urban men were rather active in domestic work).[146]

Speaking of a group of women interviewed in Moscow in 1978, Carola Hansson and Karen Lidén say this:

Even if the women rarely explained *why* their situation was unfair, they agreed, almost without exception, that it *was*. But when we looked for the desire for change, suggestions for solutions, a unified stand among women and a fighting spirit—what did we find? Almost none of these. It may seem callous to ask for struggle and protest in a country where the opportunities for such action are so much more restricted than in ours. But we seldom found even indignation.[147]

"Their attitude was one of resignation," the authors add. The most common approach these women took to their double burden was "being able to endure."

The relevant Russian word here is "terpenie" (patience). Soviet opera singer Galina Vishnevskaia, after living abroad for some years, observed: "No other woman in the world would agree [soglasilas' by] to live the way our Russian women live. Endless patience [beskonechnoe terpenie] and endurance for dragging everything on to oneself and still, if necessary, forgetting and forgiving everything—that's what a Russian woman is!"[148]

"Terpenie" has always been an important lexical item in the mind of the Russian masochist. Tsarist censor and former serf Aleksandr Nikitenko once wrote: "Patience, patience, patience. Wisdom is patience [Mudrost' est' terpenie]. There is no evil which people cannot bear. It's all a matter of getting used to it."[149]

A curiously positive attitude toward the double burden was sometimes expressed: "Of course we're grossly overburdened," said one Soviet woman interviewed by Francine du Plessix Gray. "But we're so used to it we wouldn't give it up for the world. We take such *pride* in surviving it."[150] This declaration falls, again, into the category of masochistic braggadocio. Gray quotes a proverb that captures this attitude very well: "Women can do everything; men can do the rest."[151] Here the very servitude of women is flaunted as omnipotence. There is a slightly sadistic jab at men, but men can appreciate the joke too. Both men and women can smile at this proverb because, from an ontogenetic viewpoint, it allows them to access the threatening memory of the mother's omnipotence, while at the same time canceling that memory with the reality of the mother's slavery.

The aspect of the double burden which Soviet women considered to be the most difficult was routine domestic labor such as cleaning, washing, and cooking. One despairing woman interviewed in Moscow said that "housework will continue to impede and hinder women's progress for the next hundred years." [152]

Yet, however much women claimed to dislike this work, they still did it (if the statistics are to be believed). As Zoia Iankova emphasizes, women took on even their difficult tasks voluntarily: "The Soviet woman's choice of activities is made freely, consciously, on the basis of her internal motives and needs." [153] There is of course no explicit discussion of whether any of the motives and needs in question were masochistic in nature. But the expression this sociologist uses to describe a woman's domestic chores is psychologically revealing: "domashnii trud po obsluzhivaniiu sem'i," literally, "domestic labor for servicing the family." [154] The somewhat slavish overtone in Iankova's oft-repeated "obsluzhivanie" (servicing) is evidently intended, for at one point she quotes Lenin's writings of 1919 on the topic: "housekeeping is, in the majority of cases, the most unproductive, the most preposterous [samim dikim] and the most onerous work [samim tiazhkim trudom] that a woman performs." [155] "A woman continues to remain a *domestic slave [domashnei rabynei]*, despite all the emancipating laws, for *trivial housekeeping tasks* press upon her, stifle her, stupefy and humiliate her." [156] Lenin complained that not enough efforts had been made in the new Soviet Russia to release women from their "condition of a domestic slave." [157] The expressions "domestic slave" ("domashniaia rabynia") and "domestic slavery" ("domashnee rabstvo") seem to have been favorites of Lenin's. [158] Such words were of course spoken by a connoisseur of Russian slave soul. Lenin seems, however, to have gotten his idea from Friedrich Engels, who had expounded on "the open or concealed domestic slavery of the wife" which supposedly characterized the *bourgeois* family. [159]

A woman interviewed in the late 1970s in Moscow declared that "some way has to be found to lighten women's household tasks." Yet this same woman passively accepted her husband's idleness:

Of course my husband has more free time. After dinner when I'm busy with the baby and other things he sits and reads and rests. But we never argue about that. Since I have to take care of the baby I might as well do the other chores as well.[160]

From a Western viewpoint this admission reads somewhat like a Jewish mother joke. But it is no joke at all. It is a factual description of a Russian woman's masochistic attitude. A similar attitude was expressed by the wife of a Stakhanovite fitter in 1936:

I help my husband in every possible way. I try to be cheerful and do not make him worry about taking care of the home. I assume most of the chores myself. At the same time I try to help my husband by advising him.[161]

In this case the husband was no idler, but an accomplished shock worker. For the husband to sacrifice himself to the state, however, does not lessen the sacrifice the woman was herself making to the husband.

The increased participation of women in the workforce during the Soviet period clearly was not matched by an increased contribution of men in the domestic area. The sociologist N. G. Iurkevich expressed some indignation at this state of affairs:

If women had remained within the family, in order to produce the same quantity of material wealth it would have been necessary for men to work almost twice as much. From this point of view it is possible to say that women liberated men from half of their heavy work. Why, then, should some men not wish, in their turn, to take upon themselves half of "light" women's work?[162]

A possible answer: because men are not as masochistic as women. I am sure that Iurkevich would not have anticipated such an answer to what was no doubt intended as merely a rhetorical question (the rhetoric being accomplished with a gentle laugh at men's alleged physical prowess). But the very possibility of lesser masochism of men in the relations between the sexes (or its logical equivalent, greater masochism of women in such relations) was never given serious consideration by either Soviet or Western scholars.

To characterize Soviet Russian women as masochistic because they, for the most part, accepted their double burden, is not to deny that other factors contributed to their double burden. At the economic level, a history of labor shortages in the Soviet Union has to be taken into account. At the ideological level, there was an ongoing double glorification, as it were, of female participation in the workforce and heroism in the domestic sphere, pushing every Soviet woman to be a super-woman.[163] And of course feminist scholars have pointed to the sexist male psyche.

The Male Ego and the Male Organ

Russian women have always understood the potentially harmful consequences of undermining male authority. Much of Russian female masochism is in the service of pampering the Russian male ego, and this pampering, in turn, can help elicit altruism from the man who is likely to be the biological father of a woman's children. For a variety of reasons—all of them ultimately deriving from an underlying biological-Darwinian cause—the normal heterosexual woman anywhere does not *want* to be a single mother.[164] Even Murphy Brown would like to have a good man. The majority of adults in Russia, as everywhere else, are married. Other things being equal, the woman who receives assistance in rearing offspring will be more successful at replicating genes than the woman who does not.

Assuming that the stability of a marriage is worth something to a woman, it should not be altogether surprising that she takes steps aimed at maintaining that stability. One step she can take is to avoid attempting to put constraints on her husband's freedom of action and independence (one Leningrad study showed that men are significantly more likely to value freedom of action than women).[165] Another step a woman can take is to avoid being dominant. Iankova found that women were dominant (i.e., made the major decisions and acted as head of the family) in 33.3 percent of the unstable marriages in a Moscow sample, but that they were dominant in only 7.4 percent of the most stable marriages.[166] Iankova also found that 75 percent of marital conflicts broke out in families where the wife was the "leader." [167] Psychologist Valerii Maksimenko found that, in "families in crisis" in Soviet urban areas, it was usually the wife who held the purse strings.[168]

Male, not female dominance was considered the norm, especially by men. The typical Soviet Russian male, although he may not have been the despot that ruled the pre-Bolshevik extended peasant family, liked to think that he was in charge of his wife and children. He may not in fact have been in charge, and there may have been real equality, or division of authority into various spheres of action. But his sense of moral authority ("vlast'," "glavenstvo") in the family was important to him.[169] As a result, Soviet women often found themselves walking what Susan Allott called "the tightrope between their own self-respect and the demands of the male ego."[170]

Vera Dunham, in her very interesting article on the "strong-woman motif" in Russian literature, demonstrates that literary works of the Soviet period reflect these concerns:

> The woman's success must not threaten the male ego. She saved the economy of the country during the war. However, her armor had to be laid down when the man returned. She did not always have to give up her status-gratifying job, but her attitude had to become more humble. In this double posture, she spurs him on should he show a trace of indolence. He must do the same for her. But here, the woman more than the man must know where to stop. The woman must keep deciding between occupational drives and sacrifices for the sake of mellowing marital strains.[171]

Whether it was in the lyrics of Margarita Aliger, or the postwar kolkhoz prose of Grigory Medynsky, Sergei Voronin, and others, *the wife* was the one who had to make the "sacrifices." And the ultimate "sacrifice," the one a husband was physically incapable of making, was to bear children. Dunham quotes the words of a high-ranking agronomist to her underling husband in a 1950 story by Yuri Kapusto: "Come along, help me out, catch up. I can't be the boss forever. I'll be having children."[172]

A Soviet Russian man who wished to have power in the family was not inclined to take on household tasks that had been traditionally performed by women. In my opinion this was not so much due to the actual energetic expenditure that would have been required by such labor as to the *meaning* such labor had in the Russian cultural context.

In Russia domestic labor such as cleaning and cooking is semiotically loaded. It *signifies* femininity and low status. It is therefore a *threat* to masculinity and to male authority within the family. A traditional Russian man feels that it is beneath his dignity to cook and clean and shop: "a man often feels embarrassed to do household or household-related chores," said one woman interviewed in Moscow.[173] Both men and women tend to say that such work is for the "weak," and a man is supposed to be "strong"—not merely in the physical sense (for, again, then he could perfectly well do the work), but in the sense of having power and responsibility, that is, in what some Soviet Russian commentators called the moral ("nravstvennyi") sense.[174]

It is one thing for the "strong" man to cede his seat in the metro to a pregnant woman. It is quite another to cook and clean. When the Russian husband does housework, it is typically a grudging service, almost enslavement to his wife. One male respondent, who regarded liberated Soviet women as "cowboys," wrote in *Literaturnaia gazeta* that "many self-respecting men do not aspire to absolute rule in the family, but the role of the wife's orderly [rol' denshchikov pri suprugakh] does not suit them either." [175]

Zoia Iankova says that, although women should not be restricted to the domestic role, they are nonetheless in danger of becoming overly masculinized if they begin to think that equality with men means being identical to them: " . . . women . . . become coarse [grubeiut] and acquire masculine patterns of behavior [muzhskie manery povedeniia], including masculine patterns of resolving family conflicts. They lose a preference for the kind of domestic behavior and interpersonal relations that has been tested by the centuries." [176]

The modern Soviet woman became a serious threat to the traditional Russian male ego. In one study of two hundred Leningraders the majority of both male and female respondents agreed that "masculinization" and a "domineering effect" ("effekt dominirovaniia") could be observed in women employed in the workforce. [177]

Igor' Kon, in his article on the "masculinization of women" and the "feminization of men" which took place in the wake of massive participation by women in the Soviet workforce, pointed to the "style of thinking, self-assurance, manner of conduct, smoking, etc." which became more common in women. [178] Actress Larisa Malevannaia, attempting to explain why Soviet men were having a hard time finding wives, said, "We're all the same—trousers, boots, cigarettes, a profession." [179] The pedagogues A. G. Khripkova and D. V. Kolesov said that smoking, loud speech, and other behaviors perceived as masculine were appropriate for women who sought a merely comradely relationship with men, but that such behaviors were harmful to love and marriage. [180] The playwright Leonid Zhukhovitskii, in a feisty article that asked "Where are the real men disappearing to?" said that a "strong" wife injures a man's self-esteem (and that a woman really "wants to be weak" anyway). [181]

One of the most intimidating "strengths" of the modern Soviet woman was financial. A female respondent to Zhukhovitskii's article, after describing how she bent over backwards to please her recently alcoholic husband, mentioned in passing that her salary is nearly twice her husband's.[182] Tamara Afanas'eva wrote: "The title of family bread-winner—an honourable and responsible title—has always helped the man to realize his significance and his essentialness to the people closest to him. Without this role the very earth slips from beneath his feet." [183] The traditional male role of father-provider ("otets-kormilets") would not die easily.

The Soviet Russian male did not just want to dominate. He also wanted to be in a position to *render altruism* to a woman and her offspring. When he was displaced from this position he felt threatened. Kon says: "However offensive this may be to the strong and proud sex, the man, no longer the sole provider and regulator of the family budget, is falling more and more *under* the influence of the woman [vse bol'she *pod*padaet *pod* vliianie zhenshchiny]." [184]

I emphasize the original Russian of the final clause here because it is so suggestive of the traditional Russian fear of dominance by a woman, for example, "He is *under* her shoe" ("On *pod* bashmakom u nee"), roughly equivalent to English "She wears the pants in the family." Compare Zhukhovitskii's vocabulary of degradation: "After a series of fights, and having with difficulty driven her spouse *under* her heel [zag-nav supruga *pod* kabluk], a woman suddenly and with despair and irritation realizes that she is the wife of a wimp [osoznaet sebia zhenoi *podkabluchnika*]." [185] Unfortunately, even the English word "wimp" cannot begin to convey the contempt a "real man" feels toward a husband who has turned into a "podkabluchnik," literally, "one under the heel."

Arkadii Vaksberg, offended by a call for greater participation of men in domestic labor, believed that men should not be mobilized to "wash floors" ("mobilizuia muzhchin na myt'e polov"). According to Vaksberg, "The emancipation [raskreposhchenie] of the woman from housework is not achieved by the 'enserfment [zakreposhcheniem] of the man.' " [186] N. G. Iurkevich quite justifiably criticized Vaksberg for reacting this way, asserting that it would be a long time before labor-saving devices were sufficiently developed to help Soviet women in their domestic work, and that men should therefore not sit idly by but do their fair share of work in the household too.[187] But Vaksberg's reaction was nonetheless indicative of typical masculine feelings: participation in domestic labor was not only a form of slavery, it was somehow "low", on the level of the very floor which had to be washed.

There was something distinctly sexual in the humiliation a man could feel before a powerful woman. Literary scholar Vera Dunham, referring to passages in Soviet prose works from the 1940s, says that "it does not seem right that the man be *emasculated*"; "She offers to support his research out of her own savings. He stands up to this *castrating* assault." [188]

Dunham is speaking metaphorically here, but it is worth mentioning that castration *literally* occurs in many of the obscene folktales that have been gathered in Russia. A good example is the tale "A Man Does Woman's Work," which was gathered by Afanasii Afanas'ev in the middle of the nineteenth century. [189] In this disturbing little masterpiece a male peasant is depicted as staying home in the hut to do his wife's work one day, while the wife goes out into the fields to harvest the crops. The husband of course proceeds to make a mess of everything in the household. Then he loses all his clothes in the river where he was going to do a wash, so he covers his penis with grass to hide his embarrassment. A mare standing nearby sees the grass and chomps off the penis in one bite. The moral is unstated, but clear nonetheless: a man should not do a woman's work, otherwise he will be castrated. Or, more generally: a man should not try to *be* a woman (cf. the proverb "He who gets mixed up with women will be a woman [Kto s baboi sviazhet-sia—sam baba budet]"). [190] In the sexist male imagination the danger in becoming a woman is castration.

Nikita, the simple peasant hero of Andrei Platonov's 1937 story *Potudan River,* suffers a somewhat less cruel fate than literal castration. [191] He doesn't mind doing housework for the highly educated woman he eventually marries. He especially likes to wash the floor. But he is impotent with the woman. That is, he suffers a metaphorical form of castration, for a penis that does not function is as good as no penis at all.

Kon comes close to being sexually explicit about the feeling of humiliation a "strong" woman can elicit in a man: "Women on their part do not always take into consideration the heightened sensitivity of men towards anything which is connected with their ideas about masculinity: a too energetic and pushy woman (especially in love) is involuntarily perceived as an infringer of male 'sovereignty.' " [192]

Lynne Attwood's comment on this statement is rather blunt: "This does not offer much hope to the cause of women's equality."[193] But women's equality does not depend intrinsically on what goes on in the bedroom. To teach women to be sensitive to the possibility of male sexual impotence is not necessarily to bar their way to equality in the outside world. Perhaps Attwood does not understand that Kon is talking about what sexologists call psychogenic impotence—though Kon himself did not wish to be absolutely explicit about this in a Soviet publication that appeared in 1980.[194]

Leningrad sexologist Lev Shcheglov put it this way: "I'm finding increasing male impotence among those couples in which women dominate. . . . The powerful women who say, 'I want this, I want that, do it this way'—men deeply fear them. They're afraid of still another oppressor."[195]

The greatest threat to a man's masculinity is a threat to his penis, and a "strong" woman in the bedroom is precisely such a threat. The trouble with the typical Russian male, however, is that even outside of the bedroom he often cannot handle a "strong" woman, or even just an "equal" one. He behaves as though a woman were a sexual threat even when the interaction is not sexual (e.g., at the workplace, in the kitchen).

Although there is much evidence that a Russian man fears domination by a woman, there is little indication that a Russian woman *fears* domination by a man. Perhaps the reason for this is precisely the sexual element: a man's sexuality is threatened by a powerful woman, but a woman's sexuality is not necessarily threatened by a powerful man (indeed, it may be enhanced).[196] A psychologist is not likely to be surprised by this, but for some reason other scholars always seem to be surprised at the idea that it is sexuality which lies at the heart of the relationship between the sexes.

From this very fundamental biological dichotomy we may thus perceive yet another reason why the slave soul of Russia is a gendered—that is, a female—object: acceptance of domination by a powerful partner is easier for the sex that does not have a penis to preserve.

This easier acceptance by women is not intrinsically masochistic in nature, but it can quickly become masochistic—and all too often does—if it spreads beyond the bedroom and takes on self-destructive qualities in interaction with men. Russian men, meantime, are no less masochistic in *their* world of primarily *male-male* interaction. But to ask whether the slave soul of Russia is a gendered object is to focus on what goes on *between* the sexes. There is no gender without gender difference, and there is no gender difference without differences between the sexes. In relations between the sexes in Russia, it is the woman who is most likely to be the moral masochist (despite the fact that it is the man who is likely to be the erotogenic masochist). What Dr. Nemilov said more than half a century ago still applies:

The condescension and contempt marked in the attitude toward woman is so general that often we even fail to notice it. Moreover, women themselves have become so thoroughly inured to it that they are prone to regard a radically different attitude as something unworthy of the male or even as evidence of weakness and *perhaps impotence on his part.*[197]

A woman who thinks a man must have a low opinion of her in order to have an erection has a low opinion of herself without even realizing it. Without knowing, however, how she feels about herself, she will inevitably act out her feelings instead, that is, she will behave in a self-destructive or masochistic fashion.

The Guilt Factor

In addition to bearing their double burden of domestic and extra-domestic work, Soviet women endured the resulting psychological strain. Attwood says that, "Just as the grafting of professional work on to their former domestic roles has resulted in a double work-load, the grafting of a range of hitherto 'masculine' psychological traits on to their traditional 'feminine' personalities has resulted in a psychological double burden."[198] Lapidus speaks of the "extreme degree of nervous strain and fatigue" which was sometimes damaging to health, and which could hinder a woman's functioning both on the job and in the family situation.[199] The "strain," "tension," "contradictions," and "conflict" between women's two roles were often mentioned in the literature on women in the Soviet Union, though usually these phenomena were not treated in any psychological depth.[200]

The psychological strain was not simply a matter of playing two roles instead of one. Guilt was also involved. Alix Holt, who interviewed several Soviet women in 1978, says that working women with young children felt "a certain amount of guilt."[201] In her introduction to the collection of interviews titled *Moscow Women,* Lapidus says that "an undercurrent of guilt" runs through many of the interviews, that is, guilt over not being able to devote enough time and energy to children.[202] Susan Bridger points to articles aimed at rural women which encouraged self-denial in the family and fostered guilt feelings if the proper attitude of self-sacrifice was not maintained.[203]

The Soviet working woman's guilt was double. In trying to do two jobs she felt that she never did either job quite right. The double burden meant double guilt. But guilt feelings toward the family came first. This is true not only historically, but psychologically. Guilt toward the family was primary and weighed more heavily on the working mother.

Olga, the protagonist of Natal'ia Baranskaia's insightful novella *A Week Like Any Other* (1969) is repeatedly late for work, does not get enough work done when she is at work, is reprimanded by her boss, is scolded by her colleagues, etc. All this makes her feel guilty, but she feels even more guilty about the fact that she sometimes neglects her children in order to accommodate work demands. At a political training session she cannot contain her frustration and declares: "I have a degree in chemical engineering, I love my work, I want to work better. But I feel sorry for the children." The next day, even while apologizing to her colleagues for making life difficult for them, she cannot stop thinking about her children: "A mysli moi v'iutsia vokrug rebiat."[204] She is especially upset that her sick daughter is in daycare that day when she should really be at home—but then *she* would have to be at home to look after the child.

The novella ends with Olga waking up in the middle of the night in a state of inexplicable anxiety. She goes to her two peacefully sleeping children, rearranges the bedding, strokes their little heads. Everything is quiet. She does not know why she is anxious: "Chto zhe trevozhit menia?"

This is a serious question. It indicates anxiety and guilt. Such feelings are the lot of mothers everywhere. A child, from a Darwinian viewpoint, is a guilt-inducing machine. This is one way the child elicits the altruism it requires to survive. When a mother, for whatever reason, withholds care and attention from the child, she may be expected to feel even more guilty than usual. Working full-time outside of the domestic sphere is one way, from the (especially preschool) child's viewpoint, to withhold care and attention. A sensitive mother cannot avoid feeling guilt in such a situation (this is quite apart from the ideological question of whether mothers should or should not enter the workplace).

What is of psychoanalytic consequence is this: holding down a full-time job outside of the home is *difficult,* especially if one continues to do the majority of domestic chores as well. This difficulty, however, is itself quite handy, for it can make one feel virtuous, that is, it can assuage the guilt felt about withholding care from the children (and from the child-like spouse). It would thus appear that the extradomestic burden carried by Soviet (and now many post-Soviet) women represents not only an increase in needed financial resources, and not only an enhancer of self-esteem, but is also a means of expiating the very guilt it produces. Much of the "tension" and "strain" reported in the literature on the double burden points to the ever-changing psychological dialectic between guilt and punishment.

As we saw above, Soviet women who bore the double burden tended to approve of the extent of the involvement of their husbands in domestic work (Baranskaia's Olga rebels, but only briefly and superficially). Yet we also saw that these women recognized the inequality, even the unfairness of their situation. If, then, they were not blaming their husbands, who *were* they blaming? Who, indeed, if not themselves?

Women who accepted the double burden accepted responsibility for what they were doing. They were not, in fact, responsible, or at least were only partially responsible, because their husbands were responsible as well. Yet still they accepted the responsibility for themselves, and this acceptance was an ongoing act of masochism. Every woman who accepted her double burden was reasoning as Dmitrii Karamazov did when he accepted Siberia *on behalf of others, for the "babe."*

An overworked Soviet woman interviewed by Hansson and Lidén declared: "I'm a disgusting mother! I bring up my son on the run." This is very typical. Obviously this mother felt guilty, yet she managed also to relieve herself of guilt:

Naturally, a good mother has to take care of her baby, take it out for walks and make sure it develops physically. But she should also give the child moral guidance—a feeling that life has a spiritual dimension. A mother who is concerned only with the child's health and safety is not a good mother. Of course she has to be a social being as well—she has to suffer the sorrows of her people. Then her child will turn out well. I'm quite convinced of that.[205]

This is a marvelous example of magical thinking. As long as the mother suffers *in some way,* then the child will somehow be alright. In this particular case the mother has to "suffer the sorrows of her people," which is a very Russian way of describing a mother's double burden (see the discussion below on masochism and the collective).

Late Soviet and Post-Soviet Developments

Toward the end of the Soviet period there were growing indications of resistance to suffering on the part of Soviet women (these began to appear well before the onset of political and economic deterioration in the late 1980s). For example, nearly a quarter of the women in a Moscow sample disapproved of the extent of their husbands' participation in housework.[206] Some studies indicated a correlation of marital instability with unfair workload on the wife.[207] Attwood, basing herself on statistics provided by Larisa Kuznetsova, asked a quite sensible rhetorical question: "If women are naturally so suited to family life, why is it that they initiate 70 to 80 percent of divorces, and are much less inclined than men to risk marriage a second time?"[208] Again, to supply a psychoanalytic answer to the kind of rhetorical question that feminists so often ask: many women were divorcing their men because they were beginning to understand how self-destructive and self-defeating, that is, how masochistic it would have been to remain with them.

In particular, some Soviet women were coming to understand how undesirable life with an alcoholic could be: male alcoholism was the single most important cause of divorce in the late Soviet period.[209] The overworked woman who tolerated an idle husband was less likely to tolerate him when he became a violent drunkard as well.

One of Francine du Plessix Gray's Moscow women nicely summed up the reasons for getting rid of a man: "Any young woman in her right mind is better off living alone with her child than sitting home with a man who constrains her by never wanting to go out anywhere, and doesn't lift a finger at home, and creates scandals with his drinking. . . . Why should any woman be stuck with *two* children?"[210]

This latter image of the husband as a mere child occurred again and again in the literature on gender roles in late Soviet Russia.[211] The popular media in the late Soviet period also presented images of the husband as a child.[212] The phrase "infantile husbands" became a commonplace.[213] Even when the husband was present in the family, he was often absent as an active, responsible adult. He became, in effect, a child in the Russian matrifocal world.

Many late Soviet women explicitly rejected traditional female masochism: "At last we're fed up with being martyrs and heroines, we want fairness, justice," said one Leningrad woman interviewed by Gray.[214] Irma Mamaladze declared that, "in a society of equal responsibilities women are not up to sacrificiality, compliance, and softness."[215] Women were rightly throwing away their "traditional virtues." They became tougher, more authoritarian even ("avtoritarnee"), but men should not be intimidated by this, she said.

There were also calls to subsidize women's household labor in some way. One idea was to allow women more time at home for childbearing and childrearing, without cutting their pay.[216] The idea of part-time employment (for women, not men!) also became attractive,[217] although women's employers were usually reluctant to make the necessary adjustments.

Relieving women of part of their heavy burden was not necessarily an end in itself, however. Sociologist Tatiana Zaslavskaya, for example, was concerned about the *children* of working mothers: "We have a generation of children who have been raised without mothers, who were all out working—an abandoned generation. These children have a lot of problems, including a sharp drop in morality among them. No one can replace a mother."[218] An anthropologist might interpret this as a plea to retain traditional Russian matrifocality.

Zaslavskaya said that "many Soviet women would like to leave the workforce if their husband's salary were large enough."[219] This statement reveals a concern not only with a married couple's financial total, but with the relative male versus female contributions to the total as well. Elsewhere Zaslavskaya refered to sociological research showing that 40 percent of women would prefer to work part-time. She added that, "to make this possible, however, men's wages must be raised."[220]

Men's wages? Zaslavskaya wanted to aggravate the already existing wage differential between the sexes. The idea struck some Soviet scholars as retrograde in the extreme.[221] Besides, it did not even make mathematical sense. For example, assume that the savings accrued from women cutting back to one-half-time is available for increasing wages.

It turns out that, if male and female wages are roughly equal at the start, then equally increasing *both* women's and men's wages would result in nearly the same income for a couple as increasing *only men's* salaries.[222] Why the sophisticated sociologist Zaslavskaya did not think of this can only be explained by her respect for the delicate male ego and/or her low opinion of the value of woman's labor. There is no *intrinsic* need to devalue woman's (or overvalue men's) labor in the workforce just because many women wish to work part-time.

There were indications of political action as well. An open airing of women's dissatisfaction with their undue domestic burden was made at the 1987 All-Union Conference of Women, and a declaration was made by the Conference: "We strive to achieve the situation in which husband and wife carry out household chores equally and take responsibility for childrearing."[223] The concluding document of the First Independent Women's Forum held in Dubna in March of 1991 supported "a family founded on partnership relations, with equal participation of both parents in raising children, performing everyday tasks, and maintaining a good emotional climate."[224]

As the Russian economy is being transformed downward in the post-Soviet 1990s, and as women are losing their jobs in droves, there are conflicting reports on whether and to what extent women *want* to retreat to the domestic sphere. There is a so-called "Go home" ("Idi domoi") movement being supported by antifeminist women's groups such as *Rossiia*.[225] A recent poll reported in the *New York Times* indicates that only 20 percent of Russian women wish to remain at home.[226] A recent volume edited by Iu. V. Arutiunian reports that a third of Russian men and less than half of Russian women think that wives should continue working when the family is financially secure.[227]

Of course financial security is now uncommon, to put it mildly. Many women have no choice but to look for work. Unemployment lines, like most other lines in Russia, consist mostly of women. Approximately 75 to 80 percent of the people signed up in the unemployment offices are women. Many women are losing jobs or finding it extremely difficult to find new jobs because they have small children, and employers do not want to deal with childbirth leave and days lost to sick children. Women over age forty are having difficulty because they are considered too old to work efficiently.[228]

Already overburdened during the relatively affluent Brezhnev era, women in the post-Soviet depression are under even more pressure to bring in more income for their families. Some succeed in doing this by engaging in "unofficial" work ranging from production of handmade arts and crafts to prostitution.[229]

A poor economy is not good for women. It is not good for men either, but men control resources and are in a position to demand greater control over those to whom they allocate scarcer resources. It remains to be seen whether the slight antimasochistic drift in Russian women during the late Soviet period will be canceled by these economic developments.

EIGHT

Born in a Bania: The Masochism of Russian Bathhouse Rituals

A favorite theater of pain in Russia is the communal bathhouse ("bania"). This idea may seem strange to the Westerner who is accustomed to the lonely pleasure of a tepid bathtub, or the bracing spray of a shower. A proper Russian bath, however, is not just relaxing, or bracing. It truly hurts. The Russian does not merely soap up and rinse off, but endures additional quotas of suffering. The water (or beer, or kvass) thrown on to the stones or bricks atop a special bathhouse stove (termed "kamenka" in the countryside) produces steam which is so hot as to bring out a profuse sweat in the bathers. The eyes and nostrils sting from the heat. Moreover, the naked bathers flail one another (or themselves) with a bundle of leafy birch twigs (termed a "venik"). This mild flagellation supposedly assists the steam in flushing out the pores of the skin, and leaves behind the pleasant fragrance of the birch. Sometimes the hot portion of the bath is followed up with a roll in the snow, or a dip in a nearby river or lake, or a cold shower. The hot bath may then be repeated.[1]

Russians of all social strata perform the bathhouse ritual willingly, and often follow it up with a hearty meal and drinks. Russians who do not know how to perform the ritual are rare. A criminal character in Vasilii Shukshin's novella *Snowball Berry Red* has spent so much of his time either in prison or on the run that he does not know how to make proper use of a bania: instead of pouring more water on the kamenka, he pours it on a fellow-bather, scalding him. He is called a "halfwit" ("poludurok") for such incredible ignorance.[2]

Cleansing Body and Soul

Pain is essential to the bania. In the *Primary Chronicle* it was said of ancient Novgorodian bathers that "they make of the act not a mere washing but a veritable torment."[3] Adam Olearius, who partook of a bania in Astrakhan in the middle of the seventeenth century, declared that the combined heating and beating was "unbearable for me."[4] Soviet writer V. Kabanov conjures up the cries of pain/delight uttered by peasant bathers as they would lash one another in the traditional bania: "Gradually, with growing excitement, the bathers would pass the venik from hand to hand, not letting a moment go by without using it. The sweaters would cry out rapturously, "okh!," "akh!," "ukh!," and would ask those down below to put on more steam."[5]

It doesn't take a clinician to recognize the masochistic element in this practice. Journalist Hedrick Smith, who visited the famous Sandunov Baths in Moscow, refers to the "special twist of Russian masochism" in Russian public bathing. He adds: "The *banya* is supposed to produce a sense of well-being but in my experience Russians do not really enjoy that without a preliminary dash of masochism."[6]

Russians themselves, though they may enjoy it, think of the bania as a kind of punishment as well. The colloquialism "zadat' baniu" (literally, "to give a bath") means "to give it (to someone) hot," "to let 'em have it," as in a reprimand. Earlier, according to Dahl's dictionary, this expression meant "to flog" ("vysech' "), as in: "Dam baniu, chto do novykh venikov ne zabudesh' " (lit., "I'll give you such a bath that you won't forget it before the next veniki").[7] Elsewhere, in his collection of proverbs, Dahl provides some related expressions:

> They gave him such a bath that he was scared out of his wits (or: that the very devils were sickened) (Takuiu baniu zadali, chto nebo s ovchinku pokazalos' [ili: chto chertiam toshno stalo]).
>
> You'll remember (or: you won't forget) this bath till the next veniki (Budesh' baniu etu pomnit' [ili: ne zabudesh'] do novykh venikov).
>
> Don't mention banias, for there are veniki for you as well (Ne pominai bani: est' veniki i pro tebia).[8]

The last item is paradoxical. It refers to someone who lives well and has so much leisure time as to be able to take a bania often. But this person should not brag, that is, should not mention the bania, for he or she will encounter misfortune in the future as well, will be punished by veniki just as everyone else is.

The bania cleans not only the body, but the soul. That is, it removes guilt: "Bania vse grekhi smoet" [9] ("The bania will wash away all sins"). Were there no pain involved in going to the bania, this would not be the case. An American hot shower does not wash away sins, but a Russian bania does. Guilt is removed by means of punishment. A bania is a handy device for periodically dealing with the chronic, low-level guilt feelings of most Russians.

"The essence of the steam bath," says ethnographer Dmitrii Zelenin, "is to be beaten over the body with a hot venik." [10] The veniki are understood to be the chief instruments of punishment in the bania. The organ they stimulate is the skin, which becomes red with irritation. The process might be termed skin masochism of a non-erotogenic type. Apparently there is no real damage to the skin, although there are fantasies of severe damage, such as the narrations about bathhouse demons who peel away a person's skin. [11] In a hellish scene in Dostoevsky's *House of the Dead* the prisoners' scars from previous floggings turn a bright, glistening red in the bathhouse steam. [12]

When wet the veniki are soft and do not hurt very much. Were someone to be beaten ("steamed") with a dry venik the pain would be much greater ("Poparit' sukhim venikom"). [13] The venik can also be personified: "Venik v bane vsekh (i tsaria) starshe" ("The venik in the bania is older than everybody, including the tsar," i.e., is the highest authority). There is also: "Venik v bane vsem gospodin/nachal'nik," [14] literally, "The venik in the bania is everybody's master/boss." This expression might be used in a context where, in English, someone would say "I'm the boss here!" But the venik has its limits: "Bez pereviasla i venik rassypalsia" [15] ("Without its binding the venik would fall apart").

In Mikhail Zoshchenko's famous 1924 short story *Bania* the customary veniki are never once mentioned. However, the narrator manages to "beat himself" throughout the course of the story by means of laughter. It takes an hour for him just to find a tub to use for washing himself. He then has to wash standing up, and he is so irritated by noisy, soap-splattering fellow bathers that he decides to go home to finish bathing. Upon leaving he discovers that one of his claim checks has been lost, and someone else's trousers are returned to him. The joke is on him—or on urban Soviet bathhouses generally, which do not measure up to (fantasized) American bathhouses.[16]

There is a series of delightful paintings by the contemporary artist Sima Vasil'eva depicting the bania. One pair from this series is reproduced in a volume of the *Biblioteka russkogo fol'klora*.[17] These two pictures illustrate, among many other things, contrasting attitudes toward the venik. In the first picture, titled "Ban'ka," the interior of a normal Russian village bania is represented. The men and women inside are naked, and are flailing themselves with veniki. A woman on the roof of the bania is sitting astride a venik, about to fly off. In the other picture, titled "Alternative Bania," sits a group of staid, fully dressed Soviet officials. Some veniki are hung up on the wall, others are being held as if they were rifles by two policemen, one on each side of the bania. The veniki connote punishment in both pictures, but whereas in the first they are instruments of an erotically charged masochism, in the second they will be wielded sadistically by the policemen against anyone who might dare approach the bania.

Digression on Russian Birches

Normally the veniki used in a bania are prepared from small branches cut from a birch tree ("bereza"). This is done in the spring when the leaves are just coming out on the twigs, and birch fragrance is at a maximum. Appropriately enough, the birch itself has connotations of punishment and pain.

> The birch makes one smarter, *about the rod* (Bereza uma daet, o rozgakh).
>
> Sent away to count birches, *sent off to Siberia, along the great road* (Uslan berezki schitat', *soslan v Sibir', po bol'shoi doroge*).
>
> To feed somebody birch kasha, *to whip* (Nakormit' kogo berezovoi kashei, *postegat'*).[18]

These expressions are as comprehensible to Russians today as they were over a century ago, when the birch switch was commonly used as a means of administering corporal punishment.[19] They might be compared with the somewhat pale English verb "to birch," that is, to whip with a birch rod. As for the "birch kasha," it refers to the greenish mess that a venik turns into when it has been used to hit someone over and over again. The image is curiously oral, suggesting that eating is a punishment (cf. English "eat crow"). A threat to punish someone might be stated as: "You'll find out what birch kasha tastes like" ("Uznaesh' vkus berezovoi kashi").[20] There is also a *denial* that the birch is dangerous: "The birch is no threat—it rustles but can't move" ("Bereza ne ugroza: gde stoit, tam i shumit").[21] The English equivalent might be: "All bark and no bite" (macaronic pun unintended).

The birch is of course the favorite tree of Russian peasant culture. This no doubt has something to do with the fact that various species of the birch genus *(Betula)* are common throughout vast stretches of European and Asian Russia. Dahl reports that, in the Saint Petersburg area, "bereza" was simply the generic term for any deciduous tree.[22] In the spring the birch tree provides a tasty and healthful sap (from which a birch kvas might also be made). The birch's freshly green branches, in addition to being cut for making bathhouse veniki, were formerly used to decorate the interior of the peasant hut. During Semik week (seventh after Easter) and on Whitsun (Troitsa) young girls would dance around a special birch tree, some of whose branches they had "curled" ("zavivali"), that is, twisted into the form of wreaths. The top branches of the tree would be bent over and tied to the ground, or two birches standing side by side might be tied together at the top. Girls who kissed through the wreaths ("kumit'sia") were said to be friends for life. Sometimes the girls decorated the birch wreaths with flowers or ribbons and wore them on their heads. The birch might be cut down, dressed in human (usually a woman's) clothing, and later abandoned in a rye field (to promote crop growth) or thrown into a river. Birch wreaths, too, were thrown into water in fortunetelling rituals. Birch buds were supposed to have special curative and protective powers. Mermaids ("rusalki") might choose to live in the branches of the birch tree. Patriotic Soviet films almost invariably featured birch imagery. During the late Soviet period an early summer holiday, termed "Russkaia berezka," was celebrated in some areas. As Russian national self-awareness intensified during the late Soviet period, birch references became common in such conservative journals as *Sovetskaia Rossiia,* where one could find such slogans as: "the birch is the symbol of the Russian land."[23]

Clearly the birch was and still is an important cultural object for Russians, especially for women. Its importance in women's agricultural rituals of growth was established by Soviet folklorist Vladimir Propp. To this day the birch is regarded as something like the Russian national tree. When in 1992 Bulat Okudzhava opened an article with the words "There is no peace under the birches" ("Net mira pod berezami"), his readers automatically understood that he was referring to unrest going on specifically in Russia.[24]

The fact that the birch was traditionally personified in some way is what is of psychoanalytic interest. It was dressed in a woman's clothing, for example. During the Semik-Troitsa rituals girls would sing loud songs to it. They would address their wishes and requests to it. It would be dragged into peasant huts and offered food. In some wedding songs it was forced to submit to the wind by "bowing down" in the direction the wind blows.[25] In the lyric songs generally it was associated with the sadness, suffering, and overall miserable lot of women.[26] But precisely which person, which woman might she ("bereza" is a feminine noun) have represented?

Here Propp unknowingly lends the analyst a hand when he interprets the belief that a birch tree thrown into a pond insures adequate rainfall for the summer: "The harvest [urozhai] depended on earth and water, and on their union. The same little birch that was supposed to provide the fields with the earth's birthing strength [rozhdaiushchei siloi zemli] was obliged to provide them with the moisture, without which the earth will not give birth [rodit' ne budet]."[27]

Who, if not a mother, could this imagery possibly refer to? If the birch was not a mother herself, then at least she was a midwife who, by some contagious fertility, assisted "mother earth" in producing a crop ("urozhai") of rye ("rozh' "), itself often imaged as a mother ("matushka rozh'," "rzhitsa-matushka").

Before the Soviet period women prayed to birch trees in the area of Svetloiar (near Nizhnii-Novgorod), addressing the trees as "birch mother" ("bereza matushka").[28] A topos in some of the Russian spells placed the *Mother* of God beside a birch tree: "U beloi berezy sidit mat' presviataia bogoroditsa."[29] The maternal suggestiveness of the birch is also more recent. Tat'iana Tolstaia quotes a Soviet popular song from the 1970s: "And the motherland generously fed me birch juice, birch juice" ("I rodina shchedro poila menia berezovym sokom, berezovym sokom").[30]

On the other hand, the birch in the girls' songs could also refer to the girls themselves who participated in the spring rituals, for it bore such names as "devushka" (girl), "krasota" (beauty), "nevesta" (bride), and "kuma" (girlfriend). According to folklorist Tat'iana Bernshtam the decorated birch is a "maidenly symbol" ("devichii simvol").[31] Philologist Paul Friedrich speculates that the birch is an ancient symbol of "young, virginal femininity" that goes back to the Proto-Indo-Europeans of five thousand years ago.[32]

The psychoanalytic consequence of this double semantic potential of the birch is most interesting. During the Semik-Troitsa rituals the girls treated the birch totem in a rather violent fashion. They twisted and tied the birch branches in various ways, they ripped branches off the tree ("zalomati"), they cut the tree down, sometimes they stripped off the bark ("obdiraia kak belochku"), and they chopped it up into little pieces, or set it afire, or they hurled it into a body of water to the accompaniment of funeral-like songs ("otpevanie berezki").[33]

If the birch is, indeed, a maternal icon, then is this any way to treat a mother? If, on the other hand, the birch is a maidenly symbol, as Bernshtam says it is, then is this any way for a girl to treat *herself?* Is it sadism or is it masochism that is being signified?

True, the girls would sing sad songs to the little birch as they conducted it to its place of destruction. But such behavior does seem to be a ritualized form of anger and rejection. Each girl who actively participated in the Semik-Troitsa destruction ritual was either acting out a sadistic fantasy against her mother, or she was playing a masochistic fantasy against herself. Possibly she was doing both, given the task of breaking with the mother that adolescent girls normally have to work through.

The participants in the rituals apparently did feel some guilt over what they did to the birch tree. Shein reports that, in the village of Kornilovka in Muromsk uyezd, the "curling" ("zavivanie") of the birch was considered to be a sin ("grekh"), and that the girls tried to hide this ceremony from the older members of the collective.[34] It is worth noting that, in many areas of Russia, during most times of the year there was a taboo on felling trees or cutting off tree branches.[35]

In the village of Mstera, according to Shein, girls shouted "Toni, semik, topi serditykh muzhei" ("Sink, Semik, drown angry husbands!") as they threw the little birch into a river. This would seem to indicate anxiety about the way that their future husbands were going to treat them, or the way their fathers were treating their mothers. A song they sang earlier around the birch reveals rather strong emotions about wife beating:

> Гей ты берёзка, белая, кудрявая,
> В поле на долине стояла;
> Мы тебя срубили,
> Мы тебя сгубили,
> Сгуби и ты мужа,
> Сломи ему голову,
> На правую сторону,
> С правой да на левую.

> Hi, you little white curly birch,
> In a field in the valley you stood.
> We cut you down,
> We ruined you,
> So you, too, ruin your husband,
> Cut his head off,
> On the right side,
> From the right to the left![36]

The rather sudden transition in line five suggests that the birch tree was an object on which the girls would vent their frustration concerning the violent relationship of spouses. If the spouses in question were their parents, then the girls seemed to be blaming mothers who allowed themselves to be mistreated by their husbands. In effect: if you allow your husband to ruin you, we will ruin you too, so you ruin him instead.

If, on the other hand, the husband to be ruined was their own, that is, if they were thinking about the future, then the girls seemed to be directing their anger both at themselves and their abusive husbands: we will ruin any husbands who ruin us.

Whatever the meaning of the ritualized birch-abuse, the song does indicate a high degree of sadomasochistic ideation. If the birch is a mother, then the fantasy basis of the abuse is sadistic. If the birch is the singer herself (e.g., as future, married woman), then the fantasy basis is masochistic.

More folkloric examples of the association of the birch tree with sadomasochistic ideas could be adduced. At this point it is enough to observe that such an association exists, and that the "birching" which goes on in a Russian bathhouse is therefore consistent with the overall picture. That is, the use of birch veniki in the bathhouse flagellation ritual seems to fit into an overall sadomasochistic complex of attitudes concerning the birch tree.[37]

The Bania-Mother

As observed earlier, clinicians link masochistic behaviors and attitudes to early interaction with the mother. We have just seen that the birch has unmistakable maternal attributes. But what about the bania itself? There could hardly be a more maternal image in Russia than the bania. One enjoys the bania in the nude, that is, in the equivalent of what we would call a birthday suit ("v chem mat' rodila"). In his dictionary Dahl quotes these peasant sayings: "The bania is a second mother" or "The bania is one's own mother" ("Bania mat' vtoraia *ili* mat' rodnaia")[38] (recall that the same assertion is made about the stove in a peasant hut; the bania, like the hut, contains the essential stove). There are some very good reasons why the peasant would make this blatant equation.

First of all, the bania is perceived as a place one goes to cure all ills: "The bania fixes up everything" ("Bania vse pravit"); "If it weren't for the bania we would all be done for" ("Koli b ne bania, vse b my propali"). These sayings are listed right after the "second mother" reference in Dahl's dictionary, and they reflect a typical childish attitude, to the effect that "mother will take care of everything." In Illiustrov's dictionary of proverbs the connection is direct: "The bania is our mother, it will straighten the bones and fix up the whole body" ("Bania—mat' nasha, kosti raspravit, i vse telo popravit").[39]

Second, the inside of a bania is very wet. Water is thrown upon hot bricks or stones to produce steam, which condenses everywhere within the bania. The whole interior becomes dripping wet, warm, womblike. Francine du Plessix Gray describes her experience in the "mother-hot darkness" of the Siberian variant of a bania:

Coddled in that dark maternal warmth, inhaling the dry, hot smell of pine and eucalyptus and birch leaves and of the smoldering stove, the perfume of the tea and jam in the room next door, I was transported to the arms of the Russian women who had cared for me so well when I was a small child, my great-grandmother, my great-aunt; to the fragrant intimacy of the tiny icon-filled rooms of their Paris exile, to memories of their own nurturing warmth, cheer, gentleness, selflessness, stoic patience—qualities which have given me whatever strength I've had in life.[40]

The association of water with the mother is of course well established in Russian lore. "Mother earth" is specifically "moist" ("mat' *syra* zemlia"). Rivers are often called "mother." One must not spit into a body of water, because that would be the same thing as spitting into one's own mother's eyes ("Plevat' na vodu, vse odno, chto materi v glaza").[41] The plural form "vody" in Russian, like the English plural "waters," refers specifically to the amniotic fluid in the mother's womb.[42] As Joanna Hubbs points out, peasants in many parts of Russia simply addressed water as "mother."[43]

The maternal connotations of water are not only Russian. In the dreams, folklore, mythology, etc. of many peoples water imagery is associated with childbirth. Psychoanalyst Otto Rank devotes much attention to this connection in his classic 1909 study *The Myth of the Birth of the Hero*. For example, while the Persian King Cyrus was being born his mother dreamt that "so much water passed away from her that it became as a large stream, inundating all Asia, and flowing as far as the sea."[44] Other psychoanalytic scholars have also studied the maternal significance of water imagery.[45]

The bania itself was traditionally built near a body of water, such as a lake or a river. An illustration to Kabanov's article shows two bani actually *in* the water of a large lake.[46]

Even more maternally significant than the aquatic associations is the fact that, well into the Soviet period, childbirth itself typically took place right in the bania.[47] A dialectal meaning of the verb "banit' " ("to wash," related to "bania") is "to perform midwifery."[48] The "bath prayer" ("bannaia molitva") referred specifically to a prayer a priest would recite on behalf of the woman about to give birth.[49] Of a stillborn child, or of a newborn child that quickly died, it was said: "Right from the bania and into the pit" ("Iz ban'ki da v iamku").[50]

If the wetness of the bania makes it a metaphor for the mother, its physical contiguity to her during the parturition process made it a metonymy for her. The connection of the bania with the mother was thus a semantic double whammy in the peasant imagination.

The bania was a good place to give birth because it was usually located some distance away from the rest of the population, and hot water was readily available there. This is not to say, however, that either privacy or cleanliness were of any concern. Indeed, the notion of privacy has never had much currency in Russia, and today's notions of hygienic medical practice were not known to the peasants. A mother giving birth was considered both unclean ("nechistaia") in the ritualistic sense and vulnerable to possible evil wishes of others. It was therefore best that she be isolated from most of the people she knew during childbirth (although at least a midwife was likely to be present).[51] As for hygiene, David Ransel points out that, "until very late in the imperial era it was rare to find a village midwife who bothered to wash her hands before testing cervical dilation." [52]

Apparently it was a widespread practice for the midwife ("povitukha," "povival'naia babka") to actually administer a steam bath to a woman during labor and/or after delivery. In some areas this included a beating about the mother's abdomen with the standard veniki. A treatise on midwifery published in 1784 by the physician Nestor Ambodik states that peasant midwives, "disregarding the fact that they [women in labor] are sweating enormously, mercilessly rub their bellies with coarse veniki and treat them to irritating drinks, with the intent of speeding up the process of childbirth." [53] In difficult or prolonged labor rather extreme measures were taken. Various ways of shaking the woman, hanging her upside down, rubbing her abdomen, and giving her drinks to induce vomiting are described by Professor Rein in his 1889 paper.

Even more horrifying was the treatment accorded the newborn child. Antonio Sanches, in a treatise published in 1779, reports that it was common for the mother to steam the child along with herself within hours after birth.[54] Ambodik says that, when the infant was taken to the bania to be washed, it was placed on a shelf high up, near the ceiling, so as to receive the maximum amount of steam and heat. In addition, it was scourged with veniki, then doused with cold water.[55] Another medical doctor, E. A. Pokrovskii writing in 1884, reports that steaming of the newborn child was standard practice in northern and central regions of Russia, and among Russians living in Siberia. The term "steaming" ("parenie") refers both to heating by means of steam and flogging with birch veniki (e.g., "parenie venikami").[56] Pokrovskii refers to infants developing a special type of rash from this treatment.[57]

The mother and newborn child, while recovering from the trauma of parturition, were treated to more than one round of steaming and flagellation with veniki in the bania. Various lullabies sung to the new-born infant (by the midwife or the mother), and various spells pronounced by the midwife, refer to "steaming" ("parit' ") the infant.[58] According to T. A. Listova, one of the main reasons for the midwife to stay on a few days after the birth took place (second half of the nineteenth century) was to administer steam baths to mother and child. She quotes the "widespread" rule that "the midwife may leave only after three baths" ("povitukha dolzhna uiti tol'ko posle trekh ban' ").[59] Again, the use of the word "bania" here suggests the usual application of both steam and veniki. Listova also quotes Zelenin to the effect that the village midwife would "steam" ("poparit") mother and child.[60]

An illustration in Pokrovskii's book shows an exhausted young mother lying on a bed of straw in a bathhouse. Several women are shown entering the doorway of the bathhouse, bringing food with them. Barely visible in the steamy upper left corner is the midwife. She is beating a naked newborn child with veniki.[61]

From day one, then, the Russian peasant child was subjected to the intense thermal and tactual stimulation of the bania. This postpartum treatment was repeated on an almost daily basis for several weeks.[62] When the midwife left, the (by definition pre-Oedipal) mother was the one who would "steam" her child. As the child grew, it became quite accustomed to the bania experience. Images of the bania must have been among the early memories of every adult peasant.

Typically the peasant would go to the bania once a week, on Saturday. This was often a family affair. Not only was there often a mixing of the sexes in both the peasant and commercial baths of tsarist times, there was also a mixing of the generations. Several of the illustrations provided by Professor Cross in his excellent article bear this out. A drawing by Jean-Baptiste Le Prince, who had spent some years in Russia in the second half of the eighteenth century, depicts a bania full of children and adults, including a woman pouring water over a child. A drawing done by one P. Iw (Ivanov?) in the mid-nineteenth century shows a woman with a child on her lap. An etching by Mikhail Kozlovskii (late eighteenth century) shows an assortment of children and adults, including an infant at its mother's breast. All of the mothers and children in these works are of course naked.[63] An eighteenth-century popular print ("lubok") shows several naked women in a bathhouse, including one holding a naked child.[64] A more recent work by A. A. Plastov shows a naked mother adjusting her young daughter's scarf just outside a bathhouse.[65]

Charles Masson, in his somewhat hostile memoir of Russia under Catherine, says:

> In the country, the baths are still on the old footing; that is to say, persons of all ages and both sexes use them together, and a family consisting of a father of forty, a mother of thirty-five, a son of twenty, and a daughter of fifteen, appear together in a state of innocence, and mutually rub down each other.[66]

According to Masson, the Russian peasant is not excited at the sight of others unclad, for "from his infancy he has seen and examined everything."[67]

The two occasions where mixing of the sexes did *not* occur were postpartum bathing (discussed above) and the prenuptial bath. The latter is nearly as important as the former for understanding the Russian bathhouse culture.

The Prenuptial Bath

The bania played an essential role in the traditional peasant marriage ceremonials ("svad'ba") in rural areas. The bride underwent an emotionally charged prenuptial bath with her girlfriends. Sometimes the groom would bathe with his male friends too. Typically the bride and groom bathed together after consummation of the marriage.

Of these various wedding baths the bride's prenuptial bath was of particular significance. An anthropologist would classify it as a rite of passage, or more specifically, a rite of separation.[68] Not the wedding itself, but the prenuptial bath severed the bride from her family. At some point, usually the day before the actual wedding took place, the bride was accompanied by her girlfriends to the bania. Males were usually not allowed.[69] Ethnographic descriptions of the prenuptial bath vary enormously, in part because there was considerable regional variation, and in part because some scholars are more willing than others to go into detail. Most authorities on this subject agree that the girlfriends in fact washed the bride and rearranged her hair in some way.[70] They also agree that this bath symbolized a washing away of maidenly "beauty" ("krasota") and/or "freedom" ("volia"). The "krasota" was not just an abstract idea, but was normally represented by some concrete physical object worn on the head, such as a ribbon set in beads and plaited in with the braid, or a headband. This headgear might reluctantly be cast off and entrusted to a girlfriend or sister during the prenuptial bath, or before or after it at a gathering termed the "devichnik." At some point the bride's braid would be unplaited and then replaited into a single braid for the last time (later it would be split into the double braid traditionally worn by married women).[71]

The loss of the "krasota" or the "volia" could conceivably be interpreted as loss of virginity. A bride was "officially" expected to be a virgin, as is clear from the ritualized examination of her shift for traces of blood after consummation of the marriage. The groom was regarded as "the one who drove away maidenly beauty" ("otgonitel' dev'ei krasoty").[72]

However, there is evidence for premarital sexual activity among Russian peasant girls, particularly at those traditional mixed-sex gatherings termed "posidelki," [73] so the virginity test must often have been faked. Also, female virginity became less of an issue as rural Russia became industrialized and young women gained some degree of freedom from their families by going off to work in factories.[74] Certainly the value of premarital virginity declined among rural women in the Soviet period.

In addition, there are other, more iconic signifiers of the loss of virginity, such as the various fruits and berries which pervade the love songs and wedding songs,[75] or the traditional splitting of the tightly woven, hairy braid ("kosa") into two parts. The literal meaning of the loss of "krasota" and "volia" is actually more suggestive of bondage than of sexuality. True, the bride was now supposed to have sex with her husband, and he supposedly "drove away" her virginity. But after that she no longer had sexual *choice*. For her to lose her "krasota" and "volia" suggests that she literally gained their opposites, that is, "nekrasota" and "nevolia" (ugliness and slavery).[76]

A girl of course did not literally lose her beauty just because she took a ritual bath and got married, and she did not literally don a set of chains. But the cultural expectations were such that it was *as if* the bride were now ugly and enslaved. Her beauty was no longer relevant, it no longer empowered her, for she was not supposed to be attracting males the way she had been during her premarital romps with the local village boys. She no longer was in charge of her beauty for the purpose of exercising sexual choice. There was no choice if she was sexually bonded with, and thereby bound by her husband.

As pointed out earlier, the bride had to emit signs of submission to her husband at the wedding itself, such as bowing down to him and pulling off his boots. Later the husband would be free to discipline her with beatings. Naturally, she hoped her husband would not do such a thing. In Luzhskoi uezd, for example, the girls would not bring a venik to the prenuptial bath, for otherwise "The husband will beat you." [77] In many areas, however, not only was a decorated venik brought along to the prenuptial bath, but the road taken by the girls to the bania was itself marked with veniki. The bride had to endure what might be called stations of the venik. In Vetluzhskii krai the girls would flagellate the bride with veniki and would not let her down from an upper shelf of the bania until she uttered the first name and patronymic of her husband-to-be. The longer a bride could bear this punishment without uttering the name, the more highly respected she was among her girlfriends. [78]

Even if the bride had participated in choosing her husband, and even if she happened to be in love with him, that did not mean he would later refrain from exercising his tacit right to abuse her. At the bathhouse ritual in some areas she and her girlfriends had tried not to disturb the smoldering brands in the fire, for a quiet fire portended a home life free of beatings by the husband. [79] Yet at this very ritual the venik she used to beat herself had previously been obtained from the groom in a ceremonial exchange of veniki. *Smirenie* toward her husband was what she anticipated.

The songs sung about the ritual bath give a better indication of how the bride actually felt at that moment than do the ethnographic descriptions. They are termed laments ("prichitaniia," "prichety"), or sometimes just plain howling ("voi"). They were sung by the bride, by her friends, or sometimes even by a professional wailer (which does not lessen their psychological value, any more than well-played organ music at a funeral lessens the sadness of the mourners there). They express agony, and at the same time a submission to that agony *(smirenie)*. The line "I will beat [my forehead], I will bow down low" occurs repeatedly in the wedding laments. Often the bride will sing "Thank you" for the horrible things that are being done to her. The following excerpts are from Kolpakova's marvelous chrestomathy of wedding lyrics:

Не убойся, жарка баенка!
Что не туча поднимается,
Не солдатов идет армия,
Не государь идет со армией:
Я иду со девицами,
Со девицами со красными.
Я грузным иду грузнёхонько,
Тяжелым да тяжелёхонько!

Don't be afraid, hot bathhouse!
It's not a cloud rising up,
It's not an army of soldiers walking along,
It's not the sovereign with his army:
It's just me and the girls,
The beautiful girls.
I walk along weighted down,
And with oh so heavy heart.

Я недолго в бане парилась,
Да уж я много с себя спарила:
Да уж я смыла, молодешенька,
С себя девью да красоту!

I did not steam in the bath for long,
But much I steamed away from myself:
For I, young one, washed away
From myself my maidenly beauty!

Не могла я тоски смыть,
Не могла слез да сполоскать....

I was not able to wash away the anguish,
I was not able to rinse away the tears. . . .

Раскатись, жарка парна баенка,
Но единому да бревешку!
Не могла я тоски смыти,
Не могла я да сполоскати, —
Вдвое, втрое да тоски прибыло!..

Roll away, hot steam bath,
One log after another!
I could not wash away the anguish,

I could not rinse it away.
Twice, three times greater the anguish grew![80]

Although the bride goes willingly with her girlfriends to the bania, her emotional pain is obviously great. It is evident that, within herself at least, she is putting up a fight. She wants time to stop, she does not want to go forward into a threatening future.[81] She even wants the bania to dismantle itself, as if time could go backward. In another song she wishes that the logs return to the stumps of the trees from which they were cut: "Uzh vy stan'te, eti brevnyshki, / Chto na starye na penushki." She goes on to sing:

Ты постой, да жарка баенка,
Для престарелого да всхожа солнышка,
Для желанной моей мамушки,
Для родимых моих брателков!

You stop, hot little bath,
For the sake of the aged, rising sun,
For the sake of my dear mamushka,
For the sake of my dear brothers.[82]

The bride is expressing intense ambivalence about her mother here. She tears apart the bania, her "second mother" in fantasy (cf. the nasty treatment accorded the birch tree during Semik ceremonies). Yet she also wants to maintain the relationship with the loving mother. She wants everything she is going through to stop ("Ty postoi"), so that the relationship with the mother can be preserved as is: "For the sake of my dear mamushka."

The break with the mother was very important. In another song the "krasota" to be washed away in the bania is the mother herself: "Matushka—div'ia krasota."[83]

The future was indeed bleak for the bride. She was about to be separated from the very friends who were bathing her. She was also about to be separated from her parents, to acquire an "alien mother" ("chuzhaia matushka") and an "alien father" ("chuzhoi batiushka")[84] in her new, patrilocal domicile. What is more, she was about to become the lowest-ranking individual in the new household, with only her (possibly abusive) husband to protect her. The groom suffered no comparable trauma, and it is hardly surprising that there are practically no wedding laments for men, or sung by men.

The new restrictions being placed on the bride added up to a loss of her former "volia." This loss was sustained not at the wedding itself, but earlier, at the prenuptial bath:

Как зашла я в теплу парну эвту баенку,—
Моя волюшка с головушки кидаласе....

As I stepped into this warm bath
My freedom flew away from my little head.[85]

Kolpakova quite rightly pays close attention to those bridal laments which depict the loss of the "volia." In her desperation the bride gives the "volia" many forms: " . . . it throws itself onto the walls and ceiling in the form of a white swan, it turns into white steam, in the wash-tub it ends up being a little duck, it transforms itself first into a venik, then soap, then fire, until finally it turns into a bird and flies out the window or door of the bania." [86] The bride's "volia" does not stay in one place, it does not remain one thing, it is a very slippery creature. According to Kolpakova it is a kind of werewolf or shapeshifter ("oboroten' "). Sometimes it is a girlfriend of the bride, sometimes even the bride's double. Its ability to metamorphose is remarkable. In its very slipperiness it is the epitome of freedom, "volia." To part with it is very painful for the bride, for the next stage of her life will be the epitome of unfreedom, that is, bondage, "nevolia." But part with it she does, and voluntarily. The prenuptial bath she submits herself to is emblematic of the masochism which will characterize the rest of her life. Not pulling off the boot of her new, paternal husband, but losing her "volia" in the maternal bania represents her true *sud'ba*.

If the bania is indeed a "second mother," as Dahl's informant says, then it is also possible to view the prenuptial bath as a "second birth," that is, a rebirth. The bride might in fact have been born in the very bania where her prenuptial ritual was taking place.[87] One song in the Propp collection makes an explicit reference to birth:

Я пошла, молодешенька,
Во теплую баенку
Со милыма со подружкамы
Помыться-попариться,—
Не смыть бы мне девью красу,
Отроду мне не во первые,
А во девьей красе в последние.

I set off, young one,
For the warm bania
With my dear girlfriends
To wash myself, to steam myself.
I cannot /don't want to wash away my maidenly beauty,
Not for the first time since birth,
But for the last time in my maidenly beauty.[88]

This girl has been to the bania many times since she was born
("otrodu"), but this time is special, for it is her last time as a maiden. All
subsequent times will be in a new, married life. By bathing ritually the
girl becomes a new person, the old person being taken away in met-
onymized form—the "krasota"—and hung up on a birch tree (but the
birch will be chopped down), or thrown into a field among flowers (but
the flowers will be mown down).[89] Or, the old person might be dried
from the skin of the newly-washed, newly-born person and wrapped in
a towel—rather like an infant wrapped in swaddling clothes:

Мы пошли, белые лебеди,
В жарку парну баенку
По твою да девью красоту.
Отворили двери узёхонько,
Заходили потихохонько;
Взяли твою девью красоту,
Завернули в полотенушко.

Off we went, white swans,
To the hot steam bath
After your maidenly beauty.
We opened the door a little,
We went in very quietly.
We took your maidenly beauty
And wrapped it in a little towel.[90]

In some cases water wrung out of the towel used to wash the bride was
utilized to bake dumplings ("pirogi"), which the groom would later eat.
In some areas, milk was poured on the bride, then dried from her body
with dough to be used in the dumplings. The milk poured over the
bride's body might even be fed directly to the groom.[91] These practices
were supposed to increase the groom's love for the bride. Van Gennep
would term these rites of union.[92] Psychoanalytically viewed, they represent an oral destruction of the "old" person, so that the "new," reborn
masochist can function.

Despite a few indications, the idea of rebirth does not play a very important role in the bridal rites. The life a bride could look forward to was not bright enough. If anything, indeed, her new life might better be characterized as death. In one song the bride describes herself as having died during the prenuptial bath (" . . . umerla-de krasna devushka / Vo toi, vo bane zharkoi").[93] Scholars have in fact noticed the considerable similarity between bridal rites and funeral practices in Russia.[94] As Natalie Moyle says, "In many senses, Russian women are considered to die at marriage."[95] Moyle notes, for example, that the ritual washing in the bania resembles the washing of a corpse. In some areas the bride is removed from her home the way a corpse is removed, that is, through a window rather than through a door.

The symbolism here is important, but the bride did in fact remain alive after the wedding. Without her no family could form, no children could come into the world. She may have been "dead" in some sense, but she was very much alive and would become the central masochist around which her family would grow.

The bania, then, is not just a physical facility where one may wash oneself. It is a cultural practice permeating many aspects of Russian life, it is an archaic institution of pain distributed over a diverse geographic space. For any individual Russian it extends (or extended) across the entire life span, from birth to death.[96]

The masochism of the bania is both physical and moral. On the one hand there is the welcomed heat and flagellation. This intense physical stimulation is apparently pleasurable for most Russians, and for some it may even be erotically gratifying (although it would be a mistake, despite Vasil'eva's paintings, to claim that the bania is normally a theater of erotogenic masochism, properly speaking).

On the other hand, the bania offers a scene for playing out moral masochism. This is especially evident in the bride's prenuptial bath, where freedom ("volia") is definitively relinquished, and future bondage to a parental substitute is implied. The prenuptial bath was an opportunity to master anxiety about future abnegation. It was itself an anticipatory abnegation of self.

The bania is a particularly clear instance of the psychoanalytic notion that masochism originates in painful interaction with the early (pre-Oedipal) mother. Not only was the bania traditionally referred to as a "second mother," it was one place where early interaction with the mother was painful, for the child must initially have experienced the "steaming" and flagellation by the midwife, and later by the mother herself, as painful. As the child developed, this manner of abusing the child was incorporated into the child's own repertoire of activities, that is, the child learned to abuse himself or herself within the body of that famous maternal icon, the Russian bania.

NINE

Masochism and the Collective

In Russia, as in most other large cultures outside of the Western world (Japan, China, India, etc.), emphasis is placed on the collective. What cross-cultural social psychologists call collectivism predominates over individualism. To oversimplify somewhat: the beliefs, needs, and goals of the "in-group" are accepted as being more important than those of the private self, and to some extent are not distinguished from those of the self; mutual cooperation is expected within the collective; the interests of others come before one's own interests.[1]

What It Means to Be a Zero

Masochism, as has been observed more than once in this book, is a phenomenon of the individual. Individuals do exist in collectivist cultures, even if their interests are de-emphasized. Indeed, such de-emphasis serves to encourage masochism.

Much individual masochism in Russia is enacted in relation to the collective, as opposed to another concrete person. The collective does act on the individual, but the individual is an actor as well—in contexts ranging all the way from Slavophilic *sobornost'* to Stalinist totalitarianism.[2] The collective cannot itself act without some cooperation from the individual. In Russia such cooperation often takes the form of sacrifice, suffering, or humiliation.

For example, the individual Russian peasant in tsarist Russia would on some occasions be obliged literally to bow down before the collective. Here is the ritualized utterance of a young bride newly arrived in the village of Podzovalovo, Orlov province, in 1898, as she repeatedly bowed in all four directions to the crowd surrounding her, first from the waist, the second time a little lower, the third time almost to the ground: "I bow low to the beautiful girls, to the young married women, to the bachelor fellows, to the grandfathers, to the uncles, to the grandmothers, to the aunties! To the matchmaker men and the matchmaker women, to all in one swoop! I beg you to accept me into your fold, and if not, to drive me away!" The first and second time around this servile act was met with silence by the collective, the third time around, that is, after a grand total of twelve bows, it was greeted with an enthusiastic chorus of song, followed by more servile utterances by the young woman. Those dissatisfied with the woman's performance heckled her: "Little mother, submit and bow lower!" [3]

My concern here will not be to judge what constitutes too much or too little exercise of power by the collective, or to estimate to what degree the individual should or should not act in servile fashion toward, or sacrifice himself or herself to the collective. Rather, I will simply attempt to examine the underlying psychodynamics of individuals who characteristically welcome humiliation, suffering, or defeat specifically at the hands of the collective in Russia.

By collective I mean any group of psychological importance to the individual, be it the nuclear family, the extended peasant family, the artel or other work collective, the tsarist rural commune ("obshchina" or "mir"), the Orthodox church congregation, temporary get-togethers (e.g., "posidelka," "khorovod"), the schoolroom, the Soviet Komsomol, the military unit, the Soviet village or collective farm, the Party, the tsar's court, the Motherland, and so on. There are (or were) many kinds of collectives in Russia, and any one individual could belong to several collectives simultaneously. Here I will be concerned with various collectives within Russia, as well as with Russia herself.

The family is of course the most basic type of collective, the fundamental "cell" ("iacheika") of society, as the Soviet sociologists used to say. That this is so can be seen in the directionality certain metaphors take. The Russian tsar was customarily referred to as "little father" ("batiushka"), but the father in the traditional peasant family was not normally called "tsar." Similarly, Russia itself is called "mother," but mothers are not called "Russia." This directionality may seem extremely obvious, yet it is usually neglected.

One reason why the moral masochism of the individual in Russia has not been overly visible is because Russians prefer to emphasize the collective rather than *de*-emphasize the individual. Sometimes the de-emphasis of the individual is even denied, as in this statement by the Soviet writer A. Ivanov: "The chief feature which the Slavophiles valued in the Russian people was not *smirenie* at all, but the communal spirit, or as we would put it today, the feeling of collectivism as opposed to the individualism and egoism of the bourgeois West."[4] In fact, however, the "communal spirit" implies *smirenie*, collectivism entails masochism of the individual. The two are logically connected, even if conscious attention is directed toward one at the expense of the other. The bride who bowed down twelve times before her collective was expressing "communal spirit" *and* was behaving masochistically.

Russians like to emphasize their collectivism by making a grandiose metaphor of the ordinary pronoun "we" (Russian "my"). Late in 1991, as the Soviet Union was disintegrating, writer and critic Viktor Erofeev commented: "What was imported in Western Marxism will vanish. . . . But Communism will not disappear, inasmuch as the spirit of collectivism is at the heart of this nation. The nation will always say 'we' rather than the Anglo-Saxon 'I'."[5]

Erofeev's metaphor may seem hackneyed to the Westerner, but it is both true and affectively loaded for the ordinary Russian. Russians have always emphasized the "we" at the expense of the "I." Evgenii Zamiatin satirized this emphasis in his distopian novel *We*, Vladimir Kirillov glorified it in his revolutionary poem "We," and Aleksei Peskov attempted to analyze it historically in his 1992 essay "We."[6] The Russians love a title with this word in it: "Time and We" (an emigré journal); "The World and We" (the international page in *Moskovskie novosti*); "Hellenism and We" (a chapter title in Viacheslav Ivanov); "Dostoevsky and We" (a chapter of Berdiaev's book on Dostoevsky); *I and We* (*Ia i my*, the title of a 1969 book by psychiatrist Vladimir Levi); "Bread and We" (a title on the front page of *Literaturnaia gazeta*, 11 August 1993), and so on. During the "liquidation of illiteracy" ("likbez") campaign in the early Soviet period a favorite slogan was the pun "Raby—ne my" (either "Slaves are not us" or "Slaves are mute"). As it turned out, of course, education did not eliminate slavishness.

Russian collectivism can take gigantic proportions. For example, for many millions of Soviet individuals the Communist Party was everything. It was an enormous machine, and individuals were mere "cogs" ("vintiki," to use Mikhail Heller's metaphor). People actually believed such slogans as "The Party is our steering wheel" ("Partiia—nash rulevoi"), or "The Party is the mind, honor, and conscience of our epoch" ("Partiia—um, chest' i sovest' nashei epokhi")[7]—as if individuals did not have their own minds and consciences to guide them.

Indeed it was considered best if they did not. If the party was everything, then the individual was nothing, morally. To quote Vladimir Mayakovsky's long poem deifying the Party with Lenin at its head:

Единица — вздор,
   единица — ноль.

The individual is nonsense,
  The individual is zero.[8]

Although Mayakovsky proclaims that there will be no more slaves and masters in his country ("bez rabov i gospod"), his utter self-abnegation as a "zero," or at best a tiny particle ("chastitsa") within the collective, is a most effective propaganda for slavishness.

Any Westerner who has visited Russia for an appreciable length of time knows how it feels to be treated as a "zero" by the collective. Consider, for example, the abuse accorded to individuals in crowds. On a bus, in a train, or in a crowded subway, one has to expect a certain amount of pushing, elbowing, even punching from others as they struggle to get wherever they are going. The remarkable thing, from a Western viewpoint, is that no one seems to mind. The abuse is just accepted by Russians as normal. Furthermore, it is not individuals who are perceived as pushing and shoving other individuals. Wright Miller has captured this phenomenon:

The secret of it all seems to be that the crowd pushes, but no one person pushes, so that there is no one to get angry with. Unless perhaps it is a foreigner like myself, who was made to feel mortally ashamed once when I lost my temper and lashed out back, sides, and front at my neighbours to get some breathing-space. "To have to travel with such people!" they said with indignant scorn.[9]

"Such people" means in this case a Britisher who was not so accepting of abuse, not so masochistic as Russians are.

The individual's insignificance also becomes apparent in attempts to obtain the most rudimentary goods and services in Russia. I recall how I approached a restaurant along Moscow's Arbat on a day in September of 1991. It was dinnertime, and I was hungry. But on the door was posted the following notice: "CLOSED FOR DINNER." A few restaurant workers were eating inside of the mostly empty restaurant.

Even workers in the recently formed cooperative restaurants often behave as if they do not know what is good for them. In one instance I waited forty-five minutes just to order a meal. The waiter was surly, and the food turned out to be mediocre. Naturally I left a one kopeck tip. But I am not a Russian.

There are anecdotes galore on this topic in Hedrick Smith's book *The New Russians* and in other accounts by Westerners.[10] Even Russians have written about the problem, which is to say that certainly not all Russians find that abuse of the individual by the "system" is acceptable. An example is Vladimir Voinovich's *Anti-Soviet Soviet Union* (1985), a compendium of painful, satirical essays the very title of which suggests a collective kind of masochism.

Sticking One's Neck Out in the Collective

I am hardly the first to notice the masochistic tinge to Russian collectivism. Jeffry Klugman says, for example, that Soviet Russians grew up in families and went to schools which fostered "the total warmth of *submissive* belonging."[11] Earlier in this century Berdiaev wrote that "the Russian people has a public gift of submissiveness, of *smirenie* of the person to the collective."[12] Writing in 1898, A. Nikol'skii asserted that "in the overall social life of the peasantry, the personal element is sacrificed to the communal element."[13] Nikol'skii makes it clear that such sacrifice is unnecessary and excessive, that is, masochistic in nature. He refers to the "passivity" and "profound quietism" of the communal peasant, and he expresses admiration for the enterprising peasant who acts out of self-interest, or who moves away to the city and thereby casts off the "yoke of communal life."[14]

To take an example from the immediate post-Soviet period, we have Bulat Okudzhava talking about the collective talent of Russians to accomplish great deeds, but only when under threat of the stick ("iz-pod palki"). Emerging from their "recent enslavement," Russians are still plagued by their tendency to submit unnecessarily to the collective: "Our misfortune resides in the fact that we are all one society [vse my odno obshchestvo] with a poorly developed ability to think independently, an enviable capability for submission [podchiniat'sia], and an inability to take individual risks or responsibility."[15]

When someone does take individual risk or initiative, the collective (or a representative of the collective) is likely to express disapproval and, more important for the theme of this book, the individual is likely to give in. In 1991 Moscow psychoanalyst Vera Loseva related an anecdote to me which graphically captures this situation:

Two beggars are sitting on a street corner. A third beggar arrives, sits down, and starts playing the harmonica. One of the other beggars gets up, comes over to the harmonica player and starts hitting him on the head, saying: "You can't do that, you have to beg the same way the rest of us beggars do!" The would-be musician puts away his harmonica and apologizes profusely.

The beggar who strikes the harmonica player is enforcing the sadistic will of the collective (however small, in this case a grand total of three beggars). The beggar who complies, on the other hand, is a moral masochist. He willingly accepts the harm done to him, that is, he accedes to both the blows and the reduction of his efficiency as a beggar.

If in America the inventor of a better mousetrap is rewarded, in Russia the more efficient beggar is punished.

Of course the harmonica player could resist, and this might bring even more punishment. So hasn't he chosen the *less* masochistic solution by complying? Perhaps yes in the short run, but that does not make his original solution non-masochistic. And besides, without a masochistic mind-set he (and others in his position) might *think* of ways of resisting the pressures of the collective, such as striking back at the other beggars, avoiding streetcorners where other beggars are present, or hiring beggars as bodyguards with the profits made from begging by harmonica.

But, "don't stick out!" ("Ne vysovyvaites'!"), says the proverb. The tallest blade of grass, after all, is the one to get cut down. Hedrick Smith points to the masochistic essence of this attitude toward the collective: "The Russians are long-suffering people who can bear the pain of their misery, so long as they see that others are sharing it. The collective jealousy can be fierce against those who rise above the crowd."[16] In other words, masochistic conformity can have a sadistic side-effect. Among Smith's numerous examples of this mentality are the following:

Valentin Berezhkov, a former Soviet diplomat, told me of a farmer he knew in a town outside of Moscow whose horse and few cows were set free and whose barn was set afire by neighboring farm workers who were jealous of his modest prosperity. The Soviet press is full of stories about attacks on privately owned cooperative restaurants and other small service shops, the perpetrators people who resent seeing others do well. In the debates at the Supreme Soviet, the most potent arguments, the ones with the strongest resonance among the populace, are the passionate accusations that the free market will yield speculators getting rich from profiteering and exploiting the working class.[17]

In an article that appeared in a 1992 issue of *Literaturnaia gazeta*, N. Zenova refuses to name the location of collective farm property taken over by an enterprising group of people for semi-private development. The reason is clear: some envious readers might do physical harm to the developers.[18]

If in America misery loves company, in Russia misery often *requires* company. In effect: "If I am going to live poorly, let *them* live poorly too."[19] Any attempt to improve oneself will meet with resistance. To quote a saying that was widely applied in late Soviet Russia: "Sobaka na sene" ("A dog [lying] on the hay"). Even if a dog has no use for hay, it will not let anyone *else* get at it.[20]

The members of the collective all have to be equally miserable—otherwise it becomes too obvious that one's own personal misery is not really necessary, that is, is masochistic in essence. The happy non-masochist is quite correctly perceived as alien ("chuzhoi"), not part of "us" ("svoi") any more.[21]

Not all members of the collective will necessarily feel hostile toward another's success, indeed in most cases not even the majority will necessarily feel this way. But the spiteful proportion of the population is nonetheless significant, as recent sociological surveys have shown. For example, when a jewelry cooperative in a town in the Crimea was closed down because the authorities thought the workers there were making too much money, an opinion poll showed that 30 percent of the public agreed with the closure (14 percent thought the closure was not in the spirit of glasnost, and 56 percent thought it was wrong).[22]

A century earlier envy was also common. Among the peasantry, for example, there were those enterprising individuals ("predpriimchivye liudi") who managed to acquire large amounts of land and/or other property,[23] but not without provoking resentment among neighbors. The communal envy portrayed in the classic ethnographic descriptions confirm Smith's assertion[24] that today's attitudes are pre-Soviet in historical origin. Semenova-Tian-Shanskaia, for example, describes the envy which richer peasants had to deal with in the late tsarist period:

> Those who are somewhat richer complain bitterly about their fellow-villagers' attitude toward them. "They hate you (envy you) constantly, saying: 'what makes you think you're better than we are, hold on, aren't you getting a little uppity, taking it into your head to plant a little apple tree? Ha! You've decided to plant a garden, think you're a landlord, eh? We sit hungry, and he plants a garden, and even fences it off!'" Then they smash the fence and drag off the apple tree that has been planted. Or if the apple tree grows up and produces apples, they feel obliged to make raids on it.[25]

Such envy must have been very common, to judge from just some of the numerous proverbs gathered on the subject by Dahl:

> The neighbor interferes with sleep because he lives well (Sosed spat' ne daet: khorosho zhivet).

> It's not offensive that the wine is expensive, but it's offensive that the inn-keeper is getting rich (Ne to obida, chto vino dorogo, a to obida, chto tseloval'nik bogateet).

> Beat to death the one who lives better than we do (Ubei togo do smerti, kto luchshe nashego zhivet).

> The envious one will not spare his own two eyes (Zavistlivyi svoikh dvukh glaz ne pozhaleet).[26]

Not only the one who submits to such envious attitudes is behaving masochistically, but sometimes, as the last item indicates, the envious person himself or herself can be engaged in a masochistic enterprise as well. If the envious peasant set fire to his neighbor's hut, for example, his own was likely to burn down too, since the peasants' wooden huts were built exceedingly close to one another.

A masochistic attitude toward the collective is of course not the only thing that prevents the individual from "sticking out" in Russia. There are likely to be other reasons as well, depending on the situation. A would-be family farmer in the late Soviet and post-Soviet period, for example, is thwarted by a host of daunting problems. Where will the fertilizer, seeds, tractors, and other items necessary for farming be obtained? How much should be invested in livestock? What crops would bring a profit, what crops should be avoided? Will government policies change in the midst of farming operations?—And so on, to name a few of the issues cogently discussed by Hedrick Smith.[27] But the existence of non-psychological factors does not rule out psychological factors, including masochism. When Smith asked state farm director Dmitrii Starodubtsev in 1989 why the new opportunities for leasing land were not catching on, the reply took a curiously psychological form:

"You see," he said, "the land was confiscated from the peasants in the thirties, even in the twenties. Sixty years ago. So the new generation never owned the land. They are not used to the land. They are afraid of it. It has become alien to them. The livestock they are willing to take. To breed animals, that's OK. But the land, they're afraid of it. Our people have lost the feeling of being masters of the land."[28]

With the image of "masters of the land" Starodubtsev raises, perhaps unintentionally, a sadomasochistic issue: if the peasants are *not* "masters of the land," perhaps they are its slaves instead? And given the maternal significance of "land" ("zemlia," e.g., "matushka zemlia") which is so prevalent in Russian tradition, perhaps Starodubtsev is suggesting that would-be farmers fear having to deal with an old maternal image. I will have more to say about such imagery.

A Post-Soviet Antimasochistic Trend?

It is true that efforts are now being made in Russia to reduce the importance of the collective and to emphasize the value of the individual. Psychoanalyst Aron Belkin observes that perestroika encouraged people to emerge from their previous "inhibited, infantile state," to "think independently, to get to know themselves and their environment, to evaluate for themselves their attitude to the historical past and to their native land."[29] Belkin believes that psychoanalytic therapy itself can help individuals who have suffered under a totalitarian system gain some sense of their own freedom and autonomy. To get rid of one's "slave psychology" (part of which is masochism—a term Belkin avoids), one might try some *free* association.

In the late Soviet and post-Soviet Russian media there are numerous references to something called "sovereignty of the person" ("suverenitet lichnosti"). This represents a major change of approach to human relations among Russians. The very phrase, however, is a metaphor based on the idea of a *collective:* "sovereignty" is (in Russian as in English) an attribute of a state. Lidiia Grafova, in a fascinating article under this rubric, introduces further collective metaphors in her attempt to convey her disgust at the masochism in an individual: "I don't know about you, reader, but I personally discover with shame something totalitarian in myself." Or: "Can we be free from our internal slavery and fear?" Again, "something totalitarian" and "slavery" are collective, not individual phenomena. But it is clear that Grafova has personal freedom in mind, as when she deconstructs the metaphor of "sovereignty of the person": "the secret wish of Soviet people [liudei] (not only republics) is to gain independence."[30]

Soviet psychologist Boris Kochubei made a particularly explicit and eloquent statement of the importance of the individual in an article that appeared at the end of 1990. According to Kochubei, socialism failed in Russia because it intensified the already native collectivist mentality of Russians: "From an underdeveloped 'I' in Russian culture we moved to a complete repression of the 'I' in the name of the 'we.'" After lamenting the "primitive collectivism" and the tendency toward "identification of the self with the group" among his fellow citizens, Kochubei declares: "It's high time to understand that there is nothing apart from the single, private person (the very one that people call a philistine and a clod), with his small happiness and his big sorrow." Everything else—the Party, the class, the nationality, the government, the Motherland, all of society itself—exists only for the individual. Only in a society which places the individual above all else is there a chance that "reason and conscience" will prevail.[31]

Some Theoretical Considerations

What is a collective, from the viewpoint of the individual? How do psychoanalysts characterize the individual's conscious and unconscious attitudes toward the collective?

For one thing, the collective is itself *like* an individual, and a very special individual at that. It tends to get personified, and the personification is usually maternal in nature. Semiotically speaking, the collective is an icon of the mother.

Russian culture richly exemplifies this analytic view: "Mother Russia," "Mother Moscow," and "the mother Party" are obvious examples. Sometimes this maternal metaphor is displaced beyond the collective itself and on to some abstract entity which in turn governs the collective, for example, the "mother ideology" which guides the Party or the "mother history" from which lessons must be learned. Sometimes the maternal metaphor is extended in the rhetorical sense, as when Dmitrii Likhachev tries to represent both positive and negative feelings toward Russia:

To divide up the territory of Russia the way the newly formed "independent governments" are now dividing her can only be accomplished by eliminating memory, cultural and historical memory, memory indeed of the motherland [pamiat' rodiny]—regardless of what value one may place on this motherland. Perhaps she was a stepmother [machekhoi] for many, rather than a mother [mater'iu], but still, she did exist.[32]

Another example is offered by Nina Katerli and Iurii Shmidt in their extension of the maternal personification of the Party. Writing in a recent issue of *Literaturnaia gazeta,* they assert that the enemies of democracy have mastered the art of provocation: "They have sucked in this art with the milk of the mother KPSS [Communist Party of the Soviet Union]."[33]

Here is how psychiatrist Aron Belkin depicts the child's acquisition of a submissive attitude toward the collective in Russia:

Having barely learned to distinguish words from one another, we find out that "I" [ia] is the last word of the [Russian] alphabet. *We have taken in with mother's milk* the conviction that whatever value or meaning each of us might have is only as a particle of the collective, inseparable from the overall mass.[34]

In this indirect fashion Belkin recognizes that a masochistic attitude toward the collective derives from early interaction with the mother.

If the collective is maternal, then its members are children. *We Are All Children of Russia (Vse my—deti Rossii)*—proclaims the title of a recent book by conservative literary critic Iurii Prokushev.[35] The phrase "children of Russia" has also come to refer to Russians living in non-Russian, formerly Soviet republics, and who may feel endangered and isolated from their true motherland. Since the breakup of the Soviet Union a column titled "The Children of Russia" has been running in *Literaturnaia gazeta.* A recent instance is introduced with these words: "We are all your children, Russia, both those of us living on the land of our ancestors, and those living beyond her borders. We have the same roots, we have had the same fate. And now there is pain, desperation, anxiety." [36]

Sometimes the maternal personification of the collective is slightly less obvious, as in the terms "rodina'" ("motherland," literally "birthland") and "narod" ("the people" or "the folk")—both of which are related to the verb "rodit'" ("to give birth") and "rod" ("birth," as in "ot rodu," "from birth"), and thereby indirectly suggest the mother.

Usually, however, collectives are not personified or characterized in *explicitly* maternal terms at all, even in Russia. But there is evidence from psychoanalytic theory, and there are passages from some of Russia's great philosophers and literary artists—which indicate that the collective to which one submits is always maternal at the level of deep fantasy. Below I will examine key passages in Losev, Berdiaev, Blok, and Dostoevsky to support this idea. Here I wish to offer a few psychoanalytic considerations.

Surprisingly little psychoanalytic work has been done on attitudes toward the collective. Perhaps this is because psychoanalysis, for the most part, developed in the West, where individualism rather than collectivism flourishes. Nonetheless, there are some studies which ought to be mentioned.

Didier Anzieu, reporting on his psychoanalytic work with large groups (up to eighty persons), says that significant anxiety is provoked by the impersonal nature of such a collective. It is impossible to know most of the others in the group, and this is threatening. Not knowing who the "other" is actually raises the question of who the self is: "The group situation in which I don't know who 'they' are and they don't know who 'I' am is, as such, a source of anxiety." [37] There is thus a "danger of losing one's ego identity." [38] The question "Who am I?" is, as Anzieu says, "the most difficult question that the group situation forces on its members." [39]

This question, however, is precisely the question being addressed by the child that is in the process of differentiating itself from the mother and forming itself into a unity that coheres: "The group draws the individual far into his past, to early childhood where he did not yet have consciousness of himself as subject, where he felt incoherent." [40]

Fragmentation is a persistent concern of both the pre-Oedipal child and the group member. In the case of the group member the concern is dealt with by means of an "illusion" (Anzieu) whereby the group itself coheres as a person of some kind. Attention is thus defensively displaced from the narcissistic problems of an individual person to the group as person. In other words, the collective is defensively personified.

Another way to view the problem faced by the individual in a collective is in terms of the individual's ego ideal. This Freudian construct is supposed to have developed in the early interaction of every individual with the parents. It is an internal model to which the ego seeks to conform. But the model can be replaced in intense interaction with the collective by some fictive group ego or group ego ideal. That is, the individual can project certain desired qualities of the ego on to some aspect of the group.[41]

The individual in a collective is always confronted with the issue of boundaries: where does the individual self leave off and the collective begin? Again, the issue is an old one, that is, a pre-Oedipal one. The most regressive solution is to avoid a boundary altogether, to fantasize fusion or merging with the collective other. Psychoanalyst Janine Chasseguet-Smirgel (influenced by Anzieu) says: "It is as if the group formation represented of itself the hallucinatory realization of the wish to take possession of the mother by the sibship, through a very regressive mode, that of fusion."

If the group is felt to be unquestionable, all-powerful, ideal, then, says Chasseguet-Smirgel, it "is itself an omnipotent mother."[42] If the group palliates the narcissistic wounds of individuals within it, it is serving as an idealized "breast-mother"—to quote Otto Kernberg's discussion of Anzieu.[43]

All of these issues—coherence of the self in relation to the "other," self-definition or boundary in relation to the "other," and idealization of the maternal "other"—are also paramount for masochism, as we saw earlier in the clinical chapter. For some reason, however, Anzieu, Chasseguet-Smirgel, and their Kleinian predecessors pay little attention to masochism in their discussions of the psychology of individuals in the collective. Again, this probably testifies to a cultural difference between Western European and Russian attitudes toward the collective. There is no a priori reason to believe that the sophisticated psychotherapeutic trainees in Anzieu's large groups, for example, should react the same way ordinary Russians would in a similar situation. But the issues dealt with—in particular the identity of the self in contiguity with the collective—are intrinsically the same in any culture. Anzieu's French subjects appear to be more individualistic and to resist submission in situations where Russian subjects would more likely behave masochistically.

Submission to the "Will" of the Commune in Tsarist Russia

The typical Russian peasant in the imperial period was not only under the thumb of the gentry landlord and the family patriarch ("bol'shak"), but was also beholden to a collective of fellow peasants known as the commune ("obshchina" or, more commonly among the peasants, "mir"), the administrative actions of which were usually carried out by an all-male village assembly ("sel'skii skhod"). The commune played a very important role in the emotional life of the peasant. It was also an important political and economic structure, of course, but here I am concerned with how the peasant *felt* about the commune. It is possible to address this psychological issue without getting entangled in complex economic questions, and in particular without pretending to settle the hotly disputed issues of just how ancient or how genuinely Russian the peasant commune was.[44]

The commune seems to have gained even more control over the lives of individual peasants after the emancipation of 1861 than it held previously. The emancipated peasant in most cases still was not able to own arable land, but depended on the commune to parcel it out periodically. The commune did not assign land, moreover, to the peasant as an individual, but to the extended peasant household on the basis of the number of "tiagla" per household. A "tiaglo" was usually a married couple between the ages of eighteen and sixty (sometimes land was assigned instead on the basis of the number of adult males per household, or the number of mouths to be fed). This economic disregard for the individual peasant could not but have psychological consequences.

Although the peasant worked the land, it was not in most cases his or hers to sell or to pass on to offspring. There was no truly private property, other than the hut and the immediately surrounding farmstead land and buildings, and, for women, the dowry. The typical peasant was at best a temporary landholder, not a landowner. In addition, the postemancipation peasant was required to work the exclusively collective portions of the commune's land, that is, the arable land from which funds were earned to pay assistance to landless widows, herders, teachers, doctors, etc., as well as to pay for road, bridge, and church repair.

The commune did have its advantages. The members, for example, might collectively come to the aid of a family in distress (e.g., rebuilding a hut destroyed by fire, helping a family stricken by disease, etc.; this practice was called "pomoch'").[45] Successful agricultural innovation initiated by one member might end up benefiting all members (if the majority went along with the innovation). The peasant commune also offered the psychological advantage of comfortable group identity and solidarity (this solidarity was maintained even by members who left the commune for varying periods of time in order to earn money elsewhere: "zemliaki," individuals from the same village—literally from the same "zemlia" or "land"—tended to live together in the working-class neighborhoods of large cities). Another psychological advantage to the individual member of the peasant collective was an option in some contexts to shift blame or responsibility for morally questionable actions on to the collective (see below, 237).

The commune retained enormous power over its members in exchange for the advantages it offered, however. Some, indeed, have argued that the commune enslaved the individual peasant to a greater extent than did the serf-owning landlord.[46] Certainly the typical peasant felt a much greater sense of devotion to the commune than to the landowner. Here we may cite a typical response by a serf when asked by a provincial governor whether he would obey his master: "As the mir goes, so will I." After twenty-five blows with a birch switch, the serf still gave the same response.[47]

The commune's power was manifested in a wide variety of spheres. With good reason Leroy-Beaulieu speaks of "communal despotism."[48] The commune determined land allotments for each household. It determined how much each household was to pay in taxes (there was much grumbling by individuals who had to pay higher taxes when other individuals in the household slacked off, e.g., out of drunkenness).[49] It determined which young males would be recruited into the military. In many cases the commune could prevent an individual from setting up a separate household. By various means it could pressure individuals to participate in a "pomoch'."[50] It could force an individual member to participate in a new agricultural project, such as draining a swamp, or it could prevent an individual member from introducing an agricultural innovation.[51] It could arrange for the public shaming or other disciplining of any member who stepped out of line. It dictated whether an individual peasant could receive the passport needed to reside elsewhere than on the commune (the internal passport requirement later became a fact of Soviet life as well). The commune could even interfere in family matters. For example, the powerful head ("bol'shak") of a multiple family household could be deposed by the commune if he did not see to it that his household fulfilled its communal obligations (e.g., if he became a drunkard and squandered patrimonial property).[52]

The ability of the traditional peasant collective to formally shame a member is striking evidence of the collective's power over the individual. Among the numerous examples adduced by Christine Worobec is the following:

In 1887, in the hamlet of Iazykova in Petrov district, Saratov province, the gates to two homes in which marriageable girls lived had been tarred [signifying premarital sexual activity on the part of the girls]. The girls' parents informed the village assembly that they suspected three village girls with whom their daughters had quarreled over suitors. Since the quarrel was common knowledge in the community, the assembly held the parents of the accused party responsible for their daughters' actions and ordered them to treat the assembly members to fifteen rubles' worth of vodka. Moreover, each of the guilty girls was shamed publicly by having a tarred piece of string tied round her neck. A crowd then led them to the tarred gates and forced the girls to kiss them. Such public humiliation weakened the offenders' chances for making ideal marriage matches.[53]

Two layers of collective coercion of the individual are evident in this *charivari*. First, the collective took it upon itself to regulate women's sexuality. It is clear that a woman's sexual behavior was not her own business. She and her entire family might be humiliated in the eyes of the larger collective by a premarital sexual adventure (while the man and his family were not, although there were cases where the collective forced a man to marry a woman he had impregnated). Second, the collective could punish those who falsely accused a woman of not conforming to the collective's demands on her sexuality. In effect, it could humiliate attempted humiliators, and thereby adversely affect their future lives in the collective. Apparently it was quite rare for the individual to resist or openly repudiate humiliation being meted out by the collective.

*Charivari*s were apparently most frequently directed against suspected petty thieves. Very often the victim was forced to treat those assembled to vodka or wine, which was supposed to effect a kind of reconciliation with the collective. In cases of more serious crimes, such as horse thievery, the suspected criminal might be tortured and beaten to death by a mob. Individuals accused of witchcraft or sorcery might also be murdered by a communal mob.[54]

Numerous proverbs attest to the psychological power which the traditional peasant collective wielded over the individual, or more accurately, to the power the individual *felt* the collective wielded. In effect, these proverbs express *smirenie*, an acceptance that one must *submit*, however reluctantly, to an omnipotent collective:

> What the mir has ordained is what God has decided (Chto mir poriadil, to Bog rassudil).
>
> As the mir wishes, judges, ordains, establishes, wants, sentences, decides; the will of the mir (Kak mir zakhochet, rassudit, poriadit, postavit, povolit, prigovorit, polozhit; mirskaia volia).
>
> When the mir roars, the forests groan / the forest bows (Mir zarevet, tak lesy stonyt [les klonitsia]).
>
> Wherever the hand of the mir is, my head is [in agreement] (Gde u mira ruka, tam moia golova).
>
> The mir cannot be judged, but its members can be beaten (Mir nesudim, a mirian b'iut).
>
> If the mir goes crazy, still you can't put it in chains (Mir s uma soidet—na tsep' ne posadish').
>
> Who would be greater than the mir? You don't argue with the mir (Kto bol'she mira budet? S mirom ne posporish').
>
> The neck of the mir is tough: it stretches but does not break (Mir-skaia sheia tuga: tianetsia, da ne rvetsia).
>
> No member of the mir can be opposed to the mir (Nikakoi mirianin ot mira ne proch').
>
> The people's voice betrayed / crucified Christ (Glas naroda Khrista predal [raspial]).[55]

Language is used in a personifying fashion in most of these sayings. That is, it is clear that the collective is understood to be a person. It has a "will" of its own. It has body parts, such as a "hand" that directs, or a "neck" that is strong. It is capable of doing things persons do: it "wishes," "judges," "ordains," "decides," "passes sentence on," "roars," "goes crazy," and so on. In effect, the proverbs give the commune a human face.

The proverbs may state outright that the commune is a person. In a positive vein we have: "The mir is a great person" ("Mir—velik chelovek"). On the negative side, however, there is "The mir is an aggressor/destroyer" ("Mir—nasil'nik-razoritel'").[56] From these contrasting examples provided by A. A. Rittikh it is clear that the peasant had ambivalent feelings about the personified commune.

What the commune-person does is require submission from real persons, its members. And the members go along, they submit. There is a certain passivity and fatalism to the proverbs. The commune is not to be questioned. The imagery for its members is abject. A forest "bows" to it, a member is powerless to "argue" or be "opposed" to it, one's "head" is in automatic agreement with it. One can be "beaten" by it, one can even be "crucified" by it, as was the case with Christ, the ultimate willing victim for a Russian ("Glas naroda Khrista raspial"). Here it is worth mentioning that the saying about Christ's crucifixion is the one which concludes the section of Dahl's handbook which I have been quoting from, while another one with a very similar wording begins the same section: "The people's voice is God's voice" ("Glas naroda—glas bozhii"). Evidently Dahl intended to convey a message with this symmetrical construction, namely: the voice of the commune is the voice of God the father, who demands the sacrifice of his son Christ. The commune member is thus a child, while the personified commune is a parent.

The commune member *sometimes* resists the commune, especially if its collective activity does not seem very intelligent:

The mir was in session for days, smoked up the sky [accomplished nothing], and then dispersed (Mir sutki stoial, nebo podkoptil i razoshelsia).

The people is stupid—it gathers itself into a heap (Narod glup: vse v kuchu lezet).

The peasant is smart, but the mir is a fool (Muzhik umen, da mir durak).[57]

These particular sayings suggest a certain degree of "dissidence" from the will of the collective, but it must be admitted that they are few and far between. The great majority of expressions Dahl collected on this topic favor submission over resistance. Psychoanalytically speaking, the masochistic solution is to be preferred.

The submission is particularly evident in the advice to conform. To live in the commune is to accept being lowered to the level of a dog:

> If you live with wolves, howl like a wolf (S volkami zhit'—po-volch'i vyt').

> You've landed in a pack, so whether you bark or not you'd better wag your tail (otherwise you'll be eaten) (Popal v staiu, lai ne lai, a khvostom viliai [a to zaediat]).

> Don't run ahead, but don't lag behind your own either (Vpered ne zabegai, a ot svoikh ne otstavai!).

> Though you may be in the rear, you're still in the same herd. If you lag behind, you become an orphan (Khot' na zade . . . , da v tom zhe stade. Otstal—sirotoiu stal).[58]

The implication of the last item is that the individual is a child, the commune a parent. To fail to go along with the commune is to lose a parent, to become an orphan (in Russian one becomes a "sirota" with the loss of either or both parents). The only element missing in this practically psychoanalytic characterization of masochistic conformity to the collective is a specification of which parent—mother or father—the commune represents.

The communal mentality on moral matters might thus be para-phrased as: whenever there is any doubt, the commune is right and the individual is wrong. Or, the commune is innocent and the individual is guilty. Or, to quote the poetic formulation made by one of my Russian informants to explain this whole series of proverbs: "the commune is God and the individual is shit [govno]." The masochistic orientation of anyone who actually accepts this idea of himself or herself should be self-evident.

Even death is not so bad, as long as it occurs in the context of the commune (or among people generally): "Even death is beautiful when you have got people round you" ("Na miru [Na liudiakh, S liud'mi] i smert' krasna").[59] Perhaps the attitude expressed by this proverb was not shared by all Russian collectivists, just as the comparable "Misery loves company" does not necessarily reflect the attitude of most English speakers. Yet there is something striking about the way the Russian proverb expresses fondness for company. The English proverb does not suggest that one welcomes misery, while the Russian proverb suggests an actual welcoming of death in the context of a collective (Fedotov speaks of a "zhazhda unichtozheniia v kollektive").[60] An individual may be mortal, but that is trivial because the collective with which one merges is immortal. It is even an honor to die in public.

As normally happens in masochism, the individual experiences an unclear psychical boundary with the object, in this case, with the commune. Numerous proverbs attest to the experience of identification with the group or its members:

I am such as those with whom I am (S kem ia, tem ia).

You are known by the company you keep (S kem zhivesh', tem i slyvesh').

Tell me who you are acquainted with, and I will tell you what kind of person you are (Skazhi, s kem ty znakom, i ia skazhu, kto ty takov).

You bear a resemblance to the one with whom you break bread (S kem khleb-sol' vodish', na togo i pokhodish').[61]

The Soviet historian Boris Mironov seems to have these proverbs (and others cited earlier) in mind when he discusses the individual's place in the post-emancipation commune:

Although an individual peasant's role depended on his personal qualities and immediate circumstances, the socialization process and the strong social control exercised by the commune did not allow a distinction between the individual and the group: the peasant's "I" merged with the communal "we." The result, though imperceptible and unnoticed by the peasant himself, was a far-reaching regulation of the peasant's whole life and the observance (more often unconsciously than consciously) of those stereotypes and models existing in the commune.

It is important to note that the peasant did not perceive his fusion with the commune as a violation of his individual rights, that he did not feel enslaved by the commune. Because the feeling of "I" was only inadequately developed, the individual peasant voluntarily sought to immerse himself in the "we" of the commune. The most striking example of this was the fact that decisions in the assembly were ordinarily expected to be unanimous, and if that unanimity was wanting, the commune made long, stubborn efforts to achieve it through compromise and suasion. Although the fusion of the individual peasant with the commune could have meant the forcible subordination of the minority to the majority, this was rarely the case . . , and the peasants regarded involuntary subordination as both extraordinary and undesirable. The relationship between peasant and commune may be called organic, voluntary conformism. This conformism was political, intellectual, moral, and social, and it made for standardization of the peasants' needs and interests.[62]

The conformism was also psychological, of course, as Mironov's own metaphors indicate: the peasant's "I" achieved "fusion" with the communal "we"—"more often unconsciously than consciously," as Mironov says. Parts of Mironov's article actually read like a psychoanalytic study of large group processes (cf. psychoanalyst Geoffrey Gorer's discussion of the "feeling of being merged into a larger group" which occurs in members of both tsarist and post-tsarist collectives,[63] or Margaret Mead's assertion that the *mir* stressed "merging of the individual in the group").[64] But Mironov does not specify (1) who the "we" might be a personification of in early ontogeny, and (2) he does not explicitly grant that the individual's attitude to the group was masochistic. The masochism is implicit, however, in Mironov's formulation (just as it was implicit in Slavophile writings about the commune over a century earlier): the individual commune member did not *feel* enslaved, there was not a *forcible* subordination of the individual—ergo the subordination was voluntary, was welcomed, even if "unconsciously" so. The subordination was thus masochistic by definition.

It was Petr Arkad'evich Stolypin (1863–1911), Russia's premier and interior minister under the last tsar, who initiated a series of agrarian reforms aimed at improving productivity and eliminating the peasant's slavish dependance on the commune. Stolypin and his fellow reformers made it possible for the peasant actually to own land privately. Their proposals were attractive enough to induce many peasants to overcome not only the fear of losing the security of the commune,[65] but related masochistic attitudes toward the commune as well. However, although almost two-thirds of peasant households obtained title to land by the end of the period 1906–17,[66] the reform did not stick. After the events of 1917 massive re-communalization took place. As Michael Confino and others have pointed out, 95 percent of peasant land in Russia during the 1920s was held on communal tenure.[67] After forced collectivization of agriculture occurred under Stalin in the early 1930s, private ownership of course remained totally out of the question. Not until the late 1980s and early 1990s were there any signs that individuals might get out from under the thumb of statewide collective control of arable land.

In the meantime, however, psychological attitudes toward the land had not changed. In December of 1990, when the Russian Parliament was taking steps for the privatization of farmland, President Boris Yeltsin made the following remarks to foreign correspondents: "You would never understand the spirit of Russians who never have become accustomed to the terminology and even more to the practice of selling and buying land—the motherland, as we call it." Yeltsin added: "As some legislators used to say, 'One can not sell his or her mother.'" "It is a psychological issue," declared the Russian leader.[68] The traditional idea of the Russian "land" as mother was thus alive and well late in the twentieth century. "You pick up the soil and it's like holding your mother's hand," said a collective farm worker to a reporter in 1988.[69] This is an extremely common sentiment in the Russian countryside.

To understand just how restrictive the Russian Parliament was on "selling the mother," one need only consider some of the details of its legislation: an individual who obtained land from the government was required to keep it for a minimum of ten years, and then could sell it only back to the government—not to other individuals in Russia, and not to foreigners. Such limitations on access to the agricultural "mother" would certainly be unacceptable to farmers in the West.

State ownership of land in the Soviet period fostered the same psychology as did communal ownership in previous times, that is, a masochistic attitude toward collective authority.[70] Only private ownership, free of collective control and individual submissiveness, profoundly motivates farmers to produce. True, self-interest can result in abuses too (e.g., the owner's greed can be harmful to hired hands). But self-interest is generally better than self-harm, even for the larger collective. For example, on the eve of the First World War, as a result of the Stolypin reforms, Russia became the world's second-largest exporter of grain.[71] The small private plots that were permitted during the Soviet period made a disproportionately large contribution to overall Soviet agricultural productivity by comparison with collectivized agriculture.[72]

The idea that Stolypin's agricultural reforms countered a previously masochistic (not merely repressive) arrangement between the peasant and the commune is not entirely new. There is a very interesting passage in Aleksandr Solzhenitsyn's *August 1914* which demonstrates an awareness of the psychological essence of agrarian reform in Russia. Solzhenitsyn begins by succinctly characterizing Stolypin's project:

> Stolypin's idea was one of shining simplicity—yet too complicated to be grasped or accepted. The repartitional commune reduced the fertility of the land, took from nature what it did not return, and denied the peasant both freedom and prosperity. The peasant's allotment must become his permanent property.

Solzhenitsyn then pauses to consider the psychological consequences of this momentous change, wondering whether the proposed reforms might deprive the peasant of a traditional outlet for moral masochism. Solzhenitsyn does not express himself in psychoanalytic terms, of course. But his neo-Slavophilic terminology clearly refers to what psychoanalysts mean by moral masochism:

> Perhaps, though, *in this self-denial, this harmonization of the will of the individual with that of the commune* [v etom umeren'i, soglasii svoei voli s mirskoi], this mutual aid and curbing of wild willfulness, there lay something more valuable than harvests and material well-being? Perhaps the people could look forward to something better than the development of private property? Perhaps the commune was not just a system of paternalistic constraints, cramping the freedom of the individual, perhaps it reflected the people's philosophy of life, its faith? Perhaps there was a paradox here which went beyond the commune, indeed beyond Russia itself: freedom of action and prosperity are necessary if man is to stand up to his full height on this earth, *but spiritual greatness dwells in eternal subordination, in awareness of oneself as an insignificant particle* [no v izvechnoi sviazannosti, v soznanii sebia lish' krokhoi obshchego blaga vitaet dukhovnaia vysota].

This little masochistic fantasy is then dispelled by Solzhenitsyn, who is trying to capture Stolypin's thought processes: "Thinking that way makes action impossible. Stolypin was always a realist." [73] In the meantime, however, Solzhenitsyn has given the reader a very effective summary of the broad psychological issues ("beyond Russia itself") involved in an individual's willing submission to a collective.

Aleksei Losev: Masochism and Matriotism

The most extreme Russian patriots are matriots at heart. By this I mean that their devotion to "Mother Russia" is so intense that the underlying maternal fantasy basis of patriotism comes to the surface as maternal imagery, while paternal imagery fades away. At the same time there is a willingness to indulge in or act out masochistic fantasies with respect to the maternal image.

For the Russian matriot Russia is nothing if not a suffering collective, a maternal icon in pain. But she does not suffer alone, she calls on her own to suffer as well—or at least she seems to for those who emulate her or find it difficult to distinguish themselves from her.

The philosopher Aleksei Fedorovich Losev (1893–1988), who had served time in a Soviet labor camp during the 1930s and lost loved ones during the German bombing of Moscow in 1941, expressed what it meant to suffer willingly "on the maternal bosom of the Motherland [na materinskom lone svoei Rodiny]." As Nazi troops pressed close to Moscow, he wrote:

> The very concept and appellation of "sacrifice [zhertva]" sounds elevated and exciting, ennobling and heroic. This is because we are born not just by "being," not just by "matter," not just by "reality" or "life"—all this is non-human and supra-human, impersonal and speculative—but we are born by our Motherland [rozhdaet nas Rodina], by that mother and that family which are already worthy of existence, already something great and bright, something sacred and pure. The dictates of this Motherland [Veleniia etoi Materi Rodiny] are indisputable. Sacrifices for the sake of this Motherland are inevitable. A sacrifice to a faceless and unseeing force of a community is meaningless. However, this is not a sacrifice, either. It is simply a meaningless, unnecessary and absurd conglomeration of births and deaths, tedium and bustle of a universal, but at the same time bestial womb. A sacrifice for the sake of the glory of our Motherland is sweet and holy. This sacrifice is the only thing that makes life meaningful. . . . either there is something above us that is our own [rodnoe], great, bright, common for us all, intimately and innately ours, essentially and eternally ours, namely, our Motherland, or our life is meaningless, our suffering irredeemable, and human tears interminable.[74]

Losev's desire to suffer is explicit, that is, the masochistic attitude is not even unconscious: "suffering, struggle, and death itself are nothing but desirable and full of meaning."[75] But the masochism is not a gratuitously individualistic enterprise. It is in the service of union with a collective maternal figure. A true "son of the Motherland" does not distinguish his own interests from those of the Motherland. Indeed he is one with her. This is the meaning of matriotism:

> We know the thorny path traversed by our country; we know the long and agonizing years of struggle, shortages, and suffering. But to a son of his Motherland [dlia syna svoei Rodiny], this is all his own [svoe], inalienably part of his flesh and blood [rodnoe]. He lives and dies with it; he *is* it, and it *is* him.[76]

The virtual synonymy of mother and child is also clear from the ease with which Losev moves back and forth between child-imagery and mother-imagery. At one point he says that what draws us on, what is worth sacrificing ourselves for is "you, Motherland-Mother," while two paragraphs later he asserts that what is worth dying for is "something dear [rodnoe] and lovely, something child-like, even infant-like." It is as if Losev were looking into his suffering mother's eyes and seeing himself, as child, reflected. The sacrificial death is itself a fusion of mother and child:

> He who loves dies peacefully. He who has a Motherland dies in comfort [ui-utno], if not for her, then at least in her, like a baby falling asleep in its warm and soft cradle—whether that be death in combat, or the death of a pilot who has fallen thousands of meters to the rocky earth. Only our Motherland is capable of giving internal comfort [uiut] because everything that is of the Motherland [rodnoe] is comforting, and comfort alone is triumph over fate and death.[77]

The "comfort" Losev's Motherland offers is, to say the least, severe. To an outside observer it looks more like punishment. A violent death for the Motherland can be characterized as "comforting" only because mothers typically comfort children in distress. But a child may get into trouble precisely in order to be comforted by a mother with whom it is having a problematical relationship. It may, in other words, behave masochistically. Losev is in a position to recommend masochism on behalf of the all-important Motherland because every child has experienced moments of masochism in dealing with the all-important mother. This is not to make a moral judgment of Losev's recommendation, but to point to the ontogenetic origin of its appeal. Indeed, the extreme patriotism, that is, matriotism of Soviet citizens may have saved the world from German Fascism.

Berdiaev's Prison Ecstasy

Nikolai Berdiaev was a very different kind of philosopher from Losev. He would have rejected Losev's extreme Russophilia. He was not a particularly masochistic individual by Russian standards. Yet masochistic episodes did occur by his own admission. They were connected with the terms he served in both tsarist and Soviet jails, and they reveal something of his attitude toward the collective: "during arrest and at interrogations, as in all the catastrophic events in my life, I was characteristically disinclined to experience depression. On the contrary, I was always animated and in a bellicose mood." "With no exaggeration," Berdiaev declares, "I can say that prison felt very pleasant to me." The "near ecstasy" that Berdiaev experienced upon being arrested, that is, his masochistic ebullience, was in part determined by his escape from himself or his merger with the collective: "I never experienced so fully such a feeling of oneness with the *communauté,* I was in a less individualistic mood than ever." [78]

Here it is curious that Russia's greatest philosophical advocate of freedom ("svoboda") should be claiming to achieve happiness precisely at those moments when he was deprived of his freedom, that is, when he was masochistically welcoming imprisonment.

The profound contradiction between the individual and the collective was of lasting concern to Berdiaev. Soviet communism and West-European fascism, for example, constituted unacceptable domination of the individual by the collective, for they treated the individual as a mere object, not a subject, not a person ("lichnost'"). But, as we have just seen, Berdiaev was also very interested in the potential fusion of the individual with the collective. His prime example of this was the phenomenon of *sobornost'* (or what he sometimes called "kommiunotarnost'," i.e., "communitarianism," not to be confused with "communism" or "collectivism"—both negative, authoritarian phenomena for Berdiaev). *Sobornost',* in the original sense of Khomiakov,[79] was for Berdiaev an acceptable, even desirable way for the individual to come under the complete sway of the collective.

According to Berdiaev, no domination, force, or violence is entailed by *sobornost'* (he, like Khomiakov, conveniently disregards dominance of, or violence against the self). To experience *sobornost'* is to retain the sense of one's own person while at the same time experiencing union with other persons in the collective, or with the collective as a whole. *Sobornost'* is, moreover, a divine experience, for God mediates in the union of individual and collective: "the *sobornost'* of the church is not some sort of authority, be it authority of a council of bishops or even of ecumenical councils, but is an immersion in interaction and in love of the church folk and of the Holy Spirit." [80] There are no external signs of this process, there are only internal, spiritual vicissitudes: "communitarianism is the unmediated relationship of a person with another person through God, who is the internal foundation of life." [81] Thus only God can erase boundaries between individuals. If God is absent, *sobornost'* or communitarianism degenerates into mere communism, or fascism, that is, authoritarian domination of the collective over the individual. [82]

God (the Father, Christ, or the Holy Spirit) is important to Berdiaev as an eraser of boundaries. For example, God and the human being (or to translate more traditionally, God and Man) are "inseparably connected to one another." [83] "Humanity is the basic attribute of God. The human being is rooted in God, as God is rooted in the human being." [84]

Berdiaev's favorite person of the Holy Trinity is of course Christ, the one who most blends with humankind. Berdiaev's designation "Christ the God-man" ("Khrist Bogochelovek") itself questions boundaries between persons. [85] Christ is the one person of the Trinity to become human ("stal chelovekom") as well as to be God. Christ is also precisely the person who suffers, or rather, the one who welcomes suffering. Christ is the masochistic person of God:

One can believe in God only if there exists God the Son, the Redeemer and Liberator, the God of sacrifice and love. The redeeming sufferings of the Son of God do not constitute a reconciliation of God with the human being, but rather a reconciliation of the human being with God. Only a suffering God can reconcile [one] with the sufferings of creation. [86]

Note that the word "reconciliation" here is applied both to the relationship of God and the human person ("primirenie cheloveka s Bogom") and to the relationship of the human person with suffering ("primiriaet so stradaniiami tvoreniia"). To welcome suffering is really the same thing as to blur the boundary between persons. Berdiaev can believe in God the Son *because*, in suffering, God the Son erases the boundary between God and humans.

Berdiaev admits that he is an admirer of *The Imitation of Christ*.[87] To imitate Christ is to accept suffering freely. No Christianity worthy of that designation can ever be forced upon anyone. Indeed, to believe in God *is* to be free: "God is my freedom." [88] But to be free is to be free to suffer. As I already observed in connection with the discussion of Khomiakov earlier in this book, this is a rather masochistic notion of freedom.

Berdiaev welcomes the communitarianism of *sobornost'* because it brings one closer to God. That is, immersion in the collective (which was very difficult for Berdiaev, personally) can bring one to the very feet of Christ on the cross. But neither the collective nor the suffering Christ is a particularly maternal icon (whereas Losev's motherland is starkly, almost parodistically maternal). But this does not mean that Berdiaev's ideal is not maternal nonetheless. Because Berdiaev is trapped in genderless imagery of the collective, or in the traditionally sexist imagery of God and the Holy Trinity (Father, Son, Holy Ghost), there can by definition be little hint of the maternal in his discourse on these matters.

However, it is clear from his personal religious-philosophical development that Berdiaev originally conceived of the collective as a maternal icon. The early Berdiaev, in his characterization of the "inadequate development of the personal factor in Russian life," says, "The Russian people has always loved to live in the warmth of the collective, in a kind of dissolution in the earthy element, in the bosom of the mother [v kakoi-to rastvorennosti v stikhii zemli, v lone materi]." [89] Russian religion is an example of this, according to young Berdiaev:

The universal spirit of Christ, the masculine universal logos is imprisoned by the feminine national element, by the Russian earth in her pagan primevalness. Thus was formed the religion of dissolution in mother-earth, in the collective national element, in animal warmth.[90]

From a psychoanalytic viewpoint, the maternal imagery here is striking. Berdiaev attributes not merely feminine, but specifically maternal qualities to the enslaving ("plenen") Russian collective. Religion in Russia is " . . . not so much a religion of Christ as a religion of the Mother of God, a religion of mother-earth, of a feminine deity illuminating fleshly being." [91] Here Berdiaev is being historically accurate as well as self-revealing.

Even Berdiaev's later writings will sometimes characterize union with God in maternal terms. Describing the creative potential of the God-human, Berdiaev says:

God's idea of the human being is infinitely higher than traditional, orthodox notions of the human being born [porozhdennykh] of a depressed and narrowed consciousness. The idea of God is the greatest human idea. The idea of the human being is the greatest divine idea. The human being awaits the birth of God within. God awaits the birth of the human being within [Chelovek zhdet rozhdeniia v nem Boga. Bog zhdet rozhdeniia v Nem cheloveka].[92]

With so much birthing going on, it is difficult to escape the conclusion that God is a mother after all—or that God-man is really God-woman.

One wonders whether Berdiaev thought about his mother in those ecstatic moments when he himself was thrown into prison. Certainly he experienced a sense of merger or fusion with his social-democratic collective ("oneness with the *communauté*"), as we have seen. But in the context he does not define that collective as maternal. Yet, the only thing he remembers an important official saying to him and his fellow prisoners the time he was arrested in Kiev does bear a strikingly maternal image: "Your error is that you do not see that the social process is organic rather than logical, and that a child cannot be born any earlier than in the ninth month."[93]

A Blok Poem: Suffering Begins at the Breast

The poet Aleksandr Blok (1880–1921), moved by the sufferings of his fellow Russians during the First World War, produced a poem which very explicitly depicts a mother's inculcation of masochism in her child:

КОРШУН

Чертя за кругом плавный круг,
Над сонным лугом коршун кружит
И смотрит на пустынный луг.—
В избушке мать над сыном тужит:
«На́ хлеба, на́, на́ грудь, соси,
Расти, покорствуй, крест неси».

Идут века, шумит война,
Встает мятеж, горят деревни,
А ты всё та ж, моя страна,

В красе заплаканной и древней.—
Доколе матери тужить?
Доколе коршуну кружить?

A buzzard flies the drowsy field,
Smooth circle after circle weaving.
He scans bare lands. A shack's revealed;
A mother for her son is grieving.
'Here, take this bread and suck this tit.
Mind! Grow! Here's your cross; carry it!'

Centuries pass, the war's at hand.
Rebellion came; each village sears.
And you are still the same, my land,
In your old beauty, stained with tears.
O how long must the mother grieve?
How long—the circling buzzard weave? [94]

Misfortune in the form of a buzzard [95] circles ("kruzhit") over a meadow, just as a mother grieves ("tuzhit") over her child. The striking parallel between the menacing buzzard and the breast-feeding mother is repeated in the final couplet by means of a grammatical parallelism involving the archaic "dokole" ("how long") plus a dative-infinitive construction. This suggests that the parallel actions are both really unavoidable, in effect: how long is the mother *fated* to grieve, how long is the buzzard *fated* to circle?

But how does a mother resemble a dangerous bird of prey? One historical explanation recently offered by E. Obukhova runs as follows: Blok was acquainted with Dmitrii Merezhkovskii's novelistic biography of Leonardo da Vinci in which da Vinci, in a dream of himself as an infant, is approached from above by a buzzard ("korshun") which proceeds to stroke his lips with its wings. Blok was probably also aware of the fact (possibly from Freud's own biography of Leonardo) that a buzzard was used to represent the mother in ancient Egyptian hieroglyphs. [96]

I would add that the theme of mother addressing child is common in the poetry of Blok's predecessor, Nikolai Nekrasov. In particular Nekrasov's mother figures are exemplary sufferers who often teach their children to endure. In one poem a mother, taking a break during the hard work of the harvest time ("strada," the "suffering time"), stands over her child in an open field:

Пой ему песню о вечном терпении,
   Пой, терпеливая мать!..[97]

Sing him [the child] a song of eternal endurance,
   Sing, enduring mother!

So often Nekrasov's message is this: you must suffer as all Russian mothers suffer, as Mother Russia herself suffers.

This historical background, which the typical reader of Blok's poem may or may not be aware of, can only support an intuition that the hovering buzzard represents something maternal. Yet a buzzard aggressively attacks what it is about to eat, while the mother depicted here encourages her child to eat. She foists food upon the child, force-feeds the child even (accented "na" occurs three times in one line).

A buzzard eats its prey, while a child "eats" its mother. This is a curious symmetry. In psychoanalytic experience,[98] a child's devouring attitude toward the mother's breast can result in compensatory paranoid fears about *being* devoured by the mother (cf. the well-known folktale figure of Baba Iaga, who likes to devour little children, or the charm against a mother who drinks her son's blood).[99]

By offering the breast so insistently, the mother in Blok's poem seems to be saying: "it's alright, you can eat me, I won't eat you—but the buzzard might." That is, the mother's contextual poetic equivalent may do the damage.

What might the damage be? This question is answered in the second stanza. The children grow up, war and revolution come. The children, in other words, start killing each other. Their dead bodies would probably make fine food for the buzzard circling overhead.

Not that the mother is pleased with this outcome. She grieves, after all, just as the buzzard weaves circles in the sky. Yet the terrible things which are happening are her fault at some level. She it was who taught her children to suffer: "Grow, be submissive, carry your cross!"—this would be a literal translation of her words uttered in the sixth line. There could hardly be a more explicit instruction to behave masochistically.[100] What is more, the masochism is encouraged amid overt breast imagery ("suck this tit!"). A common Russian metaphor, "to take in with mother's milk" ("vpityvat' s molokom materi") is realized, as it were: masochism is taken in with mother's milk.

The scene is strictly pre-Oedipal (or perhaps a-Oedipal would be a better term here). Not only is the child at the mother's breast, there is no competing paternal figure to fill out an Oedipal triangle. Blok thus demonstrates an intuitive knowledge of what psychoanalysts regard as the ontogenetic origin of moral masochism. One might even say that Blok's knowledge is deeper than Freud's here because he avoids Oedipal imagery, going directly to the child's primal, pre-Oedipal interaction with the mother. Freud, as we saw earlier, was reluctant to give the mother her due in his account of the origin of moral masochism.

In the poem's second stanza the scene shifts from mother and child to (Mother) Russia and the poet. The poet addresses his country ("strana") with the familiar "ty," much as a boy would address his mother. The country is in tears, much as the mother in the first stanza was.

How long must Mother Russia grieve over her sons?—the poet seems to be asking in the last couplet. A psychoanalytic answer to the question would be: as long as Russian mothers imbue masochism in their sons. If the mothers had not instilled masochism in them, they would not feel obliged to go off and destroy themselves in warfare, or destroy each other in revolution. If villages were not burning, if uprisings were not taking place, mothers would be spared their grief.

Curiously, then, mothers are the cause of their own grief. Or, Mother Russia is the cause of her own grief (by the end of the poem it is no longer possible to distinguish the personal mother from the maternal country, the "Rodina" which serves as title of the cycle which this poem culminates). Both sons and mothers suffer, of course, but the mother/Mother Russia is ultimately to blame for the suffering overall.

This is of course a sexist idea, and the implicit image of the mother as a bird of prey who might gobble up her sons seems to place inordinate blame on women for the male masochism of warfare. Yet behind Blok's sexism is an insight familiar to psychoanalysts—including women psychoanalysts who place the origin of masochism in the pre-Oedipal mother-infant scene.

Perhaps if the Russian father got more involved in "mothering" his mate's infant, there would be less reason to think that Russian masochism originated in the mother-infant relationship. This alternative is not present in Blok's poem, however, nor is it a likely prospect in Russian reality.

Blok's very graphic allusion to the maternal breast, which effectively becomes the breast of Mother Russia by the end of the poem, is not altogether original. In 1835 the Slavophile Aleksei Khomiakov wrote a poem about the bounteousness of Russia:

В твоей груди, моя Россия,
Есть также тихий, светлый ключ;
Он также воды льет живые,
Сокрыт, безвестен, но могуч.

In your breast, my Russia,
There is also a quiet, bright spring;
It too, hidden, unknown, but powerful,
Pours forth living waters.[101]

This breast, however, is rather abstract and idealized by comparison to the one in Blok's poem.

There is a sequence in Blok's unfinished long poem "Retribution" ("Vozmezdie") where another bird of prey, this time a hawk, circles over a meadow in search of a victim. Suddenly the hawk plunges down and captures a baby bird in its claws. There is a sad squeaking of little chicks, feathers fly, and again a maternal image appears:

Россия-мать, как птица, тужит
О детях; но — ее судьба,
Чтоб их терзали ястреба.

Mother Russia, like a bird, grieves
Over her children; but her *sud'ba*
Is that hawks tear them to pieces.[102]

In this case it is Mother Russia herself who has to learn to accept suffering, that is, the repeated victimization of her offspring. This is her fate *(sud'ba)*—a notion so often associated with the mother, as we saw earlier. Mother Russia has no choice, her children have no choice but to suffer. Here, however, she is not so much to blame as in the other poem, for she does not admonish her offspring to submissively carry a cross. The *hawk* is the source of any resulting masochism. The passage is not sexist, but it is also less insightful psychoanalytically, than "Korshun."

Dostoevsky's Maternal Collective

We saw earlier that Dmitrii Karamazov welcomes the punishment about to be meted out to him by the collective which arrested and imprisoned him: "I accept the torture of accusation, and my public shame, I want to suffer and by suffering I shall be purified." The motivation for this, as we saw, had something to do with the dream-image of a babe at the dried-out breast of its mother: "It's for that babe I am going to Siberia now." But Dmitrii is not satisfied to limit the psychological problem to himself. He needs to involve the collective as well. At his pretrial hearing he declares: "Gentlemen, we're all cruel, we're all monsters, we all make men weep, and mothers, and babes at the breast. . . . "[103] Not only the individual Dmitrii, then, but all of society around him is guilty. How Dmitrii should happen to know so much about the moral character of those individuals around him is unexplained. Indeed he does not "know" whether others are actually guilty monsters, he surmises that they are, he *projects* his own guilt on to others. The boundary between himself and the collective breaks down even further when he declares:

One may thaw and revive a frozen heart in [the] convict, one may wait upon him for years, and at last bring up from the dark depths a lofty soul, a feeling, suffering creature; one may bring forth an angel, create a hero! There are so many of them, hundreds of them, and we are all to blame for them. Why was it I dreamed of that "babe" at such a moment? "Why is the babe so poor?" That was a sign to me at that moment. It's for the babe I'm going. Because we are all responsible for all [vse za vsekh vinovaty]. For all the "babes," for there are big children as well as little children. All are "babes." I go for all because someone must go for all.[104]

We may gather from this somewhat incoherent discourse that Dmitrii is taking on the guilt of others, that is, of the collective which he can hardly distinguish himself from any more. In his masochistic ecstasy he feels that he can withstand the Siberia others deserve for *their* sins, because the boundary between these others and himself no longer obtains. When "all are responsible for all," or to translate more accurately, "all are guilty for all,"[105] individuals hardly matter anymore. Dmitrii loses himself in something greater than himself, he merges with the collective, fuses with it and this makes his suffering tolerable, even welcome.

The idea of "all guilty for all" occurs again and again in the novel. The monastic elder Zosima goes so far as to ask the birds in the heavens for forgiveness. At one point Zosima bows down before Dmitrii because *he* feels responsible for *another* man's patricidal impulse. His advice on the obligation to suffer for others is practically psychoanalytic in its explicitness:

> If the evil doing of men moves you to indignation and overwhelming distress, even to a desire for vengeance on the evildoers, shun above all things that feeling. Go at once and seek suffering for yourself [idi i ishchi sebe muk], as though you were yourself guilty for that wrong. Accept that suffering and bear it and your heart will find comfort, and you will understand that you too are guilty.[106]

If normal guilt feelings over one's own transgressions have a slightly masochistic tinge, guilt over the sins of others is certainly masochistic, involving as it does a gratuitous disregard for the boundaries between individuals.

It is curious that Zosima acquired this masochistic philosophy from his brother Markel who, in turn, developed it specifically in the context of trying to please his *mother*. Markel was originally an atheist, but when he learned that he was dying of consumption he deliberately started going to church for his mother's sake. In his conversations with her shortly before he died he would say such things as: "Mother, little heart of mine ... my joy, believe me, everyone is really responsible [vinovat] to all men for all men and for everything." [107] By this time he is sincere about his masochism, and his mother weeps with joy and grief.[108]

The idea of "all guilty for all" is not original with Dostoevsky. Gary L. Browning has pointed to sources in the Russian Orthodox liturgy, in the philosopher Nikolai Fedorov, in French utopian socialism, and elsewhere.[109] The idea accords well with the typically Russian attitude—especially among the peasantry—about the displaceability of responsibility between individuals, or between the individual and the collective. For example, Dahl's 1862 collection of proverbs contains the following items:

> Dump [everything] on to the mir: the mir will bear anything (Vali na mir: mir vse sneset).

> A hateful tiaglo has fallen upon the mir (during apportionment; a tiaglo which no one would take on) (Postyloe tiaglo na mir poleglo [pri raskladke; tiaglo, kotoroe nikto na sebia ne prinimaet]).

> In the mir no one is guilty. You can't find the culprit in a mir (V miru vinovatogo net. V miru vinovatogo ne syshchesh').

All for one, and one for all. Mutual responsibility (Vse za odnogo, a odin za vsekh. Krugovaia poruka).[110]

In most of these examples responsibility is being shifted away from the individual and on to the collective—a decidedly non-masochistic move, but one in which boundaries are questioned nonetheless. In the last item the direction of the shift can be projective ("all for one") or introjective and masochistic ("one for all"—Dmitrii Karamazov's position precisely).

As for the curious expression "krugovaia poruka," it has taken on a derogatory meaning similar to English "passing the buck." In English, however, "the buck stops" (e.g., President Truman's famous phrase, "The buck stops here"). In Russia the buck tends not to stop (or the attitude is that it does not stop). Rather, it goes on in endless circles ("krugovaia"), so that *no* one individual ever has to end up taking the blame for a morally questionable act. The collective answers for the irresponsible action of an individual.[111]

This is an exaggeration, of course, for in Russia there have been and there are individuals who take personal responsibility. Indeed, there are those Dostoevskian masochists who take *more* responsibility than is really their due—yet another manifestation of the fuzziness of Russian interpersonal boundaries.

The notoriously Russian question "Who is to blame?" ("Kto vinovat?," as in the title of Herzen's novel) would not come up so often in Russia if the answer were not so elusive. But the answer would not be so elusive if the individual person were more distinctly delineated from other persons or from the collective.

In the second half of the twentieth century the guilty individual continues to be elusive. When the post-Soviet Russian government tried to identify a culprit for some of the atrocities perpetrated during the Soviet period, the defendant in the courtroom was not an individual, but a collective, that is, the Communist Party of the Soviet Union (imagine trying the Republican Party rather than, say, Caspar Weinberger or Oliver North for the Iran-Contra affair!). When on the front page of *Moskovskie novosti* in late 1990 Aleksandr Kabakov described a religious gathering on the notorious Lubianka Square, he referred to the location as a "symbol of our *general* inescapable guilt," and declared that spiritual cleansing entails "the soul of the people [dusha narodnaia]," and not "just our individual souls."[112] When journalist Oleg Moroz criticized the Russian congress for not permitting a referendum early in 1993, he castigated *everyone* for having brought such a congress into existence. His rhetoric, moreover, was rather picturesque: "In the last analysis, we are all guilty of the fact that we are sitting up to our ears in shit [my vse sami povinny v tom, chto sidim po ushi v der'me]."[113]

In his 1973 essay "Repentance and Self-Limitation in the Life of Nations" Aleksandr Solzhenitsyn urged his countrymen to repent for their sins under Soviet rule. But in this work Solzhenitsyn did not so much name names as blame everyone generally, including himself:

No country in the twentieth century has suffered like ours, which within its own borders has destroyed as many as seventy million people over and above those lost in the world wars—no one in modern history has experienced such destruction. And it is true: it is painful to chide where one must pity. But repentance is always painful, otherwise it would have no moral value. These people were not the victims of flood or earthquake. There were innocent victims and guilty victims, but they would never have reached such a terrifying total if they had suffered only at the hands of others: *we, all of us,* Russia herself, were the necessary accomplices.[114]

Solzhenitsyn's article is nothing less than a call for "general repentance" among Russians. Anticipating protests that certain individuals or groups of individuals (e.g., members of the secret police) might be more blameworthy than others, Solzhenitsyn holds his ground: "But we must all answer for everything [vse—za vsë]."[115] Dostoevsky would certainly have agreed with this conflation of the innocent with the guilty. Better that everyone be slightly guilty than separate the truly guilty from the truly innocent. That way no one has to be *very* guilty. Better that everyone engage in the mild masochism of breast-beating than engage in sadistic revenge against real, specific criminals. In this essay Solzhenitsyn does not seem to understand that general repentance precludes real justice. One cannot hold a Nuremberg-style trial, one cannot bring genuine, individual criminals to justice by operating in an impractical fantasy world which blurs distinctions between individuals and the collective.[116]

But to return to Dostoevsky. When Dmitrii Karamazov asserted that "all are guilty for all," he was failing to see boundaries within a Russian context. But such a failure need not happen only in such a context. In *The Diary of a Writer,* for example (particularly in the so-called "Pushkin Speech"), the ideal Russian is characterized as some kind of universal human being ("vsechelovek"). The boundary between Russian and non-Russian is itself questioned. In grandiose fashion Dostoevsky asserts that "among all nations the Russian soul [russkaia dusha], the genius of the Russian people is, perhaps, most apt to embrace the idea of the universal fellowship of man, of brotherly love." [117]

According to Dostoevsky, the Russian national poet Aleksandr Pushkin is so great that he possesses "the faculty of completely reincarnating in himself an alien nationality." Pushkin's version of *Don Juan* seems utterly Spanish, *A Feast During the Plague* is perfectly in tune with "the genius of England," and the *Imitations of the Koran* captures the very spirit of Mohammedanism (whereas Shakespeare's Italians are "invariably Englishmen").[118] This alleged quality of Pushkin's is, however, specifically Russian:

> It is exactly in this that his national, Russian strength revealed itself most—the national character [narodnost'] of his poetry, the national spirit [narodnost'] in its future development, and the national spirit [narodnost'] in our future, which is concealed in that which is already present—and this has been prophetically revealed by Pushkin. For what else is the strength of the Russian national spirit [sila dukha russkoi narodnosti] than the aspiration, in its ultimate goal, for universality and all-embracing humanitarianism [ko vsemirnosti i ko vsechelovechnosti]? [119]

I have had to doctor up the translation a bit in order to capture the striking repetition of the Russian word "narodnost'" (which derives from "narod," "people" or "folk," and is cognate with such words as "rodina," "motherland" and "rodit'sia," "to be born"). Dostoevsky's grandiose idea of Pushkin seems inseparable from the Russian folk idea.

A little later in the same essay grandiosity takes the form of a reaching out to all of humankind by the Russian people:

> Yes, the Russian's destiny is incontestably all-European and universal. To become a genuine and all-round Russian means, perhaps (and this you should remember), to become brother of all men, *a universal man [vsechelovekom]*, if you please. Oh, all this Slavophilism and this Westernism is a great, although historically inevitable, misunderstanding. To a genuine Russian, Europe and the destiny of the great Aryan race are as dear as Russia herself, as the fate of his native land [svoei rodnoi zemli], because our destiny is universality acquired not by the sword but by the force of brotherhood and our brotherly longing for fellowship of men.

I am speaking merely of the brotherhood of men and of the fact that the Russian heart is more adapted to universal, all-humanitarian brotherly fellowship than any other nation [iz vsekh narodov]. I perceive this in our history, in our gifted men, in the creative genius of Pushkin. Let our land be poor, but this destitute land "Christ, in a slave's garb, has traversed, to and fro, with blessing." Why shouldn't we embrace His ultimate word? Wasn't He Himself born [rodilsia] in a manger? I repeat: at least we are already in a position to point to Pushkin, to the universality and all-humanitarianism of his genius. For wasn't he capable of embracing in his soul foreign geniuses as his own [kak rodnye]? [120]

The grandiosity exists despite the humble character of Russia and of Russians. The collective known as Russia is destitute ("nishchaia"), it has been visited and blessed by Christ "in a slave's garb" (Dostoevsky is quoting the famous line from Tiutchev). Humble Russia has "served" Europe, and so on. All of these ideas have clear masochistic implications.

It was also in the Pushkin Speech that Dostoevsky gave his most famous exhortation to moral masochism. The context is a discussion of Pushkin's long poem *The Gypsies,* in which a world-weary, Byronic hero named Aleko falls in love with a Gypsy girl, lives with her among a group of Gypsies for two years, then kills her when he learns that she has taken a lover. Dostoevsky quotes the words with which the girl's father sends Aleko away from the Gypsy encampment forever:

> Оставь нас, гордый человек;
> Мы дики, нет у нас законов,
> Мы не терзаем, не казним.

> Depart from us, thou haughty man:
> We're wild, we have no binding laws,
> We neither punish nor torment. [121]

According to Dostoevsky, this passage suggests a "Russian solution" to the problem of pride—even though it is a Gypsy who is speaking against pride, and a Russian who is being offensively proud. In any case, disregarding Dostoevsky's poor logic, we may quote his famous formula for *smirenie* which he believes is in accord with the faith and the truth of the Russian folk: "Humble thyself [smiris'], proud man; above all, break thy haughtiness! Humble thyself, idle man, and, first of all, labor on thy native land!" [122]

It is important to keep in mind that this is not some wizened, obscure monk perverting a fresh novice in ancient Rus', but the great

Dostoevsky speaking to the cream of the Russian intelligentsia in 1880. And, to judge from the intensity of the reaction (both positive and negative) by that intelligentsia,[123] Dostoevsky must have hit a very sensitive, Russian nerve.

The humiliation which Dostoevsky calls for is essentially the same as what had been advocated by the Slavophiles, namely, a bowing-down to the collective, here designated as the people ("narod," whereas the Slavophiles had focused on the commune, i.e., the "obshchina" or "mir"). The road to salvation lies in humble communication with the people ("smirennogo obshcheniia s narodom"). Yet, as was also the case with the Slavophiles, the truth lies within oneself: "Truth is within— not without thee. Find thyself within thyself. Subdue thyself; be master of thyself [podchini sebia sebe, ovladei soboi]."[124]

It may well be that one can find oneself in humbling oneself before the collective, but Dostoevsky does not really explain how this is so. Again, as with the Slavophiles, the self to be found is confused with that collective object toward which one takes a masochistic stance.

And again, as with Losev, that object is maternal. Dostoevsky is being matriotic in these passages. "Narod," Dostoevsky's key to achieving a high level of moral masochism, is a suggestive word. It and several other words containing the Russian root morpheme -*rod*-, which connotes birth and generativity, occur repeatedly in the passage.[125] Dostoevsky says Aleko is an "unhappy wanderer in his native land [v *rod*noi zemle], that traditional Russian sufferer detached from the people [ot na*rod*a]"—by which he also means such literary characters as Onegin, Pechorin, and Andrei Bolkonsky, as well as real Russians such as those members of the intelligentsia who feel alienated from Russia. This kind of person came into existence ("za*rod*ilsia") roughly a century after the reforms of Peter the Great, in the midst of an intelligentsia detached from the people, from the people's might ("ot na*rod*a, ot na*rod*noi sily"). These "homeless Russian ramblers," though they may belong to the hereditary nobility ("k *rod*ovomu dvorianstvu"), may seek solace "in the bosom of nature [na lone pri*rod*y]." Aleko himself suffered a longing for nature ("toska po pri*rod*e"), although he eventually came into conflict with it ("s usloviiami etoi dikoi pri*rod*y").

Elsewhere in the essay on Pushkin there are more clumps of these -*rod*- words: humble Tat'iana's childhood past is a "contact with the

motherland, with the native people [s rodinoi, s rodnym narodom]";
no writer experienced such a heartfelt union with the Russian people
("rodstvenno s narodom svoim") as did Pushkin.[126]

The accumulation of words containing the maternally suggestive
root -rod- is remarkable, particularly in the admonition itself to masochism, and in the immediately following words: " 'labor on thy native field
[na rodnoi nive]!'—Such is the solution according to the people's truth
and wisdom [po narodnoi pravde i narodnomu razumu]." [127]

The field ("niva") too is suggestive, for it is a feminine noun referring specifically to the kind of field one plants and makes fertile.[128]
Moreover, a related word with clear maternal overtones, "zemlia,"
meaning "land" or "earth" also occurs repeatedly in the essay on Pushkin (especially the phrase "rodnaia zemlia," "native land"; compare
Konstantin Aksakov's equation of "narod" and "zemlia").[129] Here it is
also worth keeping in mind that Dostoevsky was one of the pochvenniki
or "men of the soil" (from "pochva," "soil"),[130] who encouraged the
educated class to find its roots with the folk masses without necessarily
rejecting the West as the Slavophiles did. The pochvenniki too were real
Russian matriots.[131]

Dostoevsky's fantasy of masochistic bondage to a maternal figure
flows quite naturally out of an awareness of the agriculturally dependent
position of the Russian peasant. As Christine Worobec points out in her
book on the peasant in post-emancipation Russia, "Peasant societies are,
by definition, built on relations firmly tied to the land. Land generally
provides the means for peasant existence, and around that foundation
institutions develop in turn to perpetuate peasant society." [132] Although
the analysis provided by Worobec is primarily economic and cultural
in nature, she recognizes the important psychological backdrop in the
peasant's relationship to the land: "Despite the natural odds against
them, Russian peasants concentrated their attention on the land, maintaining a sacred, devotional attachment to it. Mother Earth was all-
powerful, providing peasants with sustenance and definition of
purpose." [133]

The land quite literally fed the peasant, just as a mother feeds a
child. The land had a certain degree of control over its inhabitants, much
as a mother has control over her child. There was an unavoidable
motivation to submit masochistically to that control. Dostoevsky in-
stinctively understood the emotional needs of the peasant.

The most explicit linkage of moral masochism to troubled interaction with the maternal figure of Russia comes in an earlier passage of Dostoevsky's *Diary:*

> It is we who have to bow before the people [preklonit'sia pered narodom] and await from them everything—both thought and expression; it is we who must bow before the people's truth [preklonit'sia pered pravdoi narodnoi] and recognize it as such—even in that dreadful event if it has partly emerged out of the *Chet'i Minei* [a Russian martyrology]. In a word: we must bow like prodigal children [sklonit'sia, kak bludnye deti] who, for two hundred years, have been absent from home, but who nevertheless have returned Russians—which, by the way, is our great merit.[134]

The uprooted Russian comes crawling back *as a child* to Russia which, although not explicitly characterized as a mother, is nonetheless the Russian folk, the "narod" with its repeated, maternally suggestive root morpheme *-rod-*. In returning home the *intelligent* can experience union ("soedinenie") with the "narod," can actually *be* a Russian. The underlying fantasy that Dostoevsky caters to is masochistic submission to and merger with the pre-Oedipal mother.

It is right after this passage that the famous "Peasant Marei" episode is recorded. Marei is a member of the "narod," a kind and gentle peasant that Dostoevsky vividly remembers from his childhood. Once, in late summer when he was nine years old, little Fedor was walking outdoors when, all of a sudden he heard a cry: "A wolf is coming!" Apparently this was just a hallucination, but the child was extremely frightened and ran for protection to a nearby peasant named Marei, who was plowing a field. Marei quite naturally comforted the boy, addressing him as "rodnyi" ("dear one"), caressing him, and urging him to cross himself. Dostoevsky remembers the peasant's "almost feminine tenderness" and, more important, mentions his "motherly smile" ("materinskaia ulybka," "materinski ulybaias'") three times in the course of the narration.[135] Two of Dostoevsky's psychoanalytic critics have (independently) noted the similarity of the name *Marei* to the name of Dostoevsky's mother, *Mariia*.[136] Clearly, as psychoanalyst Louis Breger observes, Marei is a "loving mother."

The memory of this encounter with a simple Russian peasant in an open field is very special for Dostoevsky. It is pressed into the service of a fantasy about an idealized Russian folk, a "narod" that is explicitly "maternal" even in the person of a male peasant, a peasant who willingly suffers deprivation ("he had no expectation, no notion of his own freedom") and who himself repeatedly admonishes his little master to obey ("Christ be with you, cross yourself"; "Christ be with you, get moving now").

Dostoevsky considers his maternal Marei to be the very highest example of moral perfection, the ideal representative of the collective "narod" before whom one must "bow down." Psychoanalytically, Marei confirms the maternal essence of the object, the "narod," before whom one must behave in masochistic fashion, and from whom one must acquire masochistic habits in order to become a true Russian matriot.[137]

The individual in traditional Russian culture is strongly inclined to submit to the collective. In effect: *Doleo, ergo sumus.* Such submission is yet another of the many forms of moral masochism which Russians may enact for themselves. Ordinarily, the deep structure of this posture is not available to consciousness. But, when we closely examine some specific imagery of the collective concocted by certain selected, highly creative individual Russians—Losev, Berdiaev, Blok, Dostoevsky—then the collective's maternal face becomes visible.

T E N
Conclusion

At the beginning of this book I stated that, over the centuries, Russians have enacted for themselves a culture of moral masochism. By this I did not so much mean to characterize Russians as to offer a characteristic of many, perhaps most Russians. Perhaps masochism is even the essence of the Russian soul, but such a claim would really have to be the topic of another book. A psychological trait, not national character, has been my focus here.

There is much more that could be said about Russian masochism, of course. In some areas I have only scratched the surface. For example, I have said practically nothing about Russian apocalypticism, although this phenomenon bears remarkable resemblances to the discourse of impending doom which emanates from some masochistic patients on the couch.[1] But the sheer quantity of evidence I have adduced should indicate that moral masochism has been and continues to be a force in Russia.

There are many other aspects of Russian culture that are worthy of psychoanalytic study. A whole book could be written about Russian xenophobia, for example (indeed, whole books could be written about the xenophobia of every existing ethnic group on our planet). The overall phenomenon of Russian nationalism, both in earlier periods and in the current period of post-Soviet disintegration, awaits detailed psychoanalytic study. Russian orality (from the famous vodka-fixation to the abundance of food-imagery in Russian literature) is another interesting psychological phenomenon that would bear investigation. A psychoanalysis of Russian Orthodox religiosity (apart from its masochism) would make a fascinating study. The psychodynamics of self-esteem in Russia have yet to be examined in any detail. And of course the psychoanalytic consequences of the enormous economic and sociopolitical changes that are going on in Russia right now deserve scrutiny.

There is so much more to the Russian soul than its masochistic aspect. Yet the masochism is there. It permeates that soul, that psyche, that culture—from the self-immolations of Old Believer communities to the self-sacrifices of the nineteenth-century intelligentsia; from the foolishness of holy fools to the antics of Ivan the fool; from the tolerance of spousal abuse to the acceptance of iron rule by the collective.

If I have tended to speak interchangeably of the culture of moral masochism on the one hand, and individual masochism on the other, if I have quoted Russian cultural practices as often as I have quoted individual Russians—it is because there is so much overlap between culture and the individual psyche ("dusha"). Every individual immersed in a culture carries that culture around in his or her own psyche. Psychoanalysis studies the individual, as I emphasized in the Introduction to this book. But the individual interiorizes a culture, so it is difficult to psychoanalyze an individual without also psychoanalyzing culture. Furthermore, culture cannot be enacted except by individuals. They may not be a sufficient condition, but they are a necessary condition for culture. Thus culture is as much in the individual psyche as the individual psyche is in culture.

Culture is not to be equated with the collective, however. In Russia the collective is a tyrant, and the individual typically gives in. Culture, on the other hand, is not a tyrant. Or rather, tyranny is only one of its many potential features. Among its other features is personal agency ("lichnost'"). A culture implies personal agents because it needs personal agents to bear and enact it.

In particular, a culture of moral masochism is borne and enacted by personal agents, because at the very heart of moral masochism is an agent acting—consciously or unconsciously—against his or her own personal interests. Even if the social environment is exceedingly rich in opportunities to suffer harm or humiliation, personal agents do not just disappear. Masochism does become more likely, but masochistic persons are there too. To assert that they are not would be to imply that the culture in question is perpetrated by something less than persons—some kind of automata, or "savages," for example—and *that* position would be both inaccurate and racist.

Some years ago I came across a book titled *Russians as People*. The author, Wright Miller, had not written a bad book, actually. But his title did provoke me to think: What on earth might Russians be, if *not* people? The implications were unfortunate.

Masochists are people. It makes more logical and moral sense to recognize their masochism than to deny their personhood. Whether the masochism itself is "pathological," or is a "disorder" that ought to be "cured"—is another question. My own inclination is to leave Russians be. I have no practical recommendations or prescriptions to make. Not all psychoanalysts are therapists, and besides, masochists are extraordinarily difficult to cure on the couch. A change in identity is required.

Russians have to find their own way. Perhaps they will even figure out how to harness masochism for economic advancement. Some of the Old Believers and sectarians did become fabulously wealthy.

In his book on Dostoevsky Berdiaev says: "There is a hunger for self-destruction in the Russian soul, there is a danger of intoxication with ruin."[2] I confess that I have sometimes found it exhilarating to observe this danger—from afar.

For me, masochism is part of the very attractiveness and beauty of Russian culture. Where would Tatiana Larina or Dmitrii Karamazov or Anna Karenina be without their masochism? To "cure" them of their masochism would be to detract considerably from their aesthetic appeal. The beauty of masochism, however, like all beauty, resides in the mind of the beholder.

Notes

1. For example: Dallin and Nicolaevsky 1947, 88–107; Hellie 1982, 711; Kiva 1990.
2. The phrase is from a famous passage in *The Diary of a Writer* (1873). See Dostoevskii 1972–88, vol. 21, 36.
3. Vakar 1961, 40.
4. Voznesenskii 1991, 12.
5. Grossman 1973, 176–80. For a historical overview of the term "Russian soul" ("russkaia dusha") see Williams 1970. Wierzbicka (1992, 31–63) offers insightful remarks on the semantics of the Russian term "dusha."
6. Ivanov 1909, 327. Cf. Merezhkovskii 1914, vol. 15, 169.
7. Ivanov 1909, 330.
8. Merezhkovskii 1914, vol. 15, 157.
9. Belkin 1991b, 14.
10. Some others have already applied this term to Russians, e.g., Hingley 1977, 195. Aleksandr Solzhenitsyn declares that the idea of a "perennial Russian slave mentality" is a "persistent and tendentious generalization" concocted by people who do not really understand Russia (1977, 187). One of the purposes of this book is to prove Solzhenitsyn wrong.

    By the English term "mentality" I do not mean to be translating French "mentalité"—as in the "histoire des mentalités" approach which has recently established itself in Russian studies (cf. Perrie 1989), and which, incidentally, I heartily endorse. In any case, English "mentality" suggests a more strictly psychological phenomenon, which is the concern of this book.
11. Gorskii 1977 (1969), 378.
12. As quoted in Golovanov 1992, 13.
13. Leopold von Sacher-Masoch (1836–95), in his semi-pornographic *Venus in Furs,* describes a man who obtains sexual gratification from being whipped,

trampled upon, or otherwise humiliated by a woman. For a discussion of Sacher-Masoch's writing, see Lenzer 1975. The term "masochism" was coined by the pioneering sexologist Richard von Krafft-Ebing (1840–1902) in his *Psychopathia Sexualis* (1866; English edition 1929, 132). Freud moved away from the erotogenic orientation of the term with his notion of "moral masochism" (see chap. 5 of this volume). As if it were an unprintable swear word, the Russian term "mazokhizm" is missing from many Russian dictionaries, including the authoritative seventeen-volume Academy dictionary (ANSSSR 1950–65). It has recently emerged, however, in the post-Soviet Russian press. For example, Freud's essay on masochism ("Ekonomicheskaia problema *mazokhizma*") has recently appeared in Russian, appended to a translation of Sacher-Masoch's *Venus in Furs* (Zakher-Mazokh 1992, 349–64).

14. As defined by Katz 1990, 226.
15. Freud, *SE,* vol. 19, 165–70.
16. See, for example, Freud's "Beyond the Pleasure Principle," in *SE,* vol. 18, 7–64. The death instinct is sometimes equated with a "primary masochism" by Freud (e.g., *SE,* vol. 18, 55). If such a species of masochism exists (and most psychoanalysts think not), it is in any case not the topic of this book. Incidentally, Freud's notion of the death instinct supposedly has a "Russian" origin, namely, the idea of the "destruction instinct" advanced by the Russian psychoanalyst Sabina Spielrein (see Rice 1982; Leibin 1990, 61).

As for Russian nonerotogenic sadism ("zhestokost' "), it too is a large and legitimate object of study, but it is not a topic that I can even begin to treat in this book.

17. For abundant examples, see Kohn 1960.
18. See Heller 1988 (1985). Heller would probably accept the idea that masochism became at least one of the traits of *Homo sovieticus,* although he does not use the psychoanalytic term. For example, speaking of the brutal collectivization of the peasantry in the early 1930s, Heller says: "The massacre of the peasantry allowed the state to turn the survivors into a submissive, inert mass of state citizens" (39). Or, paraphrasing a passage from Zamiatin's novel *We,* Heller says individuals should "wish" to be "welded together into a collective" (6). At one point Heller agrees with Igor Shafarevich's claim that socialism is "one of the aspects of the impulse of mankind's yearning for self-destruction and nothingness" (as quoted by Heller, 9).

A current, derogatory term for *Homo sovieticus* is "Sovok," acronym for "sovetskii chelovek," but also homonym of "sovok" (dustpan). Russians who refer to themselves with this humiliating term are behaving masochistically.

19. Dicks 1952. See also Dicks 1960.
20. Dicks 1952, 153.
21. Ibid., 153–54.
22. The late Felix Dreizin says, for example: "Russian culture strongly encour-

ages masochistic tendencies in individual psychology," and he backs this up with some revealing quotations from Aleksandr Solzhenitsyn about the supposed moral superiority of prison life. See Dreizin 1990, 182–85.

In his essay on Maksim Gor'kii, Erik Erikson speaks of "that pattern of masochistic identification with authority which apparently has been a strong collective force in the history of Russia" (1963, 371).

Without using the term "masochism," Nathan Leites adduces examples illustrating his thesis that Russian Bolsheviks operate on the principle that "Life is sacrifice" (Leites 1953, 132–41).

In his interesting quasi-psychoanalytic study of Russian culture, *Le tsarévitch immolé,* Alain Besançon is willing to grant that there is at least an "analogie d'expérience" between Russian religious asceticism and what Freud meant by moral masochism (1967, 75).

Others who have made passing references to Russian masochism—or who have treated it without necessarily using the term—will be quoted in the course of this book.

23. Dal' 1955 (1880–82), vol. 4, 5.
24. ANSSSR 1950–65, vol. 12, 7.
25. Ibid.
26. As quoted by Berdiaev 1971 (1946), 151.
27. Gor'kii 1978 (1912), 306.
28. For historical and socioeconomic analyses of slavery in Russia, see Pipes 1974, 148 ff.; Kolchin 1987; Blum 1961; Hellie 1982; Hoch 1986. These and related works will occasionally yield interesting information about psychological matters, but their focus is elsewhere.
29. See, for example, Perrie 1989.
30. See especially Daniel Field's book *Rebels in the Name of the Tsar* (1989 [1976]).
31. Kolchin 1987, 269. On some psychological aspects of serf rebelliousness, see Litvak 1971.
32. This is not to suggest that masochism was the only reason why serfs tended not to rebel. There were other (psychological, economic, political, etc.) reasons as well. For example, the economic interests of the serf owner and the patriarchal heads of serf households overlapped considerably, as Steven Hoch has shown (1986, chap. 3). Nonetheless, there has been little study in this area. Historians, for example, are more likely to be concerned with why peasants rebel than with why they do not.
33. Olearius 1967 (1656), 147.
34. Fletcher 1966 (1591), 46.
35. Hingley 1977, 194.
36. Dal' 1984 (1862), vol. 1, 347.
37. Ibid., 167, 168, 169, 194.
38. Ibid., 108, 180, 182.
39. See, for example, the studies of inmates of the German concentration camps or slaves on southern American plantations by Bettelheim 1980, 3–83;

Elkins 1963, 81–139; Stampp 1971. As Belkin (1991b, 23–24) points out, some of the *children* of parents who were arrested during the Stalin period live out their lives in fear.

40. Here I concur with Hellie's (1987, 183–5) refutation of Keenan's (1986) dismissal of the slavishness of persons surrounding the tsar in Muscovy.

41. For example, between the years 1959 and 1989 the proportion of ethnic Russians in the Russian Federation ranged from 81.5 to 83.3 percent (Arutiunian 1992, 21, table 3).

42. Examples provided by Cherniavsky 1961, 216–17.

43. Voloshin 1989, 11.

44. Likhachev 1988, 5.

45. Borisov 1976, 204. Cf. Borisov 1974 for the condensed Russian version of this article.

46. Berdyaev 1944, 164ff.; Berdiaev 1939, 137ff. Early in his career Berdiaev himself yielded to the temptation to personify Russia; see 229 herein.

47. Flugel 1950 (1921), 126.

48. For example: Flugel 1950 (1921), 125–28; Erikson 1969, 155, 157, 222; DeMause 1982, 175; Koenigsberg 1977; Anzieu 1984 (1975); Chasseguet-Smirgel 1985, 76–93; GAP 1987.

49. See, for example: Heller 1988, chap. 4; Cox 1989; Rzhevskii 1987.

NOTES TO CHAPTER 2

1. Lunt 1990.

2. Averintsev 1988, 332.

3. Toporov 1987, 234, 244.

4. Berdiaev 1971 (1946), 9.

5. As translated from the *Primary Chronicle* by Fedotov 1975, vol. 1, 106 (italics added).

6. As quoted by Fedotov 1975, vol. 1, 109.

7. Toporov 1987, 243.

8. Fedotov 1975, vol. 1, 105.

9. See Cherniavsky 1961, chap. 1.

10. Fedotov 1975, vol. 1, 104.

11. As quoted by Fedotov 1975, vol. 2, 57, 75, 77, 93, resp.

12. Fedotov 1975, vol. 1, 117–19.

13. Ibid., 119.

14. As quoted by Fedotov 1975, vol. 2, 210.

15. Bolshakoff 1977, 53.

16. Ibid., 124.

17. Meehan-Waters 1991, 41.

18. Fedotov 1975, vol. 1, 149–50.

19. Bolshakoff 1977, 47–48.

20. Ibid., 58, 101. For more detailed figures, see Smolitsch 1953, 538.

21. I am hardly the first to note the masochistic element in ascetic practices. Psychoanalyst Otto Fenichel, for example, considers that masochism is essential to "the psychology of asceticism" (1945, 364). Shirley Panken says that "the Christian ethic has sanctified masochism in such religious practices as mortification and its most extreme variant, asceticism" (Panken 1973, 12). Stuart L. Charme (1983, 224) points to numerous biblical examples where one's suffering is interpreted as a sign of God's love, e.g., "the Lord disciplines him whom He loves" (Hebrews 12:6). Sociologist Peter L. Berger, discussing the problem of theodicy, says that religious surrender of the self always has masochistic overtones. When Job declared "Though he slay me, yet will I trust in him," he was engaging in a "pure form of religious masochism *vis à vis* the Biblical God." The Calvinist vision of "the damned themselves joining in the glorification of that same God who has sentenced them to damnation" is also a "pure form of the masochistic attitude" (Berger 1967, 75).

The New Testament is of course full of exhortations to "turn the other cheek" and "take up the cross." Gary Liaboe and James Guy (1985) argue that these ideas should not be taken too seriously, lest Christians fall into a masochistic "distortion of servanthood." But they do not notice that very little of the Christian idea of "servanthood" is left when the masochism is subtracted from it. It is hard to miss the masochism in Saint Paul's boastful descriptions of his own sufferings, yet Dale Martin's recent treatise (1990) on the metaphor of slavery in Pauline Christianity (as in "slave of Christ") makes no mention of clinical issues or the psychoanalysis of masochism. In general, scholarly treatments of the central Judeo-Christian texts are bound to be incomplete without a consideration of masochism.

22. Billington 1968, 65, 204.
23. Fedotov 1975, vol. 1, 341.
24. Pyle 1989.
25. Kireevskii 1984, 232.
26. Fletcher 1966 (1591), 90.
27. Kovalevskii 1895, 147.
28. Gor'kii 1937, 158.
29. Wortman 1967, 66.
30. There is a considerable (and contentious) literature on holy foolishness in Russia which includes: Kovalevskii 1895; Fedotov 1942; Fedotov 1975, vol. 2, 316–43; Thompson 1987; Likhachev 1987, vol. 2, 427–30; Likhachev and Panchenko 1976; Ziolkowski 1988, 131ff; Murav 1992.
31. Billington 1968, 60.
32. Saward 1980, 22. Cf. Kovalevskii 1895, 135–36.
33. Valuable sources on the Raskol and the Old Believers include: Zen'kovskii 1970; Cherniavsky 1966; Crummey 1970.
34. Avvakum 1979 (1673), 52.
35. Ibid., 61.
36. Cf. Likhachev in Likhachev and Panchenko 1976, 75–89.

37. Hunt 1985, 29.
38. Ibid., 30.
39. Kenneth Brostrom in his introduction to Avvakum 1979, 22. In his discussion of Avvakum's "rock-ribbed passivity" (161) Brostrom comes close to recognizing that Avvakum was a masochist.
40. Sapozhnikov 1891, 123.
41. Ibid., end flap; cf. Crummey 1970, 39–57.
42. Crummey 1970, 51, 46. As Crummey points out, some Old Believers had the good sense to avoid suicidal confrontations with the authorities, and advocated avoidance of self-immolation.
43. Ziolkowski 1988, 197–217.
44. Some useful and heterogeneous sources from the enormous literature on Russian sectarianism include: Klibanov 1982 (1965); Leroy-Beaulieu 1902–5, vol. 3, 399–507; Billington 1968, 174–80; Munro 1980; Grass 1907–14; Mel'gunov 1919; Kutepov 1900; Steeves 1983. A chapter of Mel'gunov's book (157–202) vigorously defends sectarians against such labels as "pathological" and "degenerate" attached to them by pre-psychoanalytic psychiatrists in Russia.

   Yuri Glazov compares the all-male sadomasochistic collective of "thieves" ("vory") in the Soviet gulag with the Khlysty. The "thieves" were hardened criminals who killed ordinary prisoners without compunction, and who took great pride in being able to inflict various mutilations upon themselves, such as swallowing broken glass or cutting off a finger or a hand (1985, 43–44).
45. Billington 1968, 179.
46. Averintsev 1988.
47. Toporov 1987, 246.
48. As quoted by Fedotov 1975, vol. 2, 210.
49. In Avvakum 1979, 189–91.
50. As quoted by Dunlop 1972, 137.
51. Szamuely 1974, 64; Toporov 1987, 219; Siniavskii 1991, 172–73.
52. Thanks to Yuri Druzhnikov for this proverb.
53. Dunlop 1972, 123.
54. Ibid., 41.
55. As translated by Gorodetzky 1973, 34. For the Russian original see Gogol' 1937–52, vol. 8, 348. For a comprehensive study of Gogol's "forgotten book," see Sobel 1981.
56. As translated by Gorodetzky 1973, 34.
57. E.g., Fedotov 1942, 35; 1975, vol. 2, 210.
58. Gorodetzky 1973 (1938), ix. Cf. Ziolkowski 1988, 126ff.
59. Fedotov 1942, 35.
60. This according to Clark and Holquist 1984, 84–87, 128. I have made some remarks on Bakhtin's masochistic epistemology (Rancour-Laferriere 1990, 524).
61. Berdiaev 1971 (1946), 30.

62. Radishchev 1958, 146; Russian original is Radishchev 1961 (1790), 89.
63. Radishchev 1958, 152; Radishchev 1961, 93.
64. Radishchev 1958, 214; 1961, 145.
65. Pushkin 1962–65, vol. 7, 291.
66. Marina Gromyko, in her fascinating compendium *Mir russkoi derevni*, quotes the same passage from Pushkin as evidence for the positive and worthy features of the Russian peasant (1991, 94). She also quotes extensively from various published and unpublished ethnographic sources to demonstrate the existence of such qualities as intelligence, generosity, industry, honesty, and dignity among the peasants. Evidence for the peasant's less admirable qualities, however, is played down by Gromyko—as if diverse or even contradictory qualities could not coexist. This is a perhaps understandable reaction against the brutal treatment of peasants and peasant culture by Soviet authority, and against the negative characterizations of the peasantry which had been offered by Soviet scholars and pseudo-scholars in the past.
67. Chaadayev 1969, 58. For the French original, see Tchaadaev 1970, 75.
68. Chaadayev 1969, 36.
69. Ibid., 37.
70. Chaadaev 1989, 204. For the French original, only recently published in Russia, see Chaadaev 1991, vol. 1, 256. See also Kamenskii 1986.
71. Chaadaev 1991, vol. 1, 256.
72. Chaadaev 1969, 57.
73. Gertsen 1962 (1852–68), vol. 1, 449.
74. See also Chaadaev 1989, 210–211.
75. Chaadayev 1969, 178; Tchaadaev 1970, 211.
76. Chaadaev 1989, 203. For the French original, see Chaadaev 1991, vol. 1, 255.
77. As quoted by Pipes 1974, 266.
78. The ambivalence tended to get resolved in favor of submissiveness. For example, although Chaadaev spoke of the existence of free will, he saw it as illusory (Chaadayev 1969, 89). He repeatedly insisted on the need for *submission* to some higher intellect or some moral imperative in life. For example: "The mind is powerful only because it is submissive" (70; see also pp. 69, 71, 73, 75).

   Boris Tarasov, writing in a recent issue of *Literaturnaia gazeta*, detects (but does not psychoanalyze) the ambivalence of Chaadaev's feelings on a variety of topics, e.g., on whether or not Christianity is good for Russia. See Tarasov 1990; see also Lednicki (1954, 29) on the "inconsistent mind" of Chaadaev, and Z. A. Kamenskii's introduction to the 1991 edition (vol. 1, 9–85) on the "paradoxes of Chaadaev."

   Philip Pomper detects Chaadaev's own masochistic strain when he refers to the "luxuriant self-castigation" in a passage from *The Philosophical Letters* (Pomper 1970, 36). In this case, too, psychoanalysis is not actually applied, but is implicit.

   Julia Brun-Zejmis, in a very interesting recent article about national inferiority feelings in Russia, recognizes Chaadaev's masochistic side: "Chaadaev's pessimistic pronouncements about Russia answered a need for self-condemnation" (1991, 649).

79. Mickiewicz 1974, 306. Thanks to David Brodsky for the English translation.

80. Letter of 13 February 1991.

81. Lednicki 1954, 51.

82. See Kennan 1971 and Erofeev's 1990 review of Custine 1989. For the original French I rely here on Custine 1843, in four volumes.

Custine's travelogue is not without its problems. The author did not visit all of the major cities in Russia, nor did he communicate with Russians of all social classes. He was able to converse only with those Russians who knew French or some other Western language, which is to say that his in-depth contacts were limited primarily to members of the Russian nobility or government officials of various kinds. Custine does tend to ramble (he admits to "the wandering character of my thoughts," 282). The book is also repetitive, especially concerning those Russian practices that Custine does not like, such as the tendency of the Russian nobility to ape the French. As Kennan has observed (1971, 75), Custine holds contradictory views toward Tsar Nicholas, and these are symptoms of a "most painful, almost tortured, ambivalence." Custine does tend to exaggerate what is bad about Russia (ibid., 120). Sometimes Custine is wrong in matters of fact, as when he applies his observations about Russians to "Slavonians" generally (e.g., "All the Slavonian peasants [tous les paysans slaves] are thieves" [496], a sweeping statement that is not necessarily true even if limited to Russians). Custine can also be quite mistaken in interpretative matters, as when he dismisses the importance of Pushkin's poetry (289) or harshly judges the art inside of Russian Orthodox churches (e.g., 424).

But most critics agree that Custine's book is remarkably insightful. Alexander Herzen declared that it was "unquestionably the most diverting and intelligent book written about Russia by a foreigner," and Viktor Erofeev writes that "Herzen's words are still true today, despite the thousands of books written about Russia since that time" (Erofeev 1990, 23). Custine spoke with "true bearded Russians," even if in French. As he quite correctly observes at the end of his book, "I have not fully seen, but I have fully divined" (617).

In Yuri Druzhnikov's recent novel *Angels on the Head of a Pin* (1989), a condensed samizdat version of Custine's work turns up on the desk of a Soviet newspaper editor. The antics which follow demonstrate that Custine's ideas are every bit as relevant to Brezhnev-era Russia as to the Russia of Nicholas I. As the author of the novel points out, a complete and uncensored Russian translation of Custine's work has yet to be published.

83. Custine 1989, 595; 1843, vol. 4, 313.

84. Custine 1989, 619.

85. Olearius 1967 (1656), 147.

86. Chaadaev 1989, 202. Kennan is inclined to believe that Custine was influenced by Chaadaev's *First Philosophical Letter* (1971, 39–40). For a more detailed comparison of Chaadaev and Custine, see Lednicki 1954, 56ff.
87. Masaryk 1955–67, vol. 1, 135.
88. Custine 1989, 21.
89. Ibid., 234.
90. Ibid., 16.
91. Ibid., 205.
92. Ibid., 171.
93. Lermontov 1961–62, vol. 1, 524. The poem was apparently written in April of 1841 on the occasion of Lermontov's last exile from Russia to the Caucasus (Viskovatyi 1891, 379).
94. As translated by Liberman 1983, 556.
95. For a psychoanalytic study of this poem, see Rancour-Laferriere 1993b. It is worth noting that Lermontov's poem is still offensive to many in Russia. For example, when filmmakers El'dar Riazanov and Grigorii Gorin attempted to include the poem in a film they were making about Lermontov in 1980, officials from Gosteleradio forced them to delete it (see Tucker 1991, 39).
96. For more on the multifarious connections between these writers (excluding Radishchev), see Lednicki 1954, 21–104. I wish to thank David Brodsky for bringing Lednicki's book to my attention.
97. Kolakowski 1992, 5.
98. Custine 1989, 195, italics added; 1843, vol. 2, 46.
99. Custine 1989, 361. Cf. 274.
100. Ibid., 362.
101. Dostoievsky 1949, vol. 1, 186. For the Russian original: Dostoevskii 1972–88, vol. 22, 29.
102. Dostoievsky 1949, vol. 1, 186; Dostoevskii 1972–88, vol. 22, 29.
103. Custine 1989, 362, italics added.
104. Khomiakov 1955, 115.
105. Leatherbarrow and Offord 1987, 99. For the Russian original, see Brodskii 1910, 78.
106. Leatherbarrow and Offord 1987, 98; Brodskii 1910, 74.
107. Leatherbarrow and Offord 1987, 104; original in Brodskii 1910, 88. Cf. Ivan Kireevsky (Kireevskii 1984, 209), who says that the Tatars, Poles, Hungarians, Germans, and other scourges sent upon the Russians by Providence were not able to change the essential "inner and social life" of the Russians—as if the "inner" and the "social" were the same thing.
108. Billington 1968, 19.
109. Walicki 1989, 192.
110. Leatherbarrow and Offord 1987, 65. On the problem of translating *sobornost'*, see Christoff 1961, 139ff.
111. Arsen'ev 1959, 66–109.

112. Solzhenitsyn 1991 (1990), 101.
113. Leatherbarrow and Offord 1987, 94. For the Russian original, see Khomiakov 1955, 182. See Riasanovsky 1955 for a detailed study of *sobornost'* in Khomiakov's works.
114. For a useful review of the contentious literature on the genesis and development of the commune in Russia, see Shanin 1985, 78–81. For more on the psychology of communal life, see 215–24 herein.
115. Kireevskii 1984, 226.
116. Walicki 1989, 256.
117. Aksakov, 1861–80, vol. 1, 291–92, as translated in Walicki 1989, 256–57.
118. See Ivanov 1971–79, vol. 2, 219.
119. Aksakov 1861–80, vol. 1, 629 (mistakenly paginated as 229).
120. Young 1979, 139; cf. 154–56.
121. Solov'ev 1966–69, vol. 3, 113; Billington 1968, 468. See Mochul'skii 1951, 179, for further examples of Solov'ev's contradictory ideas on freedom.
122. Solzhenitsyn 1976, 136.
123. See, for example, Ivanov 1969, 131.
124. Cf. Walicki 1989, 197–99.
125. Stein suggests that the idealized collective was, for Khomiakov, maternal in nature (1976, 428). This is consonant with the general psychoanalytic findings on the attitude of the individual to the collective in Russia and elsewhere (see chap. 9).
126. Kireevskii 1984, 122.
127. Translated in Leatherbarrow and Offord 1987, 147 from Gertsen 1954–65, vol. 7, 333.
128. Gertsen 1954–65, vol. 7, 113/243.
129. Ibid., 322–23.
130. See especially Venturi 1960.
131. For example: *"Bless you, prison,* for having been in my life!" See Solzhenitsyn 1975a, 610, 611, 617; 1974, 598, 599.
132. Ulam 1976, 29. Pomper (1970, 102) refers to Chernyshevsky's "almost pathological self-subordination to his wife."
133. Blanchard 1984, 58.
134. Ibid., 58.
135. See Pipes 1989, 103–121.
136. Billington 1968, 394.
137. Fedotov 1942, 29.
138. Szamuely 1974, 152.
139. As quoted by Gorodetzky 1973, 89.
140. Gorodetzky 1973, 90 is quoting socialist thinker Petr L. Lavrov.
141. Fedotov 1942, 33.
142. Wortman 1967, 7.
143. Ibid., 8.

144. Ibid., 54.
145. Terrorists could be masochistic as well as sadistic, for their aggressive acts were often impractical and self-defeating. Thus Dmitrii Karakazov, who made an attempt on the life of Tsar Alexander in 1866, is characterized by Pomper (1970, 91) as "a miserable and suicidal person, one of those who place their self-destructive impulse in the service of some larger cause."
146. *Vekhi* 1909, 20; Fedotov 1954 (1938), 4; Hubbs 1988, 230.
147. Szamuely 1974, 160, 161; cf. Masaryk 1955–67, vol. 2, 108.
148. Dunham 1960, 482; cf. 476 on self-laceration.
149. Berlin 1979, 125.
150. Ibid., 168; cf. Chances 1978 (16) on Belinsky's praise of humility (*smirenie*) and self-renunciation (*samootrechenie*) during this period.
151. Merezhkovskii 1914, vol. 15, 173.
152. Ibid., 61.
153. Ibid., 147. Nikitenko himself speaks of the "servile spirit" of Russians ("nashemu kholopskomu dukhu"—ibid., 154).
154. Ibid., 146.
155. Ibid., 178.
156. Ibid., 66.
157. See discussion on 93–94, on the essentials of "moral masochism."
158. The story is in the collection *Black on White* (Gippius 1908), 95–105.
159. As quoted by Merezhkovskii 1914, vol. 15, 60.
160. Ibid., 174, italics added.
161. E.g., Toporov 1987, 220; Ivanov 1909, 331.
162. Merezhkovskii 1914, vol. 15, 175–76.
163. Ibid., 178.
164. Rozanov 1990b, 414.
165. Ibid., 100–102.
166. Rozanov 1990a, 253.
167. Rozanov 1990b, 351. Gor'kii was quite right to speak of Rozanov's slavishness before God ("rabstvo pered bogom Vashe"—1978 [1912], 306).
168. E.g., Berdiaev 1990, 38–39.
169. Cf. Crone 1978, 28–30.
170. Rozanov 1990b, 106.
171. Fedorov 1906–13; 1928–29. For a clear treatment of Fedorov's life and work, see Young 1979. For new information on Fedorov's biography, see Semenova 1990 (who unfortunately disregards most Western research on Fedorov).
172. Fedorov 1928–29, part I, 5.
173. E.g., Fedorov 1906–13, vol. 2, 205.
174. Fedorov 1928–29, part I, 34. See also Wiles (1965, 133–34) on Fedorov's devaluation of mothers.
175. As quoted by Young 1979, 67.
176. Ibid., 75.
177. Ivanov 1909, 361.

178. Berdyaev 1944 (1939), 48.
179. Ibid., 27.
180. Ibid., 138.
181. Berdiaev 1971 (1946), 81.
182. Ibid., 13.
183. Ibid., 145, 255.
184. Berdiaev 1991, 15.
185. Berdiaev 1990, 13.
186. Berdiaev 1991, 14.
187. Ibid., 59. Many have noticed the prevalence and importance of words with the root -*rod*- in the Russian language (e.g., Likhachev 1987, vol. 2, 421–22), although no one has considered this word-nest from a psychoanalytic angle. As will be seen repeatedly in this book (particularly in connection with the discussion of Dostoevsky's maternal collective, below, 241–42), Russians like to exploit the maternal suggestiveness of -*rod*- words.
188. Berdiaev 1991, 56. This statement is repeated on the next page as well.
189. Berdiaev 1990, 12.
190. Russian original and English translation in Markov and Sparks 1967, 510–11.
191. Grossman 1973, 176 (cf. 90 herein). Actually, the metaphor of Russia as bride and Russia's leader as groom is quite ancient (although it is not nearly as commonplace as the related imagery of Russia as mother and its leader as father). See, for example: Uspenskii 1988, 117–18; Hubbs 1988, 187–90.
192. Lenin 1958–65, vol. 26, 107. I wish to thank my colleague Yuri Druzhnikov for bringing Lenin's article to my attention.
193. Lenin 1958–65, vol. 26, 107.
194. Ibid., 108.
195. Ibid.
196. Custine 1989, 608, italics added.
197. Kennan 1971, 124; cf. Tucker 1991, 38.
198. Ibid., 131, italics added.
199. See Brun-Zejmis 1991. This author's idea that Russian messianism is a compensation for feelings of national inferiority is psychoanalytic in essence (one is reminded of the work of Adler and Kohut in particular).
200. Altaev 1977 (1969), 131, italics added.
201. Evtushenko 1988, 13.
202. Excerpts of Evtushenko (1988) were translated for *Time* magazine by Antonina Bouis (Yevtushenko 1988).
203. Yevtushenko 1988, 31.
204. Custine 1989, 474–75; 1843, vol. 4, 49.
205. Yevtushenko 1988, 31.
206. As quoted from the Western digest version of *Nezavisimaia gazeta,* vol. 1, issue 20–21, July 1992, p. 1.
207. *Literaturnaia gazeta,* no. 41, 7 October 1992, p. 1. In the poem Voznesen-

skii compares Russia to the famous poet Marina Tsvetaeva, who committed suicide.
208. Grafova 1991, 6.
209. Solzhenitsyn 1991, 4–5; for the original, see Solzhenitsyn 1990, 3.
210. *Moskovskie novosti*, no. 42, 18 October 1992, p. 23.
211. Tsipko 1991, 7.
212. Golovanov 1992, 13.
213. Zaslavskaya 1984, 106.
214. As quoted by Mikhail Heller 1988, 134 (= Geller 1985, 151). For a documentary study of alcoholism in the Soviet Union, see Boris Segal's fascinating book *The Drunken Society* (1990).
215. Belkin 1991a, 4.
216. E.g., Tkachenko and Iakubova 1992.

NOTES TO CHAPTER 3

1. Dal' 1984 (1862), vol. 2, 191–92.
2. Wierzbicka 1992, 189.
3. *Vekhi* 1909, 48ff.
4. Berdiaev 1991, 64.
5. Berdiaev 1990, 76. If in some of his writings Berdiaev manifests a positive attitude toward *smirenie,* as Wierzbicka has shown (1992, 189–90), this means that he is ambivalent about the subject. In any case I cannot agree with Wierzbicka's idea that *smirenie* is a consistently positive and exclusively religious notion.
6. Freud 1989 (1928), 41.
7. Khomiakov 1955, 83.
8. Ibid., 397.
9. Ibid., 83.
10. Berdiaev 1968 (1921), 164.
11. As quoted by Wierzbicka 1992, 188.
12. Dal' 1984 (1862), vol. 2, 194.
13. Custine 1989, 501, italics added.
14. Custine 1843, vol. 4, 103.
15. Fenichel 1945, 364.
16. Sarnoff 1988, 209.
17. Pipes 1974, 161.
18. Kavelin 1882, 151.
19. Wierzbicka 1992, 67.
20. As quoted by Wierzbicka 1992, 72.
21. See Andreev's motif-index of folktales (1929, 67), which includes about a dozen items on *sud'ba* and the related "dolia" (roughly, "one's lot in life").
22. Example furnished by Yuri Druzhnikov. Recently in the Russian press the word *sud'ba* has been frequently appearing in the plural form (e.g., "sud'by

naroda," "sud'by otechestva"). Mikhail Epshtein has written about this phenomenon (1989, 312ff.). This is no doubt yet another reflection of the increasing "pluralism" of Russian society.

23. Cherniavsky 1961, 132. I have modified his translation somewhat.
24. Wierzbicka 1992, 70.
25. Mel'chuk and Zholkovskii 1984, 857–66.
26. Dal' 1955 (1880–82), vol. 4, 356.
27. Wierzbicka 1992, 108; cf. esp. the section on "not being in control," 413–30.
28. As quoted by Wierzbicka 1992, 113.
29. Hubbs 1990, 59.
30. For examples, see Dal' 1984 (1862), vol. 1, 39–40. See also Fedotov 1975, 1, 349–50.
31. Cf. Martynova 1978, 182.
32. Martynova 1978, 178.
33. Anikin 1991, 68.
34. See Farnsworth 1992, 149. Eremina (1992) attempts to show that the death-wish lullabies were really an attempt to "deceive death," to ward off the child's possible death by concocting an apotropaic "contact with death."
35. Dal' 1984, vol. 1, 298.
36. Dunn 1974, 384.
37. Ransel 1988, 266ff.; Ransel 1991. Cf. Semenova-Tian-Shanskaia 1914, 57; Dunn 1974, 388ff.; Hoch 1986, 68–69.
38. Ransel 1991, 120.
39. Baiburin 1993, 52.
40. Dal' 1984 (1862), vol. 1, 221.
41. Ibid., 45.
42. See, for example, Selivanov 1991, 73.
43. Ibid.
44. Reik 1963, 163.
45. Infanticide did sometimes occur among the peasantry. An illegitimate infant might be drowned, suffocated, or poisoned, for example (e.g., Semenova-Tian-Shanskaia 1914, 57–58).
46. Mel'chuk and Zholkovskii 1984, 860.
47. Gertsen 1954–65, vol. 7, 185.
48. Nekrasov 1967, vol. 2, 274.
49. Durova 1988 (1836), 34.
50. Boiko 1988, 197.

NOTES TO CHAPTER 4

1. Merezhkovskii 1914, vol. 16, 166–67. Compare Maksim Gor'kii's assertion that Russian writers (including the greats, Dostoevsky and Tolstoy) offer

an "apology for passivity" and support violence "by preaching patience, reconciliation, forgiveness, justification" (Gor'kii 1937 [1905], 8, 9).
2. Gorodetzky 1973, 27–74. Cf. Fedotov 1942, which bears some curious resemblances to Gorodetzky, although Fedotov writes more clearly.
3. Ziolkowski 1988.
4. As translated by Gorodetzky 1973, 42. For the Russian original, see Turgenev 1960–68, vol. 10, 175.
5. Translated by Gorodetzky 1973, 39. Cf. Turgenev 1960–68, vol. 4, 358.
6. See Rancour-Laferriere 1993a; 1993d. On Tolstoy's own masochism, see Blanchard 1984, 31–43.
7. Rosen 1993, 430.
8. Wasiolek 1964, 54.
9. There is an enormous psychoanalytic literature on Dostoevsky which gives due attention to the roles of guilt, abjection, suffering, humiliation, punishment, and related psychological issues in the life and works of this great author. See, for example: Freud 1989 (1928); Rancour-Laferriere 1989b, 6–10; Geha 1970; Bonaparte 1962; Kristeva 1982, 18–20; Paris 1973; Dalton 1979, 68ff.; Breger 1989, 25ff., 102, 196; Rosen 1993. Gorodetzky (1973, 59–69) treats Dostoevsky in terms of the humiliated Christ, and numerous other non-psychoanalytic critics have also paid ample attention to Dostoevsky's cult of suffering.
10. Dostoyevsky 1980, 415, 433.
11. Ibid., 438.
12. Saltykov-Shchedrin 1980, 36. The Russian original is Saltykov-Shchedrin 1965–77, vol. 8, 292.
13. Saltykov-Shchedrin 1980, 10. The Russian original is Saltykov-Shchedrin 1965–77, vol. 8, 270.
14. Saltykov-Shchedrin 1980, 98, 152; 1965–77, vol. 8, 350, 401.
15. Seifrid 1992.
16. Smirnov 1987; 1990.
17. Clark 1985, 178.
18. Solzhenitsyn 1989, 361–62; 1978–, vol. 11, 426–27.
19. Pipes 1991, 213.
20. Dostoyevsky 1950, 618, italics added; Dostoevskii 1972–88, vol. 14, 458. Cf. Wierzbicka 1992, 71.
21. Dostoyevsky 1950, 615–16; Dostoevskii 1972–88, vol. 14, 456–57.
22. Dostoyevsky 1950, 617, italics added; Dostoevskii 1972–88, vol. 14, 458.
23. Dostoyevsky 1950, 617–18, italics added. I have had to make some corrections in the Garnett translation. Cf. Dostoevskii 1972–88, vol. 14, 458.
24. See Chaitin 1972, 80ff.; Besançon 1968, 348. I agree with Chaitin's suggestion that Dmitrii's desire for imprisonment is the result of Oedipal guilt. Having wished to kill his father, and having gained possession of the maternal Grushenka, his father's mistress, Dmitrii deserves the Oedipal talion punishment.

But this Oedipal reading does not exclude a pre-Oedipal one, for the desire for punishment can be overdetermined (see chap. 5 herein).

25. See Rozanov 1903, vol. 2, 98.
26. Pushkin 1962–66, vol. 5, 70–71.
27. Nabokov 1981, vol. 1, 166.
28. Dostoevskii 1972–1988, vol. 26, 140. Cf. Hubbs 1988, 216.
29. Nabokov 1981, vol. 1, 228.
30. Ibid., 185; Pushkin 1962–66, vol. 5, 86.
31. Cf. Hubbs 1988, 216.
32. Nabokov 1981, vol. 1, 205; Pushkin 1962–66, vol. 5, 100.
33. See Rancour-Laferriere 1989a.
34. See, for example Freud, *SE,* vol. 9, 220; Fenichel 1945, 214.
35. For a psychoanalytic interpretation of Tat'iana's dream, see Rancour-Laferriere 1989a.
36. It is in any case normal, cross-culturally, for the object of love in adulthood to be a parental figure from the past. Biologists, anthropologists, and psychologists of various stripes (including of course psychoanalysts) have studied this phenomenon. See Rancour-Laferriere 1985, 108ff., 196ff.
37. Nabokov 1981, vol. I, 161; Pushkin 1962–66, vol. 5, 66.
38. Nabokov 1981, vol. 1, 304–5; Pushkin 1962–66, vol. 5, 187.
39. Pushkin 1962–66, 187–88.
40. Nabokov 1981, 305.
41. Pushkin 1962–66, 188.
42. Nabokov 1981, 306.
43. Grossman 1973, 173.
44. Grossman 1973, 174, 175. The freedom/slavery opposition also plays an important role in *Life and Fate.* See Garrard 1991b. For Chaadaev's influence on Grossman, see Brun-Zejmis 1991, 649–50.
45. Grossman 1973, 30.
46. Ibid., 176–77.
47. Ibid., 180.
48. Ibid., 181.
49. See Svirskii 1979, 300.
50. On this controversy, see the attack by Antonov, Klykov, and Shafarevich (1989) on Anatolii Anan'ev, who had published *Forever Flowing* in his journal *Oktiabr'* (he was later fired, then reinstated). See also: Bocharov and Lobanov 1989; Anan'ev 1990; Garrard 1991a.
51. Anan'ev 1990, 14.
52. Grossman 1973, 175, 178, 183. Cf. also 70–71.

NOTES TO CHAPTER 5

1. Freud, *SE,* vol. 19, 165.
2. Horney 1964 (1937), 228, italics added.

3. Freud, *SE,* vol. 22, 106–7.
4. Freud, *SE,* vol. 19, 168. Cf. Dicks 1952, 139.
5. Loewenstein 1957, 230.
6. Freud 1989 (1928), 47.
7. Freud, *SE,* vol. 19, 169.
8. See, for example: Bergler 1949; Winnicott 1960; Kohut 1971; Dinnerstein 1976; Chodorow 1978; Mahler et al. 1975; Rancour-Laferriere 1985, 196ff.; Brunswick 1940; Fisher and Greenberg 1977, 187ff.; Klein 1977 (1921–45); Greenberg and Mitchell 1983; Asch 1988; Meyers 1988; Stern 1977; Koenigsberg 1989; Horner 1992.
9. Bergler 1949, 5. The idea that the painful experience is a compulsive *repetition* of some previous experience goes back of course to Freud's idea of the "repetition compulsion" ("Wiederholungszwang") as a means of mastering previous trauma. See 98 herein.
10. Cf. Socarides 1958, 588.
11. Novick and Novick 1987, 360.
12. Dinnerstein 1976, 166. Cf. Rancour-Laferriere 1985, 120; 260ff.
13. See Reik 1941, 427–33.
14. Cooper 1988, 120.
15. Katz 1990, 235.
16. Stern 1977, 122–23.
17. See, for example: Freud, *SE,* vol. 14, 127–29; Fenichel 1945, 360ff. In his later work Freud came to view masochism as a manifestation of the so-called "death instinct" (e.g., *SE,* vol. 19, 164, 170). Psychoanalysts have not received this idea with enthusiasm.
18. Bieber 1966, 268. Compare a scene described by McDevitt (1983, 281): "During his eighth month, when his father's arm interfered with his water play, Peter tried to push it aside and then bit it. Later, when his mother said, "No," when he started to bite her, he bit himself instead."
19. Bieber 1966, 267.
20. Fenichel 1945, 542.
21. Freud, *SE,* vol. 18, 3–64.
22. As phrased by Cooper 1988, 122. See also Bergler 1949.
23. Reik (1941, 156ff.) is very good on the assertiveness and defiance inherent in masochistic behavior.
24. Cooper 1988, 123.
25. Bergler 1949, 6, italics added.
26. Kernberg 1988, 68.
27. Ibid., 69.
28. Bergler 1949, 203ff.
29. Kernberg 1988, 63; cf. Asch 1988, 110.
30. Berliner 1958, 46.
31. Fenichel 1945, 363.
32. Socarides 1958, 589.
33. Berliner 1958, 44.

34. Menaker 1979, 66.
35. Freud, *SE*, vol. 14, 248.
36. Dostoyevsky 1950, 692; Dostoevskii 1972–88, vol. 15, 10.
37. Fedotov 1975, vol. 1, 294.
38. Hunt 1974, 333.
39. Kinsey et al. 1965 (1953), 677; Hunt 1974, 333.
40. For some of the abundant cross-cultural evidence that men typically have higher social status and power than women, see Rancour-Laferriere 1985, chap. 40.
41. See Baumeister 1989, 147ff.
42. Chancer 1992, 29.
43. Freud, *SE*, vol. 19, 161–62.
44. Compare, for example, Deutsch 1930 with Blum 1977. See also Rancour-Laferriere 1985, 280–82.
45. See, for example, Caplan 1985, who suggests that not only is there no female masochism, there is no such thing as masochism, period.
46. Kass 1987.
47. Rosewater 1987, 191.
48. Ibid., 192.
49. See, for example, the review of the research in this area by Brody 1985.
50. Rosewater 1987, 191.
51. Ibid., 194.
52. See, for example, Walker 1987, 186; Walker and Browne 1985, 186.
53. Walker and Browne 1985, 187.
54. Walker 1987, 186.
55. Rancour-Laferriere 1988a.
56. Asch 1988, 107. For a discussion of the many problems involved in treating masochistic patients, see Panken 1973, 143–95.
57. Asch 1988, 108.
58. Meyers 1988, 180.
59. Ibid., 1988, 183–84.
60. Ibid., 184.
61. See, for example: Cooper 1988, 127; Caplan 1985, 88. See also Baumeister's formulation: "I hurt, therefore I am" (1989, 75).
62. Stolorow 1975, 442. Cf. Warren 1985 (104), who argues that masochists "actively seek pain because feeling pain has become an essential part of their identity (e.g., they see themselves as victims)."
63. Stolorow 1975, 443.
64. Baumeister 1989, 201.
65. Baumeister attempts to reconcile his theory with Stolorow's in a somewhat different way (1989, 195–99).
66. Horney 1964 (1937), 230. Horney credits this idea to another analyst, Erich Fromm.
67. Fromm 1965 (1941).

68. Lane, Hull, and Foehrenbach 1991, 399, italics added.
69. Ibid., 397, italics added.
70. Warren 1985, 116.
71. As quoted by Walicki 1989, 248.
72. Leatherbarrow and Offord 1987, 105.
73. Shafarevich 1989, 173.
74. Kohut 1971.
75. Stolorow 1975, 444. Cf.: Berliner 1958; Menaker 1979; Loewenstein 1957.
76. Cf. Berger 1967, 74.
77. Avvakum 1979 (1673), 112.
78. Nydes 1963, 248.
79. Brenner 1959, 224.
80. See, for example, LaPlanche and Pontalis 1973, 414–15.
81. As quoted by Bolshakoff 1977, 192, italics added.
82. See Rancour-Laferriere 1988b.
83. But see Horney 1967, 214–33; Bergler 1949, 108; Cooper 1988, 125.
84. Condee and Padunov 1987, 316.
85. Toporov 1987, 220.
86. Gromyko 1991, 126–29.
87. Dal' 1984 (1862), vol. 1, 162–63; cf. Illiustrov 1904, 317ff.
88. Cf. the discussion of Russian "universal guilt" in Mead 1951, 27–29, 91–93.
89. Tolstoi 1928–64, vol. 23, 469–70, as modified from the translation by Gustafson 1986, 20.
90. See Laplanche and Pontalis 1973, 411. Tolstoy himself says that he is not certain whether this incident (and some others in this particular memoir) really took place or he dreamed it (469). He also states that he doesn't know whether the incident took place while he was still nursing and less than a year old, or later when he had an outbreak of sores and was swaddled to prevent scratching (470).
91. See especially Gorer and Rickman 1962; Benedict 1949; Mead 1954; Whiting 1981; Kluckhohn 1962, 237ff.; Erikson 1963 (1950), 388–92; Dunn 1974, 386–87; Lipton et al. 1965; Chisholm 1983; Dundes 1984, 93ff. For a rare Soviet contribution on the swaddling hypothesis, see Kon 1968, 222.
92. Dunn 1974, 387.
93. Gorer in Gorer and Rickman 1962, 123, 128.
94. See especially Lipton et al. 1965.
95. Kluckhohn 1962, 237–40.
96. Bronfenbrenner 1972, 9–10.
97. Semenova-Tian-Shanskaia 1914, 29.

NOTES TO CHAPTER 6

1. Dal' 1984 (1862), vol. 1, 341.
2. Shafarevich 1989, 190.
3. *Moskovskie novosti,* no. 43, 27 October 1991, p. 2.
4. *Literaturnaia gazeta,* no. 33, 21 August 1991, p. 1.
5. Gel'man 1992, 24.
6. See especially Likhachev and Panchenko 1976, and the discussion of Fools in Christ herein, 21–22.
7. As in Nikolai Zlatovratskii's narodnik novel *Foundations* (1951 [1878–83], 24).
8. Items 1204, 1240, 1244, 1681, 1685, 1716 in Barag et al. 1979.
9. Dal' 1984, vol. 1, 343; Smirnov-Kutachevskii 1905, 22.
10. Dal' 1984, vol. 1, 342.
11. Ibid., 339, 343.
12. Merezhkovskii 1914, vol. 15, 173.
13. See, for example: Leroy-Beaulieu 1902–5, vol. 2, 278ff., 384ff.; Eklof 1991; Worobec 1991, 211–13; Kolchin 1987, 71–77, 120–26, 304; Belliustin 1985 (1858), 73; Hoch 1986, 160–86; Evreinov 1979 (1913?). For a plethora of proverbs on corporal punishment, see Illiustrov 1904, 327ff. There is an exceptionally large entry in Dahl's dictionary under the verb "bit'" ("to beat," vol. 1, 88–90). See also the discussion of birch rods herein, 184. There are indications that corporal punishment of children is still common in Russia (Gamaiunov 1992).

    Flogging was very common during the period of serfdom. For example, Hoch calculates that for the period 1826–28 in the village of Petrovskoe in Tambov province, there was a mean of 0.27 floggings per adult worker per year; based on thirteen years of complete data for the mid-nineteenth century in Petrovskoe, "roughly one-quarter of all adult male serfs were disciplined at least once during the course of a year" (Hoch 1986, 162–63).
14. Dal' 1984 (1862), vol. 1, 347, 348.
15. Example provided by Yuri Druzhnikov. Cf. English: "It takes one to know one" (thanks to Catherine Chvany for this example).
16. Dal' 1984 (1862), vol. 1, 348.
17. Okudzhava 1982, 95.
18. Dal' 1984 (1862), vol. 1, 346; Carey 1972, 47.
19. For a good overall description (as opposed to a scholarly analysis) of the figure of Ivan the Fool, see Siniavskii 1991, 34ff.
20. Siniavskii 1991, 34.
21. Meletinskii 1958, 227.
22. Smirnov-Kutachevskii 1905.
23. A positive outcome is naturally gratifying to the listener. The nature of this gratification has been ably psychoanalyzed by Bruno Bettelheim in his essay on "The Youngest Child as Simpleton" (1977, 102–11).

24. To phrase this more in terms of Freud's key essay on "Jokes and Their Relation to the Unconscious" (*SE*, vol. 8), we may say: psychical energy or cathexis previously required to repress both sadistic impulses (against objects in the outside world) and masochistic fantasies (especially self-humiliation) is freed up by the figure of the fool, finding momentary outlet in the physiological outburst known as laughter. The behavior of Ivan the fool thus sets off psychological processes which resemble those occurring in what Freud called the "tendentious joke."

25. Cf. Smirnov-Kutachevskii 1905, 15.

26. Not all Ivans are fools, of course. There are other, different kinds of Ivans in Russian folklore: Ivan the tsar's son, Ivan the Bear's ear, Ivan the son of a bitch, Ivan the Terrible, Ivan the son of a mare, Ivan the cow's son, etc. Another way to put this is to say that masochism is only one aspect of Russian national character.

An interesting variation on foolish Ivan's name is the name *Ibanov*, invented by the anti-Soviet satirist Aleksandr Zinoviev, author of *The Yawning Heights* (Zinov'ev 1976). All characters in this novel are named Ibanov. They are a bunch of sad sack intellectuals living in the allegorical land of Ibansk (from "ebat'" ["fuck"] and "Ivan"), admirably translated by Edward J. Brown (1982, 381) as "Fuckupia." All the masochists of Ibansk are, as it were, fucked up. The numerous obscenities in the novel justify this characterization.

27. Semenova-Tian-Shanskaia 1914.

28. Gor'kii 1937, 154–63.

29. Smirnov-Kutachevskii 1905, 44.

30. Likhachev 1987, vol. 2, 425–30.

31. Meletinskij 1975, 242; cf. also Smirnov-Kutachevskii 1905.

32. Likhachev 1987, vol. 2, 428–29.

33. Smirnov-Kutachevskii 1905, 57.

34. Hubbs 1988, 147.

35. See Barag et al. 1979, item 1677.

36. Shergin 1990.

37. Rancour-Laferriere 1985, 200ff.

38. Cf. Rank 1973 (1929), 112. I wish to thank my student Ellen Crecelius for bringing this reference to my attention.

39. Meletinskii 1958, 223.

40. "Pech' nam mat' rodnaia." See Dal' 1955 (1880–82), vol. 3, 108. Sometimes the term "pechka-matushka" is used (Eremina 1991, 158; cf. Hubbs 1988, 58). Freud listed the stove and oven as dream-symbols for the uterus (*SE*, vol. 15, 156, 162). Without mentioning Freud, Toporkov has recently demonstrated the uterine significance of the stove into which a sick child was supposed to be inserted for "re-baking" ("perepekanie") in some East Slavic areas (1992, 115). See also Baiburin 1993 (53–54) on this topic.

41. There is an anal sub-motif within the category of Russian foolishness. We have, for example, the classic Russian self-deprecation: "The Russian is

strong on hindsight," or more literally, "is strong by means of the rear brain" ("Russkii chelovek zadnim umom krepok"). A Russian who is behaving foolishly may be characterized as "thinking with the ass" ("dumat' zhopoi"). The medieval Russian "world of laughter" (Likhachev) also sometimes featured a rear end covered with ash or feces.

42. See Hubbs 1988, 146–47 on the fool's dependency on his mother; Meletinskij 1975, 238–39 (= Meletinskii 1958, 224ff.) on his overall passivity.

43. Dal' 1984 (1862), vol. 1, 345, 340. The root morpheme -rod- is remarkably common among the proverbs about fools.

44. Smirnov-Kutachevskii 1905, 22.

45. Dal' 1984 (1862), vol. 1, 341.

46. Ibid., 339.

47. Ibid., 340.

48. The closest thing to an exception is the subgenre of obscene tales narrated by men, the so-called "zavetnye skazki." Here hostility toward women is frequently expressed by the representation of women as "stupid" regarding sexual matters. For example: a young woman thinks that it is a piglet that a man is putting under her dress (when in fact it is his penis); a girl believes that penises are detachable; a son shows his father that he can get a return on his investment by making a "horny noblewoman" pay for sex with him; etc. (see Afanas'ev 1975 [1872]). It should be noted that the misogynistic sentiments of these tales are often coupled with intense castration anxiety.

49. Cf. Meletinskii 1958, 239.

50. Afanas'ev 1984–85, vol. 3, 117. See also the Andreev (1929) motif-index, no. 1685, and Barag et al. 1979 (same no.).

51. Afanas'ev 1984–85, vol. 3, 116, 117. Cf. Meletinskij 1975, 247. There are numerous psychological variants on this theme where the hero gains riches not directly by means of his mother's dead body, but by destroying objects (a birch tree, a stump, etc.) which turn out to have money inside them, or underneath them. These objects would appear to be substitutes for the maternal body.

52. Zelenin 1991 (1914), 60.

53. Only very rarely does the fool's closeness to the mother have any sexual overtones, e.g.: "Such a fool is the ram: before the feast of Saint Peter he sucks his mother, then after the feast of Saint Peter he fucks her" ("Durak-to baran: do Petrova-dnia matku soset, a posle Petrova-dnia matku ebet") (Carey 1972, 47). The rarity of references to the fool's sexual interaction with the mother (even in the openly obscene lore) is testimony to the essentially pre-Oedipal nature of his relationship with her.

54. See Barag et al. 1979, item no. 1696.

55. Afanasiev 1973, 334–35. For the original Russian, see Afanas'ev 1984–85 (1873), vol. 3, 130–31. I have corrected some infelicities in the Guterman translation.

56. Thanks to Yuri Druzhnikov for pointing this out.

57. Baranskaia 1989, 283.

58. Likhachev 1987, vol. 2, 427.
59. Kruglov 1988–89, vol. 3, 400–403.
60. Tolstoi 1960–65, vol. 10, 48–54. Professor Gary Jahn of the University of Minnesota has pointed out to me that the Tolstoi variant is based on a tale collected by Kirsha Danilov in the late eighteenth century.
61. Thanks to Catherine Chvany for the latter suggestion.

NOTES TO CHAPTER 7

1. As quoted from a 1982 issue of *Krest'ianka* by Bridger 1987, 140.
2. See Rozanov's *Semeinyi vopros,* 1903, vol. 1, 311–12.
3. Dal' 1984, vol. 1, 291.
4. Stites 1990 (1978), 7.
5. E.g., Semenova-Tian-Shanskaia 1914, 19–20.
6. Ibid., 29.
7. Ibid., 6.
8. Worobec 1991, 213.
9. See Cherniavsky 1961 on the ruler myth in tsarist Russia.
10. See, among others: Antonov-Ovseyenko 1983, 229, 269, 306; Rancour-Laferriere 1988a, 112; Belkin 1991a, 4.
11. Bolshakoff 1977, 176–77 is quoting the mystic Alexander Putilov, also known as Anthony (italics added).
12. Friedrich 1972, 285.
13. Kuznetsova 1980, 98.
14. Hansson and Lidén 1983, 153.
15. See, for example: Chodorow 1978; Rancour-Laferriere 1985, 260–67.
16. Smith 1973; Rancour-Laferriere 1985, 123–24. Cf. Maksimenko (1988), who discusses the "matrifocalization" of the urban Russian family during the late Soviet period. Bronfenbrenner speaks of the "mother-centered family" and even "matriarchal patterns" in the Soviet Union (1972, 71ff.).
17. The Soviet anthropological/sociological tradition, influenced by Johann Bachofen's *Das Mutterrecht* (1861) and Friedrich Engels's *The Origin of the Family, Private Property and the State* (1884), has tended to support a "matriarchal" theory of human origins (see: Plotkin and Howe 1985; Kharchev 1979, 10ff.; Kosven 1948; Matorin 1931; Meletinskij 1975, 253; Reshetov 1970 is a daring exception). The book by Kosven, titled *The Matriarchate,* alternates between erudition and Stalinist crudity. Even the ex-Soviet feminist Tatyana Mamonova speaks of "matriarchal Rus'" and the "matriarchal roots in Russian folklore" (1989, 3–8).

   Professional anthropologists in the West and various other scholars have rightly rejected the notion of "matriarchy." No evidence has been found for a society characterized by matrifocal family relations, matrilineal inheritance, and pervasive female dominance of *adult* males. See Rancour-Laferriere 1985, 118–24, for a review of the literature. As feminist Sherry

Ortner says, "the search for a genuinely egalitarian, let alone matriarchal, culture has proved fruitless" (1974, 70).
18. Sakharov 1989 (1885), 50–51.
19. Dicks 1952, 143.
20. Berdiaev 1971, 10. Early Berdiaev is more revealing on this topic. See Berdiaev 1990 (1918), 8–36.
21. Nekrasov 1967, vol. 3, 244, as translated by Gorodetzky 1973, 78.
22. Many of the maternal phenomena that I have enumerated in this section are discussed by Joanna Hubbs in her interesting recent book *Mother Russia* (1988). The enormous literature on motherhood and mother imagery in Russian culture also includes, among others, the following valuable sources: Maksimov 1909, vol. 18, 259ff,; Rybakov 1981, 379–92, 438–70; 1987, 244–47, 437–38; Dicks 1952; Vakar 1961, 67ff.; Barker 1986; Kogan 1982, 97–114; Strotmann 1959; Billington 1968, 19–20; Dunham 1960; Kalustova 1985; Fedotov 1975, vol. 1, 11–20, 296–98, 348–51, 358–62; vol. 2, 135–39; Isaiia 1989; Matorin 1931; Uspenskii 1988; Dal' 1955 (1880–82), vol. 2, 307–8; Ivanits 1989, 15–16, 20–21; Levin 1991; Ransel 1988; 1991; Becker 1990, 110ff.; Siniavskii 1991, 181–92. The figure on "Heroine Mother" awards comes from an anonymous article in *Argumenty i fakty* (3–9 March 1990, p. 1).
23. Drummond and Perkins 1987, 26; Dreizin and Priestly 1982, 42–43; Rancour-Laferriere 1985, 226; Isačenko 1976, 362–64; Uspenskii 1988.
24. Quoted by Uspenskii 1988, 215, from a collection of lore gathered in the Smolensk area in the late nineteenth century.
25. Uspenskii's assertion (1988, 245) that the basis of mat is the image of a dog defiling mother earth has historical validity. But the massive body of historical and comparative linguistic evidence which Uspenskii brings to bear on the phrase "Eb tvoiu mat'" is not something today's Russian (or any Russian in the past) could possibly have been aware of. The Russian who exclaims "Eb tvoiu mat'!" is not making learned allusions, but is expressing gut feelings about maternal sexuality.
26. Uspenskii 1988, 210.
27. Siniavskii 1992, 3.
28. Coe 1984, 44–58.
29. E.g., Kanzer 1948; Besançon 1967, 182–218.
30. Merezhkovskii 1914, vol. 15, 145–66; cf. Cherniavsky 1961, 214.
31. Siniavskii 1974, 183.
32. See the poem "Na dne preispodnei" in Markov and Sparks 1967, 520.
33. Solzhenitsyn 1975, 358.
34. See Hackel 1975, 174, 212.
35. Semenova-Tian-Shanskaia 1914, 18.
36. Ibid., 19.
37. Dal' 1984 (1862), vol. 1, 287.
38. Ibid., 291.

39. I have argued elsewhere (Rancour-Laferriere 1985) that this type of semiosis is a cross-cultural universal.
40. Abandonment of the wife is another alternative frequently resorted to by men in matrifocal cultures. For example, among the Minankabau of Sumatra, or the Black Carib of Belize, or American ghetto blacks, a man is very likely to abandon his mate (Rancour-Laferriere 1985, 123–24, 192–95). In Russia abandonment did not become widespread until the Soviet period, but a husband could always legitimately express hostility by beating the mother of his children. Indeed, a man who *neither* beat a woman *nor* abandoned her was considered a strange fellow (see 154 herein).
41. Dicks 1960, 643.
42. Cf. Dicks 1952, 143, 145.
43. An exception would be the "tsar-father," who was sometimes said to suffer in Christlike fashion (e.g., Cherniavsky 1961, 187; Zhivov and Uspenskii 1987).
44. Nekrasov 1967, vol. 3, 240.
45. Thompson 1989, 503.
46. Pasternak 1989 (1956), 294.
47. Dicks 1960, 643.
48. As quoted by Merezhkovskii 1914, vol. 15, 159.
49. Koenigsberg 1977, 6.
50. Billington 1968, 20.
51. Dostoievsky 1949 (1877), vol. 2, 846.
52. Nekrasov 1967, vol. 2, 274.
53. As quoted by Gray 1990, 168.
54. Hansson and Lidén 1983, 16.
55. Siniavskii 1991, 185.
56. Ivanits 1989, 21.
57. Strotmann 1959, 195.
58. Ibid., 195.
59. Isaiia 1989, 122.
60. Ibid., 123.
61. Solov'ev 1966–69, vol. 9, 188.
62. Siniavskii 1991, 186.
63. Uspenskii 1988, 272.
64. See 141 herein.
65. Hubbs 1988, 112.
66. For example Matorin 1931, 5; Kovalevskii 1895, 150.
67. Dal' 1984 (1862), vol. 1, 294, 302.
68. Ibid., 274.
69. Nekrasov 1967, vol. 2, 371; cf. Heldt 1987, 34.
70. Heldt 1987, 35.
71. Lermontov 1961–62, vol. 4, 396.
72. Tolstoi 1960–65, vol. 7, 298, 301.

73. Pasternak 1989, 47–48.
74. Akhmatova 1973, 98.
75. Gromyko 1989, 16. Warner and Kustovskii are particularly clear and informative on Russian laments: 1990, 38–49, 71–77, 81–86, 105–6.
76. Pushkin 1962–66, vol. 7, 287.
77. Efimenko 1884, 81.
78. Ibid., 83.
79. Kuznetsova 1980, 50.
80. Ibid., 109.
81. Ibid., 150.
82. Kharchev 1970, 18.
83. Sysenko 1981, 7, 27.
84. Worobec 1991, 177.
85. Elsewhere (Rancour-Laferriere 1985, 247–59) I have developed a sociobiological explanation for why, cross-culturally, female deference tends to go with male dominance.
86. E.g., Myl'nikova and Tsintsius 1926, 147; Worobec 1991, 167–70.
87. As quoted from the tsarist law code of 1857 by Kharchev 1979, 123.
88. E.g., Pevin 1893, 247; Semenova-Tian-Shanskaia 1914, 68; Myl'nikova and Tsintsius 1926, 147.
89. Worobec 1991, 187.
90. Ibid., 188.
91. Dal' 1984 (1862), vol. 1, 289, 290, 291, 293.
92. Worobec 1991, 189.
93. Efimenko 1884, 114.
94. Worobec 1991, 189.
95. Kollmann 1991, 70, italics added.
96. Semenova-Tian-Shanskaia 1914, 6.
97. Dal' 1984 (1862), vol. 1, 288, 290, 291.
98. Efimenko 1884, 82.
99. Krafft-Ebing 1929, 36.
100. Kovalevsky 1891, 45.
101. Ralston 1872, 10.
102. As defined by Laplanche and Pontalis 1973, 335.
103. SE, vol. 17, 45.
104. Maksimenko 1988, 145.
105. Freud, SE, vol. 17, 47.
106. Rancour-Laferriere 1985, 277.
107. Nemilov 1932 (1930), 130.
108. The same is true of the verb "parit'" ("to steam," "to beat") (Baiburin 1993, 73).
109. De Armond 1971, 103.
110. He might lie on top of her all night long, but still he would not be able to perform. Cf. Semenova-Tian-Shanskaia 1914, 14.
111. Information provided by Yuri Druzhnikov.

112. Horney 1967, 223–24.
113. Hansson and Lidén 1983, 24, italics added.
114. Attwood 1990, 212. The "double burden" is not an altogether Soviet invention. Russian women who labored in factories before the Bolshevik Revolution often complained about it. Rose Glickman quotes a woman textile worker who, in 1908, declared: "We women have two burdens. At the factory we serve the boss, and at home the husband is our ruler. Nowhere do they see the woman as a real person" (Glickman 1984, 26). Christine Worobec has also pointed to precursors of the woman's double burden in post-emancipation peasant life, e.g., field work added to domestic labor during the short harvest season (Worobec 1991, 206–8).
115. The audience obliges with "prolonged applause." See Brezhnev 1977, 1.
116. Hansson and Lidén 1983, 15.
117. Lapidus points out that in 1946 there were 59 men for every 100 women in the 35–59 age group (1988, 91). For more figures, see Buckley 1989, 189.
118. Lapidus 1988, 92–93. See also Kharchev and Golod 1971, 42, 137; Zaslavskaya 1990, 94.
119. Lapidus 1988, 93; Iankova 1975, 43; Kuznetsova 1980, 19; Sysenko 1981, 76; Shlapentokh 1984, 179; Shineleva 1990, 35; Arutiunian 1992, 171. Although employment is of intrinsic value to a woman, it is of even greater value to a man. For example, Boiko (1988, 103) found that, in a large sample of Leningraders, a good position at work is rated significantly higher by men than by women.
120. Hansson and Lidén 1983, 165.
121. See, for example Lapidus 1978, 171ff.; 1988, 93–99.
122. Tereshkova 1987, 3. For a detailed analysis of women's labor in the Soviet countryside, see Bridger 1987.
123. Goskomstat 1990, 41, 42.
124. Shineleva 1990, 47.
125. Ibid., 37.
126. Lapidus 1988, 103.
127. Iankova (1978, 99) says women in urban areas spend 30–35 hours per week on domestic work, women in rural areas 45–55 hours, and men 15–20 hours. Kharchev (1979, 281) cites some Leningrad data showing that women spend 30.5 hours per week, men 10.5. See also Shlapentokh 1984, 191–93; Bridger 1987, 101, 108–13.
128. *The World's Women* (1991), 101, table 7.
129. Robinson et al. 1989, 133.
130. Shlapentokh 1984, 190.
131. Remennick 1993, 51.
132. Goskomstat 1990, 42–43.
133. Ispa 1983, 5.
134. Iankova 1978, 78, 108.
135. Alexandrova 1984, 49.
136. Marshall 1991, 6.

137. Sarnoff 1988, 209. Cf. Fenichel 1945, 364; Leites 1979, 14–15; Asch 1988, 100, 113.
138. Lapidus 1988, 107.
139. Peers 1985, 124; cf. Allott 1985, 196, who speaks of the "parasitic behaviour" of many Soviet men.
140. Iankova 1975, 48.
141. Sysenko 1981, 53, referring to the work of A. E. Kotliar and S. Ia. Turchaninova.
142. Khanga 1991, A15.
143. Kuznetsova 1988, 47.
144. See, for example, Allott 1985.
145. Golod 1984, 51.
146. Sysenko 1981, 86.
147. Hansson and Lidén 1983, 191.
148. As quoted in an interview with Feliks Medvedev 1992, 97.
149. Quoted by Merezhkovskii 1914, vol. 15, 148.
150. Gray 1990, 39.
151. Ibid., 47.
152. Hansson and Lidén 1983, 183.
153. Iankova 1978, 111.
154. Ibid., 99
155. Lenin 1958–65, vol. 39, 202.
156. Ibid., 24 (italics Lenin's). Cf. Iankova 1978, 99.
157. Lenin 1958–65, vol. 39, 202.
158. See also Lenin 1958–65, vol. 42, 368–69.
159. Engels 1985 (1884), 105. Engels is famous for comparing the woman in a marriage to the exploited proletariat, the man to an exploiting bourgeois (ibid.). Engels also regarded the bourgeois marriage as a financial transaction in which the husband essentially supported a prostitute for life. For a very informative essay on the attitudes of early Marxist theoreticians toward the women's movement, see Meyer 1977.
160. Hansson and Lidén 1983, 76.
161. As translated by Mary Buckley from the stenographic report of a conference of the wives of shock workers held in 1936 (Buckley 1989, 116).
162. Iurkevich 1970, 192, as translated by Lapidus 1988, 113.
163. See especially Buckley 1989, 136.
164. Rancour-Laferriere 1985, 108ff.
165. Boiko 1988, 103.
166. Iankova 1979, 110. Cf. Shlapentokh 1984, 203. The figures given by Arutiunian (1992, 182–83, table 18) appear to indicate that, the more respondents say the wife makes the major decisions in the family, the less stable the marriage is likely to be.
167. As cited by Maksimenko 1988, 152.
168. Ibid.
169. Kharchev 1979, 258.

170. Allott 1985, 197.
171. Dunham 1960, 481.
172. As translated by Dunham 1979, 223.
173. Hansson and Lidén 1983, 13.
174. See, for example: Kharchev 1979, 222; Kuznetsova 1980, 167.
175. Molodtsov 1976, 11.
176. Iankova 1978, 128.
177. Boiko 1988, 201.
178. Kon 1970, 11.
179. As quoted from a 1982 issue of *Krest'ianka* by Bridger 1987, 135.
180. Khripkova and Kolesov 1981, 120–21.
181. Zhukhovitskii 1984. Compare Kharchev (1979, 222), who says that a woman is disappointed and humiliated when her husband tries to run away from his traditional role of moral superiority and responsibility, that is, when he attempts to "surpass her in weakness."
182. Grafova 1984, 13.
183. As quoted from a 1977 issue of *Nedelia* by Attwood 1990, 167.
184. Kon 1970, 11, italics added.
185. Zhukhovitskii 1984, 12, italics added.
186. Vaksberg 1965, 2.
187. Iurkevich 1970, 193ff.
188. Dunham 1979, 216, 218, italics added.
189. Afanas'ev 1975 (1872), 45–49.
190. Dal' 1984 (1862), vol. 1, 275.
191. Platonov 1984–85, vol. 2, 178–204.
192. From Kon's interview with Larisa Kuznetsova 1980, 189.
193. Attwood 1990, 95.
194. But see Kharchev 1979, 201–2, 230, where impotence is explicitly (but very briefly) discussed.
   In his recent book on sexology Kon says that "in contemporary society" (he does not refer specifically to Russian or Soviet society) "the emancipation of women" can sometimes cause "psychogenic impotence" in men reared according to traditional ideas of male dominance. See Kon 1988, 120–21. For a detailed theoretical discussion of the causes of psychogenic impotence, see Rancour-Laferriere 1985, 317–30.
195. As quoted by Francine du Plessix Gray 1990, 76.
196. For detailed arguments on this topic, see my *Signs of the Flesh* (1985).
197. Nemilov 1932 (1930), 194–95, italics added.
198. Attwood 1990, 127.
199. Lapidus 1978, 288.
200. See, for example: Kharchev 1970, 18; Kharchev and Golod 1971, 162, 163; Lapidus 1978, 287; Iankova 1978, 126; Attwood 1990, 170ff.; Boiko 1988, 194.
201. Holt 1980, 45.
202. Hansson and Lidén 1983, xv.

203. Bridger 1987, 136–38.
204. Baranskaia 1989 (1969), 301.
205. Hansson and Lidén 1983, 16.
206. Sysenko 1981, 67.
207. For example, Rodzinskaia 1981, 109; Bridger 1987, 138ff.
208. Attwood 1990, 177; Kuznetsova 1987, 23. Cf. Shlapentokh 1984, 208; Bridger 1987, 142ff.
209. Shlapentokh 1984, 182; Bridger 1987, 142ff.
210. Gray 1990, 69.
211. For example: Gray 1990, 59; Allott 1985, 197; Shineleva 1990, 84.
212. See, for example, a cartoon by A. Gartvich which appeared on the back page of *Literaturnaia gazeta*, 8 May 1991.
213. Goldberg 1992, 8.
214. Gray 1990, 83.
215. Mamaladze 1985, 11.
216. Lapidus 1988, 111; Shlapentokh 1984, 176.
217. See, for example, Sysenko 1981, 77; Boiko 1988, 209; Buckley 1989, 197.
218. Zaslavskaya 1989, 137.
219. Ibid.
220. Zaslavskaya 1990, 95.
221. E.g., Shineleva 1990, 84.
222. Thanks to Barbara Milman for the algebra.
223. As quoted from *Izvestiia* by Buckley 1989, 203.
224. Quoted from a flyer published in *Women East-West*, September, 1991, p. 17.
225. Scott 1992, 18.
226. Heuvel 1992, 13.
227. Arutiunian 1992, 189.
228. See Gurova 1992, 10; Azhgikhina 1993.
229. Goldberg 1992, 8.

NOTES TO CHAPTER 8

1. Among the observed physiological effects of the bania on the bather are: increased pulse, increased respiratory rate, slightly increased body temperature, significant decrease in body weight (due to heavy perspiration), decreased muscle strength, etc. Flagellation by means of the veniki supposedly increases peripheral blood circulation. See Godlevskii 1883.
2. Shukshin 1975, vol. 1, 447.
3. As quoted by Cross 1991, 34.
4. Olearius 1967 (1656), 161.
5. Kabanov 1986, 136.
6. Smith 1976, 117, 118.
7. Dal' 1955 (1880–82), vol. 1, 45.

8. Dal' 1984 (1862), vol. 1, 170, 173.
9. Dal' 1955 (1880–82), vol. 1, 45.
10. Zelenin 1991 (1927), 284.
11. See Ivanits 1989, 60, 161–62.
12. Thanks to Gary Rosenshield for pointing out this passage.
13. Dal' 1984 (1862), vol. 1, 170.
14. Dal' 1955 (1880–82), vol. 1, 45, 331.
15. Dal' 1984 (1862), vol. 1, 193.
16. Zoshchenko 1978, vol. 1, 107–9.
17. Selivanov 1990, Illustrations 60 and 61.
18. Dal' 1955 (1880–82), vol. 1, 83.
19. For examples of flogging by means of the birch, see: Kolchin 1987, 73, 76, 124, 262; Belliustin 1985 (1858), 73. Steven Hoch (1986) reports that, of 4,187 recorded instances of punishment meted out to serfs on the estate of Petrovskoe in Tambov province in the early to mid-nineteenth century, 97.8 percent consisted of whipping by means of a birch rod ("rozga").
20. Dal' 1984 (1862), vol. 1, 173.
21. Ibid., 175.
22. Dal' 1955 (1880–82), vol. 1, 83.
23. See: Sakharov 1989 (1885), 347ff.; Shein 1898, 344ff.; Shapovalova 1977; Sokolova 1979, 188ff.; Gromyko 1986, 181–93; Gromyko 1991, 345–60; Bernshtam 1988, 175ff.; Zelenin 1991 (1927), 153, 395; Propp 1963, 58ff., 75ff., 95ff.; Propp 1975, 7; Hubbs 1988, 71–74; Brudnyi 1968, 97–100; Warner and Kustovskii 1990, 28–30; Arutiunian 1992, 394; Stites 1992, 114, 140, 172. See also Roberta Reeder's informative comments to Propp 1975, 81ff.
24. Okudzhava 1992, 5. The subtext is the title of a Soviet film "There Is No Peace Beneath the Olives" (thanks to Yuri Druzhnikov for this information).
25. E.g., Propp 1961, 298. Tree names were utilized as signals during match-making ceremonies (Dal' 1955, vol. 1, 83). The droopy flexibility of the birch probably explains why "birch" was a code word for "yes" during matchmaking, while the inflexible uprightness of the pine, fir, and oak is the likely reason why these trees represented a negative reply to the match-maker.
26. Klimas 1991.
27. Propp 1963, 77.
28. Komarovich 1982 (1936), 9.
29. For example Matorin 1931, 22.
30. Tolstaia 1992, 22.
31. Bernshtam 1988, 175.
32. Friedrich 1970, 157–58.
33. There is also a series of folktales in which a fool chops open the trunk of a birch tree and finds treasure there (e.g., Afanas'ev 1984–85 [1873], vol. 3, 128–29).
34. Shein 1898, 344.

35. For example Dmitrieva 1988, 212.
36. Translated from Shein 1898, 346.
37. Dmitrieva (1988, 209–12) suggests that ritual steaming with birch veniki in the bania is connected to ancient worship of a birch-totem. The psychoanalytic theory being offered here would seem to complement this hypothesis because it posits that both the birch tree and the bania are maternal icons tied to sadomasochistic ideas. That is, the hypothesised historical connection is supported by a psychological connection.
38. Dal' 1955 (1880–82), vol. 1, 45. Cf. Vahros 1966, 25.
39. Illiustrov 1904, 308.
40. Gray 1990, 207.
41. Dal' 1955 (1880–82), vol. 2, 307.
42. ANSSSR 1950–65, vol. 2, 494.
43. Hubbs 1988, 56.
44. Rank 1964 (1914), 38.
45. For example: Niederland 1956–57; Dundes 1986; Rancour-Laferriere 1993c. For an interesting recent study of water imagery in Dostoevsky's *Crime and Punishment,* see Syrkin 1991.
46. Kabanov 1986, 137.
47. Other places where women would give birth included the peasant hut (sometimes inside of the large stove), a cattle shed or storehouse, or, at harvest time, an open field or woods. Scholars do not always agree on which place was the most commonly used for childbirth. There was, no doubt, much regional variation, with the bania apparently predominating as a birthing site in the more northern and central regions. See: Pokrovskii 1884, 41ff.; Rein 1889, 8ff.; Zelenin 1991 (1927), 319–22; Baiburin 1993, 91; Dunn 1974, 385; Ramer 1978, 229; Ransel 1988, 267.
48. Dal' 1955 (1880–82), vol. 1, 45.
49. Pokrovskii 1884, 41.
50. Dal' 1955 (1880–82), vol. 1, 45.
51. Ransel (1991, 116) cites several ethnographic sources on the ritual uncleanliness of birthing mothers. Cf. Pokrovskii 1884, 41–48; Rein 1889, 10; Baiburin 1993, 91ff.
52. Ransel 1991, 116. Cf. Rein 1889, 18.
53. Ambodik 1784, part I, xviii.
54. Sanches 1779, 11ff.
55. Ambodik 1784, part I, xxiii.
56. Cf. one current meaning of the verb "parit'," i.e., "to flog" (Gamaiunov 1992, 13).
57. Pokrovskii 1884, 42, 46, 77–78, 83–88. Cf. Ransel 1991, 117; Dunn 1974, 389.
58. Martynova 1978, 181.
59. Listova 1989, 148. Cf. Pokrovskii 1884, 46.
60. Listova 1989, 148.
61. Pokrovskii 1884, 47.

62. Ibid., 84.
63. Cross 1991, plates 1, 3, 8.
64. Likhachev and Panchenko 1976, 73.
65. Kabanov 1986, 136.
66. Masson 1800, vol. 2, 119.
67. Ibid., 120.
68. Gennep 1960, 130.
69. Zelenin, however, mentions cases where not the girlfriends, but a male sorcerer ("znakhar' ") would wash the naked bride to protect her from evil influences (1991 [1927], 340). Cf. also Myl'nikova and Tsintsius 1926, 66, 68; Baiburin 1993, 73.
70. For example: Pevin 1893; Myl'nikova and Tsintsius 1926, 60–69; Vahros 1966, 136, 168ff.; Propp 1975, 21–23; Pushkareva and Shmeleva 1974, 348; Worobec 1991, 161–62; Zorin 1981, 93–95.
71. See especially: Kolesnitskaia and Telegina 1977; Gvozdikova and Shapovalova 1982. During parts of the marriage sequence besides the prenuptial bath the "krasota" could take forms other than a headpiece, e.g., a little birch tree or a little fir tree. There is considerable potential for further psychoanalytic study here.
72. Kolpakova 1973, 254.
73. Bernshtam 1988, 242 ff.; cf. id. 1978, 52, 67–68.
74. See Engel 1989, 231–33.
75. See: Rancour-Laferriere 1989a, 238–40; Bernshtam 1991. In some areas the very nightshirt the bride wore to consummate her marriage was called "kalina," i.e., "snowball berry" (Worobec 1991, 170).
76. Cf. Baiburin's characterization of a woman's marriage as deprivation of her right to further participate in youthful carousals, i.e., "nastuplenie nevoli" (1993, 69).
77. Myl'nikova and Tsintsius 1926, 67.
78. Ibid. Cf. Smirnov 1877, 28.
79. Worobec 1991, 161.
80. Kolpakova 1973, 230, 231.
81. Pushkareva and Shmeleva (1974, 348) speak of a ritual of "beating off the dawn" ("otbivanie zor'") before the wedding.
82. Kolpakova 1973, 231.
83. Gvozdikova and Shapovalova 1982, 271.
84. In the marriage lyrics there are numerous uses of the word "alien" ("chuzhoi") to characterize the bride's new in-laws (e.g., Kolpakova 1973, 26, 59, 62, 97, etc.).
85. Istomin 1892, 141.
86. Kolpakova 1973, 260; cf. Pevin 1893, 233.
87. There was even a possibility that she might in the near future give birth to a child in the same bania, although this was much less likely because she would be living with her husband's family elsewhere.
88. Propp 1961, 268.

89. See Propp 1975, 22.
90. Kolpakova 1973, 232.
91. See: Pevin 1893, 232; Worobec 1991, 161.
92. Gennep 1960, 132.
93. Gvozdikova and Shapovalova 1982, 272.
94. See especially Eremina 1991.
95. Moyle 1987, 229.
96. Many ethnographic and folkloristic discussions of the bania have in the past focused on its "unclean" and "pagan" aspects, rather than on the masochistic aspect. The bania was devoid of Christian icons, for example, or one was not supposed to go to church on the same day that one went to the bania. The bania had its own demon-in-residence, termed a "bannik" or "baennik" (just as most other significant places in Russian traditional culture had their special spirits: the peasant hut had its "domovoi," the threshing-barn its "ovinnik," the forest its "leshii," bodies of water a "vodianoi," the open field a "polevoi," etc.).

    The bannik and other local demons would themselves take steam baths, preferring to be fourth in line after three rounds of steaming by humans (a person who tried to go fourth might be burned or even killed by the bathhouse demon). Various witches, evil spirits, and unclean dead might gather in the bania. One was not supposed to make loud noises there. Both the mother who gave birth there and her midwife were considered unclean until they performed a special cleansing ceremony, usually a joint handwashing. A mother's newborn child could not be left in the bania, for fear an evil spirit might steal it before it could be baptized. And so on. See, for example Maksimov 1909, vol. 18, 51–57; Vahros 1966, 79–95; Ivanits 1989, 59–60; Levin 1991; Zelenin 1991 (1927), 283–85, 319ff.; Listova 1989.

    These beliefs reveal an overall sense of unease about the bania, and they are no doubt related to the very real dangers associated with its use. For example, people were known to suffocate in the bania, most likely as a result of carbon monoxide poisoning from lack of ventilation and improper timing in firing the stove. This danger would have a certain appeal to a masochist, although it was hardly the primary aspect of the bania which appealed to masochistic impulses.

    The most dangerous event to occur in a bania was of course childbirth. Mother and/or child could die, or some complication could occur, leading to serious illness. Furthermore, there was little that could be done. Nature took its course because peasant midwives were largely ignorant of real medicine. Superstition thrives on a soil of fear compounded by ignorance. Even without complications childbirth was painful. Women suffered unspeakable torments giving birth in the bania. The ritual postpartum cleansing must have helped the participants suppress some very unpleasant memories. The rule that one was supposed to speak quietly and avoid any noisy behavior in a bania was undoubtedly connected to the fact that a woman screamed her heart out while giving birth there. The notion that the bannik could do painful things to you was probably related to the intense pain of childbirth, for the newborn was typically referred to as a "little devil" ("chertenok").

The various superstitions and apotropaic practices concerning the bania would themselves make an interesting subject for detailed psychoanalytic study. For the most part they are not connected to masochism, however, which is why I am not investigating them here. Masochism plays very little role when there is absolutely no choice. One did not *have* to steam and beat oneself with veniki, but, when labor started, a woman *had* to endure.

NOTES TO CHAPTER 9

1. For example, Alan Roland (1988) writes about the "we-self" of Japan and India, as opposed to the "I-self" of Western countries. Triandis (1990) provides an extensive survey of the sophisticated empirical studies which have been done on individualism and collectivism in a variety of cultures. Unfortunately, almost nothing is said about Russia. It is clear from what Triandis says, however, that ethnic Russians would fit at the collectivist end of the spectrum. For example, Triandis finds that a sharp distinction between "ingroup" and "outgroup" characterizes collectivism (56). This terminology perfectly reflects the important cultural opposition of "svoi" ("own") vs. "chuzhoi" ("other") in Russia.

   Inkeles, Hanfmann, and Beier (1958), utilizing some standard psychological tests, found a much stronger need for *affiliation* in a sample of former Soviet Russian citizens than in a comparable sample of American subjects.

   Urie Bronfenbrenner's book *Two Worlds of Childhood: U.S. and U.S.S.R.* (1972) provides substantial documentation of the contrast between the collectivist orientation of child upbringing ("vospitanie") in Soviet Russia and the somewhat haphazard individualism fostered by American child rearing.

   Boris Segal (1990) demonstrates an awareness of the cross-cultural studies, and explicitly discusses the "communal spirit that was the foundation of the old Russian society" as well as the "low degree of individualism" in Soviet society (503).

2. See Esaulov 1992 who, although he argues that the extremes of *sobornost'* and totalitarianism are "two faces of Russian culture," does not deal with the underlying masochism that unites the apparent polarity.

3. Gromyko 1986, 167.

4. Ivanov 1969, 131.

5. As quoted by Schmemann 1991, A9.

6. See Peskov 1992.
7. Examples provided by Belkin 1991b, 13.
8. Maiakovskii 1970 (1924), vol. 3, 217.
9. Miller 1961, 68.
10. See the section titled (after Mayakovsky) "The Individual Is Nothing" in Smith 1991, 194–99.
11. Klugman 1989, 205, italics added. Urie Bronfenbrenner provides chilling examples of how grade school teachers in the Soviet Union manipulated the student group itself into disciplining individual students (Bronfenbrenner 1972, 57ff.).
12. Berdiaev 1990, 39.
13. Nikol'skii 1898, 66. By comparison, says Nikol'skii, educated Russians have a downright "cult of personality" ("kul't lichnosti"). Clearly this phrase was not invented just to describe Joseph Stalin.
14. Nikol'skii 1898, 83–84.
15. Okudzhava 1992, 5.
16. Smith 1991, 199.
17. Ibid., 202.
18. Zenova 1992.
19. Here I translate a typical attitude paraphrased to me by Irina Bukina in Moscow in May of 1990: "Esli ia budu zhit' plokho, pust' i oni budut zhit' plokho."
20. Example kindly provided by Konstantin Pimkin.
21. Cf. Siniavskii 1992, 3.
22. Zaslavskaya 1990, 126.
23. See, for example, Gromyko 1991, 57–63, for extensive documentation.
24. Smith 1991, 203.
25. Semenova-Tian-Shanskaia 1914, 95.
26. Dal' 1984 (1862), vol. 2, 148, 149.
27. See Smith 1991, chap. 11.
28. Conversation with Dmitrii Starodubtsev in Smith 1991, 229.
29. Belkin 1991b, 15.
30. Grafova 1991, 6.
31. Kochubei 1990, 13.
32. Likhachev 1992, 6.
33. Katerli and Shmidt 1992, 12.
34. Belkin 1993, 185, italics added.
35. Prokushev 1990.
36. From an anonymous introduction in *Literaturnaia gazeta*, 9 October, 1991, p. 2.
37. Anzieu 1984 (1975), 118.
38. Ibid., 73.
39. Ibid., 118.
40. Ibid., 122. Cf. GAP 1987, 5, and various items in 252 n. 48 above.
41. Anzieu 1984, 73–76, 140–41. Cf. Freud (*SE*, vol. 18, 127) who believes

that it is a paternal leader of the group, rather than the group itself which takes the place of the ego ideal.

42. Chasseguet-Smirgel 1985 (1975), 82. Cf. Koenigsberg on "the country as an omnipotent mother" (1977, 6 ff.).

43. Kernberg 1984, 15.

44. There is an enormous literature on the Russian land commune. For a generous sampling of recent views, see the volume edited by Bartlett (1990). An excellent Soviet study is Aleksandrov (1976). See Worobec (1991) for a clear and engaging treatment of the complexities of peasant economic life in post-emancipation Russia. Hoch (1986, chap. 4) gives a good discussion of communal functions in the pre-emancipation period. Gromyko (1991, 155ff.) provides a well-documented but rather idealized view of the peasant's relationship to the commune in the eighteenth and nineteenth centuries. None of these works pays much attention to the psychology (and particularly the masochism) of the individual commune member.

45. See especially Gromyko 1991, 73–85.

46. See, for example Nikol'skii 1898, 72–73.

47. As quoted in Kolchin 1987, 332.

48. Leroy-Beaulieu 1902–5, vol. 2, 43.

49. E.g., Semenova-Tian-Shanskaia 1914, 95.

50. Gromyko 1991, 73–85.

51. Kingston-Mann 1991, 43.

52. Worobec 1991, 45. See Aleksandrov (1976, 294–313) on the commune's powerful influence in family affairs.

53. Worobec 1991, 147.

54. See Frank 1990 for a detailed treatment of Russian *charivari*s and other collective punishments.

55. Dal' 1984 (1862), vol. 1, 315–16.

56. Rittikh 1903, 51.

57. Dal' 1984 (1862), vol. 1, 316.

58. Ibid.

59. Kuz'min and Shadrin 1989, 138.

60. Fedotov 1981 (1949), 166.

61. Illiustrov 1904, 312–13.

62. Mironov 1990 (1985), 18–19.

63. Gorer and Rickman 1962 (1949), 135.

64. Mead 1951, 26.

65. See especially Macey 1990, 227–28.

66. Treadgold 1959, 107.

67. Confino 1985, 42.

68. Clines 1990, p. A2.

69. Taubman 1988, p. A6.

70. This is not to deny that there are many differences as well (social, economic, political) between the tsarist peasant commune and the Soviet collective farm. See, for example: Kerblay 1985; Medvedev 1987.

71. See, for example Seliunin 1989, 202 (= Seliunin 1988, 186).
72. Medvedev 1987, 362–65.
73. Solzhenitsyn 1989, 530–31, italics added. The Russian original is Solzhenitsyn 1978–, vol. 12, 168.
74. Losev 1990b (1941), 15. For the Russian original, see Losev 1990a, 6.
75. Ibid. I have had to make some corrections in the translation.
76. Ibid.
77. Ibid.
78. Berdiaev 1991 (1949), 120–21.
79. Ibid., 151 ff.
80. Berdiaev 1990, 295.
81. Ibid., 294.
82. Here it is appropriate to note a general tendency in Russian philosophy: things should be "united" in some fashion. Selves should somehow be joined to others. This is already apparent in Chaadaev, it is especially clear in the Slavophile notion of the union of self and collective (e.g., Khomiakov's *sobornost'*), it becomes "total unity" ("vsëedinstvo") in Solov'ev, and appears as "multi-unity" or "all-unity" ("mnogoedinstvo," "vseedinstvo") in the works of Fedorov. George Young's comments on this philosophical topic are quite pertinent: "In all these models, the individual is incomplete in and of itself. The individual completes himself, becomes whole, only by becoming part of a greater whole. Russian thinkers, like Russian composers, love the strong chorus" (Young 1979, 179). The "greater whole" that Young speaks of here implies an asymmetrical relationship with something lesser, i.e., the self as an isolated, insignificant individual. It is this obligatory lesser status, this acknowledgment of one's own personal insignificance in the face of the all—that comprises the masochistic element in Russian mystical philosophy. One submits "freely," says Solov'ev, i.e., masochistically. Even the great antimasochist Fedorov, who resists submission to death with such vehemence, and who rejects altruism as "slavery" and "self-destruction" (Fedorov 1906–13, vol. 2, 201), envisages a masochistic submission of the many to the all as the ideal alternative. Otherwise the "project" he proposes could not have been termed the "*general* task" ("obshchee delo"). Fedorov does not want the "blind force of nature" to coerce humankind, but his own writing is ultimately coercive, or conversely, it invites moral masochism in readers. Here it is ironic that Fedorov resisted making his writings *generally* available ("not for sale" is printed on the title page of the Vernyi edition). He must have sensed that widespread, popular acceptance of his ideas would have been uncomfortably close to acceptance of the "blind force of nature."
83. Berdiaev 1990, 297.
84. Berdiaev 1991, 179.
85. The notion of "Godhumanhood" ("Bogochelovechestvo") is of course not original with Berdiaev. Among Russians it played an especially important

role in the thinking of Vladimir Solov'ev, and it endures to this day in Russian theology (e.g., Men' 1991, 127–29). The epithet "God-human" is an ancient one, referring to Christ, who was God become human (Greek "theandros" or "theanthropos").

86. Berdiaev 1991, 177.
87. Ibid., 189.
88. Ibid., 177. Berdiaev mistakenly believes that his idea of freedom contradicts the traditional Russian idea of *smirenie* (he speaks of a "lozhnoe uchenie o smirenii"—ibid.).
89. Berdiaev 1990, 13.
90. Ibid., 17.
91. Ibid.
92. Berdiaev 1991, 209.
93. Ibid., 121.
94. Blok 1971, vol. 3, 178. As translated in Markov and Sparks 1967, 183.
95. Fellow bird-watchers please note that "korshun" is really a "kite," but English "buzzard" comes closer to the menacing connotation of the Russian word.
96. Obukhova 1989. Another possible subtext for Blok's poem is a poem by Ivan Savvich Nikitin (1824–61) about a falcon ("sokol") which has been chained in the steppes of Rus' for a thousand years, and which tears out its own breast in vexation (see Prokushev 1990, 31–32).
97. Nekrasov 1967, vol. 2, 144.
98. Freud, *SE*, vol. 21, 237.
99. See "Zagovor na ukroshchenie gneva rodimoi matushki" in Sakharov 1989 (1885), 50–51.
100. Obukhova comes close to this conclusion by means of religious imagery: "It is out of this that the personality of the Son striving for crucifixion began" (1989, 209).
101. Khomiakov 1955, 50.
102. My translation of Blok 1971, vol. 3, 208. Again, apologies to my ornithologist friends. The bird in question is an accipiter of some kind.
103. Dostoyevsky 1950, 617.
104. Ibid., 720; Dostoevskii 1972–88, vol. 15, 31.
105. See Browning 1989, 516.
106. Dostoyevsky 1950, 386; Dostoevskii 1972–88, vol. 14, 291–92.
107. Dostoyevsky 1950, 344; Dostoevskii 1972–88, vol. 14, 262.
108. The grandiose idea of bearing the guilt of others can apply temporally as well as spatially. In 1846 Khomiakov wrote a poem in which he asserted that Russians are responsible for, and should ask forgiveness for, the sins of their fathers ("Za temnye otsov deian'ia," 1955, 61). In the twentieth century we have Aleksandr Solzhenitsyn saying essentially the same thing in his essay on repentance and self-limitation in the life of nations: "It is impossible to imagine a nation which throughout the course of its whole

existence has no cause for repentance." Or: "The nation is mystically welded together in a community of guilt, and its inescapable destiny is common repentance" (1976, 110, 112).

109. Browning 1989, 517.
110. Dal' 1984, vol. 1, 315.
111. In Soviet politics such avoidance of responsibility was often referred to as "perestrakhovka," which might be translated as "mutually playing safe."
112. Kabakov 1990, 1, italics added.
113. Moroz 1993, 2.
114. Solzhenitsyn 1976, 118; Solzhenitsyn 1978–, vol. 9, 57.
115. Solzhenitsyn 1976, 132; Solzhenitsyn 1978–, vol. 9, 69.
116. In his recent essay *Rebuilding Russia* (1990) Solzhenitsyn gets more practical. He calls for "public repentance" from the Party, but he also notes that no one among the "former toadies of Brezhnevism" has expressed *"personal* repentance" (italics Solzhenitsyn's). He also laments the fact that specific criminals such as Molotov and Kaganovich (the latter still alive at the time) had not been brought to justice (1991 [1990], 49–51).

It seems to me that those who engage in loud cries of repentance are precisely the ones who need least to repent. Such breast-beating is masochistic in nature, and is not in character with the sadism required of a *real* murderer. A Solzhenitsyn will repent, but not a Molotov or a Kaganovich.

In the late Soviet period calls for repentance, or outright acts of public repentance became common. The distinguished Russian philologist Dmitrii Likhachev, for example, declared that all Soviet citizens were responsible for not resisting their leaders, and should therefore repent. The prominent economist Oleg Bogomolov, in a 1990 article titled "I Cannot Absolve Myself from Guilt" castigated himself for failing to speak out against abuses under Brezhnev (see Teague 1990).

117. Dostoievsky 1949, vol. 2, 962; Dostoevskii 1972–88, vol. 26, 131.
118. Dostoievsky 1949, vol. 2, 977.
119. Ibid., 978–79; Dostoevskii 1972–88, vol. 26, 147.
120. Dostoievsky 1949, vol. 2, 979, 980; Dostoevskii 1972–88, vol. 26, 147, 148.
121. Quoted by Dostoevskii 1972–88, vol. 26, 139, translation in Dostoievsky 1949, vol. 2, 970.
122. Dostoievsky 1949, vol. 2, 970; Dostoevskii 1972–88, vol. 26, 139.
123. See Levitt 1989, 122–46.
124. Dostoievsky 1949, vol. 2, 970; Dostoevskii 1972–88, vol. 26, 139.
125. Cf. Fasmer 1986–87, vol. 2, 45, 490–93, and Townsend 1968, 251, on the linguistic aspects of this root morpheme. We should perhaps also keep in mind the ancient East Slavic pagan fertility figures of Rod and Rozhanitsa (cf. Ivanits 1989, 14–15; Fedotov 1975, vol. 1, 348–51; Hubbs 1988, 15, 81). Young (1979, 83–84) gives an interesting discussion of the use of -*rod*- words in Fedorov's philosophy. Kathleen Parthé (1992, 8–9) finds

that *-rod-* words play an important role in Russian Village Prose of the 1960s and 1970s.

126. Dostoevskii 1972–88, vol. 26, 143, 144.
127. Dostoievsky 1949, vol. 2, 968–70; Dostoevskii 1972–88, vol. 26, 137–39.
128. Cf. the maternal association in Nikolai Nekrasov's lines " . . . Tseluias' s mater'iu-zemleiu, / Kolos'ia beskonechnykh niv" (Nekrasov 1967, vol. 2, 13).
129. E.g., Aksakov 1861–80, vol. 1, 298.
130. See, for example: Chances 1978, chap. 4; Dowler 1982. The focus on a fruitful womb in the form of "pochva" (soil), "zemlia" (land), "lono" (bosom), etc. is also characteristic of today's village-prose writers in Russia, such as Vasilii Belov and Valentin Rasputin, as Natal'ia Ivanova has recently observed in a controversial article (1992, 200).
131. Breger has offered an interesting explanation for Dostoevsky's emotionalism about Pushkin in the *Diary*. It happens that Pushkin died about the same time that Dostoevsky's mother died. Dostoevsky would thus have been mourning these two deaths simultaneously. Later on, in Breger's view, Pushkin's "idealized love for his mother was displaced onto Pushkin" (1989, 60). All the more reason, then, to expect covert maternal imagery in the Pushkin passages of the *Diary*.

     Breger also believes that Dostoevsky's idealization of the Russian people is a remnant of his idealization of his mother (e.g., 150). But Breger does not concern himself with the masochistic aspects of this problem, nor does he adduce intrinsic evidence for maternal imagery from the original Russian text.
132. Worobec 1991, 6.
133. Ibid., 19.
134. Dostoievsky 1949, vol. 1, 204; Dostoevskii 1972–88, vol. 22, 45.
135. Dostoevskii 1972–88, vol. 22, 48–49.
136. See Rice 1989; Breger 1989, 150.
137. There is much else of psychoanalytic interest in this episode. See, for example: Rice 1989; Rosen 1993, 423–25.

NOTES TO CHAPTER 10

1. For a detailed study of apocalypticism in modern Russian fiction, see Bethea 1989.
2. Berdiaev 1968 (1921), 230.

Bibliography

Afanas'ev, A. N. 1975 (1872). *Russkie zavetnye skazki,* 2d ed. Ste. Geneviève-des-Bois: Imprimerie R.G.M.

———. 1984–85 (1873). *Narodnye russkie skazki.* Edited by L. G. Barag and N. V. Novikov. Moscow: Nauka, 3 vols.

Afanasiev, A. N. 1973 (1873). *Russian Fairy Tales.* Translated by N. Guterman. New York: Pantheon.

Akhmatova, Anna. 1973. *Poems of Akhmatova/Izbrannye stikhi.* Translated by S. Kunitz and M. Hayward. Boston: Little, Brown and Co.

Aksakov, Konstantin S. 1861–80. *Polnoe sobranie sochinenii.* Moscow: Tipografiia P. Bakhmeteva and M. Katkov, 3 vols.

Aleksandrov, V. A. 1976. *Sel'skaia obshchina v Rossii (XVII-nachalo XIX v.).* Moscow: Nauka.

Alexandrova, Ekaterina. 1984. "Why Soviet Women Want to Get Married." *Women and Russia: Feminist Writings from the Soviet Union.* Edited by Tatyana Mamonova. Boston: Beacon Press, 31–50.

Allott, Susan. 1985. "Soviet Rural Women: Employment and Family Life." *Soviet Sisterhood: British Feminists on Women in the USSR.* Edited by B. Holland. London: Fourth Estate, 177–206.

Altaev, O. 1977 (1969). "The Dual Consciousness of the Intelligentsia and Pseudo-Culture." *The Political, Social and Religious Thought of Russian "Samizdat"—An Anthology.* Edited by M. Meerson-Aksenov and B. Shragin. Belmont, Mass.: Nordland, 116–47.

Ambodik, Nestor Maksimovich. 1784. *Iskusstva povivaniia ili nauki o bab-ich'em dele.* Saint Petersburg, part I.

Anan'ev, Anatolii. 1990. "Uvolen za ubezhdeniia." *Moskovskie novosti,* no. 2, 14 January, p. 14.

Andreev, N. P. 1929. *Ukazatel' skazochnykh siuzhetov po sisteme Aarne.* Leningrad: Gosud. russ. geogr. obshchestvo.

Anikin, V. P. 1991. *Mudrost' narodnaia: zhizn' cheloveka v russkom fol'klore. Vypusk pervyi. Mladenchestvo, detstvo.* Moscow: Khudozhestvennaia literatura.

ANSSSR. 1950–1965. *Slovar' sovremennogo russkogo literaturnogo iazyka.* Moscow-Leningrad: Nauka, 17 vols.

Antonov, M. F., V. M. Klykov, and I. R. Shafarevich. 1989. "Pis'mo v sekretariat pravleniia Soiuza Pisatelei RSFSR." *Literaturnaia Rossiia* no. 31, 4 August, p. 4.

Antonov-Ovseyenko, Anton. 1983 (1980). *The Time of Stalin: Portrait of a Tyranny.* Translated by G. Saunders. New York: Harper and Row.

Anzieu, Didier. 1984 (1975). *The Group and the Unconscious.* Translated by B. Kilborne. London: Routledge and Kegan Paul.

Arsen'ev, N. S. 1959. *Iz russkoi kul'turnoi i tvorcheskoi traditsii.* Frankfurt: Posev.

Arutiunian, Iu. V., editor-in-chief. 1992. *Russkie: etnosotsiologicheskie ocherki.* Moscow: Nauka.

Asch, Stuart S. 1988. "The Analytic Concepts of Masochism: A Reevaluation." *Masochism: Current Psychoanalytic Perspectives.* Edited by R. Glick and D. Meyers. Hillsdale, N.J.: Analytic Press, 93–115.

Atkinson, Dorothy. 1977. "Society and the Sexes in the Russian Past." *Women in Russia.* Edited by D. Atkinson, A. Dallin, and G. Warshofsky Lapidus. Stanford: Stanford University Press, 1–38.

Attwood, Lynne. 1990. *The New Soviet Man and Woman: Sex Role Socialization in the USSR.* Bloomington: Indiana University Press.

Averintsev, S. S. 1988. "Vizantiia i Rus': dva tipa dukhovnosti—stat'ia vtoraia." *Novyi mir,* no. 9, 227–39.

Avvakum. 1960 (1673). *Zhitie protopopa Avvakuma im samim napisannoe i arkhiv ego sochieneiia.* Edited by N. K. Gudzii. Moscow: Gosudarstvennoe izdatel'stvo khudozhestvennoi literatury.

———. 1979 (1673). *Archpriest Avvakum: The Life Written by Himself.* Translations, annotations, commentary by K. N. Brostrom. Ann Arbor: Michigan Slavic Publications.

Azhgikhina, Nadezhda. 1993. "Believing the Impossible." *Women's Review of Books* 10, 4–5.

Baiburin, A. K. 1993. *Ritual v traditsionnoi kul'ture.* Saint Petersburg: Nauka.

Barag, L. G., I. P. Berezovskii, K. P. Kabashnikov, and N. V. Novikov. 1979. *Sravnitel'nyi ukazatel' siuzhetov: vostochnoslavianskaia skazka.* Leningrad: Nauka.

Baranskaia, Natal'ia. 1989 (1969). *Den' pominoveniia.* Moscow: Sovetskii pisatel'.

Barker, Adele. 1986. *The Mother Syndrome in the Russian Folk Imagination.* Columbus: Slavica Publishers.

Bartlett, Roger, ed. 1990. *Land Commune and Peasant Community in Russia.* London: Macmillan.

Baumeister, Roy F. 1989. *Masochism and the Self.* Hillsdale, N.J.: Lawrence Erlbaum Associates.

Becker, Richarda. 1990. *Die weibliche Initiation im ostslawischen Zaubermärchen.* Wiesbaden: Harrassowitz.

Belkin, Aron. 1991a. "Chto skazal by o nas Freid?" *Sovetskaia kul'tura*, 27 July, p. 4.

———. 1991b. "Sovremennye sotsial'nye problemy v svete psikhoanaliza (priglashenie k diskussii)." *Rossiiskii psikhoanaliticheskii vestnik* 1, 9–31.

———. 1993. *Pochemu my takie? Psikhologicheskie etiudy*. Moscow: Tipografiia A/O "Vneshtorgizdat."

Belliustin, I. S. 1985 (1858). *Description of the Clergy in Rural Russia*. Translated and edited by G. L. Freeze. Ithaca: Cornell University Press.

Benedict, Ruth. 1949. "Child Rearing in Certain European Countries." *American Journal of Orthopsychiatry* 19, 342–50.

Berdiaev, Nikolai. 1939. *O rabstve i svobode cheloveka*. Paris: YMCA-Press.

———. 1968 (1921). *Mirosozertsanie Dostoevskago*. Paris: YMCA-Press.

———. 1971 (1946). *Russkaia ideia: Osnovnye problemy russkoi mysli XIX veka i nachala XX veka*. Paris: YMCA-Press.

———. 1990 (1918). *Sud'ba Rossii*. Moscow: Sovetskii pisatel'.

———. 1991 (1949). *Samopoznanie*. Moscow: Kniga.

Berdyaev, Nikolai. 1944 (1939). *Slavery and Freedom*. Translated by R. M. French. New York: Charles Scribner's Sons.

Berger, Peter L. 1967. *The Sacred Canopy: Elements of a Sociological Theory of Religion*. Garden City: Doubleday.

Bergler, Edmund. 1949. *The Basic Neurosis: Oral Regression and Psychic Masochism*. New York: Grune and Stratton.

Berlin, Isaiah. 1979. *Russian Thinkers*. New York: Penguin.

Berliner, Bernhard. 1958. "The Role of Object Relations in Moral Masochism." *Psychoanalytic Quarterly* 27, 38–56.

Bernshtam, T. A. 1978. "Devushka-nevesta i predbrachnaia obriadnost' v Pomor'e v XIX-nachale XX v." *Russkii narodnyi svadebnyi obriad: issledovaniia i materialy*. Edited by K. V. Chistov and T. A. Bernshtam. Leningrad: Nauka, 48–71.

———. 1988. *Molodezh' v obriadovoi zhizni russkoi obshchiny XIX—nachala XX v.* Leningrad: Nauka.

———. 1991. "Sovershennoletie devushki v metaforakh igrovogo fol'klora (traditsionnyi aspekt russkoi kul'tury)." *Etnicheskie stereotipy muzhskogo i zhenskogo povedeniia*. Edited by A. K. Baiburin and I. Kon. Saint Petersburg: Nauka, 234–57.

Besançon, Alain. 1967. *Le tsarévitch immolé: La symbolique de la loi dans la culture russe*. Paris: Plon.

———. 1968. "Fonction du rêve dans le roman russe." *Cahiers du monde russe et soviétique* 9, 337–52.

Bethea, David M. 1989. *The Shape of Apocalypse in Modern Russian Fiction*. Princeton: Princeton University Press.

Bettelheim, Bruno. 1977. *The Uses of Enchantment: The Meaning and Importance of Fairy Tales*. New York: Vintage.

———. 1980. *Surviving and Other Essays*. New York: Random House.

Bieber, Irving. 1966. "Sadism and Masochism." *American Handbook of Psychiatry.* Edited by S. Arieti. New York: Basic Books, vol. 3, 256–70.

Billington, James H. 1968. *The Icon and the Axe: An Interpretive History of Russian Culture.* New York: Alfred A. Knopf.

Blanchard, William H. 1984. *Revolutionary Morality: A Psychosexual Analysis of Twelve Revolutionists.* Santa Barbara: ABC-Clio Information Services.

Blok, Aleksandr. 1971. *Sobranie sochinenii v shesti tomakh.* Moscow: Pravda, 6 vols.

Blum, Harold P. 1977. "Masochism, the Ego Ideal, and the Psychology of Women." *Female Psychology: Contemporary Psychoanalytic Views.* Edited by H. P. Blum. New York: International Universities Press, 157–91.

Blum, Jerome. 1961. *Lord and Peasant in Russia from the Ninth to the Nineteenth Century.* Princeton: Princeton University Press.

Bocharov, Anatolii, and Mikhail Lobanov. 1989. "Samokritika ili samooplevyvanie?" *Literaturnaia gazeta* no. 36, 6 September, p. 2.

Boiko, V. V. 1988. *Malodetnaia sem'ia: sotsial'no-psikhologicheskii aspekt.* Moscow: Mysl'.

Bolshakoff, Sergius. 1977. *Russian Mystics.* Kalamazoo: Cistercian Publications.

Bonaparte, Marie. 1962. "L'épilepsie et le sado-masochisme dans la vie et l'oeuvre de Dostoievski." *Revue française de psychanalyse* 26, 715–30.

Borisov, Vadim. 1974. "Natsional'noe vozrozhdenie i natsiia-lichnost'." *Iz-pod glyb.* Paris: YMCA-Press, 199–215.

———. 1976. "Personality and National Awareness." *From Under the Rubble.* New York: Bantam, 193–228.

Breger, Louis. 1989. *Dostoevsky: The Author as Psychoanalyst.* New York: New York University Press.

Brenner, Charles. 1959. "The Masochistic Character: Genesis and Treatment." *Journal of the American Psychoanalytic Association* 7, 197–226.

Brezhnev, Leonid. 1977. "Sovetskie profsoiuzy—vliiatel'naia sila nashego obshchestva." *Pravda,* 22 March, pp. 1–3.

Bridger, Susan. 1987. *Women in the Soviet Countryside.* Cambridge: Cambridge University Press.

Brodskii, N. L., ed. 1910. *Rannie slavianofily.* Moscow: I. D. Sytin.

Brody, Leslie R. 1985. "Gender Differences in Emotional Development: A Review of Theories and Research." *Journal of Personality* 53, 102–49.

Bronfenbrenner, Urie. 1972 (1970). *Two Worlds of Childhood: U.S. and U.S.S.R.* New York: Simon and Schuster.

Brown, Edward J. 1982. *Russian Literature Since the Revolution.* Cambridge: Harvard University Press.

Browning, Gary L. 1989. "Zosima's 'Secret of Renewal' in *The Brothers Karamazov.*" *Slavic and East European Journal* 33, 516–29.

Brudnyi, V. I. 1968. *Obriady vchera i segodnia.* Moscow: Nauka.

Brunswick, Ruth Mack. 1940. "The Preoedipal Phase of the Libido Development." *Psychoanalytic Quarterly* 9, 293–319.

Brun-Zejmis, Julia. 1991. "Messianic Consciousness as an Expression of National Inferiority: Chaadaev and Some Samizdat Writings of the 1970s." *Slavic Review* 50, 646–58.

Buckley, Mary. 1989. *Women and Ideology in the Soviet Union*. Ann Arbor: University of Michigan Press.

Caplan, Paula. 1985. *The Myth of Women's Masochism*. New York: E. P. Dutton.

Carey, Claude. 1972. *Les proverbes érotiques russes*. The Hague: Mouton.

Chaadaev, Petr Iakovlevich. 1989. *Stat'i i pis'ma*. Moscow: Sovremennik.

———. 1991. *Polnoe sobranie sochinenii i izbrannye pis'ma*. Edited by Z. A. Kamenskii. Moscow: Nauka, 2 vols.

Chaadayev, Peter Yakovlevich. 1969. *Philosophical Letters and Apology of a Madman*. Translated by Mary-Barbara Zeldin. Knoxville: University of Tennessee Press.

Chaitin, Gilbert. 1972. "Religion as Defense: The Structure of *The Brothers Karamazov*." *Literature and Psychology* 22, 69–87.

Chancer, Lynn S. 1992. *Sadomasochism in Everyday Life: The Dynamics of Power and Powerlessness*. New Brunswick: Rutgers University Press.

Chances, Ellen B. *Conformity's Children: An Approach to the Superfluous Man in Russian Literature*. Columbus: Slavica Publishers.

Charme, Stuart L. 1983. "Religion and the Theory of Masochism." *Journal of Religion and Health* 22, 221–33.

Chasseguet-Smirgel, Janine. 1985 (1975). *The Ego Ideal: A Psychoanalytic Essay on the Malady of the Ideal*. Translated by P. Barrows. London: Free Association Books.

Cherniavsky, Michael. 1961. *Tsar and People: Studies in Russian Myths*. New Haven: Yale University Press.

———. 1966. "The Old Believers and the New Religion." *Slavic Review* 25, 1–39.

Chisholm, James S. 1983. *Navajo Infancy: An Ethological Study of Child Development*. New York: Aldine.

Chodorow, Nancy. 1978. *The Reproduction of Mothering: Psychoanalysis and the Sociology of Gender*. Berkeley: University of California Press.

Christoff, Peter K. 1961. *An Introduction to Nineteenth-Century Russian Slavophilism: A Study in Ideas, Volume I, A. S. Xomjakov*. The Hague: Mouton.

Clark, Katerina. 1985. *The Soviet Novel: History as Ritual*. Chicago: University of Chicago Press.

Clark, Katerina, and Michael Holquist. 1984. *Mikhail Bakhtin*. Cambridge: Harvard University Press.

Clines, Francis X. 1990. "Russian Republic Backs Private Farm Plan But Rejects Private Sale of Land." *New York Times*, 4 December, p. A12.

Coe, Richard N. 1984. *Reminiscences of Childhood: An Approach to a Comparative Mythology*. Leeds: Leeds Philosophical and Literary Society (= *Proceedings of the Leeds Philosophical and Literary Society, Literary and Historical Section*, vol. 19, part 6, 221–321).

Condee, Nancy, and Vladimir Padunov. 1987. "The *Soiuz* on Trial: Voinovich as Magistrate and Stage Manager." *Russian Review* 46, 315–19.

Confino, Michael. 1985. "Russian Customary Law and the Study of Peasant Mentalités." *Russian Review* 44, 35–43.

Cooper, Arnold M. 1988. "The Narcissistic-Masochistic Character." *Masochism: Current Psychoanalytic Perspectives*. Edited by R. A. Glick and D. I. Meyers. Hillsdale, N.J.: Analytic Press, 117–38.

Cox, Gary. 1989. "Can a Literature Be Neurotic? or Literary Self and Authority Structures in Russian Cultural Development." *Russian Literature and Psychoanalysis*. Edited by D. Rancour-Laferriere. Amsterdam: John Benjamins, 451–69.

Crone, Anna Lisa. 1978. *Rozanov and the End of Literature*. Würzburg: JAL-Verlag.

Cross, A. G. 1991. "The Russian *Banya* in the Descriptions of Foreign Travellers and in the Depictions of Foreign and Russian Artists." *Oxford Slavonic Papers* 24, 34–59.

Crummey, Robert O. 1970. *The Old Believers and the World of Antichrist: The Vyg Community and the Russian State, 1694–1855*. Madison: University of Wisconsin Press.

Custine, Astolphe, marquis de. 1843. *La Russie en 1839*, 2d ed. Paris: Librairie d'Amyot, 4 vols.

———. 1989 (1843). *Empire of the Czar: A Journey Through Eternal Russia*. Translation anon. New York: Anchor Books.

Dal', Vladimir. 1955 (1880–82). *Tolkovyi slovar' zhivago velikoruskago iazyka*. Moscow: Gosudarstvennoe izdatel'stvo inostrannykh i natsional'nykh slovarei, 4 vols.

———. 1984 (1862). *Poslovitsy russkogo naroda*. Moscow: Khudozhestvennaia literatura, 2 vols.

Dallin, David J., and Boris I. Nicolaevsky. 1947. *Forced Labor in Soviet Russia*. New Haven: Yale University Press.

Dalton, Elizabeth. 1979. *Unconscious Structure in* THE IDIOT. Princeton: Princeton University Press.

De Armond, Richard. 1971. "On the Russian Verb *ebat'* and Some of its Derivatives." *Studies Out in Left Field: Defamatory Essays Presented to James D. McCawley*. Edited by A. Zwicky et al. Edmonton: Linguistic Research, 99–107.

DeMause, Lloyd. 1982. *Foundations of Psychohistory*. New York: Creative Roots.

Deutsch, Helene. 1930. "The Significance of Masochism in the Mental Life of Women." *International Journal of Psycho-Analysis* 11, 48–60.

Dicks, Henry V. 1952. "Observations on Contemporary Russian Behaviour." *Human Relations* 5, 111–75.

———. 1960. "Some Notes on the Russian National Character." *The Transformation of Russian Society*. Edited by C. Black. Cambridge: Harvard University Press, 636–52.

Dinnerstein, Dorothy. 1976. *The Mermaid and the Minotaur: Sexual Arrangements and Human Malaise*. New York: Harper and Row.

Dmitrieva, S. I. 1988. *Fol'klor i narodnoe iskusstvo russkikh Evropeiskogo Severa*. Moscow: Nauka.

Dostoevskii, Fedor. 1963. *Brat'ia Karamazovy*. Moscow: Gosudarstvennoe izdatel'stvo khudozhestvennoi literatury, 2 vols.

————. 1972–88. *Polnoe sobranie sochinenii v tridtsati tomakh*. Leningrad: Nauka, 30 vols.

Dostoievsky, Feodor. 1949 (1877). *The Diary of a Writer*. Translated by B. Brasol. New York: Charles Scribner's Sons, 2 vols.

Dostoyevsky, Fyodor. 1950. *The Brothers Karamazov*. Translated by C. Garnett. New York: Random House.

————. 1980. *The Possessed*. Translated by Andrew MacAndrew. New York: Signet.

Dowler, Wayne. 1982. *Dostoevsky, Grigor'ev, and Native Soil Conservatism*. Toronto: University of Toronto Press.

Dreizin, Felix. 1990. *The Russian Soul and the Jew: Essays in Literary Ethnocriticism*. Lanham, Md.: University Press of America.

Dreizin, Felix, and T. Priestly. 1982. "A Systematic Approach to Russian Obscene Language." *Russian Linguistics* 6, 232–49.

Drummond, D. A., and G. Perkins. 1987. *Dictionary of Russian Obscenities*, 3d ed. Oakland: Scythian Books.

Druzhnikov, Iurii. 1989. *Angely na konchike igly*. New York: Liberty Publishing House.

Dundes, Alan. 1984. *Life Is Like a Chicken Coop Ladder: A Portrait of German Culture Through Folklore*. New York: Columbia University Press.

————. 1986. "The Flood as Male Myth of Creation." *Journal of Psychoanalytic Anthropology* 9, 359–72.

Dunham, Vera. 1960. "The Strong-Woman Motif." *The Transformation of Russian Society*. Edited by C. E. Black. Cambridge: Harvard University Press, 459–83.

————. 1979. *In Stalin's Time: Middleclass Values in Soviet Fiction*. Cambridge: Cambridge University Press.

Dunlop, John B. 1972. *Staretz Amvrosy: Model for Dostoevsky's Staretz Zossima*. Belmont, Mass.: Nordland.

Dunn, Patrick P. 1974. "'That Enemy Is the Baby': Childhood in Imperial Russia." *The History of Childhood*. Edited by L. deMause. New York: Psychohistory Press, 383–405.

Durova, Nadezhda. 1988 (1836). *Izbrannye sochineniia kavalerist-devitsy N. A. Durovoi*. Moscow: Moskovskii rabochii.

Edie, James M., James P. Scanlan, Mary-Barbara Zeldin, and George L. Kline, eds. 1969. *Russian Philosophy*. Chicago: Quadrangle Books, 3 vols.

Efimenko, Aleksandra. 1884. *Izsledovaniia narodnoi zhizni*. Moscow: Izdanie V. I. Kasperova, "Russkaia" tipo-litografiia, vol. 1.

Eklof, Ben. 1991. "Worlds in Conflict: Patriarchal Authority, Discipline and the Russian School, 1861–1914." *Slavic Review* 50, 792–806.

Elkins, Stanley M. 1963. *Slavery: A Problem in American Institutional and Intellectual Life.* New York: Universal Library.

Engel, Barbara Alpern. 1989. "Women, Work and Family in the Factories of Rural Russia." *Russian History* 16, 223–37.

Engels, Friedrich. 1985 (1884). *The Origin of the Family, Private Property and the State.* Harmondsworth: Penguin.

Epshtein, Mikhail. 1989. "Opyty v zhanre 'opytov'." *Zerkala* 1, 296–315.

Eremina, V. I. 1991. *Ritual i fol'klor.* Leningrad: Nauka.

———. 1992. "Zagovornye kolybel'nye pesni." *Fol'klor i etnograficheskaia deistvitel'nost'.* Edited by A. K. Baiburin. Saint Petersburg: Nauka, 29–34.

Erikson, Erik H. 1963 (1950). *Childhood and Society.* New York: W. W. Norton.

———. 1969. *Gandhi's Truth: On the Origins of Militant Nonviolence.* New York: W. W. Norton.

Erofeev, Viktor. 1990. "Neither Salvation Nor Sausage." *New York Review of Books,* 14 June, pp. 23–25.

Esaulov, I. 1992. "Totalitarnost' i sobornost': dva lika russkoi kul'tury." *Voprosy literatury,* no. 1, 148–70.

Evreinov, N., ed. 1979 (1913?). *Istoriia telesnykh nakazanii v Rossii.* New York: Chalidze Publications.

Evtushenko, Evgenii. 1988. "Priterpelost'." *Literaturnaia gazeta,* no. 19, 11 May, p. 13.

Farnsworth, Beatrice. 1992 (1985). "Village Women Experience the Revolution." *Russian Peasant Women.* Edited by B. Farnsworth and L. Viola. Oxford: Oxford University Press, 145–66.

Fasmer, Maks. 1986–87 (1950–58). *Etimologicheskii slovar' russkogo iazyka,* 2d ed. Moscow: Progress, 4 vols.

Fedorov, Nikolai Fedorovich. 1906–13. *Filosofiia obshchego dela.* Edited by V. A. Kozhevnikov and N. P. Peterson. Vernyi-Moscow, 2 vols.

———. 1928–29. *Filosofiia obshchego dela,* 2d edition. Kharbin, vol. 1.

Fedotov, George P. 1942. "The Religious Sources of Russian Populism." *Russian Review* 1/2, 27–39.

———. 1954 (1938). "The Russian." *Russian Review* 13, 3–17.

———. 1975. *The Russian Religious Mind.* Belmont, Mass.: Nordland, 2 vols.

Fedotov, Georgii. 1981. *Rossiia i svoboda (sbornik statei).* New York: Chalidze Publications.

Fenichel, Otto. 1945. *The Psychoanalytic Theory of Neurosis.* New York: W. W. Norton.

Ferenczi, Sandor. 1938. *Thalassa: A Theory of Genitality.* Translated by H. Bunker. New York: Psychoanalytic Quarterly.

Field, Daniel. 1989 (1976). *Rebels in the Name of the Tsar.* Boston: Unwin Hyman.

Fisher, Seymour, and Roger P. Greenberg. 1977. *The Scientific Credibility of Freud's Theories and Therapy.* New York: Basic Books.

Fletcher, Giles. 1966 (1591). *Of the Russe Common Wealth.* Cambridge: Harvard University Press.

Flugel, J. C. 1950 (1921). *The Psycho-Analytic Study of the Family.* London: Hogarth Press.

Frank, Stephen P. 1990. "Popular Justice, Community, and Culture Among the Russian Peasantry, 1870–1900." *The World of the Russian Peasant: Post-Emancipation Culture and Society.* Edited by B. Eklof and S. Frank. Boston: Unwin Hyman, 133–53.

Freud, Sigmund. 1953–65. *The Standard Edition of the Complete Psychological Works of Sigmund Freud.* Translated under general editorship of J. Strachey. London: Hogarth Press, 24 vols. (= *SE* in the text).

———. 1989 (1928). "Dostoevsky and Parricide." *Russian Literature and Psychoanalysis.* Edited by D. Rancour-Laferriere. Amsterdam: John Benjamins, 41–57.

Friedrich, Paul. 1970. *Proto-Indo-European Trees: The Arboreal System of a Prehistoric People.* Chicago: University of Chicago Press.

———. 1972. "Social Context and Semantic Feature: The Russian Pronominal Usage." *Directions in Sociolinguistics.* Edited by J. Gumperz and D. Hymes. New York: Holt, Rinehart and Winston, 270–300.

Fromm, Erich. 1965 (1941). *Escape from Freedom.* New York: Avon Books.

Gamaiunov, Igor'. 1992. "Posledniaia porka." *Literaturnaia gazeta,* no. 52, p. 13.

GAP (Group for the Advancement of Psychiatry). 1987. *Us and Them: The Psychology of Ethnonationalism.* New York: Brunner/Mazel.

Garrard, John G. 1991a. "A Conflict of Visions: Vasilii Grossman and the Russian Idea." *The Search for Self-Definition in Russian Literature.* Edited by Ewa Thompson. Houston: Rice University Press, 57–75.

———. 1991b. "Stepsons in the Motherland: The Architectonics of Vasilii Grossman's *Zhizn' i sud'ba.*" *Slavic Review* 50, 336–46.

Geha, Richard, Jr. 1970. "Dostoevsky and 'The Gambler': A Contribution to the Psychogenesis of Gambling, Parts I & II." *Psychoanalytic Review* 57, 95–123, 189–302.

Geller, Mikhail. 1985. *Mashina i vintiki.* London: Overseas Publications Interchange.

Gel'man, Aleksandr. 1992. "Obratno vpered." *Moskovskie novosti,* no. 32, 9 August, p. 24.

Gennep, Arnold van. 1960. *The Rites of Passage.* Translated by M. Vizedom, G. Caffee. London: Routledge and Kegan Paul.

Gertsen, A. I. 1954–65. *Sobranie sochinenii v tridtsati tomakh.* Moscow: Izdatel'stvo ANSSSR, 30 vols.

———. 1962 (1852–68). *Byloe i dumy.* Moscow: GIKhL, 2 vols.

Gippius, Zinaida. 1908. *Chernoe po belomu.* Saint Petersburg: M. V. Pirozhkov.

Glazov, Yuri. 1985. *The Russian Mind Since Stalin's Death*. Dordrecht: D. Reidel Publishing Company.

Glickman, Rose L. 1984. *Russian Factory Women: Workplace and Society, 1880–1914*. Berkeley: University of California Press.

Godlevskii, V. V. 1883. *Materialy dlia ucheniia o russkoi bane*. Saint Petersburg: M. Stasiulevich.

Gogol', N. V. 1937–52. *Polnoe sobranie sochinenii*. Moscow: ANSSSR, 14 vols.

Goldberg, Kate. 1992. "Second Thoughts on Gender Roles in Russia." *Women: East—West* 25, 8.

Golod, S. I. 1984. *Stabil'nost' sem'i: sotsiologicheskii i demograficheskii aspekty*. Leningrad: Nauka.

Golovanov, Vasilii. 1992. "V poiskakh utrachennogo smysla." *Literaturnaia gazeta*, no. 3, 15 January, p. 13.

Gorer, Geoffrey, and John Rickman. 1962 (1949). *The People of Great Russia: A Psychological Study*. New York: W. W. Norton.

Gor'kii, M. 1937 (1905). *Literaturno-kriticheskie stat'i*. Edited by S. M. Breitburg. Moscow: GIKhL.

———. 1978 (1912). "A. M. Gor'kii—V. V. Rozanovu." *Kontekst*, 300–342.

Gorodetzky, Nadejda. 1973 (1938). *The Humiliated Christ in Modern Russian Thought*. New York: AMS Press.

Gorskii, V. 1977 (1969). "Russian Messianism and the New National Consciousness." *The Political, Social and Religious Thought of Russian "Samizdat"—An Anthology*. Edited by M. Meerson-Aksenov and B. Shragin. Belmont, Mass.: Nordland, 353–93.

Goskomstat. 1990. "Novaia informatsiia Goskomstata SSSR: zhenshchiny v SSSR." *Vestnik statistiki*, no. 1, 41–64.

Grafova, L., ed. 1984. "O pape, mame i semeinoi drame." *Literaturnaia gazeta*, no. 52, 26 December, p. 13.

Grafova, L. 1991. "Bezhentsy ot samikh sebia?" *Literaturnaia gazeta*, 16 January, p. 6.

Grass, Karl Konrad. 1907–14. *Die russischen Sekten*. Leipzig: J. C. Hinrichs, 2 vols.

Gray, Francine du Plessix. 1990. *Soviet Women: Walking the Tightrope*. New York: Doubleday.

Greenberg, Jay R., and Stephen A. Mitchell. 1983. *Object Relations in Psychoanalytic Theory*. Cambridge: Harvard University Press.

Gromyko, M. M. 1986. *Traditsionnye normy povedeniia i formy obshcheniia russkikh krest'ian XIX v.* Moscow: Nauka.

———. 1989. "Sem'ia i obshchina v traditsionnoi dukhovnoi kul'ture russkikh krest'ian XVIII-XIX vv." *Russkie: semeinyi i obshchestvennyi byt*. Edited by M. M. Gromyko and T. A. Listova. Moscow: Nauka, 7–24.

———. 1991. *Mir russkoi derevni*. Moscow: Molodaia gvardiia.

Grossman, Vasilii. 1973 (1970). *Vse techet . . . .* Frankfurt: Posev.

———. 1980. *Zhizn' i sud'ba*. Lausanne: L'Age d'Homme.

Gurova, Irina. 1992. "Kuda mne teper'—na panel'?" *Literaturnaia gazeta*, 8 January, p. 10.

Gustafson, Richard F. 1986. *Leo Tolstoy: Resident and Stranger—A Study in Fiction and Theology*. Princeton: Princeton University Press.

Gvozdikova, L. S., and G. G. Shapovalova. 1982. "'Dev'ia krasota' (kartografirovanie svadebnogo obriada na materialakh Kalininskoi, Iaroslavskoi i Kostromskoi oblastei)." *Obriady i obriadovyi fol'klor*. Editd by V. K. Sokolova. Moscow: Nauka, 264–77.

Hackel, Sergei. 1975. *The Poet and the Revolution: Aleksandr Blok's "The Twelve."* Oxford: Oxford University Press.

Hansson, Carola, and Karin Lidén. 1983. *Moscow Women*. Translated by G. Bothmer, G. Blecher, and L. Blecher. New York: Pantheon Books.

Heldt, Barbara. 1987. *Terrible Perfection: Women and Russian Literature*. Bloomington: Indiana University Press.

Heller, Mikhail. 1988 (1985). *Cogs in the Wheel: The Formation of Soviet Man*. New York: Alfred A. Knopf.

Hellie, Richard. 1982. *Slavery in Russia 1450–1725*. Chicago: University of Chicago Press.

———. 1987. "Edward Keenan's Scholarly Ways." *Russian Review* 46, 177–90.

Heuvel, Katrina vanden. 1992. "Women of Russia, Unite!" *New York Times*, 12 September, p. 13.

Hingley, Ronald. 1977. *The Russian Mind*. New York: Charles Scribner's Sons.

Hoch, Steven L. 1986. *Serfdom and Social Control in Russia: Petrovskoe, A Village in Tambov*. Chicago: University of Chicago Press.

Holt, Alix. 1980. "Domestic Labour and Soviet Society." *Home, School and Leisure in the Soviet Union*. Edited by J. Brine, M. Perrie, and A. Sutton. London: George Allen and Unwin, 26–54.

Horner, Thomas M. 1992. "The Origin of the Symbiotic Wish." *Psychoanalytic Psychology* 9, 25–48.

Horney, Karen. 1964 (1937). *The Neurotic Personality of Our Time*. New York: W. W. Norton.

———. 1967. *Feminine Psychology*. Edited by H. Kelman. New York: W. W. Norton.

Hubbs, Joanna. 1988. *Mother Russia: The Feminine Myth in Russian Culture*. Bloomington: Indiana University Press.

Hunt, Morton. 1974. *Sexual Behavior in the 1970's*. Chicago: Playboy Press.

Hunt, Priscilla. 1985. "Avvakum Petrovich, Protopop (1620–82)." *Handbook of Russian Literature*. Edited by V. Terras. New Haven: Yale University Press, 29–31.

Iankova, Z. A. 1975. "Razvitie lichnosti zhenshchiny v sovetskom obshchestve." *Sotsiologicheskie issledovaniia*, no. 4, 42–51.

———. 1978. *Sovetskaia zhenshchina (sotsial'nyi portret)*. Moscow: Izdatel'stvo politicheskoi literatury.

———. 1979. *Gorodskaia sem'ia*. Moscow: Nauka.

Illiustrov, I. I. 1904. *Sbornik rossiiskikh poslovits i pogovorok.* Kiev: Tipografiia S. V. Kul'zhenko.

Inkeles, Alex, Eugenia Hanfmann, and Helen Beier. 1958. "Modal Personality and Adjustment to the Soviet Socio-Political System." *Human Relations* 11, 3–22.

Isačenko, Alexander V. 1976. *Opera Selecta.* Munich: Wilhelm Fink Verlag (= *Forum Slavicum,* vol. 45).

Isaiia (Ieromonakh). 1989. "O pochitanii Bozhiei Materi v Pravoslavnoi Tserkvi." *Pochitanie Bozhiei Materi v russkoi Pravoslavnoi Tserkvi i Rimsko-Katolicheskoi Tserkvi v Pol'she.* Warsaw / Moscow: Novum / Moskovskii Patriarkhat, 119–25.

Ispa, Jean. 1983. "Soviet and American Childbearing Experiences and Attitudes: A Comparison." *Slavic Review* 42, 1–13.

Istomin, Fedor. 1892. "O prichitaniiakh i plachakh, zapisannykh v olonetskoi i arkhangel'skoi gub." *Zhivaia starina* 2, sect. 2, 139–45.

Iurkevich, N. G. 1970. *Sovetskaia sem'ia: funktsii i usloviia stabil'nosti.* Minsk: Izdatel'stvo BGU im. V. I. Lenina.

Ivanits, Linda J. 1989. *Russian Folk Belief.* Armonk, New York: M. E. Sharpe.

Ivanov, A. 1969. "Otritsatel'noe dostoinstvo." *Voprosy literatury,* no. 7, 129–38.

Ivanov, Viacheslav. 1909. *Po zvezdam.* Saint Petersburg: Ory.

———. 1971–79. *Sobranie sochinenii.* Brussels: Foyer Oriental Chrétien, 3 vols.

Ivanova, Natal'ia. 1992. "Russkii vopros." *Znamia,* no. 1, 191–204.

Kabakov, Aleksandr. 1990. "Ochishchenie—skorbnyi i neminuemyi put'." *Moskovskie novosti,* no. 50, 16 December, p. 1.

Kabanov, V. 1986. "Khorosha russkaia bania!" *Nauka i zhizn',* no. 12, 134–37.

Kalustova, N. G. 1985. *Serdtse materi i pravda revoliutsii.* Moscow: Prosveshchenie.

Kamenskii, Z. A. 1986. "Urok Chaadaeva (P. Ia Chaadaev v 40–50–kh godakh XIX v.)." *Voprosy filosofii,* no. 1, 111–39.

Kanzer, Mark. 1948. "Dostoevsky's Matricidal Impulses." *Psychoanalytic Review* 35, 115–25.

Kass, Frederic. 1987. "Self-Defeating Personality Disorder: An Empirical Study." *Journal of Personality Disorders* 1, 168–73.

Katerli, Nina, and Iurii Shmidt. 1992. "Pochemu volkodav prav, a liudoed—net?" *Literaturnaia gazeta* 14, 12.

Katz, Anita Weinreb. 1990. "Paradoxes of Masochism." *Psychoanalytic Psychology* 7, 225–41.

Kavelin, K. D. 1882. *Krest'ianskii vopros.* Saint Petersburg: M. Stasiulevich.

Keenan, Edward L. 1986. "Muscovite Political Folkways." *Russian Review* 45, 115–81.

Kennan, George F. 1971. *The Marquis de Custine and His Russia in 1839.* Princeton: Princeton University Press.

Kerblay, Basile. 1985. *Du mir aux agrovilles.* Paris: Institut d'études slaves.

Kernberg, Otto F. 1984. "The Couch at Sea: Psychoanalytic Studies of Group and Organizational Leadership." *International Journal of Group Psychotherapy* 34, 5–23.

———. 1988. "Clinical Dimensions of Masochism." *Masochism: Current Psychoanalytic Perspectives.* Edited by R. Glick and D. Meyers. Hillsdale, N.J.: Analytic Press, 61–79.

Khanga, Yelena. 1991. "No Matryoshkas Need Apply." *New York Times,* 25 November, p. A15.

Kharchev, A. G. 1970. "Byt i sem'ia kak kategorii istoricheskogo materializma." *Problemy byta, braka i sem'i.* Edited by N. Solov'ev, Iu. Lazauskas, and Z. Iankova. Vilnius: Mintis, 9–22.

———. 1979. *Brak i sem'ia v SSSR* (2d ed.). Moscow: Mysl'.

Kharchev, A. G., and S. I. Golod. 1971. *Professional'naia rabota zhenshchin i sem'ia.* Leningrad: Nauka.

Khomiakov, Aleksei. 1955. *Izbrannye sochineniia.* Edited by N. S. Arsen'ev. New York: Izdatel'stvo Imeni Chekhova.

Khripkova, A. G., and D. V. Kolesov. 1981. *Devochka—podrostok—devushka.* Moscow: Prosveshchenie.

Kingston-Mann, Esther. 1991. "Peasant Communes and Economic Innovation: A Preliminary Inquiry." *Peasant Economy, Culture, and Politics of European Russia, 1800–1921.* Edited by E. Kingston-Mann and T. Mixter. Princeton: Princeton University Press, 23–51.

Kinsey, Alfred C., W. B. Pomeroy, C. E. Martin, and Paul H. Gebhard. 1965 (1953). *Sexual Behavior in the Human Female.* New York: Pocket Books.

Kireevskii, I. V. 1984. *Izbrannye stat'i.* Moscow: Sovremennik.

Kiva, A. 1990. "Mify ukhodiashchikh vremen." *Izvestiia,* no. 93, 2 April.

Klein, Melanie. 1977 (1921–45). *Love, Guilt and Reparation and Other Works, 1921–1945.* New York: Dell.

Klibanov, A. I. 1982 (1965). *History of Religious Sectarianism in Russia (1860s–1917).* Translated by E. Dunn. New York: Pergamon Press.

Klimas, I. S. 1991. "Spetsifika nazvanii rastenii v fol'klornoi leksike." *Russkii fol'klor* 26, 134–42.

Kline, George L. 1968. *Religious and Anti-Religious Thought in Russia.* Chicago: University of Chicago Press.

Kluckhohn, Clyde. 1962. *Culture and Behavior.* New York: Free Press.

Klugman, Jeffry. 1989. *The New Soviet Elite: How They Think and What They Want.* New York: Praeger.

Kochubei, Boris. 1990. "Dozhdemsia li my kul'ta lichnosti?" *Literaturnaia gazeta,* no. 51, 19 December, p. 13.

Koenigsberg, Richard A. 1977. *The Psychoanalysis of Racism, Revolution and Nationalism.* New York: Library of Social Science.

———. 1989. *Symbiosis and Separation: Towards a Psychology of Culture.* New York: Library of Art and Social Science.

Kogan, Emil'. 1982. *Solianoi stolp: politicheskaia psikhologiia Solzhenitsyna.* Paris: Poiski.

Kohn, Hans. 1960. *Pan-Slavism: Its History and Ideology,* 2d ed. New York: Vintage Books.

Kohut, Heinz. 1971. *The Analysis of the Self.* New York: International Universities Press.

Kolakowski, Leszek. 1992. "A Calamitous Accident." *Times Literary Supplement,* 6 November, p. 5.

Kolchin, Peter. 1987. *Unfree Labor: American Slavery and Russian Serfdom.* Cambridge: Harvard University Press.

Kolesnitskaia, I. M., and L. M. Telegina. 1977. "Kosa i krasota v svadebnom fol'klore vostochnykh slavian." *Fol'klor i etnografiia: sviazi fol'klora s drevnimi predstavleniiami i obriadami.* Edited by B. N. Putilov. Leningrad: Nauka, 112–22.

Kollmann, Nancy Shields. 1991. "Women's Honor in Early Modern Russia." *Russia's Women: Accommodation, Resistance, Transformation.* Edited by B. Clements, B. Engel, and C. Worobec. Berkeley: University of California Press, 60–73.

Kolpakova, N. P. 1973. *Lirika russkoi svad'by.* Leningrad: Nauka.

Komarovich, V. L. 1982 (1936). *Kitezhskaia legenda: Opyt izucheniia mestnykh legend.* Berkeley: Berkeley Slavic Specialties.

Kon, Igor'. 1968. "Natsional'nyi kharakter—mif ili real'nost'?" *Inostrannaia literatura,* no. 9, 215–29.

———. 1970. "Muzhestvennye zhenshchiny? Zhenstvennye muzhchiny?" *Literaturnaia gazeta,* 1 January, p. 12.

———. 1988. *Vvedenie v seksologiiu.* Moscow: Meditsina.

Kosven, M. O. 1948. *Matriarkhat: Istoriia problemy.* Moscow/Leningrad: Izdatel'stvo Akademii nauk SSSR.

Kovalevskii, I. 1895. *Iurodstvo o Khriste i Khrista radi iurodivye vostochnoi i russkoi tserkvi.* Moscow: A. I. Snegirevaia.

Kovalevsky, Maxime. 1891. *Modern Customs and Ancient Laws of Russia.* London: David Nutt.

Krafft-Ebing, Richard von. 1929 (1886). *Psychopathia Sexualis.* Translated and adapted by F. J. Rebman. Chicago: Login Brothers.

Kriegman, Daniel, and Malcolm Slavin. 1989. "The Myth of the Repetition Compulsion and the Negative Therapeutic Reaction: An Evolutionary Biological Analysis." *Progress in Self Psychology* 5, 209–53.

Kristeva, Julia. 1982. *Powers of Horror: An Essay on Abjection.* Translated by L. Roudiez. New York: Columbia University Press.

Kruglov, Iu. G., ed. 1988–89. *Biblioteka russkogo fol'klora: skazki.* Moscow: Sovetskaia Rossiia, 3 vols.

Kutepov, Konstantin. 1900. *Sekty khlystov i skoptsov,* 2d ed. Stavropol'-gubernskii: T. M. Timofeev.

Kuz'min, S. S., and N. L. Shadrin. 1989. *Russko-angliiskii slovar' poslovits i pogovorok.* Moscow: Russkii iazyk.

Kuznetsova, Larisa. 1980. *Zhenshchina na rabote i doma.* Moscow: Izdatel'stvo politicheskoi literatury.

———. 1987. "A Woman Executive: Why Not?" *New Times,* no. 25, 22–24.

———. 1988. "What Makes a Woman Happy." *New Times,* no. 37, 46–47.

Lane, Robert C., James W. Hull, and Leonore M. Foehrenbach. 1991. "The Addiction to Negativity." *Psychoanalytic Review* 78, 391–410.

Lapidus, Gail Warshofsky. 1978. *Women in Soviet Society: Equality, Development, and Social Change.* Berkeley: University of California Press.

———. 1988. "The Interaction of Women's Work and Family Roles in the U.S.S.R." *Women and Work: An Annual Review* 3, 87–121.

Laplanche, J., and J. B. Pontalis. 1973. *The Language of Psychoanalysis.* Translated by D. Nicholson-Smith. New York: W. W. Norton.

Leatherbarrow, W. J., and D. C. Offord, eds. 1987. *A Documentary History of Russian Thought: From the Enlightenment to Marxism.* Ann Arbor: Ardis.

Lednicki, Waclaw. 1954. *Russia, Poland and the West.* London: Hutchinson.

Leibin, Valerii. 1990. *Freid, psikhoanaliz i sovremennaia zapadnaia filosofiia.* Moscow: Izdatel'stvo politicheskoi literatury.

Leites, Nathan. 1953. *A Study of Bolshevism.* Glencoe: Free Press.

———. 1979. *Depression and Masochism: An Account of Mechanisms.* New York: W. W. Norton.

Lenin, Vladimir Il'ich. 1958–65. *Polnoe sobranie sochinenii,* 5th ed. Moscow: Gosudarstvennoe izdatel'stvo politicheskoi literatury, 55 vols.

Lenzer, Gertrud. 1975. "On Masochism: A Contribution to the History of a Phantasy and Its Theory." *Signs* 1, 277–324.

Lermontov, M. Iu. 1961–62. *Sobranie sochinenii v chetyrekh tomakh.* Moscow-Leningrad: Izdatel'stvo Akademii Nauk SSSR.

Leroy-Beaulieu, Anatole. 1902–5. *The Empire of the Tsars and the Russians.* Translated by Z. Ragozin. New York: G. P. Putnam's Sons, 3 vols.

Levi, Vladimir. 1969. *Ia i my.* Moscow: Molodaia gvardiia.

Levin, Eve. 1991. "Childbirth in Pre-Petrine Russia: Canon Law and Popular Traditions." *Russia's Women: Accommodation, Resistance, Transformation.* Edited by B. Clements, B. Engel, and C. Worobec. Berkeley: University of California Press, 44–59.

Levitt, Marcus C. 1989. *Russian Literary Politics and the Pushkin Celebration of 1880.* Ithaca: Cornell University Press.

Liaboe, Gary P., and James D. Guy. 1985. "Masochism and the Distortion of Servanthood." *Journal of Psychology and Theology* 13, 255–62.

Liberman, Anatoly. 1983. *Mikhail Lermontov: Major Poetical Works.* Minneapolis: University of Minnesota Press.

Likhachev, Dmitrii S. 1970. *Chelovek v literature drevnei Rusi.* Moscow: Nauka.

———. 1987. *Izbrannye raboty v trekh tomakh.* Leningrad: Khudozhestvennaia literatura, 3 vols.

———. 1988. "Rossiia." *Literaturnaia gazeta,* no. 41, 12 October, p. 5.

———. 1992. "Poverkh bar'erov." *Literaturnaia gazeta,* no. 19, 6 May, p. 6.

Likhachev, Dmitrii S., and A. M. Panchenko. 1976. *"Smekhovoi mir" drevnei Rusi.* Leningrad: Nauka.

Lipton, Earle L., Alfred Steinschneider, and Julius B. Richmond. 1965. "Swaddling, A Child Care Practice: Historical, Cultural and Experimental Observations." *Pediatrics* 35, part II, 521–67.

Listova, T. A. 1989. "Russkie obriady, obychai i pover'ia, sviazannye s povival'noi babkoi." *Russkie: semeinyi i obshchestvennyi byt.* Edited by M. M. Gromyko and T. A. Listova. Moscow: Nauka, 142–71.

Litvak, B. G. 1971. "O nekotorykh chertakh psikhologii russkikh krepostnykh pervoi poloviny XIX v." *Istoriia i psikhologiia.* Edited by B. F. Porshnev and L. I. Antsyferova. Moscow: Nauka, 199–214.

Loewenstein, Rudolph M. 1957. "A Contribution to the Psychoanalytic Theory of Masochism." *Journal of the American Psychoanalytic Association* 5, 197–234.

Losev, Aleksei. 1990a (1941). "Rodina." *Literaturnaia gazeta,* no. 4, 24 January, p. 6.

——. 1990b (1941). "Motherland." *Literary Gazette International,* no. 7, May, pp. 14–15.

Lunt, Horace G. 1990. "History, Nationalism, and the Written Language of Early Rus'." *Slavic and East European Journal* 34, 1–28.

Macey, David A. J. 1990. "The Peasant Commune and the Stolypin Reforms: Peasant Attitudes, 1906–14." *Land Commune and Peasant Community in Russia.* Edited by R. Bartlett. London: Macmillan, 219–36.

Mahler, Margaret, Fred Pine, and Anni Bergman. 1975. *The Psychological Birth of the Human Infant: Symbiosis and Individuation.* New York: Basic Books.

Maiakovskii, Vladimir. 1970 (1924). *Sochineniia v trekh tomakh.* Moscow: Khudozhestvennaia literatura.

Maksimenko, Valéry. 1988. "Le pouvoir psychologique dans la famille urbaine russe contemporaine." *L'évolution des modèles familiaux dans les pays de l'Est européen et en U.R.S.S..* Edited by B. Kerblay. Paris: Institut d'études slaves, 139–154.

Maksimov, S. V. 1909. *Sobranie sochinenii.* Saint Petersburg: Prosveshchenie, 20 vols.

Mamaladze, Irma. 1985. "Posledniaia privilegiia." *Literaturnaia gazeta,* no. 4, 23 January, p. 11.

Mamonova, Tatyana. 1989. *Russian Women's Studies: Essays on Sexism in Soviet Culture.* New York: Pergamon.

Markov, Vladimir, and Merrill Sparks, eds. 1967. *Modern Russian Poetry.* Indianapolis: Bobbs-Merrill.

Marshall, Bonnie. 1991. "A Commentary on Francine du Plessix Gray's 'Reflections (Soviet Women).'" *Women East-West,* January, pp. 6–7.

Martin, Dale B. 1990. *Slavery as Salvation: The Metaphor of Slavery in Pauline Christianity.* New Haven: Yale University Press.

Martynova, Antonina. 1978. "Life in the Pre-Revolutionary Village as Reflected in Popular Lullabies." *The Family in Imperial Russia.* Edited by D. Ransel. Urbana: University of Illinois Press, 171–85.

Masaryk, Thomas Garrigue. 1955–67 (1912). *The Spirit of Russia: Studies in History, Literature and Philosophy*. Translated by R. Bass, E. Paul, and C. Paul. London: George Allen and Unwin, 3 vols.

Masson, Charles. 1800. *Secret Memoirs of the Court of Petersburg*. London: Longman and Rees.

Matorin, N. 1931. *Zhenskoe bozhestvo v pravoslavnom kul'te: piatnitsa—bogoroditsa*. Moscow: Moskovskii rabochii.

McDevitt, John B. 1983. "The Emergence of Hostile Aggression and Its Defensive and Adaptive Modifications during the Separation-Individuation Process." *Journal of the American Psychoanalytic Association* (supplement) 31, 273–300.

Mead, Margaret. 1951. *Soviet Attitudes toward Authority*. New York: Rand/McGraw Hill.

———. 1954. "The Swaddling Hypothesis: Its Reception." *American Anthropologist* 56, 395–409.

Medvedev, Feliks. 1992. *Posle Rossii*. Moscow: Izdatel'stvo Respublika.

Medvedev, Zhores A. 1987. *Soviet Agriculture*. New York: W. W. Norton.

Meehan-Waters, Brenda. 1991. "The Authority of Holiness: Women Ascetics and Spiritual Elders in Nineteenth-Century Russia." *Church, Nation and State in Russia and Ukraine*. Edited by G. Hosking. London: Macmillan, 38–51.

Mel'chuk, Igor', and Aleksandr Zholkovskii. 1984. *Tolkovo-kombinatornyi slovar' sovremennogo russkogo iazyka*. Vienna: Wiener Slawistischer Almanach, Sonderband 14.

Meletinskii, E. M. 1958. *Geroi volshebnoi skazki: proiskhozhdenie obraza*. Moscow: Izdatel'stvo vostochnoi literatury.

Meletinskij, E. M. 1975 (1958). "The 'Low' Hero of the Fairy Tale." *The Study of Russian Folklore*. Edited by F. Oinas and S. Soudakoff. The Hague: Mouton, 235–57.

Mel'gunov, S. P. 1919. *Iz istorii religiozno-obshchestvennykh dvizhenii v Rossii XIX v*. Moscow: Zadruga.

Menaker, Esther. 1979. *Masochism and the Emergent Ego*. New York: Human Sciences Press.

Men', Aleksandr. 1991. *Syn chelovecheskii*, 4th ed. Moscow: IPTs "Vita."

Merezhkovskii, Dmitrii. 1914. *Polnoe sobranie sochinenii*. Moscow: I. D. Sytin, 24 vols.

Meyer, Alfred G. 1977. "Marxism and the Women's Movement." *Women in Russia*. Edited by D. Atkinson, A. Dallin, and G. Warshofsky Lapidus. Stanford: Stanford University Press, 85–112.

Meyers, Helen. 1988. "A Consideration of Treatment Techniques in Relation to the Functions of Masochism." *Masochism: Current Psychoanalytic Perspectives*. Edited by R. Glick and D. Meyers. Hillsdale, N.J.: Analytic Press, 175–88.

Mickiewicz, Adam. 1974. *Dziady*. Warsaw: Czytelnik.

Miller, Wright. 1961. *Russians as People*. New York: E. P. Dutton.

Mironov, Boris. 1990. "The Russian Peasant Commune After the Reforms of the 1860s." *The World of the Russian Peasant: Post-Emancipation Culture and Society*. Edited by B. Eklof and S. Frank. Boston: Unwin Hyman, 7–43.

Mochul'skii, K. 1951. *Vladimir Solov'ev: Zhizn' i uchenie*. Paris: YMCA-Press.

Molodtsov, Grigorii. 1976. "Devushka ili kovboi?" *Literaturnaia gazeta*, 24 November, p. 11.

Moroz, Oleg. 1993. "Nas snova obvedut vokrug pal'tsa!" *Literaturnaia gazeta*, no. 8, 24 February, p. 2.

Moyle, Natalie K. 1987. "Mermaids *(Rusalki)* and Russian Beliefs about Women." *New Studies in Russian Language and Literature*. Edited by A. L. Crone and C. V. Chvany. Columbus: Slavica Publishers, 221–38.

Munro, George E. 1980. "Khlysty." *Modern Encyclopedia of Russian and Soviet History*. Edited by J. Wieczynski. Gulf Breeze, Fla.: Academic International Press, vol. 16, 150–54.

Murav, Harriet. 1992. *Holy Foolishness: Dostoevsky's Novels and the Poetics of Cultural Critique*. Stanford: Stanford University Press.

Myl'nikova, K., and V. Tsintsius. 1926. "Severno-velikorusskaia svad'ba." *Materialy po svad'be i semeino-rodovomu stroiu narodov SSSR*. Edited by V. G. Bogoraz and L. Ia. Shternberg. Leningrad, 17–170.

Nabokov, Vladimir, translator, commentator. 1981. *Aleksandr Pushkin: Eugene Onegin: A Novel in Verse*. Princeton: Princeton University Press, 2 vols.

Nekrasov, N. A. 1967. *Polnoe sobranie stikhotvorenii v trekh tomakh*. Leningrad: Sovetskii pisatel'.

Nemilov, A. 1932 (1930). *The Biological Tragedy of Woman*. Translated by S. Ofental. New York: Covici, Friede, Publishers.

Niederland, William G. 1956–57. "River Symbolism." *Psychoanalytic Quarterly* 25–26, 469–504; 50–75.

Nikol'skii, A. 1898. "Lichnost' v obshchinnom bytu (K peresmotru krest'ianskogo polozheniia)." *Russkoe ekonomicheskoe obozrenie* 1, 64–95.

Novick, Kerry Kelly, and Jack Novick. 1987. "The Essence of Masochism." *Psychoanalytic Study of the Child* 42, 353–84.

Nydes, Jule. 1963. "The Paranoid-Masochistic Character." *Psychoanalytic Review* 50, 215–51.

Obukhova, E. 1989. "Zagadka blokovskogo 'Korshuna'." *Voprosy literatury*, no. 12, 200–209.

Odoevskii, A. I. 1958. *Polnoe sobranie stikhotvorenii*. Leningrad: Sovetskii pisatel'.

Okudzhava, Bulat. 1982. *65 pesen*. Ann Arbor: Ardis.

———. 1992. "Zapiski vozbuzhdennogo diletanta." *Moskovskie novosti*, no. 7, 16 February, p. 5.

Olearius, Adam. 1967 (1656). *The Travels of Olearius in Seventeenth-Century Russia*. Translated and edited by S. H. Baron. Stanford: Stanford University Press.

Ortner, Sherry. 1974. "Is Female to Male as Nature Is to Culture?" *Woman,*

Culture, and Society. Edited by M. Rosaldo and L. Lamphere. Stanford: Stanford University Press, 67–87.

Panken, Shirley. 1973. *The Joy of Suffering: Psychoanalytic Theory and Therapy of Masochism.* New York: Jason Aronson.

Paris, Bernard J. 1973. "*Notes from Underground:* A Horneyan Analysis." *PMLA* 88, 511–22.

Parthé, Kathleen F. 1992. *Russian Village Prose: The Radiant Past.* Princeton: Princeton University Press.

Pasternak, Boris Leonidovich. 1989 (1956). *Doktor Zhivago.* Moscow: Knizhnaia palata.

Peers, Jo. 1985. "Workers by Hand and Womb: Soviet Women and the Demographic Crisis." *Soviet Sisterhood: British Feminists on Women in the USSR.* Edited by B. Holland. London: Fourth Estate, 116–44.

Perrie, Maureen. 1989. "Folklore as Evidence of Peasant *Mentalité:* Social Attitudes and Values in Russian Popular Culture." *Russian Review* 48, 119–43.

Peskov, Aleksei. 1992. "My: Nekotorye istoricheskie paralleli." *Druzhba narodov,* February, pp. 215–28.

Pevin, P. 1893. "Narodnaia svad'ba v tolvuiskom prikhode, petrozavodskogo uezda, olonetskoi gubernii." *Zhivaia starina* 3, sect. 2, 219–48.

Pipes, Richard. 1974. *Russia Under the Old Regime.* New York: Charles Scribner's Sons.

———. 1989. *Russia Observed: Collected Essays on Russian and Soviet History.* Boulder, Colo.: Westview Press.

———. 1991. *The Russian Revolution.* New York: Vintage Books.

Platonov, Andrei. 1984–85. *Sobranie sochinenii v trekh tomakh.* Moscow: Sovetskaia Rossiia.

Plotkin, Vladimir, and Jovan E. Howe. 1985. "The Unknown Tradition: Continuity and Innovation in Soviet Ethnography." *Dialectical Anthropology* 9, 257–312.

Pokrovskii, E. A. 1884. *Fizicheskoe vospitanie detei u raznykh narodov preimushestvenno Rossii.* Moscow: A. A. Kartsev.

Pomper, Philip. 1970. *The Russian Revolutionary Intelligentsia.* New York: Thomas Y. Crowell.

Pribylovskii, Vladimir. 1992. *Dictionary of Political Parties and Organizations in Russia.* Washington: Center for Strategic and International Studies.

Prokushev, Iurii. 1990. *Vse my—deti Rossii.* Moscow: Sovremennik.

Propp, V. Ia. 1961. *Narodnye liricheskie pesni.* Leningrad: Sovetskii pisatel'.

———. 1963. *Russkie agrarnye prazdniki.* Leningrad: Izdatel'stvo Leningradskogo Universiteta.

———. 1975. *Down Along the Mother Volga.* Translated and edited by R. Reeder. Philadelphia: University of Pennsylvania Press.

Pushkareva, L. A., and M. N. Shmeleva. 1974 (1959). "The Contemporary Russian Peasant Wedding." *Introduction to Soviet Ethnography.* Edited by

S. Dunn and E. Dunn. Berkeley: Highgate Road Social Science Research Station, vol. 1, 343–62.

Pushkareva, N. L. 1989. *Zhenshchiny drevnei Rusi.* Moscow: Mysl'.

Pushkin, Aleksandr. 1962–66. *Polnoe sobranie sochinenii v desiati tomakh.* Moscow: Nauka, 10 vols.

Pyle, Emily. 1989. "Prospects for a Third Wave of Russian Monasticism." *Report on the USSR* 1, no. 31, 4–6.

Radishchev, Aleksandr Nikolaevich. 1958 (1790). *A Journey From St. Petersburg to Moscow.* Edited by R. Thaler. Translated by L. Wiener. Cambridge: Harvard University Press.

———. 1961 (1790). *Puteshestvie iz Peterburga v Moskvu.* Moscow: GIKhL.

Ralston, W.R.S. 1872. *The Songs of the Russian People.* London: Ellis and Green.

Ramer, Samuel C. 1978. "Childbirth and Culture: Midwifery in the Nineteenth-Century Russian Countryside." *The Family in Imperial Russia.* Edited by D. Ransel. Urbana: University of Illinois Press, 218–35.

Rancour-Laferriere, Daniel. 1985. *Signs of the Flesh: An Essay on the Evolution of Hominid Sexuality.* Berlin: Mouton de Gruyter.

———. 1988a. *The Mind of Stalin: A Psychoanalytic Study.* Ann Arbor: Ardis.

———. 1988b. "The God of Solženicyn." *The Supernatural in Slavic and Baltic Literature: Essays in Honor of Victor Terras.* Edited by A. Mandelker and R. Reeder. Columbus: Slavica, 261–74.

———. 1989a. "Pushkin's Still Unravished Bride: A Psychoanalytic Study of Tat'jana's Dream." *Russian Literature* 25, 215–58.

———. 1989b. "Russian Literature and Psychoanalysis: Four Modes of Intersection." *Russian Literature and Psychoanalysis.* Edited by D. Rancour-Laferriere. Amsterdam: John Benjamins, 1–38.

———. 1990. Review of G. S. Morson and C. Emerson, *Rethinking Bakhtin. Slavic and East European Journal* 34, 523–24.

———. 1993a. *Tolstoy's Pierre Bezukhov: A Psychoanalytic Study.* London: Bristol Classical Press.

———. 1993b. "Lermontov's Farewell to Unwashed Russia: A Study in Narcissistic Rage." *Slavic and East European Journal* 37, 293–304.

———. 1993c. "The Couvade of Peter the Great: A Psychoanalytic Aspect of *The Bronze Horseman.*" *Puškin Today.* Edited by D. Bethea. Bloomington: Indiana University Press, 73–85.

———. 1993d. "Anna's Adultery: Distal Sociobiology vs. Proximate Psychoanalysis." *Tolstoy Studies Journal* 6, 33–46.

Rank, Otto. 1964 (1914). *The Myth of the Birth of the Hero and Other Writings.* New York: Vintage.

———. 1973 (1929). *The Trauma of Birth.* New York: Harper and Row.

Ransel, David L. 1988. *Mothers of Misery: Child Abandonment in Russia.* Princeton: Princeton University Press.

———. 1991. "Infant-Care Cultures in the Russian Empire." *Russia's Women: Accommodation, Resistance, Transformation.* Edited by B. Clements, B. Engel and C. Worobec. Berkeley: University of California Press, 113–32.

Reik, Theodor. 1941. *Masochism in Modern Man.* Translated by M. Beigel and G. Kurth. New York: Farrar, Straus and Co.

———. 1963. "The Three Women in a Man's Life." *Art and Psychoanalysis.* Edited by W. Phillips. New York: Meridian, 151–64.

Rein, G. E. 1889. *O russkom narodnom akusherstve.* Saint Petersburg: M. M. Stasiulevich.

Remennick, Larissa I. 1993. "Patterns of Birth Control." *Sex and Russian Society.* Edited by I. Kon and J. Riordan. London: Pluto Press, 45–63.

Reshetov, A. M. 1970. "Ob ispol'zovanii dannykh fol'klora dlia izucheniia rannikh form semeino-brachnykh otnoshenii." *Fol'klor i etnografiia.* Edited by B. N. Putilov. Leningrad: Nauka, 237–55.

Riasanovsky, Nicholas V. 1955. "Khomiakov on *Sobornost'.*" *Continuity and Change in Russian and Soviet Thought.* Edited by E. J. Simmons. Cambridge: Harvard University Press, 183–96.

Rice, James L. 1982. "Russian Stereotypes in the Freud-Jung Correspondence." *Slavic Review* 41, 19–34.

———. 1989. "Psychoanalysis of 'Peasant Marej': Some Residual Problems." *Russian Literature and Psychoanalysis.* Edited by D. Rancour-Laferriere. Amsterdam: John Benjamins, 245–61.

Rittikh, A. A. 1903. *Zavisimost' krest'ian ot obshchiny i mira.* Saint Petersburg: Tipografiia V. F. Kirshbauma.

Robinson, John P., Vladimir G. Andreyenkov, and Vasily D. Patrushev. 1989. *The Rhythm of Everyday Life: How Soviet and American Citizens Use Time.* Boulder, Colo.: Westview Press.

Rodzinskaia, I. Iu. 1981. "Material'noe blagosostoianie i stabil'nost' sem'i." *Sotsiologicheskie issledovaniia,* no. 3, 106–12.

Roland, Alan. 1988. *In Search of Self in India and Japan.* Princeton: Princeton University Press.

Rosen, Steven J. 1993. "Homoerotic Body Language in Dostoevsky." *Psychoanalytic Review* 80, 405–32.

Rosewater, Lynne. 1987. "A Critical Analysis of the Proposed Self-Defeating Personality Disorder." *Journal of Personality Disorders* 1, 190–95.

Rozanov, V. V. 1903. *Semeinyi vopros v Rossii.* Saint Petersburg: Tipografiia M. Merkusheva, 2 vols.

———. 1990a. *Sochineniia.* Moscow: Sovetskaia Rossiia.

———. 1990b. *Uedinennoe.* Moscow: Politizdat.

Rybakov, B. A. 1981. *Iazychestvo drevnikh slavian.* Moscow: Nauka.

———. 1987. *Iazychestvo drevnei Rusi.* Moscow: Nauka.

Rzhevskii, Leon. 1987. "Kommunizm—eto molodost' mira . . ." *Sintaksis,* 3–79.

Sakharov, I. P. 1989 (1885). *Skazaniia russkogo naroda.* Moscow: Khudozhestvennaia literatura.

Saltykov-Shchedrin, M. E. 1965–77. *Sobranie sochinenii.* Moscow: Khudozhestvennaia literatura, 20 vols.

———. 1980. *The History of a Town.* Translated by I. P. Foote. Oxford: Willem A. Meeuws.

Sanches, Antonio. 1779. *O parnykh rossiiskikh baniakh*. Saint Petersburg.

Sapozhnikov, D. I. 1891. *Samosozhzhenie v russkom raskole*. Moscow (repr. Gregg International, Westmead, England).

Sarnoff, Charles A. 1988. "Adolescent Masochism." *Masochism: Current Psychoanalytic Perspectives*. Edited by R. Glick and D. Meyers. Hillsdale, N.J.: Analytic Press, 205–24.

Saward, John. 1980. *Perfect Fools: Folly for Christ's Sake in Catholic and Orthodox Spirituality*. Oxford: Oxford University Press.

Schmemann, Serge. 1991. "The Soviet State, Born of a Dream, Dies." *New York Times*, 26 December, pp. A1, A8–A9.

Scott, Helen. 1992. "Community Involvement Projects in Russia." *American Association for the Advancement of Slavic Studies Newsletter* 32/5, p. 18.

Segal, Boris M. 1990. *The Drunken Society: Alcohol Abuse and Alcoholism in the Soviet Union—A Comparative Study*. New York: Hippocrene Books.

Seifrid, Thomas. 1992. "Literature for the Masochist: 'Childish' Intonation in Platonov's Later Works." *Wiener Slawistischer Almanach (Sonderband)* 31, 463–80.

Seliunin, Vasilii. 1988. "Istoki." *Novyi mir*, no. 5, 162–89.

———. 1989 (1988). "Roots." *Soviet Historians and Perestroika: The First Phase*. Edited by D. J. Raleigh. Armonk, New York: M. E. Sharpe, 165–208.

Selivanov, F. M., ed. 1990. *Biblioteka russkogo fol'klora: chastushki*. Moscow: Sovetskaia Rossiia.

———, ed. 1991. *Stikhi dukhovnye*. Moscow: Sovetskaia Rossiia.

Semenova, Svetlana. 1990. *Nikolai Fedorov: tvorchestvo zhizni*. Moscow: Sovetskii pisatel'.

Semenova-Tian-Shanskaia, O. P. 1914. *Zhizn' "Ivana": Ocherki iz byta krest'ian odnoi iz chernozemnykh gubernii*. Saint Petersburg: M. M. Stasiulevich.

Shafarevich, Igor'. 1989. "Rusofobiia." *Nash sovremennik*, nos. 6 (167–92), 11 (162–71).

Shanin, Teodor. 1985. *Russia as a 'Developing Society'*. London: Macmillan.

Shapovalova, G. G. 1977. "Maiskii tsikl vesennikh obriadov." *Fol'klor i etnografiia: sviazi fol'klora s drevnimi predstavleniiami i obriadami*. Edited by B. N. Putilov. Leningrad: Nauka, 104–111.

Shein, P. V. 1898. *Velikoruss v svoikh pesniakh, obriadakh, obychaiakh, verovaniiakh, skazkakh, legendakh i t. p.* Saint Petersburg: Imperatorskaia Akademiia Nauk (vol. 1).

Shergin, B. V. 1990. "Van'ka Dobroi." *Tsvetok paporotnika: skazki russkikh pisatelei XVII–XX vekov*. Moscow: Moskovskii rabochii, 369–76.

Shineleva, L. T. 1990. *Zhenshchina i obshchestvo: deklaratsii i real'nost'*. Moscow: Izdatel'stvo politicheskoi literatury.

Shlapentokh, Vladimir. 1984. *Love, Marriage, and Friendship in the Soviet Union*. New York: Praeger.

Shukshin, Vasilii. 1975. *Izbrannye proizvedeniia v dvukh tomakh*. Moscow: Molodaia gvardiia, 2 vols.

Siniavskii, Andrei (Abram Terts). 1974. "Literaturnyi protsess v Rossii." *Kontinent* 1, 143–90.

———. 1991. *Ivan-durak: ocherk russkoi narodnoi very*. Paris: Sintaksis.

———. 1992. "V tupikakh svobody." *Literaturnaia gazeta*, no. 14, 1 April, p. 3.

Smirnov, Aleks. 1877. *Ocherki semeinykh otnoshenii po obychnomu pravu russkago naroda*. Moscow: M. Katkov.

Smirnov, Igor'. 1987. "Scriptum Sub Specie Sovietica." *Russian Language Journal* 41, 115–38.

———. 1990. "Scriptum Sub Specie Sovietica, 2." *Ideology in Russian Literature*. Edited by R. Freeborn and J. Grayson. London: Macmillan, 157–73.

Smirnov-Kutachevskii, A. M. 1905. "Ivanushka-durachek." *Voprosy zhizni*, no. 12, 5–73.

Smith, Hedrick. 1976. *The Russians*. New York: Quadrangle.

———. 1991. *The New Russians*. New York: Avon.

Smith, Raymond T. 1973. "The Matrifocal Family." *The Character of Kinship*. Edited by J. Goody. Cambridge: Cambridge University Press, 121–44.

Smolitsch, Igor. 1953. *Russisches Mönchtum: Entstehung, Entwicklung und Wesen, 988–1917*. Würzburg: Augustinus-Verlag.

Sobel, Ruth. 1981. *Gogol's Forgotten Book: SELECTED PASSAGES and Its Contemporary Readers*. Washington, D.C.: University Press of America.

Socarides, Charles W. 1958. "The Function of Moral Masochism: With Special Reference to the Defence Processes." *International Journal of Psycho-Analysis* 39, 587–97.

Sokolova, V. K. 1979. *Vesenne-letnie kalendarnye obriady russkikh, ukraintsev i belorusov*. Moscow: Nauka.

Solov'ev, Vladimir. 1966–69. *Sobranie sochinenii Vladimira Sergeevicha Solov'eva*. Brussels: Zhizn' s Bogom/Foyer Oriental Chrétien, 12 vols.

Solovyov, Vladimir. 1950. *A Solovyov Anthology*. Edited by S. L. Frank. Translated by N. Duddington. New York: Charles Scribner's Sons.

Solzhenitsyn, Aleksandr. 1974. *Arkhipelag GULag 1918–1956: Opyt khudozhestvennogo issledovaniia, III-IV*. Paris: YMCA-Press.

———. 1975a. *The Gulag Archipelago 1918–1956: An Experiment in Literary Investigation, III-IV*. Translated by T. Whitney. New York: Harper and Row.

———. 1975b. "Sakharov i kritika 'Pis'ma vozhdiam'." *Kontinent* 2, 350–59.

———. 1976. "Repentance and Self-Limitation in the Life of Nations." *From Under the Rubble*. Edited by M. Scammell. New York: Bantam, 104–42.

———. 1977. "Remarks at the Hoover Institution, May 24, 1976." *Russian Review* 36, 184–89.

———. 1978–. *Sobranie sochinenii*. Vermont-Paris: YMCA-Press (20 vols. published to date).

———. 1989. *August 1914*. Translated by H. Willetts. New York: Noonday Press.

———. 1990. "Kak nam obustroit' Rossiiu?" *Literaturnaia gazeta*, no. 38, 18 September, pp. 3–6.

————. 1991 (1990). *Rebuilding Russia: Reflections and Tentative Proposals.* Translated by A. Klimoff. New York: Farrar, Straus and Giroux.

Stampp, Kenneth M. 1971. "Rebels and Sambos: The Search for the Negro's Personality in Slavery." *Journal of Southern History* 37, 367–92.

Steeves, Paul D. 1983. "Skoptsy." *Modern Encyclopedia of Russian and Soviet History.* Edited by J. Wieczynski. Gulf Breeze, Fla.: Academic International Press, vol. 35, 171–75.

Stein, Howard. 1976. "Russian Nationalism and the Divided Soul of the Westernizers and Slavophiles." *Ethos* 4, 403–38.

Stern, Daniel. 1977. *The First Relationship: Mother and Infant.* Cambridge: Harvard University Press.

Stites, Richard. 1990 (1978). *The Women's Liberation Movement in Russia: Feminism, Nihilism, and Bolshevism 1860–1930.* Princeton: Princeton University Press.

————. 1992. *Russian Popular Culture: Entertainment and Society Since 1900.* Cambridge: Cambridge University Press.

Stolorow, Robert D. 1975. "The Narcissistic Function of Masochism (and Sadism)." *International Journal of Psycho-Analysis* 56, 441–48.

Strotmann, D. T. 1959. "Quelques aperçus historiques sur le culte marial en Russie." *Irénikon* 32, 178–202.

Svirskii, Grigorii. 1979. *Na lobnom meste: literatura nravstvennogo soprotivleniia (1946–1976gg.).* London: Novaia literaturnaia biblioteka.

Syrkin, A. 1991. "Zametki o 'Prestuplenii i nakazanii'." *Wiener Slawistischer Almanach* 28, 57–88.

Sysenko, V. A. 1981. *Ustoichivost' braka: problemy, faktory, usloviia.* Moscow: Finansy i statistika.

Szamuely, Tibor. 1974. *The Russian Tradition.* London: Secker and Warburg.

Tarasov, Boris. 1990. "Revoliutsionnoe oskoplenie, ili v mire ideologicheskikh zerkal." *Literaturnaia gazeta* 48, 4.

Taubman, Philip. 1988. "Down on the Soviet Farm, a Fear of Change." *New York Times,* 9 May, pp. A1, A6.

Tchaadaev, Pierre. 1970. *Lettres philosophiques addressées à une dame.* Edited by F. Rouleau. Paris: Librairie des cinq continents.

Teague, Elizabeth. 1990. "'I Cannot Absolve Myself from Guilt'." *Report on the USSR* 2/39, 4–5.

Tereshkova, V. V. 1987. "Doklad V. V. Tereshkovoi." *Izvestiia,* no. 32, 1 February, pp. 3–4.

Thompson, Ewa M. 1987. *Understanding Russia: The Holy Fool in Russian Culture.* Lanham: University Press of America.

————. 1989. "The Writer in Exile: The Good Years." *Slavic and East European Journal* 33, 499–519.

Tkachenko, A. A., and A. V. Iakubova. 1992. "Sadomazokhistskoe vlechenie i mekhanizmy psikhologicheskoi zashchity." *Rossiiskii psikhoanaliticheskii vestnik* 2, 87–100.

Tolstaia, Tat'iana. 1992. "Vot tebe, baba, blinok!" *Moskovskie novosti,* no. 29, 19 July, p. 22.

Tolstoi, L. N. 1928–64. *Polnoe sobranie sochinenii,* 91 vols. Edited by V. G. Chertkov et al. Moscow-Leningrad: Gosudarstvennoe izdatel'stvo khudozhestvennoi literatury.

———. 1960–65. *Sobranie sochinenii,* 20 vols. Edited by N. N. Akopovaia, N. K. Gudzii, N. N. Gusev, and M. B. Khrapchenko. Moscow: Gosudarstvennoe izdatel'stvo khudozhestvennoi literatury.

Toporkov, A. L. 1992. "'Perepekanie' detei v ritualakh i skazkakh vostochnykh slavian." *Fol'klor i etnograficheskaia deistvitel'nost'.* Edited by A. K. Baiburin. Saint Petersburg: Nauka, 114–118.

Toporov, V. N. 1987. "Ob odnom arkhaichnom indoevropeiskom elemente v drevnerusskoi dukhovnoi kul'ture—*svet-." *Iazyki kul'tury i problemy perevodimosti.* Edited by B. A. Uspenskii. Moscow: Nauka, 184–252.

Townsend, Charles E. 1968. *Russian Word-Formation.* New York: McGraw-Hill.

Treadgold, Donald. 1959. *Twentieth Century Russia,* 2d ed. Chicago: Rand McNally.

Triandis, Harry C. 1990. "Cross-Cultural Studies of Individualism and Collectivism." *Nebraska Symposium on Motivation* 37, 41–133.

Tsipko, Aleksandr. 1991. "Nikto ne khotel pobezhdat'." *Moskovskie novosti,* no. 8, 24 February, p. 7.

Tucker, Robert C. 1991. "What Time Is It in Russia's History?" *Perestroika: The Historical Perspective.* Edited by C. Merridale and C. Ward. London: Edward Arnold, 34–45.

Turgenev, I. S. 1960–68. *Polnoe sobranie sochinenii i pisem v dvadtsati vos'mi tomakh.* Leningrad: Nauka.

Ulam, Adam B. 1976. *Ideologies and Illusions: Revolutionary Thought from Herzen to Solzhenitsyn.* Cambridge: Harvard University Press.

Uspenskii, B. A. 1988. "Religiozno-mifologicheskii aspekt russkoi ekspressivnoi frazeologii (semantika russkogo mata v istoricheskom osveshchenii)." *Semiotics and the History of Culture: In Honor of Jurij Lotman.* Edited by M. Halle, K. Pomorska, E. Semeka-Pankratov, and B. Uspenskii. Columbus: Slavica Publishers, 197–302.

Vahros, Igor. 1966. "Zur Geschichte und Folklore der grossrussischen Sauna." *Folklore Fellows Communications* 197, 340 pp.

Vakar, Nicholas. 1961. *The Taproot of Soviet Society.* New York: Harper and Brothers.

Vaksberg, Arkadii. 1965. "107 stranits pro liubov'." *Literaturnaia gazeta,* 12 October, p. 2.

Vekhi: sbornik statei o russkoi intelligentsii (2d ed.). 1909. Moscow: Tipografiia V. M Sablina.

Venturi, Franco. 1960 (1952). *Roots of Revolution: A History of the Populist and Socialist Movements in Nineteenth Century Russia.* Translated by F. Haskell. New York: Grosset and Dunlap.

Viskovatyi, Pavel Aleksandrovich. 1891. *Mikhail Iur'evich Lermontov: zhizn' i tvorchestvo.* Moscow: V. F. Rixter.

Voinovich, Vladimir. 1985. *Antisovetskii Sovetskii Soiuz.* Ann Arbor: Ardis.

Voloshin, Maksimilian. 1989. *Stikhotvoreniia.* Moscow: Kniga.

Voznesenskii, Andrei. 1991. "Strana stradan'ia." *Literaturnaia gazeta,* no. 43, 30 October, p. 12.

Walicki, Andrzej. 1989 (1964). *The Slavophile Controversy: History of a Conservative Utopia in Nineteenth-Century Russian Thought.* Translated by H. Andrews-Rusiecka. Notre Dame, Ind.: University of Notre Dame Press.

Walker, Lenore. 1987. "Inadequacies of the Masochistic Personality Disorder Diagnosis for Women." *Journal of Personality Disorders* 1, 183–89.

Walker, Lenore, and Angela Browne. 1985. "Gender and Victimization by Intimates." *Journal of Personality* 53, 179–95.

Warner, Elizabeth A., and Evgenii S. Kustovskii. 1990. *Russian Traditional Folk Song.* Hull: Hull University Press.

Warren, Virginia L. 1985. "Explaining Masochism." *Journal for the Theory of Social Behavior* 15, 103–29.

Wasiolek, Edward. 1964. *Dostoevsky: The Major Fiction.* Cambridge: MIT Press.

Whiting, John W. M. 1981. "Environmental Constraints on Infant Care Practices." *Handbook of Cross-Cultural Human Development.* Edited by Ruth Munroe, Robert Munroe, and Beatrice Whiting. New York: Garland STPM Press, 155–79.

Wierzbicka, Anna. 1989. "Soul and Mind: Linguistic Evidence for Ethnopsychology and Cultural History." *American Anthropologist* 91, 41–58.

———. 1992. *Semantics, Culture, and Cognition: Universal Human Concepts in Culture-Specific Configurations.* Oxford: Oxford University Press.

Wiles, Peter. 1965. "On Physical Immortality: Materialism and Transcendence." *Survey,* nos. 56–57, 125–43, 142–61.

Williams, Robert C. 1970. "The Russian Soul: A Study in European Thought and Non-European Nationalism." *Journal of the History of Ideas* 31, 573–88.

Winnicott, D. W. 1960. "The Theory of the Parent-Infant Relationship." *International Journal of Psycho-Analysis* 41, 585–95.

The World's Women 1970–1990: Trends and Statistics. 1991. New York: United Nations.

Worobec, Christine D. 1991. *Peasant Russia: Family and Community in the Post-Emancipation Period.* Princeton: Princeton University Press.

Wortman, Richard. 1967. *The Crisis of Russian Populism.* Cambridge: Cambridge University Press.

Yevtushenko, Yevgeny. 1988. "We Humiliate Ourselves." *Time,* 27 June, pp. 30–31.

Young, George M., Jr. 1979. *Nikolai F. Fedorov: An Introduction*. Belmont, Mass.: Nordland.

Zakher-Mazokh, Leopol'd fon. 1992. *Venera v mekhakh*. Translated by A. V. Garadzhi. Moscow: RIK "Kul'tura."

Zaslavskaya, Tatyana. 1984 (1983). "The Novosibirsk Report." *Survey* 28, 88–108.

———. 1989. "Socialism with a Human Face." *Voices of Glasnost: Interviews with Gorbachev's Reformers*. Edited by S. Cohen and K. vanden Heuvel. New York: W. W. Norton, 115–39.

———. 1990. *The Second Socialist Revolution: An Alternative Soviet Strategy*. Translated by S. Davies and J. Warren. London: I. B. Tauris.

Zelenin, Dmitrii. 1991 (1914). *Velikorusskie skazki permskoi gubernii*. Moscow: Pravda.

———. 1991 (1927). *Vostochnoslavianskaia etnografiia*. Moscow: Nauka.

Zen'kovskii, Sergei. 1970. *Russkoe staroobriadchestvo: dukhovnye dvizheniia semnadtsatogo veka*. Munich: Wilhelm Fink Verlag.

Zenova, N. 1992. "I sebe, i liudiam." *Literaturnaia gazeta*, no. 14, 1 April, p. 15.

Zhivov, V. M., and B. A. Uspenskii. 1987. "Tsar' i Bog: Semioticheskie aspekty sakralizatsii monarkha v Rossii." *Iazyki kul'tury i problemy perevodimosti*. Edited by B. A. Uspenskii. Moscow: Nauka, 47–153.

Zhukhovitskii, Leonid. 1984. "Kuda ischezaiut nastoiashchie muzhchiny?" *Literaturnaia gazeta*, 10 October, p. 12.

Zinov'ev, Aleksandr. 1976. *Ziiaiushchie vysoty*. Lausanne: L'age d'homme.

Ziolkowski, Margaret. 1988. *Hagiography and Modern Russian Literature*. Princeton: Princeton University Press.

Zlatovratskii, N. N. 1951 (1878–83). *Ustoi: istoriia odnoi derevni*. Moscow: Goslitizdat.

Zorin, N. V. 1981. *Russkaia svad'ba v srednem Povolzh'e*. Kazan': Izdatel'stvo Kazanskogo Universiteta.

Zoshchenko, Mikhail. 1978. *Izbrannoe*. Leningrad: Khudozhestvennaia literatura, 2 vols.

Index

WITHDRAWN